JOHN MASEFIELD: *LETTERS TO REYNA*

CONTENTS

First published in 1983 by
Buchan & Enright, Publishers,
Limited
53 Fleet Street, London
EC4Y 1BE

ISBN 0 907675 14 X

Text designed by T. M. Jaques FSIAD
and Jo Angell

Decorated with John Masefield's
own sketches, which accompanied
some of his letters to "Reyna".

Typeset by CentraCet, Saffron Walden
Set in linotron baskerville
Printed and bound in Great Britain by
The Pitman Press, Bath

JOHN MASEFIELD
LETTERS TO REYNA

Edited by
William Buchan

BUCHAN & ENRIGHT, PUBLISHERS
LONDON

INTRODUCTION

A published book of letters, of numerous, long, intimate letters between close friends, must nowadays seem something of a marvel, when we consider the few smudgy ball-pointed or badly typed lines, the unrevealing notes, the occasional postcards, which are all that most of us can manage in the way of communication. The telephone is much to blame in this matter, as is the regrettable decline in frequency of the postal service. Worse is the lack of leisure—true leisure for thought and reflection, for the development of friendship, for the sharing of ideas unconnected with the struggle to keep a place in a world of continual change.

For at least seventy years of his long life John Masefield was a copious writer of letters. Once he had established a friendship, he would maintain it, broaden and deepen it by a continual flow of ideas, comment, criticism, expressions of affection, through the medium of the post. Had he written nothing else, had his letters alone survived. we should still have a clear picture of the man and the movements of his mind.

The letters in this book were all written over the fifteen years from 1952 until Masefield's death in 1967, by which time he had been Poet Laureate for thirty-seven years. Their recipient, known to the poet as "Reyna", had come into his life through a letter of appreciation which she had been moved to write on hearing a play of his on the wireless. How this came about shall be told later in Reyna's own words.

John Edward Masefield was born at Ledbury, in Herefordshire, on 1st June 1878, in a house called The Knapp. He was the third of six children of Edward and Caroline Masefield. His father was a lawyer in Ledbury, where the family firm of solicitors had been founded by John's grandfather.

Herefordshire, although it lies on the marches of Wales, and has many Welsh influences, seems to the outsider the most English of

counties. Its world of enclosed fields, thick woodland, unprecipi-
tous hills, echoes Shropshire and Gloucestershire; its hop gardens
and apple orchards recall Kent or Devon. It is a land speaking, more
than most, of antiquity. There are reminders of the Normans, and of
older conquests than theirs; of Roman settlement, and fierce
mediaeval wars. The place names are often resounding and sometimes very strange. Something remains of the great forest which once
covered the region in the oak trees scattered everywhere, the dark
woods which clothe the hills.

Ledbury's long High Street goes downhill and then up again past
the black-and-white half-timbered seventeenth-century Market
House on its stout wooden props. Many of the houses in the town
are black-and-white, and there are narrow lanes and side-streets
unchanged for centuries, where gabled houses on jutting bressum-
mers lean forwards over the pavement. The High Street is part of the
old road from Hereford to Gloucester. At its southern end it is
crossed by the road from Tewkesbury to Ross-on-Wye. Ledbury
itself lies at the edge of Gloucestershire, and thus is more English,
perhaps, than places farther to the west.

Much of Herefordshire is remote, folded away, secret: likely to be
haunted, for an imaginative child, by many ghosts, full as it is of
legends from a long and turbulent past. It is largely a rolling, gentle
pastoral of fields and orchards, made dramatic in places by hills and
valleys. The hills are not so high as the Malverns, a few miles away
to the north-east, but impressive enough for contrast, particularly
where high land sweeps down to the valley of the Wye. Wild
snowdrops grow in the woods, and lilies-of-the-valley, and wild
daffodils. The boy Jack, as his family called him—he was later to be
known to his friends as Jan—had no farther to go than the edge of
his town to find the daffodil fields which, one day, he was to make
the title of a narrative poem.

During Jack's early childhood, a coach and horses ran regularly
between Ledbury and Gloucester; animals, on market day, were
sold in the streets; the High Street shopkeepers showed their wares
behind the small, square panes of old bay-windows. Because
Ledbury and Herefordshire remained so much in John Masefield's
mind, they are worth dwelling on for a little. The town is the scene of
two long narrative poems out of three which made his fame in the
early nineteen-hundreds, *The Everlasting Mercy* and *The Widow in the
Bye Street*, and can be recognised, with the names of its inns in *The
Midnight Folk* and *The Box of Delights*. Herefordshire is certainly a
part of the hunting scene in *Reynard the Fox*, and the setting of a
novel, *The Hawbucks*. It is "the hearty land, where I was bred, my
land of heart's desire".

When Jack was in his seventh year he received a blow from which he was never quite to recover. His adored mother died suddenly of pneumonia in 1885, a few weeks after giving birth to her sixth child. She was then in her early thirties. By all accounts she was an attractive and lively person, much loved, and, for her children, a marvellous entertainer with songs and poems, and stories which she herself made up. As if the loss of so warm, so trustworthy an element in his life were not enough, troubles of many kinds were yet to come.

Jack's grandfather, George Masefield, a shrewd and successful lawyer, had come to Ledbury from Shropshire. His wife came of a Ledbury family and, when his prosperity increased, George Masefield bought their old home, a house called The Priory, by the great church of St Michael and All Angels. To the house, probably seventeenth-century or even older, he added an acceptably prosperous Victorian shell in red brick with windows mullioned and gothicised in stone.

Hard on the death of Jack's mother, both his grandparents died. During the disruption suffered by the family as a result of these three deaths, the Masefield children lived at The Priory, in the charge of a governess. This loud, vulgar and insensitive young woman was cordially loathed by the children, and by Jack most of all. He was to give her immortality later, in *The Midnight Folk*, as the wicked governess, Sylvia Daisy Pouncer, who is also a practising witch.

Further ills were to follow. At George Masefield's death it was found that the family fortunes, until then so solid-seeming, were not solid at all. John Masefield was to believe, later, that his grandfather had been speculating wildly. Whatever the reason, money—or its lack—had become a serious pre-occupation.

For Edward Masefield, Jack's father, things went badly indeed. The successive shocks of his wife's death and the discoveries about his father's finances seriously undermined his health, and it was not long before it became apparent that his mind was deranged. In 1888, when he was ten, Jack was sent away to school at Warwick; in that same year William Masefield, head of the family law firm, seeing his brother Edward's mental condition worsening, felt obliged to put him into a hospital in Gloucester where, in the following year, he died.

The six Masefield children were now orphaned. William Masefield and his wife Kate, showing a strong sense of duty, if nothing great in the way of love, and being childless themselves, decided to undertake their upbringing. They gave up their own home and moved to The Priory. (Jack's birthplace, The Knapp, had long been disposed of.) Aunt Kate, a clergyman's daughter, was affected to "muscular" Christianity. No more than the odious governess was she suited to understand a sensitive, dreamy, poetically inclined small boy. All art she regarded as soppy and futile, where not actually immoral. She jeered at Jack's story-telling, and at the poems and stories which he was beginning to write.

Having unwisely admitted to writing poetry, Jack got off to a bad start at school and for a while was made miserable by the other boys. Warwick, an ancient grammar school just, at that time, re-organised along the lines of the older public schools then so greatly admired, was probably no less severe than any other of the period upon deviations from the norm. Yet, in the end, after a wretched start, Jack came to be happy in his rather brief schooldays. He was a healthy, strong boy, and was lucky in that he enjoyed swimming and cricket, and indeed all games. Echoes of Victorian schooldays can be found here and there in his later work: in metaphors of Rugby football, and cricket, and the use by his heroes of rather antique schoolboy slang. In his letters to Reyna he allows himself few expletives—his "damns" are always "d——n" but sometimes he amuses himself by writing "Golly", and "Golly again!" to express wonder or astonishment.

Jack was not destined to enjoy his school for long. Financial stringency decided his uncle and aunt to take him away from Warwick School, and he came home to Ledbury in 1890 when he was twelve years old. He was back once more doing lessons with his sisters' governess and, in his free hours, roving the countryside. He tells in his letters of the fearful frights he had from time to time with great Hereford bulls, which gave him horrifying dreams. "I was frequently told that I was wicked—just the sort of chap a bull would know about and deal with." However, as he tells Reyna, he was to weep tears of homesickness, years later in America, at the sight of a Hereford herd.

In his letters, more than once, John Masefield quotes a Spanish proverb about the three best things of life: "Good air, good water and good bells." Ledbury church has a peal of eight bells, and an old clock which plays, every three hours, the tune of "Holy, Holy, Holy". From The Priory's big garden he could see the top of the church and the free-standing bell-tower with its tall spire, and the gilded weathercock at its top; but the church, although it fascinated him, held little solace for the boy. As for so many children, religion was less spiritual revelation than social observance. Moreover, he was frequently told that he was wicked, and his aunt's brisk, shallow brand of Christianity cannot have appealed to one whose temperament, perhaps even then, inclined strongly to mysticism. His powerful imagination imagined Hell, and the strictures and admonitions of his elders led him to suppose that Hell was his inevitable destination.

It is probable that the young John Masefield's childhood experience differed little from that of other children of his time who although comfortable enough, well clothed and fed, were nevertheless starved, or positively distorted, on their spiritual side. Although Masefield, the man, was very evidently strongly gifted for religion; although he thought long and hard, often with anguish, on life and death and life after death, it is equally evident that what the Anglican Church and his family's Christian observances sought to impose on him was something which, all his life, he would never be wholly able to accept. In a letter to Reyna about Havelock Ellis, and that writer's courageous attempts to breach certain social and sexual taboos, he writes of "the callous imbecility of those trusted with the care of the young" in Victorian times. And again, in answer to a letter of hers asking him to tell her about his childhood, he writes: "It was a shadow . . . and made me the kind of night I am." Many have remarked on the sadness of his face as an older man, and even in boyhood one can divine from the large, puzzled eyes, and a slight down-turn to the mouth, the beginnings of a settled melancholy, a melancholy derived from experience which, although often bitter, never—as these letters will show— poisoned the springs of humour.

When John Masefield was in his forties someone wrote of him: "He is the kind of figure that gives rise to legends." Two of the most persistent of these legends are, first, that he ran away to sea, and second, that he sailed before the mast. Neither legend is true, although the first is perpetuated in the *Oxford Companion to English Literature*.

When the boy was still only in his thirteenth year his uncle and aunt, still harassed by financial difficulties, were casting about for a means of putting him to a career. Aunt Kate, who evidently thought her nephew needed curing of what she saw as namby-pambiness, had the idea of having him trained for a career at sea. Family funds would not run to sending him to Dartmouth for a naval training, but there was still the merchant service. Young Jack was probably not consulted much about his future, and in any case would not have been likely to know, at that early age, and with a highly romantic view of the world, coloured by the adventure stories he read, what precisely he wished to do with his life. It was decided for him that he should join the school-ship, HMS *Conway*, for training to become an officer in the merchant service; and this, in September 1891, he did.

Although steam, at that time, was well on the way to ousting sail as a means of propelling ships, it was still thought that a training in sail gave the best possible grounding in seamanship. The school-ships had been set up by the British Government to ensure that future officers of the merchant service should have, in addition to that training, a good general education, such as had not been available in the past.

From many words and writings in later life it is clear that his time in HMS *Conway*, rigorous as parts of it were, remained with Jack as the happiest of memories: and it was there that he developed a passion for the sea, and for sailing ships, an understanding of seamanship and the hard, separate life of seamen, which were to show up in his writings again and again. It is certain that John Masefield is the only poet in the history of English literature to write about ships and the sea from a full and profound knowledge of their beauties, their moods, their terrors and their technicalities. Nobody lacking such knowledge could have produced the narrative poem *Dauber* (1913) or the poems in his first book *Salt Water Ballads* (1902).

Conway did indeed provide a good general education, and in many other things besides seamanship. Like any other new boy—or "new chum" in this case—Jack was bewildered at first by the strange terms and strange duties which no one, in an intensely busy day, seemed to have time to explain. Once he had mastered those, however, and had made one or two rewarding friendships, he fitted easily and happily into his new life. From the *Conway* he would watch the sea-life of Liverpool, then one of the busiest ports in the world, and the comings and goings of great ships. It was there that he saw the majestic four-masted barque, *Wanderer*, set out proudly on her first voyage, only to return battered and bedraggled, her sails in tatters, but still unassailably beautiful. She would always be, for Jack, the paragon of sailing ships, and he wrote about her many times. Ashore in Liverpool he made acquaintance with the Walker Art Gallery, whose collection of Pre-Raphaelite pictures was later to mean so much to him, and to which he refers more than once in his letters to Reyna. The ship had a good library and, in spare moments, of which there were not many, he read what he could, and it was then that he discovered Captain Marryat, of whom he speaks so warmly in these letters.

After two years and six months in training John Masefield left the *Conway* and, in the spring of 1894, with other apprentices, mostly older than himself, left to be taken on by one of the sailing ship companies. He was then two months short of his sixteenth birthday.

His first appointment was to a four-masted barque, the *Gilcruix*, belonging to the White Star Line, one day to be owners of the *Titanic*. Here the second part of the Masefield legend falls down. He did not sail before the mast. Being an apprentice, not a seaman, his berth was in the half-deck, a deck-house half-way down the ship.

This was cramped, and uncomfortable enough for the six apprentices who shared it, but had they been seamen their berth would have been in the forecastle, that is to say "before the mast".

The *Gilcruix* left Cardiff in April, bound for Iquique in Chile. Since the Panama Canal was not yet in existence such a voyage to South America's west coast meant, inevitably, sailing round Cape Horn. That voyage began, for John Masefield, a time of varied tribulation which would see him, three years later, back in England for good, thin, sick, exhausted, and on the edge of death from consumption, but determined heart and soul to be a writer.

Yet, he must have set out for Iquique with high hopes. The *Gilcruix* was a fine ship, although no match for the *Wanderer* with which he had for ever fallen in love. He was sailing for a far country, which had been much in his imaginings.

When the expected foul weather came, first in the Roaring Forties and then around Cape Horn, Masefield bore his part fully with the ship's company, scaling the rigging to bring flapping topsails under control in the teeth of devilish winds. Such emergencies are described with great power in *Dauber*.

Rounding the Horn, the *Gilcruix* was continually under attack for thirty-two days on end from raging gales, with seas forty feet high, the air bitter cold, so that her decks and rigging were cased in ice, and there was ice in the sea. She finally reached Iquique thirteen weeks after leaving Cardiff, and her coming must have been like that of the storm-savaged ship which, after Dauber's death, comes safely into port:

> Then in the sunset's flush they went aloft
> And unbent sails in that most lovely hour
> When the light gentles and the wind is soft,
> And beauty in the heart breaks like a flower;
> Working aloft they saw the mountain tower
> Snow to the peak; they heard the launchmen shout;
> And bright along the bay the lights came out.

There, at Iquique, John Masefield's career as a sailor really came to an end. He had withstood admirably the stresses and dangers of the three-month voyage to South America. His manhood had been handsomely proven. He had derived much good that he was always to remember from companionship, from working in close concert with strong men in dire situations. But it may be that his spirit, the complex mental and moral makeup which was the prime motor of his true vocation, had been battered and shaken more deeply than his body. At all events, he became quite seriously ill, first with sunstroke and then with a nervous collapse of some sort.

The captain of the *Gilcruix*, a kindly man, arranged with the British Consul that John Masefield should leave his ship and be sent home to England as a DBS (Distressed British Seaman). And so, after some weeks in hospital at Iquique, he was discharged from the *Gilcruix* by "mutual consent". There are no details recorded of the means by which he made his way home, but, after spending some time in hospital in Valparaiso, his biographer thinks he must have been shipped off to Callao, the port of Lima in Peru, and thence to Panama. He would have had to cross the isthmus by train to Colon, and there join a Royal Mail steamer bound for England by way of ports in the West Indies. At the end of October he was back in Ledbury.

Once or twice in the past Jack had mentioned shyly to one or another trusted friend that he wanted to be a writer, and had met with responses varying between non-comprehension and slight horror. During his journey of many weeks back to Ledbury, his wish may well have hardened to a resolve. With his mind still full of his terrible voyage, its glories and its fears, he was travelling slowly, visiting new places and finding before his eyes scenes and kinds of people as vivid, as highly coloured and as fascinating as any he had ever imagined. The boy who had dreamed of the Spanish Main was now actually travelling it. At a time of life when sixteen-year-olds of our own epoch would be struggling with "A" levels, Jack was hourly learning things that no educational system in the world could teach, and more and more feeling the need to express what he had learned in writing.

Jack was not fully recovered from illness when he finally reached Ledbury. His family found him listless, and Aunt Kate did not scruple to accuse him of weakness, of a failure to "stick it" at sea. His time at home, accordingly, was not happy; and soon family pressure which he simply, at that time, had not the power to resist, drove him back to seafaring. Through the agency of the captain of the *Conway* a place was found for him in another four-masted barque, then loading in New York for a voyage to the Far East. In the early spring of 1895 Jack sailed for America. He left England in a mood of deep depression. His biographer quotes remarks which he made to a friend at that time. He said that he felt "only a hopelessness. The sea seemed to have me in her grip. I was to pass my life beating other men's ships to port. That was to be 'life' for me. The docks, and sailor town, and all the damning and the heaving." The last sentence is significant. Although Jack had a profound sympathy for the ordinary seamen then in sail, and had loved their shanties and their strength and endurance, there were many things in "sailor

town" and much in the "damning and heaving" distasteful to the
romantic and delicate-minded boy that he seems to have been. It
was a life without light and shade, a coarse, blasphemous, drunken
existence, redeemed by skill and courage, warm in comradeship, but
philistine, uncomprehending, indifferent or positively hostile to the
values which, he was beginning to know, were most precious to him.

Eighteen years later John Masefield was to publish his long poem
Dauber which concerns an artist, a young man burning with a desire
to paint the sea as it has never been painted before, who ships as a
painter on board a sailing vessel. His job is not to paint pictures, but
to keep the ship's paintwork smart. He is an incompetent seaman,
and unwise in that he lets his true passion show by bringing out his
paints at quiet moments, by confiding to fellow sailors what that
passion is. He is met with something worse than incomprehension, a
savage hostility, expressed in curses, jeers and cruel practical jokes.
He is made to pay heavily for not being one of the herd and, finally,
when in great fear he is aloft trying to furl sails in a terrible gale, he
falls to the deck and is killed. It is not suggested that Masefield saw
himself as Dauber. The latter was a weakling and one, moreover,
who had set himself an impossible artistic goal. But the story is there
to illustrate, in one aspect, the eternal plight of the artist as
odd-man-out in an embattled and fear-ridden world.

Three thousand miles of Atlantic Ocean brought about a
crucial change in Jack's thinking. At some point in the voyage his
feelings about life at sea had crystallised to a determination never
to go to sea again. When he reached New York he simply "jumped
ship", or rather, never joined the one where he was expected. He
took off, alone, quite friendless, with £1 in his pocket and some
luggage containing clothes, into an unknown, unguessable new
world.

In a letter to Reyna, sometime in 1962, Jan (as he then signed
himself) wrote: "I worked on a farm in wild, primitive country in
New York state, when I was a boy 67 years ago. The country is now
all a vast NY suburbia, incredible, unrecognisable, where once I
drove cows and fed multitudinous poultry, and blasted out rocks
with dynamite, and planted fruit-trees that must long since have
grown past bearing." That was in the spring of 1895 when Jack was
tramping the still unviolated countryside, looking for work, any
work, with a companion whom he later spoke of as "a disreputable
ruffian". It was a time of economic depression and work was hard to
find. Many times Jack must have gone cold and hungry, and many
times slept rough, during the early months of that year.

In summer he went back to New York, to Greenwich Village

where for a while he looked for jobs in vain. Eventually he was taken on as a helper to the barman in a shady hotel.

Meanwhile the Masefields in England had completely lost sight of their wanderer. His Uncle William employed private detectives to find him, but without success. Jack was pursuing his own difficult path and it was long before he got in touch with his family again.

Meanwhile, Jack, after two months' work as junior barman and lad-of-all-work, found a new job which promised a little more money and quite a lot more leisure. He had made friends with an English boy from Shropshire who was working in a carpet factory out at Yonkers, and who managed to get him taken on to work in the cutting-room. In those days Yonkers was still only a small township on the Hudson River, north of New York, and there Jack found lodgings. His work in the factory came easily to him and, after a year, he was promoted to a more responsible job and given to understand that there was a future for him with the firm. He seems to have endured the stunning racket of the machines and thick fluff in the air well enough, although the latter can hardly have been good for one suffering from the beginnings of tuberculosis.

It has been necessary to tell of John Masefield's early life, for the stony road which had led him to the Yonkers carpet factory, and would shortly lead him back to England, led also to a rapturous awakening to the glories of literature, and his own possible contribution to it. Working in the hotel in New York he had scarcely known a moment of free time. At night he stumbled to bed exhausted; his only leisure lay in sleep. At Yonkers he had evenings and whole Sundays to himself, in which to read and write and read again. He soon found a bookshop whose friendly proprietor let him browse by the hour. Every payday he bought books. They were not expensive; good editions of fiction cost as little as five cents, and the Chaucer which was to mean so much to him cost only seventy-five. He was steeping himself in poetry: first with Malory—"the first book I bought in NY when I vowed I wouldn't be so ignorant"—then with Keats and Shelley. All was revelation. Jack had had truly a hard life. Many forces had combined to drive him against his real nature, and to deprive his mind and spirit of nourishment. He was eighteen years old, on his own, working at a humble job in a foreign land, yet once he had left the factory gates and returned to his lodgings, he was in paradise, devouring, in a blaze of happiness, an omnifarious diet of literature from Sir Thomas Browne to Hazlitt, from Molière and Dumas (in French) to Kipling and Stevenson. He knew now that his destiny was to be a writer and nothing but a writer, however bitter the struggle might be going to be.

John Masefield has sometimes been compared to Chaucer, for the reason that his best-known long poems are stories, narrative verse, told in an easy metre and uncomplicated language, yet full of poetic imagery of high quality. His discovery of Chaucer opened to him a new and different dimension of poetry from any that he had met before, and moreover, dazzled by his reading of *The Parliament of Fowls*, he found again those ideals of courtly love which had so appealed to him in Malory. In 1955, earnestly wishing to interest Reyna in Chaucer, he writes, "Please read *Troilus and Criseyde* through. It is long; but it is by a Master; tho' he is still immature he is often charming, or very charming: and if not, he is his Time speaking, and his City is there, too, tho' he calls it Troy: but most of all I long for you to feel the full tide of the tale sweeping you up into the ecstasy of the end."

From American newspapers Jack gathered something of what was going on in the English literary world, and what he read convinced him that London must be the scene of his début as a writer. It was the year of Queen Victoria's Jubilee; England was much in the news. Simple homesickness was probably added to his desire to get to London. Almost on the spur of the moment Jack, who had become increasingly withdrawn and decidedly less easy with his workmates, burnt his writings, sold or gave away all but a few of his books, and headed for the New York docks. Finding a ship bound for Liverpool, whose captain was an "Old Conway", he managed to get taken on as a steerage steward for the voyage. He landed at Liverpool in July 1897.

When Jack reached England again the elder of his sisters was shocked by his appearance, so much at variance with the glowing and exalted tone of his letters. In addition to being manifestly seriously unwell, he was also penniless, and it was his sister who found him his first London job, as a clerk in a city firm at £1 a week.

Jack's harsh experience had brought him to the verge of consumption and, in addition, he had somewhere contracted malaria which came back to him in bouts. He knew the flaring heights and leaden depths of his impending malady, and was convinced that he was going to die. Fortunately an uncle, his mother's brother, came to hear of his condition and prevailed upon William Masefield to let Jack have some of his father's money. In 1898 he also got him a rather better job, with the Capital and Counties Bank.

There followed a long period of comparative penury, but not of unhappiness. It had taken a harrowing time at sea, a tramp's life in New York State, menial service, and the infernal noise, the dull, repetitive work of the carpet factory, to produce the bursting excitement of an imagination working at full power. For all his black moods of depression, Jack never seems to have lost for long either his sense of vocation, his all-excluding need to write, or his gentle, somewhat whimsical sense of humour. Through the practical discovery of what he did not want from life, he had, at the age of nineteen, quite certainly discovered where he wished to go.

Meanwhile the young Masefield quartered central London, living in hired rooms at Fulham and Islington, amongst other places. In 1900 he moved out to Walthamstow, on the city's eastern fringe, where long walks in Epping Forest, in air that could still be called "country", helped in the restoration of his health. That early physical stamina acquired in Herefordshire, in the *Conway*, and at sea, probably saved him from an illness which, at one time, had seemed likely to be fatal.

1900, the turn of the century, was a year of great significance for John Masefield, who soon ceases to be Jack and becomes Jan. The year before he had had his first literary success, when the *Outlook* published one of his poems. However haltingly, he was on his way, and that way was to be greatly illuminated by his discovery of W. B. Yeats, whose *Collected Poems* was issued in 1899.

Jan, reading Yeats, found an excitement, an exaltation equal to that which he had felt in America when he discovered Chaucer. He was determined to follow Yeats, to get closer to him, even—and this must have cost the shy young man an effort of nerve—to approach him in the flesh.

Yeats, whose principle was always to encourage, must have responded kindly to Jan's approach, for in the autumn of 1900 their first meeting took place. Jan was invited for the evening to Yeats's London lodging at 18 Woburn Buildings in Bloomsbury, "that old room above the noisy slum", as he was later to call it. Woburn Walk lies just south of St Pancras Church in Bloomsbury and what were then called Woburn Buildings included one side of Woburn Walk, "the noisy slum", now carefully restored to its original elegance as Cubitt built it for the Duke of Bedford in 1822. More than sixty years later John Masefield, perhaps the last survivor from Yeats's Monday evenings, was asked to open the refurbished apartment, which was to be specially preserved while the whole block behind was being remodelled for a new hotel.

Writing to Reyna in 1963, Jan describes his feelings about the speech he has to make, and his memories of his visits to "Willy".

"I cannot certainly name any man or woman who is now alive to tell you of his Mondays as they were in the great days. Then, always, at a Monday there were some scholars of Righteousness: about a dozen in all, whom I never knew well, for they were men of 35 or 40, and I was only 22, but they were all wonderful beings, kind, helpful, generous and righteous, knowing (seemingly) all knowledge, somehow, and unlike anybody I had ever seen anywhere. . . . We at Willy's were all in the theories of our gang, and the hatreds that theories provoke. What a sad lot we were, but what an excitement it was, and how senseless going to bed seemed. . . . WBY was there for 25 years, for about ½ of each year, & there on all the winter Mondays he discoursed wisdom to all comers, & induced something liker wisdom, in each, than had been there before. There, too, came Synge, and . . . and . . . and . . . and . . . and . . . after 60 years, I wonder if there will be anyone next week who was there then."

Yeats lived at 18 Woburn Buildings, now 5 Woburn Walk, from 1895 to 1919. Guests at his Mondays included not only Masefield and J. M. Synge, but Rupert Brooke, Ezra Pound, Rabindranath Tagore and T. S. Eliot.

William Butler Yeats did much good in his life, but nothing better than the impetus he gave to the rather awkward, passionate young man who wore, at so early an age, an aura of legend, of strenuous action and hardship and travel in far-off lands, and who was trapped, as it seemed, clerking in a bank.

At the end of 1901 Jan moved to lodgings in Coram Street, only a few hundred yards from Woburn Buildings. He continued to frequent Yeats's Mondays, and to make a number of new friends. Among them was Laurence Binyon, who was then an admired poet. He is probably not much remembered now, although many people know his "Lines for the Fallen"—"They shall not grow old as we that are left grow old"—without knowing the name of their author.

Binyon and his friends did not think that Jan was likely to make a living out of poetry; they thought he needed some reasonably lucrative work to sustain him and this they set about providing. He was given one or two temporary jobs at which he worked with fiery energy, and the moderate ease they produced in his life enabled him to get together his very first publication, *Salt Water Ballads* (1902). There are fifty poems in this collection, many of them in vernacular, most relating to the sea, and Jan thoughtfully provided a glossary of the nautical terms used in them. To have been able to winnow fifty poems for a public showing argues that Jan must have been writing pretty constantly since his return to England, and with increasing mastery. *Salt Water Ballads* contains two poems, "Sea Fever" and "Trade Winds", which are to be found in most anthologies.

Jan was now launched as a serious writer. *Salt Water Ballads* did not drop cold from the press, but sold five hundred copies in six months. From then on he was never to cease from writing. An incomplete bibliography might list forty-eight books of poems, plays in verse, and collections of poems; twenty-three novels; and twenty-seven miscellaneous works in prose, but this would not take into account articles written and lectures given over an unremittingly busy writing career which continued until the very last year of his life.

When Jan began his career as a writer he joined the not then overcrowded ranks of a profession which an increasingly literate public held in high regard. In those days writers *wrote*, most of them punctually, professionally, continuously, and as a way of life. Nobody spoke of "writer's block"; nobody wrote a book about his inability to write books. A quite small reward from publication was adequate to keep a writer in reasonable comfort. There were many flourishing publishers interested in new authors, many literary reviews or book-sections of newspapers in which new writing might find a place.

Not the least interest of these letters to Reyna is that they display so many aspects of John Masefield's astonishingly enquiring and reflective mind, as well as the contents of that wonderful "rag-bag" (as he called it), his memory. In common with several admired contemporaries, such as H. G. Wells and Henry James, he had had no university education. It was perhaps just as well that his mind had never been seriously constricted by a syllabus, not forced into any particular mould of thought. His university was his adventures, his solitary, enraptured reading, and the enlightenment which came to him from his friendship with Yeats and Synge.

It is a marvel how Jan came to develop skill and competence as a poet, entirely on his own. Yet the ear was there, and the fire, the care for technique, the need to express feeling in that particular way, and beneath those there lay a genuine originality, a new way of looking at the world. Naturally there were influences. Later in life he was to recognise gladly a debt to Yeats, while furiously denying anything of the kind to Kipling. Housman, whose *Shropshire Lad* had come out in 1896, had all his reverence. In 1956 he writes to Reyna: "I love you to love A. E. Housman, for I have loved him dearly for 58 years now; tho' I did not often see him I admired him deeply." There are echoes of Housman in his early poems, as for instance:

> The leaves whirl in the wind's riot
> Beneath the Beacon's jutting spur,
> Quiet are clan and chief, and quiet
> Centurion and Signifer.

There is also something of Yeats in "Fragments", a poem about Troy:

> They knew all beauty—when they thought
> The air chimed like a stricken lyre,
> The elemental birds were wrought,
> The golden birds became a fire.

There are some hints of D. G. Rossetti in his sonnets, which are variable in quality. Jan was a devoted admirer of Rossetti: indeed his unstinting admiration and affection, never touched with malice even in criticism, for other writers and poets was one of the most attractive sides of his character, and one which comes out continually in his literary discourses to Reyna.

Sonnets are a constricting form of verse It is hardly surprising that the difficulty of expressing a thought, an emotion, an apprehension, in fourteen lines under very stringent rules, should sometimes cause one poet's expression to jostle another's. As Professor Saintsbury remarked with his customary genial severity, in a comment on the sonnets of Tennyson's elder brother: "His work . . . though never reaching consummateness, has as much adequacy as is possible in a medium which almost necessitates consummateness in order to be adequate."

Young Jan had been much with the world's underdogs. His experiences at sea and in America had shown him only too clearly the seamy side of the world's prosperous coat. At one time the idea of becoming a doctor, to fight yellow fever, almost ousted his desire to be a writer. It sprang, evidently, from a wish to help mankind, and that wish, and what he had seen of the helplessness of the poor and oppressed, remained with him always and coloured much of his work.

"A Consecration", the first poem in *Salt Water Ballads*, is not, as a poem, among his most distinguished, but as a confession of faith it is significant:

Others may sing of the wine and the wealth and the mirth,
The portly presence of potentates goodly in girth:-
Mine be the dirt and the dross, the dust and the scum of the earth!

Theirs be the music, the colour, the glory, the gold;
Mine be a handful of ashes, a mouthful of mould.
Of the maimed and the halt and the blind in the rain and the cold—
Of these shall my songs be fashioned, my tales be told.

We are so unused nowadays, in poetry, to galloping, trotting or tripping metres, or even any kind of strict form, that it might take a positive act of submission, for many people, to approach the long poems which, in their day, brought John Masefield so great an acclaim. *The Everlasting Mercy* is a narrative poem written almost entirely in rhymed octosyllabic couplets. *The Widow in the Bye Street*, which came out in the following year, is composed in a mode much favoured by Masefield, rhyme royal, a seven-line stanza of decasyllables rhyming a-b-a-b-b-c-c. Chaucer used this for *The Parliament of*

Fowls, as well as for *Troilus and Criseyde*, and the young Masefield, coming fresh to Chaucer, may have thought it admirable for combining dialogue and observation while maintaining the pace of a narrative. For *Dauber* (1913) the same scheme is used, as also for *The Daffodil Fields* (1913) with the difference, in that poem, of a twelve-syllable last line.

One day in 1911 a rather sombre young man stalked into the offices of the *English Review*, thumped a large manuscript onto the editors' desk, and left without a further word. The editors, Austin Harrison and Norman Douglas, read the manuscript, liked it immensely, but were alarmed by its implications. To begin with it was very long. It was also full of oaths and a kind of passionate plain-speaking to which the literary and literate worlds were not then accustomed. They debated anxiously, and then decided to publish. That number of the *English Review* sold out immediately, and the paper's circulation at once increased. A firm of publishers took over the poem, which went into many editions. The time of doubt and anxiety (but not of hard work) was over for John Masefield. He was, almost literally, famous overnight.

The Everlasting Mercy is the story of a ruffian, Saul Kane, who, having committed most offences short of murder goes on a wild rampage through a country town (based on Ledbury) and is finally brought to grace by a Quaker woman who bravely enters a pub to confront him in mid-carouse. But the great rampage, it should be added—gone into naked (another scandal) because Saul has torn off his clothes—will be seen at the end to be the first fermenting of grace in Saul, the religious fervour well-known to the evangelists. As he runs, Saul shouts in no uncertain terms what he thinks of the town's inhabitants:

> Male and female human blots
> Who would, but daren't be, whores and sots;

and much more in the same vein, flaying his listeners for their meannesses and petty vice.

The next day, after more drinks, Saul sets out into the town again and, encountering the parson, gives him a piece of his mind. This passage contains many of Masefield's strongest feelings about the poor and unprivileged, in a way fulfilling the promise made in "A Consecration". Then he goes back to the pub, and more drinks to quell a strange disquiet. Then comes the appearance of the Quaker woman and the sudden bursting of the religious fire inside him:

O glory of the lighted mind,
How dead I'd been, how dumb, how blind.
The station brook, to my new eyes,
Was babbling out of Paradise;
The waters rushing from the rain
Were singing Christ has risen again.
I thought all earthly creatures knelt
From rapture of the joy I felt.
The narrow station-wall's brick ledge,
The wild hop withering in the hedge,
The light in huntsman's upper storey
Were parts of an eternal glory . . . .

These lines may help to illustrate the special quality of Masefield's art, the quality which brought him instant recognition from a very large public. As one critic has said, "Masefield had achieved the impossible. He had made the British public read contemporary poetry, an event which had not occurred since the death of Tennyson. Here at last was a man who took Synge's advice and infused into his poetry the life he knew. Synge had said that before poetry could be real again it must learn to be brutal; that there was no true poetry which had not its roots among the clay and the worms. Masefield faithfully followed the prescription, and the foundation of his fame was laid."

In the lines quoted there is, on the one hand, the joy of a soul released from self, and dazzled by a glory newly apprehended: on the other there are "The narrow station wall's brick ledge", "the wild hop withering in the hedge" and "the light in huntsman's upper storey", to hold the narrative to the ordinary world, to give an overwhelming spiritual occurrence a simple terrestrial frame. John Masefield had no use for the ivory tower: he wrote to be understood. He was a minstrel with a story to tell, and he chose a method of telling it which anyone who could read could understand.

The Everlasting Mercy was widely praised and wildly denounced. Many were shocked by the frequent use in it of the word "bloody". (Shaw's use of it in *Pygmalion*, a year later, would also cause severe shock.) Many thought it an improper treatment of a religious theme, some simply found it to be coarse, brutal and in bad taste. Its fierce energy made the more aesthetic litterateurs, the writers about fauns and fans and cottage gardens, feel queer. Some extreme purists thought it rather low-grade versifying. Others, many distinguished writers among them, praised it to the skies; and non-conformist clergymen declaimed whole passages from it in their churches with enormous glee.

Nearly fifty years later Jan wrote to Reyna: "There will be no good narrative verse now, till the poet comes along with the power of music to make a chant that lifts like music, & thrills like music, & can go on an hour at a time enchanting hearers & leading on the story as the Iliad does in the Greek & nobody else does anywhere." It may be that narrative verse will never again be written to be enjoyed by a literate public *on paper*. But minstrelsy itself is far from dead. There is an immense audience, not only among the young, for popular music. It may be, one day, that a singer of, say, the quality of a Bob Dylan, a Lennon, a McCartney, may come to hold a multitude spellbound with great stories told in song, as stories were always told before the invention of printing. The reading public, the public for books, has dwindled greatly since Masefield's day: its eyes, like its ears, are turned elsewhere. But new means of communication may, just possibly, not kill but revive the telling of the great stories, the great myths which humanity needs for its understanding of the world. And John Masefield, who tried so hard, in middle life, through his production of plays in verse, his encouragement of verse speaking by live voices to live audiences, might very well approve.

In a much later letter he writes: "I saw the old England of 80 years ago: a dreadful land, so starved, so drunken, so untaught, so cruel, & now I cannot see any child unfed, or lousy, or beaten, or set to beg, & thrashed if unsuccessful, or sewn into clothes already ragged .... Millions and millions are now free from all this, & are now set free to so, so much: and the joy of that is, O, beyond all old hopes and prayers."

Saul Kane would not, nowadays, need to reprove Squire and Parson for their greed and worldliness, their part in the stultification of the poor:

> You teach the ground-down starving man
> That Squire's greed's Jehovah's plan.
> You get his learning circumvented
> Lest it should make him discontented
> (Better a brutal, starving nation
> Than men with thoughts above their station).

The Parson, in fact, makes a quite reasonable response to this; but, in any event, the argument nowadays has shifted ground, the accusations take another form. Squire's fine house is very likely now the headquarters of an electronics company and Parson, no longer scholarly, well-fed and locally powerful, is thin and underpaid, with a Midlands accent, a congregation of three and an anxious concern for the Third World.

Masefield cared little for practical politics, but had been greatly influenced by the ideal socialism of William Morris. "I cannot say what Morris meant to me when I first really read him." All his life he disliked what is now called "the Establishment", but nevertheless retained, from an early age, a strong devotion to the Royal Family. He speaks scornfully of the imbecilities of government, and of "skunks in skunkeries called ministries".

By the time that *The Everlasting Mercy* was published, John Masefield had given to the world three volumes of poetry and five novels. In 1903 he had married Constance Crommelin, one of the three dedicatees of *Salt Water Ballads*, a strong-willed, highly intelligent woman eleven and a half years older than himself. In 1904 their first child, a daughter, had been born, and Masefield was working desperately hard to try to make money, writing articles for several newspapers, reviewing almost incredible numbers of books, and working for five months in Manchester for the *Guardian*. He was also developing a passion for the theatre, for both play-writing and production. His first, and perhaps best play, *The Tragedy of Nan*, was produced in London in 1908 by Harley Granville-Barker, then the most admired avant-garde producer in England.

In 1909 a second child, a boy, was born and the Masefields moved to a cottage at Great Hampden in Buckinghamshire, and it was there that inspiration came for *The Everlasting Mercy*: genuine inspiration, so rarely received by writers, which came to John Masefield at a time of deep depression and unhappiness. The story has often been told of how, walking one evening, he said to himself suddenly: "I will write a poem about a blackguard who is converted," and there and then wrote down the first twenty-four lines before he even reached home.

Masefield's plain trotting metre and homely sentiment are easy to parody, and it has to be said that he sometimes lets himself down badly. Rare beauty of phrase, clumsy rhyming, and stark banality can often be found in the same stanza; but the heights, when he reaches them, are splendid. It could be said of him that he wrote, or at any rate published, too much, and was deficient in self-criticism. But is it possible to write too much, if a mind and temperament wide open to the world's beauties and the oddities of people, enthralled by every possible manifestation of human capacity, positively demand that findings about these be set down? Certainly he was an uneven writer, touching heights and depths, and sometimes merely jogging along. But had he been a composer and produced an equivalent body of symphonies, oratorios, concertos, and motets, would anybody expect equal excellence in every single piece? As Jan writes to Reyna: "In writing one sometimes meets a man of genius, a fellow who makes one say 'He has it . . . . He will knock down the bars and

let some light in', and then what joy when he ups & does it.
Excellence is rare, however, even in the very good. As a terrible
Spanish proverb says: 'There are more days than sausages.'" And
again, writing of Herman Melville: "Generally speaking, I find
something very clever and good in any books that please a lot of
people."

John Masefield certainly pleased a lot of people. Between 1923
and 1930 his *Collected Poems* sold more than 100,000 copies, and his
novels, *Sard Harker* (1924) and *Odtaa* (1926), achieved about the
same sales.

John Masefield, all his life, sought for and adored Beauty. We are
nowadays finically nervous of the great abstract words—Beauty,
Honour, Patriotism, Truth, the Soul—but they were part of the
poetic currency of his time. The Beauty he sought, and which (or
whom) he hymned so often, and often so movingly, especially in his
sonnets, was an abstraction for an extra-human force or immanence
which could illuminate the quotidian, bring peace and hope, touch
the poetic nerve by its manifestation in nature, in humanity, in
friendship, in a horse-race or a ship at sea. This Beauty, so real to
Masefield, he perceived particularly in women, and that perception
inspired a special reverence for them.

> Woman, beauty, wonder, sacred woman.
> Spirit moulding man from brute to human,
> All the beauty seen by all the wise
> Is but the body to the soul seen by your eyes.

He loved the beauty in women, and not only the physical beauty.
The lines just quoted could hardly be written today and, if they
were, they would infuriate those who are striving to turn womanhood into a different gender. No spirited girl can endure, for long,
being put on a pedestal, unless for particular reasons of tactics, but
it is possible that the general smashing of pedestals has left a certain
desolation in the sexual landscape. In any case a generation which
speaks of falling in love as "emotional involvement" and of physical
love as "having sex" can hardly be said to deserve its poets, past or
present.

Masefield was a devoted husband and father, and a man of
scrupulous honour who had always been moved by the mediaeval
conception of courtly love, but he was a man nevertheless and an
attractive one, and he had eyes in his head for feminine beauty in all
its forms. There must have been something very remarkable about
Reyna's first letter to him, for it is obvious that he was most anxious
to meet her, and had probably already made for himself a picture of
her appearance, and an idea of her personality, before she ever came

to his house. It is equally clear that he was in no way disappointed. Reyna must have fulfilled his highest expectations in every respect. His good manners would never admit of personal remarks, except on abstract matters, but he does allow himself, in an early letter, to mention Reyna's "glorious crown of hair".

When I was sixteen or so in the nineteen-thirties, I had the good fortune to know John Masefield slightly. His name and his books were often in circulation in my home; my parents knew him well; and my sister acted sometimes with his daughter Judith in the plays which he produced in his little theatre on Boar's Hill, about ten miles away from our house on the other side of Oxford. The things I remember about him are his fine appearance, his height, the breadth of his shoulders, his tanned complexion and wide-open blue eyes; and the beautiful courtesy with which he treated everyone, adult, adolescent or child. His courtesy, like all his words and deeds, was perfectly genuine and from the heart: there was nothing about it of pose, or conceit, or mockery, or condescension. He never took charge of any conversation; as Reyna says: "His aim was always to encourage others to talk, to hear *their* views, to know about *their* lives."

At that time my sister and I had set up a curtained stage in a disused barn, and this I displayed to John Masefield. He seemed really interested, and talked fascinatingly about theatres and what could be done in them. Two days later I received from him a copy of *The Midnight Folk*—a handsome copy in a special illustrated edition, signed by himself—and a letter wishing me all success with the theatre and asking whether he might be allowed to come and play a ghost in it. Down one side of the paper he had drawn a vigorous, swirling picture of a ghost.

If it were left to me to choose a handful of works by John Masefield to offer to posterity, I think that they would be the *Collected Poems*, chiefly for *Reynard the Fox*, with *Odtaa*, *Sard Harker*, *The Midnight Folk*, and *The Hawbucks*. I have not written of his novels but, had he not been before everything a poet, his output of novels would have ensured him a place in the history of twentieth-century literature, although they are, like his verse, uneven in quality. The best of them are intensely poetical in feeling. As to his poems, it seems to me that *Reynard the Fox* is likely to be read as long as printed books hold together: and I would give a high place to some of his short lyrics, such as the Ghosts' Song in *The Midnight Folk*.

In the dialogue of his novels, and in the snatches of common talk in his long poems, Masefield shows an acute ear for country speech, both that of Herefordshire, where he was born, and Oxfordshire

where he ended his days. His country people really live; more really
perhaps than his upper-class characters with whom, like Hardy, he
never seems perfectly at home. There is always something a little
stilted about their conversation. John Masefield was a countryman
from a far country and an Englishman to the bone. His England is
the England of a sporting print, of Leech as much as Alken and, in
Reynard the Fox, he celebrated the people and the ways of an older
England as he knew them in boyhood in Ledbury.

Reynard the Fox is the story of a hunt, from the meet until the end of
the day. Once the hunt is up, the story is told largely from the point
of view of the fox, but the descriptions of the hunters as they gather
for the meet, before moving off, are a series of brilliantly differenti-
ated brief portraits of country people of all classes in Victorian
times. The economy of words and accuracy of delineation of various
characters—the Squire, the Doctor, the sporting Parson, the ostlers,
the young men down from University, the women and girls, the
idlers in the inn-yard—show Masefield at his observant, trenchant
best. The poem is written in the same loosely octosyllabic rhymed
couplets as *The Everlasting Mercy*, and this mode seems to suit very
well the kind of narrative that *Reynard* is. For sharpness of description I should think some lines hard to beat, in verse or prose; here is
Major Howe:

> He was a lean, tough, liverish fellow,
> With pale blue eyes (the whites pale yellow),
> Moustache clipped toothbrush-wise, and jaws
> Shaved bluish like old partridge claws.

In *Recent Prose* (1924) we have John Masefield on his reasons for
writing *Reynard the Fox*. As a boy he had followed the Ledbury hunt
on foot at every possible chance; he knew the joy and excitement
which, in a hunting county, people felt as they saw the hunt sweep
past. He loved horses and hounds, and could feel his way into, and
describe with real immediacy, the sensations of going hard over
good country in a classic hunt such as the Ghost Heath Run of his
poem; ". . . in the English country during the autumn, winter and
early spring of each year the main sport is fox-hunting, which is not
like cricket or football, a game for a few and a spectacle for many,
but something in which all who come may take part, whether rich or
poor, mounted or on foot. It is a sport loved and followed by both
sexes and all classes. At a fox-hunt, and nowhere else in England,
except perhaps at a funeral, can you see the whole of the land's
society brought together, focused for the observer, as the Canterbury
pilgrims were for Chaucer."

The story of the Ghost Heath Run takes the reader through at a thudding pace, exciting to breathlessness: and the wild exhilaration of the riders and the hounds is counter-pointed by the fear and desperate exertion of the fox. Reynard is not caught: he wins the day by courage, strength and cunning. He goes off in the dark to kill for food:

> Then the moon came quiet and flooded full
> Light and beauty and clouds like wool,
> On a feasted fox at rest from hunting,
> In the beech-wood grey where the brocks were grunting.

Of foxes Masefield wrote: "Their grace, beauty, cleverness, and secrecy always thrilled me . . . I thought the fox a merry devil, though a bloody one. Then he is one against many, who keeps his end up and lives, often snugly, in spite of the world." Writing to Reyna he tells several stories of foxes—among them the travelling fox which had a special ruse for survival, and the fox which joined the pack unnoticed and hunted with the hounds. He also uses a most telling phrase which has meaning far beyond fox-hunting: "Hounds love the man who hunts them, not the man who feeds them."

When the austere and scholarly Robert Bridges, Poet Laureate, died in 1930, the Labour Prime Minister, Ramsay Macdonald, had to find a successor, and at the age of fifty-two, John Masefield was appointed. There was a good deal of controversy about that appointment. Some would have preferred Kipling (who was sixty-five), Yeats (also sixty-five), Housman or de la Mare. Yet it was an intelligent appointment in many ways. John Masefield wrote of England and for England. He had done fine work for his country in the First War—his plain, detailed, yet sensitive story of the Dunkirk evacuation in the Second, *The Nine Days Wonder*, has nothing imprecise or fantastic about it, which some might consider a fault of poets, but it is a poet's work nonetheless—and his proclaimed concern for the poor, the unlucky and the deprived was in accord with the ideals of the Prime Minister's party.

Some thought the whole business of the Laureateship out-of-date and meaningless. Nevertheless, it is an appointment known, however vaguely, to a great number of people. If it seems to demand a kind of poetic journalism, instant reaction in verse to Royal, national, or international events, it has other important meanings. As Constance Babington-Smith has written: "There is much more, or can be much more to the Laureateship than the writing of eulogies and dirges. If the incumbent so wishes, if he has the initiative and the will, he can do much to promote the interests of his fellow poets and of English poetry; he symbolises England's recognition of poets and poetry as worthy of honour . . . ." The Laureate's occasional verses are traditionally printed in *The Times*. It was wholly typical of John Masefield, as *The Times* revealed after his death, that he never sent his verses without a stamped addressed envelope, in case the editor should find them unsatisfactory. As we have seen he had a strong reverence for the Royal Family, so he had no reservations about accepting the appointment. In 1935, in King George V's Jubilee Honours, he was invested with the Order of Merit.

The relationship of John Masefield and "Reyna" began in the autumn of 1952, when she wrote her letter of thanks for a play of his, *Melloney Holtspur*, heard on the wireless. It is clear from Masefield's swift and grateful response, and from subsequent letters, that this was one of his works that he most cared for, but one whose message had not been comprehended. He had received only two other letters about that broadcast, one of them illiterate and abusive, and the other demanding an autograph. Reyna's impulsive act was to lead to something deeply satisfying both to herself and to Jan; to a warm, loving and enlightening exchange which was to last until his death in 1967, and elicit from him more than a thousand letters, and a now unknown quantity from herself although, in the course of nearly fifteen years, they met one another only five times.

Every writer has a special affection for some particular work, the writing of which has meant much to him, but which may not have been appreciated by his public. *Melloney Holtspur* is chiefly built on one of Masefield's persistent themes, the mistreatment of women by men; and its principal male character, a painter, is there to illustrate by his presumed talent and evident misdeeds, the plight of the artist, dedicated, and necessarily sometimes ruthless, in a conventional world. It must be a play nearly impossible to stage convincingly, since several of the leading characters are ghosts, and there is a suit of armour which speaks, and a secret hiding-place in panelling which opens and closes, all presenting severe technical problems. But in the broadcast performance which Reyna heard, it must have been that these technical difficulties did not obtrude, and that the lines came over, to one listener at least, with the fire and poignancy their author had intended.

Three years before Reyna's first appearance, when he was seventy, Jan had been very seriously ill, first with pneumonia, and then appendicitis. He had been slow to recover, and those who knew him saw how much illness had aged him physically and sapped a hitherto seemingly inexhaustible energy. He was no longer allowed to drive a car and there were restrictions on his visits away from home. Towards the end of his life also, both his eyesight and his hearing were beginning to fail.

In the last of a number of conjugal homes the Masefields had come to rest at Burcote Brook, near Dorchester in Oxfordshire. From a visit after the war I remember this as a rather large, ugly house, too large in fact for the two old people who lived in it, set on flat land with a view over the river Thames to the Berkshire downs. Constance, who, in 1952, was in her eighty-sixth year, had become very deaf. Jan and she managed as best they could with a series of housekeepers (the difficulty of finding which is the subject of a later lament by Jan to Reyna: he thinks that they must all have been murdered) and life at Burcote Brook was probably fairly uncomfortable. However, Jan had long been inured to discomfort. He had his collection of books, and a further continual supply from the London Library. He wrote every day, mostly poems, and at the time of Reyna's first visit, he was just bringing out his first chapters of an autobiography *So Long to Learn*. On top of that he must have been writing many letters and all, since he never seems to have had a secretary, in that clear consistent hand which scarcely lost its character even in his last years. Whatever a new generation of critics and younger poets might have said about him that was insulting or merely dismissive, he still had a very large number of admirers who wrote to him, and whom he felt obliged to answer. Their letters came from all over the world, and were often not simply letters but requests for help in publishing verses, or for critical advice, the kind of ruthless molestation which the celebrated have to suffer, and to which few respond as kindly and patiently as did the Poet Laureate.

Christmas was ruined for Jan by the sackfuls of mail, largely Christmas cards, which marked it. He felt he must answer everything, by hand, and every year raises a bitter complaint: "I live like a lost sheep in a kind of cold chaos", "Ankle-deep in envelopes, and in despair of ever being tidy again".

To read John Masefield's letters to Reyna is to receive a good grounding in English literature, with useful side-glances at French and Spanish as well. Reyna, when they first met, was already a serious reader. In an early letter she must have asked Masefield, who very soon became Jan to her, for some suggestions about reading, to which he responded with pleasure and a touch of diffidence. In the same manner as those delightful dons of an earlier age, who would preface an obscure literary or linguistic allusion with "As of course you know . . ." he gladly took on the role of guide, and was happy to share the fruits of his own erudition, but without, ever, the smallest touch of condescension. Thus he discoursed to Reyna, who must have prompted him with many skilful questions, on Chaucer and Langland, Shakespeare, Jonson and Fletcher; on Gray, Blake, Shelley and Keats; on Swinburne and Browning, Chatterton and Hazlitt, Defoe, Smollett, Sterne, Trollope, Yeats, and Synge, Thackeray, Dickens and Hardy, with not very approving glances at Sir Richard Burton and Oscar Wilde. Of French writers he wrote of Victor Hugo with enthusiasm, of Rabelais, Voltaire, Alexandre Dumas, Maupassant, Baudelaire, Georges Courteline and the Marquis de Sade; of Spanish, he discussed Cervantes, Quevedo and Bernal Diaz; he wrote many letters about Napoleon, by whom he was obviously fascinated; and as many about Wellington whom he greatly admired. He wrote of Homer and Sappho and Apuleius, Fielding and Richardson, of Marryat, and Conan Doyle, and of certain obscure English writers who were his special favourites. When Reyna discovered a first edition of *Lives of the Poets* he wrote to her at length about Samuel Johnson and James Boswell.

There are letters in this collection on boxing and jockeys, on eating contests and trials of strength, circuses, birds and flowers, cowboys, the San Francisco gold rush, Greek and Roman seals, shipwrecks, French prisoners of war, petrifying wells, the source of the Thames, ziggurats, Brueghel, ghosts, Wagner's golden trousers and the sad end of Sir Cloudesley Shovell. And naturally there are many letters about sailing ships and the technicalities of their rigging.

Jan had found in Reyna a lively mind and a curiosity about life and literature to match his own. After Constance's death in 1959, the ailing, lonely old man must often have found solace in his continuing epistolary conversation with Reyna. Almost to the end of his life his letters express the same eager willingness to tell and be told, the same anxious interest in everything that Reyna does.

For her part, Reyna kept up her end of the correspondence with warm affection and keen percipience. She came to know how to light or fan a spark of interest in some story, person or book, and make questions work as a catalyst of memory. This, in an extremely busy life, cannot always have been easy. Reyna had been for years a violinist with the Hallé Orchestra in Manchester; based upon Manchester, rather, for the orchestra was continually on its travels, fulfilling engagements in Africa, the Middle East, South America, Scandinavia, and Europe. In addition, she had to look after her father and mother, the latter of whom died in the course of this correspondence. She has told me of the difficulties she had in answering Jan's letters promptly, at snatched moments during rehearsals, or in trains and aeroplanes; and yet in her letters she must almost always have managed to give Jan the stories, the jokes, the queries, the comments on her reading which gave him so much pleasure and which inspired him, right until the last, to further flights of commentary and reminiscence, and to the most touching expressions of his care and affection for her.

Reyna, at the end of the last war, had spent some time in the WRNS, and her naval service together with her interest in ships and the sea, made a further bond between her and the gentle Victorian who was deeply sad for the death, in war, of Lewis his beloved son; who was, for all his celebrity, lonely, somewhat adrift in an increasingly puzzling era, and thus deeply grateful for this communion with a younger mind.

Early in their correspondence, that is to say after only three hundred or so letters, Reyna asked Jan if she might ever be allowed to publish any of them. Jan's reply was anxious. Years before, "shocked by the appalling irreverence shown to dead men by writers and editors" he had written a rhymed curse upon anyone who should seek to write his life or print his letters. He warned Reyna against the kind of literary touts who get hold of writers' letters under the pretence of writing a biography, and feared that she might, unwittingly, become their victim. In short his response was doubtful. But twelve years later, his views had changed. "May I write to you a writer's advice about publishing my letters, if after my death you should wish to make a selection from them? . . . Would you, who are you, but something of me as well, it seems to us, care to write a brief life of me to go with the letters?"

Reyna has made her selection, and upon that I have worked. Since she has decided not to write the brief life which Jan suggested, I have taken it on myself to supply something of the sort. John Masefield, although he died less than twenty years ago is, to those who remember him, indeed a creature of legend. For whose who do not, I have hoped to provide an acceptable introduction to his work.

Ledbury is very proud of its famous son. He is well-remembered in the town where there is now a John Masefield High School. For all the unhappiness of his early years, Ledbury and its countryside kept their place in his affections, and appeared in many of his works. When something went wrong with the famous church clock, and money could not be found to repair it, Masefield wrote a book, *St Katherine of Ledbury* and gave the proceeds for that purpose. (St Katherine, in the reign of Edward II, proved the truth of a revelation she had received, when she found in Ledbury what she was seeking—a town where the bells rang without human aid.) The place had had a curious attraction for writers. Sidney Smith lived in Ledbury at one time and, later, Elizabeth Barrett Browning; and Thomas Traherne is believed to have been at school there. It is odd that Masefield never mentions Traherne in his letters for, although he wrote much of John Fletcher, "whom I judge to be nearest to me of all whom I read", I should have thought that Traherne, on the quietist side of his nature, might also have come very near to him. Masefield speaks often in his letters of a belief in an ultimate Justice (not a Judgement) and the prevalence, now and hereafter, of Order, Beauty and Power. These lines from *Christian Ethicks* seem to express all that he most admired, and to be not a bad portrait of himself: "Magnanimity . . . includes all that belongs to a Great Soul: a high and mighty courage, an invincible patience, an immovable grandeur which is above the reach of injuries, a contempt of all little and feeble enjoyments, and a certain kind of majesty that is conversant with great things; a high and lofty frame of spirit, allied with the sweetness of Courtesy and Respect; a deep and stable resolution founded on humility without any baseness; an infinite hope and a vast desire; a Divine, profound, uncontrollable sense of one's own capacity; a generous confidence, and a great inclination of heroical deeds; all these conspire to complete it, with a severe and mighty expectation of Bliss incomprehensible."

I must hope that the reader will share my pleasure in these letters, for their joyful discursiveness, their mixture of the reminiscences of a most unusual career with homely jokes, snatches of music hall songs and sea-shanties, acute criticism of writers, and, throughout, for their flavour of the sea. I have not tampered with John Masefield's style of writing, since his abbreviations—"wd" for "would" and abbreviated "thoughs", for example—and his ampersands, are the necessary semi-shorthand of one who was a letter-writer on an heroic scale. His spelling of names, in one or two places, I have corrected, for consistency's sake, and have given the author of *The French Revolution* his correct form, rather than Masefield's version "Carlisle". I have also corrected one or two small errors of fact— very small ones: the wonder is that he made so few mistakes, even at an advanced age, and that his memory for facts and books and names held up until the end.

John Masefield once wrote to Reyna that poets were unlikely to be properly appreciated until fifty years after they were dead or in a madhouse. ("As I am neither, I am probably no good.") There is much about his work which many of today's readers might shy from, since lofty ideals and their expression do not seem to suit the kind of fevered banality that the arts generally have become. It is to be hoped that these notes on John Masefield's career, and the great amount that can be learned about the man from his letters, may inspire the more adventurous among readers of poetry to attempt what I believe would be a most rewarding exploration.

* * *

For such details as I have given of Masefield's early life, and of his time at sea, I am wholly indebted to Constance Babington-Smith's deeply researched and admirably written biography, *John Masefield* (1978), which must surely remain the definitive work on this remarkable life. I should like, also, to acknowledge with thanks valuable help given to me by Mr B. F. Cook, FSA, of the British Museum, Mr D. J. H. Smith, County Archivist of Gloucestershire, and Mr. E. H. H. Archibald of the National Maritime Museum at Greenwich. I owe a great deal to Miss Audrey Napier-Smith, whose kindness, patience and good humour in answering dozens of questions, and lending me certain mementoes, have made my task of editing entirely pleasurable.

The publishers would like to add their thanks to the Society of Authors for their help and their permission, on behalf of the Estate of John Masefield, to publish these letters; and to Miss Mary Griffith, Mr Peter Cotes, and Sir Peter Masefield, for all that they have done.

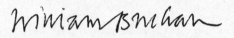

PROLOGUE

BY

"REYNA"

Ships, and deep friendships,
and remembered days . . .
John Masefield, "Biography"

The extracts in this book are all taken from the many letters which
John Masefield wrote to me, over a period of fifteen years; that is,
from 1952 until his death in 1967. It was at a time when he had
retired from active life after a severe illness: he was growing older,
and his own familiar world was fast receding from him. He must
often have felt very lonely, and only too ready to relive the past by
bringing before my eager eyes every kind of verbal coloured light
from the kaleidoscope of his vivid memory and many-sided mind.

In November 1952 I was a violinist in the Hallé Orchestra,
Manchester. Owing to wartime damage in the city, we were, at that
time, obliged to rehearse in a disused school where there was
insufficient light, one coal fire at the end of a huge room to warm
nearly ninety people, practically no ventilation, and ancient, defunct
radiators that still leaked a faint but persistent smell of gas. This
particular day, we had rehearsed for six hours, mostly badly printed
and very difficult modern music, and we were all tired to death.
Having arrived back at my flat, I switched on my wireless (which
took a moment or two to warm up in those days) and went into the
kitchen where I brewed some strong coffee to restore my shattered
self. As I returned, there was a play in progress which I had never
heard before. Within a few minutes all my troubles and weariness
were forgotten, and I was deep in the play—spellbound by the
beauty of the words and the magical atmosphere they created. When
the author's name was announced, with that of the play—John
Masefield's *Melloney Holtspur*,—I felt a surge of emotion and gratitude to him, and then and there I wrote a letter which I hoped
would convey something of the depth of my feelings. Thus began a
correspondence which continued until his death.

He wrote back at once. His first letter arrived; the beautiful hand-writing, with its eighteenth-century long S, on the envelope seemed to smile at me. "That's from somebody interesting," I thought, never dreaming it was from Masefield, for I had neither expected nor hoped for a reply. But it was from him, and this was not to be his last. At Christmas, a few weeks later, he sent me a greetings card, and with it a photograph of himself with Micky, his seventeen-year-old cat. I wrote to thank him, and from then on at least once a week an envelope addressed "Mifs Napier-Smith" in his distinctive hand would arrive, and I would reply.

About six weeks after his first letter, we met at his home near Abingdon. The orchestra was playing in Oxford that day, and between the end of the rehearsal and the beginning of the concert I had two and a half hours to spare. He sent a car to meet me, "with a reliable woman driver" as his letter had said. It turned out that both she and I had been Wren drivers during the war, so we were soon in conversation. During the drive to Burcote Brook, the Masefield's Thames-side home, I asked her, rather anxiously, what the Poet Laureate was like to meet.

"You needn't worry," she said. "Everyone loves him. He is so kind, and so full of old-world courtesy."

We drove through the tall gateway, and as we rounded the last bend of the drive, I saw him standing waiting, near the lauristinus of which he was so fond. He was dressed in a dark blue suit, his silvery hair, his white shirt and dark tie giving a kind of spruce neatness to his height and breadth of shoulder. I thought to myself: "Shake off fifty-odd years and put him in rougher clothes, and there would be the old *Conway* boy, the deep-water sailor." As we came nearer I saw his eyes, blue, far-seeing and sad, sad as those of Thomas Hardy, a dreamer's eyes. "Here is the Poet," I thought then: and when I stepped from his car and he came forward and spoke to me in his somewhat high, musical voice, using beautiful and meticulously pronounced English, I felt that I was shaking hands with the scholar, the thinker, the reader in the British Museum who had once (as he told me) held open the door for Lenin.

We sat, he and his wife, Constance, and I, and had our tea— home-made bread and scones, I remember, and honey from his own hives. Mrs Masefield made me very welcome. It set me wondering how many people she had manoeuvred graciously and tactfully in—and, particularly, out—of her famous husband's presence, so as not to overtire him. After tea he showed me his private sanctum, which he usually kept locked; a lovely room with french windows facing the river. One could see for miles, over wide stretches of long, rough grass first, and then across the Thames to the open country beyond. ("It is a pity," he wrote to me later, "that the sun did not shine for you five years ago, for then you would have seen the river shining, and far away (half a mile, about) the site of the little Roman town, now under the grass, to the R of the winter sunset . . .") Since the war, he told me, the grounds had been left to grow wild, and when, in summer, the grass grew long, broad paths were mown to give access to the river. Judith, his daughter, later showed me where she used to bathe during the hot weather.

In his room were a grand piano and a huge desk, both covered with papers ("I am revising a book on the *Conway*—a fearful job," he explained); a chesterfield (facing a big stove) with a kangaroo rug upon it: lovely blue and white Worcester porcelain on the mantelpiece; and, above that, a great picture of the sea. On top of a bookcase was a model of a full-rigged ship. In a letter he wrote later, he told me: "I made the model in the room here. It has been a bit knocked about, and I must repair it (some day). Before my illness this was our sitting-room. I worked in an outdoor shed."

As he showed me round, he gently drew me out. What was my opinion on this? My taste in that? My likes and dislikes in literature? All my life I have been a natural and deeply interested reader, but as I answered his questions the consciousness of an abysmal ignorance grew upon me.

"I am afraid I am a romantic," I confessed at last, with shame.

"That's all right." He gave a warm and kindly smile. "I am one myself."

That was my first visit to John Masefield. I only met him five times during the whole fifteen years of our correspondence. Four of these visits took place at Burcote Brook, where twice I met Mrs Masefield and twice their daughter Judith. The fifth occasion was when he went to London on a visit to the recently restored house of W. B. Yeats in Woburn Buildings (now Woburn Walk) off Southampton Row. There, sixty years before, he and other young writers had sat at the feet of the Master on his "Monday Evenings".

After seeing the restorations Masefield and I were driven to Greenwich, and he took me round the *Cutty Sark*. It was an unforgettable experience. He knew every inch of the old ship; he had, of course, immense knowledge of rigging, having himself sailed round the Horn in windships. He explained all kinds of practical things which had always puzzled me, and also made illuminating remarks such as: "This is where the hens would have been kept. We used to try to steal the eggs: we boys were always hungry." He was well-known on board, and it warmed my heart to see the "crew" muster to salute him as the old man slowly "went ashore". And very old he was, and his eyes were failing, but a chivalrous polite Victorian always, insisting upon my staying in shelter while he went out in the pouring rain to find where his chauffeur had parked the car.

Most of what I know of his character, his thoughts, his opinions, I gleaned more from his letters than from the meetings we had. His aim was always to encourage others to talk, to hear *their* views, to know about *their* lives. But he would speak, most willingly, of anything and everything other than of himself, of Hardy, of Chaucer, of America and Spain; of boxers and cricketers, of ships and the sea, pirates and the Bight of Benin. When I left after my first visit, he gave me his own copy of Johnson's *History of the Pyrates* (1724). He told me that he was sure Robert Louis Stevenson had read it before writing *Treasure Island*, as from its historic pages he had borrowed the name of Israel Hands, the Master of Blackbeard's sloop, who had been lucky enough to escape the gallows "and is alive at this time in London, begging his bread".

Gradually, over the years of his writing to me, I have been able, as it were, to dip a little more deeply into the unplumbed depths of the character and background of this man. He never invited enquiry—he discouraged biographers, preferring to write, in his own autobiographical books, mainly of things that had interested him. I never knew him when he was "tall, straight and blue-eyed" and when "no one but a strong athlete and runner could have conceived Saul Kane's tremendous sprint" (A comment made by Gerald Cumberland in *Set Down in Malice*, 1918, discussing *The Everlasting Mercy*). He was nearly eighty when we met, but still mentally young and alert, interested in almost everything, brave and gentle and kind. So much is revealed in these letters. In them may be followed the quick changes of his mind; the variety and colour of his moods; the splendour of his imagery; his little twists of irony and humour; his wonderful memory; his humanity, humility, and his great heart. Above all, and through everything, shines the clear and vivid power of his story-telling. He "had the Phantsie very strong", as someone said of Shakespeare, and the life of his imagination was the most dominant of the many aspects of this very complex character. In many ways I believe that I became a part of his "phantsie", for he hardly knew me, yet in these letters would address me with a mixture of charming Victorian delicacy and lavish warmth of affection certainly unusual between two people who had met but five times. I often wrote to say how guilty I felt that so much of his time was taken up with my silly questions, but he answered: "Please, do you not know that I am honoured by your questions;

and vain that you should think me capable of answering them. It is always a joy to me to try to answer them, as far as I can: and I hope, therefore, that you will ask whenever you think I know the answer. This can be but seldom, for I am a very ignorant man. I know less than any man I know. But ask, ask, my dearest, ask."

How fortunate that I did.

In selecting these letters I have taken great care that what is printed in this book is, word for word, Masefield's writing. I have made deletions—but only those parts of his letters that I considered of no interest to others: the formal, the trivial, the technical, and the repetitions, which, in fifteen years of frequent and long letters, were bound to occur. As the letters came to me—and often, when the Hallé was on tour, they followed me from country to country—so in that order they appear here; JM, however, never dated his letters, and although I, fortunately, numbered them as they arrived, some slight confusion was inevitable—not helped by the fact that he was apt to dart from one topic to another only to turn back later: a characteristic which adds to the letters a charming immediacy of a lively mind.

I wish to thank most gratefully Judith Masefield, Sir Peter Masefield, and Constance Babington-Smith for their kind support and encouragement; the Society of Authors who, on behalf of the Estate of John Masefield, have given permission to publish these letters; and Peter Cotes for giving such generous and invaluable help to "Reyna".

Audrey Napier Smith

1952

1

Dear Mrs [sic] Napier-Smith[1]

Many thanks for your very kind letter about *Melloney* and my other writings.

I am glad to think they had the happy fortune to give you pleasure.

Might I be allowed, do you think, just to keep the link between us still in being? Writers seldom meet with readers and are grateful to them.

Yours very sincerely
John Masefield

[1] JM's first letter to Audrey Napier-Smith in early December.

2

Dear Miss Napier-Smith

I find it hard to tell you how deeply I have been touched by the kindness of your letter, and by the grace and beauty of your gift.[1]

Now, as I said, writers seldom meet with readers, but would you consider whether you could grant the privilege of sending you a book now and then?

Let me thank you for your gift and letter, and wish you all the joy

your blessed art gives, and all happy, gladdest success in it, and in
life too, always.

Believe me, very gratefully yours,

John Masefield

[1] ANS had sent JM a photograph of herself. This letter was written on 12th
December.

A Dogger.

1953

3

Dear Miss Napier-Smith

Your very charming kind letter made me very happy. Thank you. I am so glad to know that you will not be vexed by a book now and then: and much honoured by your liking the photograph. The cat was a ginger cat, named Micky. He died aged 17, two years ago. Please do not think that I am reading any special Sage. I was looking up a word, for a cross-word puzzle, in a Dictionary of Quotations . . .

. . . About the 20th [January], when you are to play in Oxford. I have been very ill, and cannot go to hear you play, alas; but we wonder whether you would care to come out just to see us after your concert? Would that be too tiring for you, after playing? We could give you tea.

A reliable woman-driver would bring you here, if the roads should be free of fog, ice and snow. There should be a young moon, and after tea the driver would take you back to Oxford, and get you there by 6 p.m. or so. Please, dear Reader, let me arrange all this; if it will not be too cold or too tiring.

You will not find us terrifying: only glad to see a new friend who is a musician as well as a reader. We do not play, but have had much fondness for your art, and old age is touched to the quick by youth and loves every sight of it.

With many thanks for your letter and all the best wishes to you for this young year.

Gratefully yours
John Masefield

Let me add, that I am no longer ill, only unable to be very active.

Perhaps you might like the enclosed *Dalgonar*, a colossal full-rigged ship that I remember; a terror to all hands I should say, and later fatal to them, but the bows are very lovely.

4

Most kind, welcome, understanding Reader,

I know not quite how to begin this letter of thanks to you, having so very much to thank you for, first for writing to me, and then for so kindly telephoning me, and then for filling our hearts with joy of having you,[1] and then for the most precious and prized gifts.

We mean to listen to you tonight.

I have found some *Wanderer*[2] photographs for you: please keep them if they interest you, the Bristol print is rather smoky I fear.

Please, be sure that I cannot write formally to you again, and would seek the privilege of some name that you would like, possibly some name that might be just ours.

I was very mindful of your glorious crown of hair and wondered whether the name hidden in your name

AUDREY NAPIER
REYNA,[3]

the old spelling of the Spanish word for Queen, would be permitted or liked?

This is a letter of grateful thanks.
John Masefield

[1] My first visit to JM was on 20th January 1953, a date that was already important to him, and which became of significance to both of us. On my departure, JM gave me his old, and sadly battered, copy of Johnson's *History of the Pyrates* (1724), which he later had bound for me. ANS.

[2] The *Wanderer*, a four-masted barque, was first seen by JM as a boy when on the training-ship *Conway*, and remained for ever after his ideal of a sailing vessel.

[3] Pronounced Ra-eena.

5

Reyna mia

I am so glad that you liked the ship photographs and so happy that you liked the sender.

When I saw the *Wanderer* first she was very loftily rigged even more splendid than in the San Francisco, 1892, photograph: but she came down in the world, poor soul, as sailing-ships did.

I am going to send you *Dead Ned*[1] and some other matters. There is a 2nd volume of the *Pyrates* somewhere: not nearly so interesting: all about those at Madagascar whom the *Weymouth* and *Swallow* also put an end to.

. . . I must read up about violins, I see.

Bless you,

John Masefield

[1] A novel by JM, published 1938.

6

. . . I want to make up for all the 2nds [of May] I have missed in the past, please; so now and then you must not be vexed if I send you a book or two inscribed "For your Birthday". When I get the proper total duly given, never mind, but put the others to the future, for birthdays to come.

Do you care much for the poetry of Thomas Gray?

. . . I was touched & thrilled to read of your journey home.[1]

I used to go to London from Manchester every week about 50 years ago [1904–1905]. I left the paper [the *Manchester Guardian*] at midnight on Fridays & was back at the paper at 8 p.m. on Sundays.

[1] If ANS had two consecutive free days, she used to travel through the night from Manchester to Bristol to spend those days with her parents.

7

. . . I was in the *Guardian* office for 6 months, while one of the men was abroad, but I was for years a contributor and still (very rarely) review a book for them, once a year or so.

I was there under C. P. Scott, whose first wife died about that time; soon after I left I think. I met Scott and Montague[1] occasionally after I left the city. M was a remarkable man too (M was married to C. P. Scott's daughter) and a first-rate journalist like C. P.

I liked hearing of your braving Force 9 to see the eclipse, & wish that you had had better reward, and hope that you caught no cold . . .

. . . I never thought of my name seeming romantic to anyone.

Swinburne's name was wonderful to us young men, about equally suggestive of fire and water and a kind of whirling dream.

Tennyson used to put himself into a happy trance "by considering the letters of his name", but I never met others who could do this.

May I now send the little Gray? In a note on p.109 you will find the heavenly stanza he cut out . . .

[1] C. E. Montague (1867–1928), author of *Disenchantment* and other novels.

8

. . . Please, may I ask all sorts of things, if they will not seem inquisitive and impertinent? If they do, you must write the word *Cleopatra*: and that will stand for C's neat reformer:
"Thou hast damnable iteration, fellow."

. . . The Gray I have had for years. I don't care much for the Odes, except the Eton one, but I adore "Selina", and the "Elegy" and the "Long Story", and the "Impromptu" and "Tophet" and the scandalous one about Jemmy Twitcher.[1] I love all these very dearly: & as I have another Gray (2 in fact) I would like you to have this one as a special birthday gift . . .

[1] The satirical nickname for the Earl of Sandwich (1718–92).

9

. . . You ask me about the Pyrate book. Please will you someday post back the fragments to me? It is, I fear, "all over the place, like a shifting backstay". If the book interests you at all, and you would like it as a link with Jan. 20th you shall have it; but please, first, let me have it done up by a binder here.

In case you should like it, I send a print of the *Wanderer* just after she reached Kingston in 1891, with her Captain dead on board; this was as I saw her in the Mersey. Would you care to have the sail-plan and deck-plan of her?

10

. . . You must not think that writers always write because they are wise or great. Often they write not from special beauty but from special defect. We used to say that the traditional Blind Poet (the Homer of legend) was only an ordinary man, who could not do ordinary things because he was blind, & so made poetry.

What I love in Gray is his power over the 4 line ten-syllable stanza, the quatrain or elegiac stanza, so called from its fitness for elegiac or lamenting verse. The quatrain is the foundation of some more elaborate verse-forms, and Gray, in the "Elegy", the "Impromptu" & the "Tophet" uses it with extraordinary skill that I hope will delight you dearly on your long journeys sometimes when the carriage is full . . .

. . . I did once see a very lofty American ship in Liverpool docks with a moonsail yard, the 8th yard from her deck. I was never near her, for she was towed elsewhere to discharge, and I never saw another.

I think that a good many very lofty American ships set triangular moonsails without yards; the apex was hoisted up to a block or sheave at the summit of the mast.

11

. . . I used to think that there was a text in the Bible "Upon them that hope is his Mercy".[1] My Bible had a "fox" or rust-spot on the word *is*: the word is really *in* which (to me) makes it common-place.

Hope is an ever-green in the heart, and I send you two little ever-green leaves, bay and lauristinus, one from each side of the door. You passed between them on the 20th. In the Bad Winter both trees seemed killed, but they have revived and are beautiful. May they bring cheer to you; of courage and faith & kindness you have full measure: and all these things and their Causer are with you now, be very sure. May they truly guard and bless you . . .

[1] My mother had had an accident and was very ill. ANS.

12

. . . The plays of Mr Fry[1] are all competent and successful plays. I have not seen nor heard them and do not know what effects he makes by writing them in verse, nor how he trains his people to speak them.

To the Victorians, like myself, modern verse is without any inner life; to which the modern writer retorts that my own verse is without any life at all: so there we rather stick . . .

¹ Christopher Fry (born in 1907), the dramatist, best known for his verse plays *A Phoenix too Frequent* (1946), *The Lady's Not For Burning* (1948), *Venus Observed* (1950), which were extremely popular at the time.

13

. . . You mentioned the beauty of the name "moonsail"; it is beautiful, isn't it? The sail was sometimes called a moon-raker, which would be a good name for a National winner. In its triangular yardless form it was sometimes called a "Jimmy Green".

Thank you for telling me all about your writing to me in Nov.

I had 2 other letters about the broadcast: an illiterate and abusive letter, and a request for an autograph. Your genuine, gentle & lovely letter would have won any heart at any time: and coming when it did it meant much, dear girl, and means more now . . .

. . . You were asking about some modern poetry. Generally speaking, you will find truth in the remark "Good artists do not care for each others' work". In youth, after enjoying many styles, an artist sees what he can aim at, and cares for that way beyond all others. All his power, and the power of all his clique, for he will belong to a clique, will turn *to* work of that sort, and *from* work, however good, of another sort.

Velasquez could not care at all for Raphael. William the Fourth did not care for Turner: "Give me Huggins,"¹ he cried. W the 4th was not an artist, but, being a sailor, he could probably draw ships, and found Huggins a better sailor than Turner.

Generally speaking, an artist only really profoundly understands the art of his own formative years, 15 to 25. When I was young, there were two aims among writers; a way to an exquisite select perfection, to be loved and understood by very few, and a way to the heart of the multitude. All young men longed for both qualities, to suit the shrine and the market-place both.

Keats had an exquisite perfection, and threw it all away, in trying to find a verse that the many would love. Tennyson & Swinburne, in their different ways, had exquisite perfections. Since the First War, poets have been trying to find an idiom that can delight the multitude. They have lost many qualities in the attempt, and have not yet found something that will stand by the work of Masters, but they are trying; and with broadcasting to help them, they are likely to make a fine poetry based on good speech.

My school, that of the Romantics, who began with Gray, base their work on Chaucer, the early Shakespeare, & the early Milton; on choice books, that is, and a lovely general culture in which music is very important.

I understand that much talent and good invention is with the moderns, and also the modern world. But what shone, and seemed tempting, if unattainable, when I was 18, seems even more marvellous now; and I will not change; even if I could I wouldn't. I belong to the camp of Gray, Keats, Rossetti and Wm Morris and the early Yeats.

Generally speaking, the best art of any time is pretty good; and seems an improvement on its immediate predecessors. Its makers, who think thus, tend to loathe the art that follows & supplants them . . .

[1] William Huggins (1781–1845) was Marine Painter to King William IV. Three of his paintings of the Battle of Trafalgar are at Hampton Court.

14

. . . In the Shanty book, you will find "Spanish Ladies", that the "Conways"[1] of my year all sang (it isn't a shanty) and "Rolling Home" that meant all the world to sailors for years. It, too, is a song, but was used as a capstan shanty; and I think I have sung some of it (to myself) almost daily for over 60 years; and with a kind of fever, whenever coming near England from abroad.

. . . I will send you my notes on *Macbeth* before long. There can be no doubt that it was the most wonderful thing written since the *Iliad*: and altogether a divine & glorious poem *about 700 lines longer* than what we now have of it, if not even longer, but the theatre cut it, and the cuts were no doubt burned in the Globe Theatre, or lost, or burned in some later fire.

I loved your story of the children at your lunch in the churchyard: love the thought that you play to them. These children are to have enormous political power, for which their training has not and cannot fit them. Any art that may make them human now is England's hope: I see no greater hope.

. . . I was much interested in what you tell me of your Gagliano. I play no instrument except the Fool, and I am old even for that, but I have done much public speaking, and have experience of (really hundreds) halls, theatres and concert rooms; and know how they differ; and know how some of the old ones were (as I used to put it, knowing nothing about it) just like violins for resonance and delight . . .

¹ Old boys of the Merchant-Service training-ship *Conway* are always referred to as "Conways".

15

. . . I once was on a platform with a lot of writers, and heard a lady below me say "Now tell me which is which."

Her friend said, "The good-looking one is Mr de la Mare: the one with the squiggly hair is Masefield."

. . . Please you mustn't trust too far to my views of poetry. Most writers would tell you that I am obsolete or very, very old fashioned, & you who are of this time should learn of one younger what this time seeks to say. I can tell you a little of the Romantic Mov. to which I belong. Time was when I would have talked to you till breakfast about the poetry of the Romantics. Now I get tired and have to go to bed.

16

. . . Not long ago I sent you a little photograph of the *Royal George* under sail. I now send you a small card of Clevely's painting of her, down the Thames at Deptford; interesting, perhaps, as it shows (at the waterline) that she was not copper-sheathed but lime-washed in the old way, against the Teredo worm that bores through plank below water.

Said worm is a terror.

Try (some day) at Greenwich or other Naval museum, to see his work. They used to have specimens at Greenwich. You would not believe that a soft thing like a slug could play such old Harry with oak.

The *Royal George* is the ship of Cowper's poem,¹ and a man called David Ingram, who went down in her, and (unlike about 1,000 others) came up again, & wrote a vivid account of her going. Marryat took this narrative, spoiled all its simplicity, and used it in a tale of his, *Poor Jack*, which you may have read.

When I was little, men blew up some remnants of the *RG* to improve the anchorage there. The wood was bought by some publishers, who used it as binding for a little reprint of Ingram's book, and other *RG* matter. This was one of the very first books I ever read.

¹ Rear-Admiral Richard Kempenfelt gained a brilliant victory over the French in 1781. In 1782 he hoisted his flag on the *Royal George* of Lord Howe's fleet. The vessel was in a state of incomplete repair and sank. The admiralty claimed that she had been capsized by a squall, but the general opinion of the Navy was that she was rotten (see Letter 18): a large piece of her bottom fell out and she went down at once. It is estimated that at least 800 people died; Robert Southey commemorated the disaster with the poem, "The Loss of the *Royal George*".

17

. . . I have a photograph of the *Dalgonar* somewhere; not a good one . . . if I can find it you shall have it. She was a big and terrible splendid ship: and "she was overset", like the *Royal George* in the poem, and drowned all hands.

Later, she drifted 4,000 miles, & came ashore on a Pacific island, bottom up, and there she very likely lies to this day.

When the light betters, I'll try to paint her for you, as she was; and you shall mock all you like, & I'll not mind.

. . . About drowning being pleasant. I had reached the pleasant stage when ducked at Liverpool as a new chum: it was pleasant & green & sunny. The prelude to this stage was harsh . . .

18

. . . You very dearly told me of your ways of reading. I asked because I have a big one-volume Herman Melville book containing a lot of his work; & I would like you to have this, but felt that it is a heavy, ill-designed book only to be easily read from a table. I used to read him a good deal, not so much *Moby Dick* (tho' I liked the Nantucket chapter) as *Typee*, *Omoo* and *White Jacket*. *Typee* is very good; and *White Jacket* described US naval life 110 years ago: & books of real lower deck naval life are very rare. But best of all his books I liked *Redburn*, about old-time New York, and old-time Liverpool.

They had a nice show of whaling things from Nantucket in New York once; all the gear Melville saw in use. I shall send you a *Poor Jack* with the hashed-up Ingram paper.

I met an American whaler once, who told me that he once saw a whale swallow a seaman whole; and they promptly killed the whale, got out the man, & restored him to life, but by that time his hair had been completely bleached; permanently white; no more raven, nor golden, nor amber love-locks for him. I guess it taught him not to go tormenting whales another time . . .

. . . Nicholas Pocock[1] the painter must have seen the boy Chatterton at some time. He engraved a plate, "The Infant Chatterton showing Genius the way" or the other way about; you know the kind of thing. He painted moving ships very movingly. He left descendants. His great great somethings were Miss Lena Ashwell (Lady Simson) the actress and her brother R. Pocock a writer; who at one time started the ride round the USA on a horse. I suppose it would have been a ride of 11,000 miles and would have taken 2 years or so; but I think the ride was interrupted by some important matter.

. . . May I offer you an old passport photograph that has travelled with me many thousands of miles, by Nombre di Dios and Porto Bello, four times across the Atlantic, once across America, and in almost every European land except Russia. It is a much travelled piece and many suspicious police eyes have looked at it . . .

. . . You ask about my painting; alas, I have to say like Leonardo or some other great dog, "I do not paint as I would but as I can." I paint about 20 minutes or 25 minutes in a week; usually for you; & use a fine BB pencil a good deal: Turquoise blue for skies (& cobalt for the tropics) and 2 or 3 blues for seas, cyanine, prussian, ultra marine. You must laugh sometimes . . .

. . . About the *Royal George*. It seems to be a fact that the *cause* of her collapse was that she was utterly rotten & unseaworthy, and when heeled over broke her beams that held her sides together, and that this fact made the authorities very coy about trying to raise her. They feared that too much dishonesty might come to light . . .

. . . Please, you must not think that I was ever nearly a good enough seaman to be employed as a rigger. Riggers were wonders, I assure you.

I never was a sailor (worth a red cent) but loved ships, in a way, & was fond of rigging, & would have been very happy as a rigger: but knew that the law of my being was not sailorising. What it was I had to knock about the world to find out, and plenty of knocks were knocked: but I want to talk to you some day about this, not to write about it.

. . . On the 20th I mentioned a Shakespeare[2] written in a great hurry over 40 years ago. I send the last copy of the book to you. I used it daily as I wrote the revision, and sent it to you on the day that the revision was done. After 42 years, I have pretty well re-written the book, and now it may well be that though I think the old book sad stuff, the world may think the new one even sadder. It will now be a little longer than formerly, & comes no nearer to the truth, but I still feel the marvel of the man's power, and range, and verse, more, even, than formerly.

[1] Nicholas Pocock (1741–1821) English marine painter. First exhibited Royal Academy 1782.

[2] *William Shakespeare* (1911)

19

... I was charmed by your tale of the Irish Priest's description of Good Friday;[1] & by the other tale of the people doing the *Messiah*. This tale used to be applied to a Duke of Devonshire (about 1850–60, I think) who could not (in the tale of him) keep awake; and dreamed once that he was addressing the House of Lords, and woke up to find that he was.

... Thank you for telling me so much about Bulawayo.[2] Of course the ostrich is a fine foreign bird, and well worth a visit, but I'll be glad when you are with The Swan at Bibury. When at Bibury I hope that you will find that the Norman door (the North door I'm afraid I must add) of the Church has been unwrecked by time & the wars.

... You ask if the artistic gifts of writers seem sometimes to have no connection with their personalities? Well, very often, the writer is the very opposite of his art: the art completes the want in a person, or tries to complete it. The "complete man" appears in the Renaissance. Raphael, the golden youth, whom all adored: Shakespeare, "the handsome, well-shap't man" who "had the phantsie very strong"; John Fletcher,[3] whose "inimitable soul did shine through his countenance in such air and spirit that the painters confessed it was not easy to express him".

It is generally held that writers are less complete persons than a century ago. We have no-one to compare with Wordsworth, Tennyson, Dickens, Trollope: no-one.

... The "leaf-like" decoration in the Heinemann books: it is probably only the House's sign or totem, done for old Heinemann by Wm Nicholson. It is meant for a Windmill, and once was visibly a windmill, but the blocks are worn out, I think, and the impressions are no longer clear ...

[1] "The very Divil of a day in the Church". ANS.

[2] The Hallé was to go on tour there for the Rhodes Festival.

³ John Fletcher (1579–1625). He collaborated with Francis Beaumont from *c.* 1606 to 1616 in the writing of plays. *The Two Noble Kinsmen* (1634) was probably written by Fletcher and Shakespeare.

20

. . . So you have a Bosun's Call and can pipe it. I had one once, and could pipe it a little; but I have not heard one since my *Conway* time. Only one Warrant could *really* blow it there. Can you pipe belay?

Never think that I think you anything but exquisitely feminine . . . & that I can have anything but joy in this link of the sea between us. For both of us the sea means much. It was rather rammed down my throat, and from you it was barred by womanhood, but it is a gladness to me now, and a joy to be near you with it.

I have thought much of the anguish that must come to many spirited girls when they find that certain ways of life are almost shut to them. All this allotting of Destiny seems often hard upon women . . . It is all mixed with thoughts of religion & everlasting life: and I feel that I must not let you think that I am a Church man, but share what bread and salt I have with you.

21

. . . You ask about difficult poetry. New minds often seem difficult and hateful and meaningless (or blasphemous) as so often they are in rebellion against whatever is accepted. Generally, in about 6 generations, *all* in their work becomes perfectly clear—some of the difficulty (long before that) is seen to be due to perversity or weakness, defect in judgement, want of complete culture or tenderness in the creator. Much obscurity in art is due to defect in art, to unclear thought, to insufficient mastery. Art is like the sun: it makes clear: it is what gets in the way that makes shadow.

A lot of old art is obscure because the texts are corrupt, as in Aeschylus and Shakespeare; or because the paint has perished, or the fresco peeled, or the statue has had its nose & arms knocked off.

A lot of obscure poetry is bad work: the writer's thought has not been clear to him, or he hasn't cared to make it clear.

We have plenty of queer poetry, like Blake's prophetical books. Men grub into these for odd meanings, but the result is not always uplifting. Shelley is more tempting. There are all sorts of lovely wonders, as to his inner meanings, in "The Revolt of Islam", "Prometheus", & "The Sensitive Plant". Shelley was a startling spirit, fast growing more and more when he died. Some of his inner meanings are still hidden.

Shakespeare the man remains completely or very nearly completely hidden, but some of his meanings are clear enough. The chief puzzle is "The Phoenix and the Turtle";[1] but I fancy that his main design in that was playful, fanciful design and (perhaps) a very intimate word to two close friends (Sir J & Lady Salisbury).

Generally speaking Dante is the most difficult of the great poets.

[1] A poem attributed to Shakespeare, published 1601 by Robert Chester in *Love's Martyr*.

22

. . . I am at last sending you a photograph of a Wm Huggins painting.

It shows the Russian squadron near their flagship, the 74, *Azof*, at, or near, Malta, just after the battle of Navarino.[1] The Allied ships, Russians, French and English, put into Malta, to refit, land their wounded, and draw stores, etc.

The *Azof* was a good deal battered in the battle: and you will note that she has no fore nor mizen topgallant masts, only jackstaffs. She is hoisting out (or in) her launch, from the booms; and seems to be doing it in an odd way, with insufficient gear, and with no great forethought. Perhaps I am wrong about this. The boat may be something much lighter than a launch. Huggins noted it as something special to the occasion: and must well have known how very differently our own men would have done it, with extra supports to the yards that took the weight, etc. etc. (using also the foreyard).She may well have been unable to risk using her foreyard. It is a little point that puzzles me . . . I am not sure of the part the *Azof* took at Navarino, but I think she was on the left, and under fire from a fort as well as from the Turk fleet. Anyhow, she lost many more men than any single ship in action, and I expect Huggins wished to show this somehow.

She had over 60 men wounded, and perhaps every eighth man on board out of action. I will try to find out what she did, but it will take some time, and may not be very enlightening.

[1] The Battle of Navarino was fought on 20 October 1827, a naval action during the Greek War of Independence, and the last to be carried out wholly under sail. A British, French and Russian fleet defeated a Turkish and Egyptian fleet.

23

. . . Please may I send a line or two more about the *Azof*, or *Azoff*, or *Azov*?

Navarino is a big harbour with a narrow entrance. The Turks were arranged by a renegade French officer, in 3 tiers in a semi-circle inside the harbour. The entrance to the harbour is about 1,200 yards across, and under easy gunfire from the batteries on one side and the fort on the other.

The Allied Fleets sailed in two lines, the English leading the R line, with the French; and the Russians leading the left. They sailed right up to the first line of Turk ships and there anchored.

Their orders were to avoid hostilities, but to cause the Turks to cease their atrocities on the Greek inhabitants.

They took up their positions without opposition. In doing this, some of the English and other Allied ships came to the left of the Russians, so that the *Azov* was very nearly in the centre.

Near the harbour entrance, close to the fort, were some Turkish fire-ships (yellow dots on the plan). [He had drawn a plan in various colours.]

These began the battle by firing at an English boat. In a few minutes, all hands were firing, and for 4 hours were hard at it. By the end of that time most of the Turk ships were sunk or burning and blowing up. Being in the centre, the *Azov* was bound to be shattered and battered. All the Allied ships were probably hit by many of their friends' shot. With the old black powder there was dense smoke of course: few could see anything.

After the battle, the Allies had to stay in the harbour for some days, repairing rigging etc, before they could sail to Malta. All agree that Admiral Heiden, in the *Azov*, was a hero & a wonder, well deserving the big green blob I give him.

The battle was fought with nearly all ships at anchor. Many had believed that there would be no battle: and tho' the hands were at quarters some ships were not properly cleared for action: bulkheads not down, cabins not cleared away, etc; however, the battle cleared these all right.

The Russian ships came from the Baltic as the Turks could and did bar the Dardanelles. They were in high order and of new copper "of a beautiful dark rose colour", which added much to their appearance. It is possible that Huggins shows this copper: but it would not show in the photograph.

The Egyptian ships, that could sail at all, fled in the night. They were patched in their shot-holes with canvas; & a few got back to Alexandria.

The English ships were ill-supplied with gear; and the fleet discipline was not good. The marines seem to have been in bad order, with the sergeants selling liquor to the privates. However, the gunnery seems to have been good; and the victory so complete that Greece really became free from the Turks from that moment.

You may note from the plan that nearly every shot fired by the Turks' ships was bound to hit the Fort or the shore batteries if it missed the Allies. This may have cheered the many Greek slaves serving in the Turk forces.

> And things like this will often be
> In any famous victory.

The shot from the shore batteries, if it missed the Allied ships must have hit the Turk ships or gone on into the main Turk camp in the bight of the bay. Perhaps the true Moslem had some joy in the thought that it was a Moslem cannon-ball that brought him to the waiting peri.

. . . In the USA, when lecturing, it was possible to get a dress shirt and collar washed, starched, ironed & dried in about an hour, so that one could manage with only a few, with luck, except in the wilder parts.

24

. . . To think of you reading *The Three Musicians* [Beardsley]! Never think that people now look on musicians with scorn. "The Tweeded Tourist" is now extinct: but about 1895 he represented "the Philistine" of 1875: a public opinion, that is, a vast middle class opinion, as Matthew Arnold said, "purblind and hideous", loathing music, hating books, thinking culture effeminate and decadent, and giving to all Europe at all times, the sight of their ill manners and awful point of view. You cannot know what the tweeded tourist was, nor how the clever youth writhed under it and tried to mock at it. Wilde was leader of the mockery, and the tourist was helpless against Wilde; but then Wilde fell: & there was fearful exaltation in the TT camp. This was what the TT had always said: "Poetry is vile: poets ought to be hung: art is unclean: artists are the scum of all abomination and corruption: now the world can see."

However, there are now few tourists and none in tweed: the TT is gone: England the most musical land in the world & you must have the joy of knowing that you are wanted and loved: and that wherever you play you touch the national heart. Now you are going to a vast new wonderful concert-hall in a new city [Bulawayo] which in the TT's day was a savage King's Kraal and capital, newly burned by the TT's younger sons.

25

. . . What an interesting account you give of the strength of finger in the cellist.[1] I have heard nothing quite like it.

The feat that some strong men have (or are said to have) done, of tearing a pack of cards in two, and then tearing the double thickness of the two halves across, is the feat that has always impressed me. I have never seen it: nor S. Holmes bending a poker; nor John Ridd taking a bull by the horns and pushing him backwards.

. . . Mark Twain's friend from Caribou, who picked up a glass tumbler and quietly and neatly bit out of it a tidy semi-circular piece, as one might bite thin bread and butter, has also impressed me, though it was before my day.

I like quieter feats, such as that of Admiral Rodney's sailor, who to please King George III ran to the main-truck, stood on it on his hands, took off his hat with his toes, and waved it thrice around while the crew gave three cheers.

[1] André Navarra had shown me the power in the little finger of his left hand: with thumb and all fingers held lightly down on a table he could raise his little finger and bring it down on a lump of sugar with enough force to crush the sugar to small crumbs and powder. ANS.

26

Reyna dear, my grateful thanks for your welcome kind letter about the natives,[1] and your life in the wilds, and for the picture you create of yourself: still (as I read the letter) very well, deeply interested, and happy. Possibly, too, the nights are a shade less cold, or you are now equipped against them. You have certainly a seeing eye and a feeling heart, and are knowing something that will be deep in your deepest self for all your time.

I have often supposed that musicians must loathe playing for ballets. Many years ago I knew one who ran a theatre orchestra, and directed Pavlova's music until she died; but that was devotion to a rare spirit to whom all were devoted. I have often felt that those who torture the masters into being accompaniments to the dance, are not friends of the arts, either of music or the dance. But this has been a modern disease of the now dying ballet, and the ballet will die out before it has done any lasting harm, so be of good cheer; that is so easy to write, isn't it, to one far away, who has perhaps 2 3-hour performances in each day.

The heatwave was nothing: the usual Arctic blast soon followed & has continued.

I have always liked the negroes that I have seen much of: & been often impressed by the cleverness of the children. We seem heading into a racial struggle: & what can be done? No-one likes a half-breed: & few, either black or white, are without colour pride. When I have seen negroes dance, or heard them singing, I have felt "Man is but One Soul", but then, later the colour vanity returns.

I hate to think of the leopard[2] biting you, but I am glad it was not a hyena, for hyenas are said to take off most of the face at one go, while the person is asleep.

> Picture the wretched victim's horror
> Facing a mirror on the morrer.

[1] I was at the time in Bulawayo, on tour with the Hallé Orchestra. ANS.

[2] Laurence Turner, the leader of the orchestra, and an animal lover, was presented with a leopard cub which he let me hold. She eventually went to Belle Vue Zoo in Manchester. ANS.

27

. . . Thank you so very much for your most kind, vivid, interesting letter about the [Victoria] Falls. You have seen perhaps the most shattering wonder in the world, before they have begun to harness its power. All agree that Niagara is nothing to what you saw, though of course it may be said, that taking it by and large, Niagara does, on the whole, convey a general impression of dampness.

Some years ago, I read an account of a fearful chasm in the US, a kind of fossil waterfall, if I may use the term. It was (if I remember) vaster than Niagara and loftier than the Zambesi, and must at one time have emptied a kind of Amazon down its crag. The photographs of it (with all the Amazon gone) looked appalling bare hard rock, but the only water now is a surface drainage pond underneath it.

I shuddered to think that perhaps you nearly slipped into the Zambesi, & hope that you weren't hurt, nor in real danger.

You have had a wonderful time, and are one who enjoys such

things. The Spanish proverb says "To the good judge let there be a good witness." So let us say, "To the good delight let there be the good Reyna."

You ask: do I sit in the garden? No, for I have much writing to do, and of kinds needing reference to books; besides, flies are a bother in summer, tho' in old days I did write out of doors, unless it were too wet. There is a stuff called Citronella that keeps away flies (more or less).

28

. . . Thank you for the wonderful photograph, which gives me such a good notion of how you will look in a halo, a sight I do not expect to be privileged to see. The hat is indeed a triumph. How on earth have you packed and kept it thus? But perhaps it is like the great straw hats, once made by the San Blas Indians, of some very flexible strong thin straw. It took a year to make a hat, and when made it would last 150 years. It gave the shade and beauty yours gives, but *if it would not roll up so as to pass through a wedding-ring* it was not counted as a hat at all, but as one of those billycocks[1] or Morny Cannons[2] that the toughs used to wear at Races, and come home singing:

> Don't put your feet in the port wine, Joe,
> There's plenty of stale old beer.

[1] A round-crowned, brimmed hat of felt, like a bowler.

[2] This is obscure, but it appears to be some sort of hard, probably high-crowned, hat in the style of a bowler. Its name might be attributable to the Duc de Morny (1811–65), a famous dandy, racing man and leader of fashion who helped to engineer the *coup d'état* of 1851 which created the Second Empire.

29

. . . May I go on about the fossil waterfall? Very long ago the Columbia River ran in a course to the E of its present bed. It was then a vast river. It is now about twice the size of the Nile, & is still 1,400 miles long (halfway to New York). In one of the Glacial times the old river-bed was blocked, & the river shoved elsewhere & much diminished: but the old bed, called the Grand Coulee in Washington State, is seen in an awful chain of canyons and lakes. The old Fall, called Dry Falls, but it might be called with equal wit Dried Ups, is appalling. It is a crag 3½ miles long and over 400f sheer black basalt, with black canyons leading to it: and my Dear, the old Columbia River went over this crag 3½ miles wide and 100 feet deep (300 feet deep in flood time) for untold myriads of years . . .

. . . Sir Cloudislie Shovell.[1] Could Art invent such a name? Try it: You will see that it is impossible: Sir Sunburnley Pickaxe: Admiral Sir Preposterous Tongs. It cannot be. There is a ballad somewhere about a Captain Death, RN, who was a Captain Alive once, so I was told, but I do not know it.

Sir Cloudislie Shovell went ashore after sunset: the fleet knew that it was in some danger and was lying by under easy sail. I think it must have been dark thick weather, and without any proper sights for days: only soundings to go by. It was darkish anyhow, for the Admiral's stern signal lanterns were burning and were beaten out when she took the rocks. The entrance to the channel is a terrible graveyard of ships.

It is said that he made sail (easy sail) believing that he had seen some light on Sally, perhaps a recognisable light, "though a report prevailed that a great Part of the Crew had got drunk for joy, that they were within sight of land".

[1] JM uses various spellings of this name, which stands in the *DNB* as Clowdisley Shovell (1650–1707). His body was eventually taken to Plymouth in HMS *Salisbury* and buried in Westminster Abbey.

30

. . . May I send you my thanks for your exquisite playing last night at the Albert Hall? The *Symphonie Fantastique*: a work that I love.

Berlioz is one of the good writers, too; and a real Romantic, but a bit touched with the nightmare of the 1820–40 people; Byron, Beddoes, Poe: one wishes the *Marche au Supplice* and *Witches' Sabbath* away: & then the Beloved putting him out of his opium into the light.

. . . When I wrote to you [about Sir Cloudislie Shovell], I thought that he was lost on the Bishop Rock, where the light now is, that blessedest of all lights. It is not so; he was lost on the Gillston Reef, much further to the East, & was found next day below the rocks of St Mary's. One story is, that he came ashore alive & was murdered by a wicked old woman (for his emerald ring) who long afterwards confessed & gave up the ring and then died. Another much more likely story is that he was washed ashore dead, next morning: stripped at once of everything, including his emerald ring, and buried in a sandbank: & that the taker of the ring, boasting of it, was forced to give it up. The sandbank in which he was buried was long shown to travellers.

You must not think the seamen were drunk. It was thick weather, & (it is supposed that) they mistook some light or other for the primitive beacon on St Agnes. No-one knows. They may have been a little beside themselves, at the thought of being drunk later in the week, but it is unlikely that they were in that state of seamen's bliss in thick weather in soundings at the end of a cruise (where there could only have been just enough rum to preserve the poor Admiral's body).

31

. . . I had not heard the tale of Lady Mt Edgecombe.[1] But many, many years ago I was in Devon, on the coast, & saw an old man who was somewhat shunned by people. In his youth (some 100 years ago now) a wreck had come ashore there, and all hands gathered to harvest. Among the harvest was a dead lady with rings on her fingers, & this man had tried to get them off. As they would not come, he drew his knife to cut them off: "and HER GROANED".

I never heard more than this; but it was not reckoned to be quite cricket in him, or anyone, if he or her groaned: otherwise the fortune of the sea and findings-keepings.

The 2nd *Conway*, once the *Winchester*, was re-named the *Mt Edgecombe*, and I saw her ½ a dozen times: a lovely big frigate with a noble straight sheer.

. . . I had hoped to write again about Sir Cloudesly Shovell, but I cannot give you any real sense of what happened. You see, he and his were all drowned, no survivors from the three ships: but I will in time learn something about it for you. He was wrecked on the Gillston Reef about a mile E of the Bishop's Light. I have often passed Bishop's Light, but always at night, & I suspect that the reef is mainly under water at high tide. It must be as toothy a tombstone place as you would find for any pretty ship on a long summer day. The tide must have been making, I think, & the wind from some Westerly point, since the bodies were ashore on St Mary's next day. But I hope to find you some sailor's account of it. They *were* sailors: the pick of their profession: and they met with the ill-fortune of the sea. The accounts I have sent you are all by landsmen. I can only suspect a blind week with no sights, and something that deceived the flag's Master.

But fortune it will take its place
Let a man do all he can brave boys,
Let a man do all he can.

and at the entrance to the Channel fortune had a good place.

¹ It is thought that Lady Mount Edgcumbe (JM's spelling was, as has been remarked, idiosyncratic) lived to tell her story.

32

. . . The *Salisbury* 50-gun ship, put into Plymouth with Sir Cloudesly's body (and the news of his loss) a day or two after the wreck.

You will be saying very much what the man in the French Revolution said to Robespierre, "Avec thy Sir Cloudesly Shovell tu commences m'embêter."

. . . You may have heard of Rennell's Current? It is a Variable that often sets North (& North West) from the Bay of Biscay, sometimes a mile and more in an hour, probably always a quarter mile. These Variables used to kill a lot of ships—perhaps it was the final cause here: setting the poor fellows just a shade too far to the North, just on to the Gillston when they were so nearly all clear.

Looking at a chart shews that the lead couldn't help them very much just there. They knew that they weren't in safety: but may not have known in which direction safety lay.

I shall hope to clear up the point for you some day, and then you shall be no more embêted.

33

. . . Thank you for telling me about your visit to Pitcairn. It is a bold grim island with an appalling landing-place. Alas, I sent my Bligh books to the *Conway*, and among them some fine coloured views of Pitcairn. Some of the mutineers got there, and were never found till 1808, when all but one had died (or been killed).

Years ago, at the Record Office, I read all the Courts Martial on those mutineers who were caught at Tahiti and brought back to England. Some died on the way, being not very kindly treated but I think ten were tried and (I think) 2 or 3 hanged. A midshipman, palpably innocent, was condemned to death, but (mercifully) pardoned; and being wisely encouraged by good Admirals (Howe and Hood) did very well later (a captain, RN).

I have (in a sort of way) seen the *Bounty*. She was not of the Naval establishment (not a sixth-rate) but an adopted merchantman. Well, the Metro film people did a film about her; & built & rigged an image of her, which I came upon at Hollywood. The creature was brilliantly done & of intense interest. They sailed her off the California coast under her proper canvas, and not having her proper ballast they upset her (I was told) but perhaps that was part of the film: she *was* wrecked, of course.

She was the size of a topsail schooner: yet carried all told about 40 odd hands.

The Americans are a race of sailors, and at that time were doing a good many films of the olden time, with single topsails. The skill of the reconstruction was unusual.

You might not think it, but the Mutiny influenced English poetry & prose romance a good deal.

. . . You ask did I ever read *Pierre* by H. Melville? No, but I tried. When a man's brains get into his imagination they poison it. H.M. was a wanderer, and such people ought to keep wandering.

Please will you try to tell me (when you have read some more of him) if you are still interested in him. I read some books of verse by him once: all quite dead except for 2 things about ships.

. . . I have twice been to Widdicombe. Once to see the Fair there, or what should have been a Fair, but was an up & down Devon rain: once to try with friends in the Churchyard to find a stone to a Gurney, a Davy, a Hawke, a Whiddon, or a Cobleigh: for though all these lived at a distance, one or two of them might have been buried there for old time's sake. We did not find any grave of the kind, and had not the heart to consult the Parish Register (perhaps we hadn't the sense).

34

. . . I am so glad you liked *Typee*.[1] The prose is a bit long-winded, but the life must have been something like the description. All those thousands of splendid creatures, with their dances, their music, their poems, their physical perfection, all doomed to utter destruction so soon by the terrible whaler trader, and black-birder—the very scum of the earth.

I liked the early part of *Redburn*, & the Nantucket part of *Moby Dick*—a page or two of *Omoo*—& some of *White Jacket*, not for the writing (this last) but because it is *almost* the only book that describes a foremast hand's life in a sailing man of war.

. . . Generally speaking, I find something very clever and good in all books that please a lot of people: & a lot of queer knowledge, too, & queer personal preferences.

Of course, in youth, this is not so. In youth, men pass through the Middle Ages, and cry out that all heretics shall be burned, or boiled in oil, or treated to the private assassin with his dagger or a cup of cold poison.

[1] All the books mentioned in this letter are by the American writer, Herman Melville (1819–91), whose work stayed unrecognised until thirty years or so after his death.

35

. . . Thank you for writing about Lichfield and Dr Johnson. Did you ever read his *Lives of the Poets*, of the Poets of his school, Cowley to Gray? It is so wise, so witty, & so well informed. Who could write any comparable book, Gray to Yeats, say, without failure? There are a full fifty brief lives, I suppose, with pungent and exquisite comment on the poetry. The only blemish seems to be due to his fondness for Savage, who seems to most of men now to have been a blackmailer. He did not like Gray, of course, but Gray was of our school, not of his, and also of the company of some who were hostile to him.

You must be weary of this talk about books, alas, & think of the weary Duke of Gloucester[1] who cried: "Another——thick, square book. Always scribble, scribble, scribble, eh, Mr Gibbon?"

Well, that is the sort of thing one does.

[1] HRH William Henry, Duke of Gloucester (1743–1805).

36

. . . You mention the Duke of Portland. One of the Dukes was rather shy, & contrived an underground passage from his Castle to the railway station so that he might not be eyed and surveyed (and perhaps asked for an autograph).

The *real* Dukes (there were 3 I think) could drive from their country homes to their town houses on their own property. I believe they were Portland, Westminster and Marlborough.

. . . Salisbury [Cathedral] is unique: it is all of one piece: all of one style: William Longsword[1] is buried there in a fine tomb (or was).

Winchester I know well, the High Altar is said to be really floating there: a violent stream runs under it, & has given endless trouble in the last 800 years, but the chancel hasn't fallen yet.

[1] William Longsword (1198–1226) was an illegitimate son of King Henry II by an unknown mother. He became Earl of Salisbury, held many high offices under King John and was present at the signing of the Great Charter in 1215. There is no evidence for the belief that Henry II's mistress, Rosamund Clifford ("Fair Rosamond") was his mother.

37

Dear—Let me thank you for your letter, for all the interesting things you told of the ring-finger muscles.

The tale of Schumann's mad operation has always been frightful to me.

It may be that the ring-finger, in modern Western peoples, is little exercised in the year of growth. I used to be told that the really good cricket-bowlers (& baseball-pitchers) always use their third fingers (from boyhood) to get certain breaks & spins, and that their fingers are abnormal from this use. It may be true. It is so long since I bowled that I cannot recollect the dodges nor just what each one did.

Please let me thank you for your playing last night, especially the 7th Symphony. It was pleasant to think of you all done-up regardless, exceedingly ponkie and twee, with your face all happy & tense, and yourself away somewhere in Music, that I expect is something like being in Poetry, only with many more happy people near you.

I hope that you will have ever such a happy time in Bristol this weekend. If you go into Bristol Cathedral you may see a window to one Fargus,[1] an old "Conway", a novelist who died young (in 1885), just as he was beginning to grow. He wrote one very famous story; & some verse that was not bad: songs chiefly: indeed a little operetta, one of his things, was long ago done in Manchester.

I have sometimes wondered whether the Cathedral at Winchester were not specially built over a spring about which pagan rites had gathered. Springs are often holy to primitive & poetical people: and many more consecrated by the Church to keep them from some rites perhaps not too holy in Xtian eyes. You see: at a good spring, you could refresh yourself and horse, and perhaps on a feast day drown your enemy, if you had one, which wd please a primitive man as much as he hoped it wd please the god. Then after a bun & perhaps a nice piece of pig he could ride away all fresh and clean, with the enemy gone for ever, and the feeling that the god had enjoyed a really good time.

Perhaps the Normans checked something like this at Winchester. It was a great worry, having the Chancel flooded, but perhaps in time they piped the water away, but at first of course some of the Bishops & clergy must have rather rheumatically limped to Paradise. However, they would have been all right as soon as they got there.

The tomb of William Longsword at Salisbury is (or was) very fine. When you look at it again you must try to imagine what Fair Rosamund was like. She was his Mother: so perhaps Longsword was the name people knew him by: he could have had no other. "Fair" is probably meant for "beautiful". One can only hope that she wasn't a blonde: but the word would mean that now.

. . . You have a little photograph of the *Wanderer* in San Francisco in 1892. You will see in that a fine ship in exquisite order. It is hard to describe what a joy it is to make a ship exquisite to see.

The later sailing ships were of very lovely & subtle curves, all different yet all beautiful. Then in contrast to the curves came the uprights, the masts, that were never quite upright, but subtly raked, — supported by gear subtly slanting and counter slanting; and then crossed by yards that were squared to faultless order, at right angles to the other spars. The effect was one of contrasting subtle lines. But, my dear, you must be spared all this.

Bless you dear.

[1] Fargus, Frederick John (1847–1885), born in Bristol, wrote under the name of "Hugh Conway". He joined the training ship *Conway* in 1860, at the age of thirteen but did not pursue a career at sea. He took over his family's auctioneering business in 1868, and in 1883 published his first long story *Called Back*, which sold 350,000 copies within four years. Another story, *Dark Days* came out in 1884. Several works were published after his death, notably *A Family Affair*.

38

. . . About Blondes. They are apt to have startling effects on races usually dark, such as Spaniards or Red Indians. The use of the word Fair, for a Blonde, is not very ancient. The word Fair usually meant Beautiful, in form, or look, or grace, and had no connotation of colour.

39

... You were writing as though S. Holmes were a pleasing figure to you. There was a time, long before your time, as such can be called a time (it seemed long enough) when no-one knew Holmes, when not even Watson knew his methods; all was original Night: "For no live creatures lived there, no weasels moved in the dark." Doyle said, "Let Sherlock be": and all was Light.

"Ah, the wonder, the delight, the singing", and few little boys could bear the thought that one long calendar month had to pass before the next adventures could be.

As the Governor of N. Carolina said to the Governor of S. Carolina, "What weary ages"[1] (or words to that effect).

On the whole, what most writers would agree, that no creation in writing has so taken the world by storm since the death of Charles Dickens. There has been no comparable stir in my time. No figure in our fiction (our present fiction) has anything like such hold on people; one has to go back to Mrs Gamp, or the people in the early Dickens books.

The early illustrators in the *Strand Magazine* were helpful too. They helped fix the type.

... In London, you are near the scene of the life's work of G. Holst[2] where one went to see him long since in preparation for the Canterbury play,[3] of which he was the very life throughout: a most admirable, lively man, none like him for tact and glory.

... The past only exists for us by what was virtuous in it: one must not think that as an age it was virtuous. It had some virtue and much blind brutality; and perhaps Milton wrote some quite good page on the day the London merchants sold Royalist prisoners as W. Indian slaves. Shakespeare may quite well have been interrupted in writing *Macbeth* by someone being burned as a witch after being tortured into saying she was one.

[1] "It's a long time between drinks."

[2] St Paul's, Hammersmith—I used to stay at my sister's house in Barnes. ANS.

[3] JM's *The Coming of Christ* was performed in Canterbury Cathedral on 28 and 29 May 1928.

40

... Thank you for the specimen signature of your soloist [Segovia]. He writes like old Choate,[1] who wrote three different hands, 1 that he could read, 1 that his printer could read, 1 that nobody could read.

Some youths once put a beetle into an inkpot, let it free over a sheet of paper, & sent the sheet to the printer to set up. The printer set it up, but presently came to Choate to ask, "Please sir, is this word *constitution* or *emancipation?*"

... Do you ever go to the Manchester Art Gallery or was it a war-casualty?

There used to be a very fine little portrait by Millais there: a lady, sitting thinking, either of him, or of what she would wear at the party.

If you go to play at Birmingham again, please go to the Gallery there, & see if the Morris tapestries are still there. Ah, 50 odd years ago, when the pre-Raphaelites swayed all young men, that gallery, that had specialised in them, & had Burne-Jones as a local genius moreover, that gallery was a place of pilgrimage—"Myself, when young, did eagerly frequent."

... You ask about Doyle: Sherlock Holmes was something quite new: there had been nothing like it. It took the young world by storm, and made the *Strand Magazine* a success at once. His first adventure appeared in the first number.

Generally speaking writers do not value what they do with their power, but what they do with their difficulty. Doyle may well have preferred his poems or his very fine History of the S. African War.

[1] Rufus Choate (1799–1859), American lawyer, orator and statesman, US Senator 1840–45.

41

Dear. It was gentle & kind of you to write at such length: so many thanks again.

You ask about Irving & Miss Ellen Terry. Yes, I saw them both act; Irving in all his famous melodramas, never in Shakespeare: the Shakespeare was before my time: Miss Terry, only in one of two late parts. She had much charm in all that she did: a winning irresistible way. I never saw her in works of power & do not know if she ever did the great thing like Duse, or the shattering thing, like Bernhardt.

Ruskin knew nothing about acting. Dickens did; D was a very versatile good actor, and one might even say that the Surrey Theatre of Melodrama was the only real education he ever had. Perhaps that wasn't the name of it, but that was the kind of thing: Mr Crummles and his world-famous Company in *Blood Will Tell* or, *The Red Stains on the What-Not*.

Ruskin probably disliked HI's speaking of Shakespeare. Many sensitive people did. I heard him speak *Becket*, by Tennyson, & indeed, it was not pleasing. But in prose melodrama he was incomparable: there was nobody like him.

My feeling was that he was not an instinctive actor, but a superb artist, working out every least movement & accent, till perfection was attained. O the difference when another tried to do the same parts: "A mammet, quite, to me, in memories nursed." O that thou mightest see him in *The Lyons Mail*: O golly. Or in Conan Doyle's *Waterloo*: that was truly shattering: but since then wars & battles have rather dwarfed Waterloo: & it would not have the same effect, perhaps. Or do you still dream of Boney, & hope he won't land in the night? Not you: never.

You ask about heeling, graving, breaming. They are parts of the same process, of cleaning the under-water-body of an ancient ship. In all sea-going ships, barnacles and other shells, sea-weeds and sea-grasses will swiftly gather under water. Soon they will be a foot or more thick, greatly impeding the ship's progress. From very early times, men have tried to hinder these growths by tar, tallow, pitch, felt, lime-wash & all sorts of anti-fouling mixtures, but the things grew all the same. Whenever possible, the ships were heeled, that is careened or tilted on one side, or just allowed to lie on their side on the mud at low water. Ships were pretty small, and with care this heeling didn't harm them. When heeled, they could be graved, or scraped, with shovels, 3-cornered scrapers, spades, hoes, etc; but as barnacles and limpets stick like limpets, it was helpful to bream the exposed strakes.

They lit small quick fires of gorse, reeds, straw etc on the exposed growths. The fires were always small & quick. They melted the pitch or grease to which the growths stuck, and then the scrapes could just shovel them off.

That was breaming.

You will often see old prints of ships being breamed.

Sometimes, when drunk, the seamen set fire to their ships while breaming.

Sometimes, the ship after being heeled refused to right herself. I never heard of a modern ship being heeled and breamed. They can now be docked, hosed with chemicals, and then painted with poisons.

I have the facsimile Pepys book about the Navy.[1] It is a fine little book by one who mastered his profession & did honest work in a time of utter infamy in high places.

The Whitworth Institute was full of drawings when I last saw it, mostly Turner water-colours. I did not know the house full of costumes: but about 20 years ago there was a very fine show of women's costumes in London: all the fashions from 1800–1900 pretty well: some were elegant: but the stuffs were often exquisite; & the little appurtenances, fans, handbags, shoes, belts, buttons & clasps nearly always graceful; and the uses of lace and colour always subtle. (I do not remember any hats.)

Foxe's *Book of Martyrs* I only saw once (with the engravings): it rather cheered a gloomy day; but I was not then quite a child.

May blessings keep you from all harm and bring you all gladness wherever you may be . . .

[1] *The State of the Navy* (1688).

1954

42

. . . You ask about Chaucer, and the pronunciation of his poetry.

We cannot know *exactly* how men spoke it 600 years ago: but we know a good deal: and it is necessary to know, for the language & pronunciation have changed much in these 580 years.

For instance, read the first two lines of the Prologue, according to the modern method. You have—

> When that April with his showers swoot
> The drought of March have pierced to the root—

It is not practical, and the sense is not too clear. But read it in what we believe to be like the old method, and you will have—

> Whanne that Aprill-a with his show-res swoot-a
> The drought of March have perc-ed to the root-a—

a musical & dancing couplet, with the meaning made clearer.

Professor Tolkien knows more about Chaucer than any living man: and sometimes tells the Tales superbly, inimitably, just as though he were Chaucer returned.

43

Dear,

My grateful thanks again for a very kind welcome letter, and for all your gentle New Year wishes. Thank you for all these. May you, too, have a lovely year, of heart's delight & gladness: and many more such later.

I did not hear the broadcast you mention: and though I was at Lyme [Regis] once, did not hear your crier there. Criers were frequent in my youth: but they were indistinct often, not knowing how to produce, or pitch, their voices. The famous one at Shrewsbury was remarkable: he may be there still: one of the gigantic men: not tall, but with a great chest and enormous power of sound. One at Hereford Station was remarkable, too, with a fine singing tenor, announcing trains.

You asked me about Irving and the Victorian theatre: I can tell you a little about the famous study of old age, called *Waterloo* (I did tell you a little).

Conan Doyle wrote it and HI was incomparable as the Old Corporal. It was an extra-ordinary feat. He was an ageing man, with many young people in rebellion against him, and a changing time demanding fundamental changes in acting & everything else: but HI was a matchless artist, and also a spirit of dynamic power that annihilated everyone in the same house with him: he swept them all into his power and left them gasping & incoherent, yelling, sobbing, screaming: calling for him again & again.

. . . He was the great giver of his time: no-one comparable with him; but I never saw his really great things: Shylock, Richard III, Hamlet, Dante, Othello, Malvolio. (The Malvolio is the one I long for.) I wish I had seen the Dante.

But about *Waterloo*. The Corporal is very old, and receives complimentary visits from the Colonel of his old Regiment & others. He is over excited by these, & by the passing of troops, recalls Waterloo, and collapses & dies.

This seems nothing: but Irving made it everything, including a fearful half hour at Hougoumont, June 18, 1815, when powder ran short in the château. HI brought into it all war, and all England, and all old age: & no man who ever saw it ever forgot it.

In Irving's cast an actor named Belmore (either George, the son of Lionel, or Lionel the son of George B)[1] a most admirable character-actor. He played a non-com of the old Regiment paying a complimentary visit and played it superbly: for Irving's people were A1. In the last years he stage-managed the piece for Irving, and acted this part to Irving's old Corporal: & he held his own, in a way beyond praise: so often Irving's men were lifted up by him: but B was a very fine actor always.

Now towards the end of the life of Irving, King Edward asked Irving to come to play (either at Sandringham or Balmoral) before the Emperor William of Germany. So Irving gathered his men & gear (he was acting in Belfast at the time) and away he went;

meaning to play *Waterloo* & some other short scenes. Belmore as stage-manager came along.

The Kaiser had brought a Viennese orchestra & a big staff with him. HI understood that this orchestra would play all the Prelude & music in *Waterloo*. There is a clever use in the prelude & other music, of marches of various kinds, quick & solemn.

But when the orchestra was reached: lo, there was no drum: "not a drum was heard"; so a drum & drummer had to be found: not much time left: and without a drum . . . disaster: The Palace Chief of Police said that the Police Band had a Drummer. But on enquiry, this man was far away, out on his beat. He was sent for by swift horsemen & dog-carts, and brought in just in time, very weary, but a champion drummer.

The stage was ready. The cast were ready. Belmore was on the stage supervising. Suddenly the orchestra conductor said that he could not conduct the Prelude and incidental music, "there were too many changes of time".

To us, today, it seems likely that the Kaiser or his men had resolved to make a mess of our play of Waterloo; & that these were the conductor's orders.

This was not suspected at the time: but there the scene was: the conductor refusing duty: Royalty on its way to the door: no music to play them in: & the whole evening headed for the rocks . . .

Belmore saved the day. He was dressed for his part as the non-com, but he seized a baton (some say, a violinist's bow) & at once beat the time, or acted a conductor conducting, with all the usual gestures, and whatever the orchestra's orders had been, they struck up before the man in uniform and played as never before. B played his part as his cues fell and again conducted in the incidental marches. Some say, he was a good musician as well as a very good actor: but for that night he was a conquering hero, besides.

Goodnight and bless you
John Masefield.

[1] It was George, the younger Belmore. ANS.

44

. . . [Town] Cryers were of great use till about 1900, for, till then, a good many people could not read much (or at all) and there were no loud-speakers. The Hereford station announcer used to ring a big hand-bell, and then intone, or chant, or sing, in a way all his own, and melodiously, a sort of song—thus:

> Any more for Ludlow,
> Leominster
> Craven Arms
> Condover
> Shrewsbury
> Any more for the Chester Train.

As this was a song, he was heard. He announced trains thus, in day times: but I never heard such an announcer elsewhere.

. . . I am glad to think that the gales blew away your sore throat and cough. Gales can be exhilarating and helpful thus. But they can also destroy.

> Ashore went the *Northumberland*
> *The Warwick* and the *Cumberland*
> And all the seamen lost their lives.
> (But the greatest loss was to their wives.)[1]

[1] Last line supplied by JM.

45

. . . I did not know the Welsh tales you mention: nor Messrs Secker's anthology, but knew the work of many of the men of the 90s and met some of the men, too, though all the *Yellow Book* and *Savoy* set were older than I. (I only met some of them: did not know them well: save 1 or 2) Wilde had fallen, Beardsley was dying, Lionel Johnson, Dowson, Crackanthorpe & (I think) Francis Thompson were dead; & John Davidson was soon to disappear into the sea somewhere: but that may have been a year or 2 later, even more perhaps.

46

. . . The feet of mice are admirably adapted to scutter over ever-varying surface: how admirably few consider. The sole is perhaps insensitive. The Farmer's Wife tried to find out, but the mice were too swift. She was late with all 3 chops.

47

... You ask about Irving.[1] He was one of the best of the 19th cent. American writers (a very good lot) & still much read. He was Ambassador here (& in Spain). He wrote the tale of Rip Van Winkle, about a lovely place (called Sleepy Hollow) where he (and Rip) lived of old. It is up the Hudson about 25 m from NYC [ity]. It is engulfed by NYC but no doubt still lovely. He is said to be a good historian, comparable with Parkman, Motley, Prescott, but I only know his more playful things. He was very much liked over here, and his English books show that he liked us, too.

[1] Washington Irving (1783–1851).
American writer, son of an Englishman, Diplomatist, Secretary of Legation, London 1829. US Minister to Spain 1842.

48

... In the tomb of Spenser in Westminster Abbey, there may still be the pens that all the poets flung there: but who could identify each? ... It would be something to hold a pen once used by some lesser poet, Drayton, Daniel, or Campion, or Nashe, or Lyly.
... I am grieved to think of you having this week of bitter frost (& perhaps fog) and coming home late in the snow, not sure if your fingers & toes are still on, nor your ears are there, and perhaps finding all frozen when you get in.
There is a nice weather proverb:

> When Candlemass Day is past and gone
> Snow lies on a hot stone.

49

... Music is your Destiny, surely, for some large share of your intenser interests and delight. Music surely is the law of your Being, even if you feel otherwise at times. It is one of the great arts: one of the ways of "conversing with Paradise".
You are not like us young rips of the *Conway*, who used to shout, in the well-known hymn.

> O Paradise, O Paradise
> I want to sin some more.

. . . You ask what I looked like when I did the Dampier.[1] Even more repulsive than now, if possible.

It was done 3 or 4 years before the portrait.[2] I was living at Greenwich, & spent much time in the Museum & Painted Room there.

Dampier was the best of the buccaneer *writers*; & neglected at that time. His portrait is interesting. As he was the first intelligent Englishman to land in Australia (in the worst possible place) I had the portrait copied for the National Library at Canberra, where it still hangs, I believe.

[1] *Voyages of Captain William Dampier*, edited by John Masefield (Two Vols, 1906). William Dampier, buccaneer and explorer, published his *Voyages* in 1697.

[2] William Strang painted JM's portrait in 1909. It hangs in the National Portrait Gallery.

50

. . . It was only a passing mood in you about Music. I expect your normal view of Music is rosier than that of the man in Mark Twain, who discovered that it isn't half as bad as it sometimes sounds.

51

. . . Books have become costly in the last 50 years . . . Fifty years ago no-one regarded the period 1650–1800. You could buy almost any book at that time for very little. The tiny English editions of Voltaire could be found at 1d a piece (V printed them here, as no French printer wd have dared). A folio Beaumont & Fletcher only cost 30/- or £2 (the 2nd folio). One could also find amazing prints, Rembrandt & Dürer etchings & so forth, at 3d or 6d if one looked. As for the shipping prints, they were everywhere: 1/- the best & a great selection at 2d. These things are now sought for, but no doubt others as good, but very different, are now neglected.

52

. . . You ask about Shaw: and what I thought of his writing when I was young.

I did not know it when I was young, and did not care about it when I first saw it: dramatic criticism: support of Ibsen, and some of the prose novels: none of that interested the sets I moved in. We asked for poetry, for feeling, for style, for romance.

When the Court Theatre produced his plays, it was another matter; another Shaw; and *Major Barbara* made the Court Theatre the most important place in England. It was in that movement that Shaw went out of his way, at the height of his own newly won glory, to speak in public in high praise of me—a piece of generosity so great & so moving & so little deserved that it made even the brazen me a little abashed.

He was of an overwhelming, shattering generosity in many ways. I am not at all sure that he did not finance the later phases of the Court Theatre movement at the Kingsway & the Savoy & the Repertory movements elsewhere; I feel sure that this was so.

He was a violinist & a good general musician, but I never heard him play. He played in theatre orchestras for years, and wrote his early plays on the tops of buses while on his way to rehearsals, & learned the theatre there, having always a clear logical mind & an instinct for situation. Being a dramatic critic taught him all the stock situations, and all the sentimental flap-doodle of the theatre of 1870–1900 roused every intellectual needle in him to action. He put an end to a lot of the flap-doodle: but the flap-doodle was only dying romance. Romance & poetry & feeling for style are what a theatre must have. As our theatre hasn't even the shadows of them now, the world goes to the opera and the ballet, which are really only parts of the theatre, drawn apart from it instead of living limbs of it.

53

My Reyna dear,

Thank you for so very kindly answering the questions about the strain upon the player. You answer so fully that perhaps you have given yourself writer's cramp in addition to the other pangs. You were ever too generous to me (as may have been said before).

I hope that you may enjoy a long happy smooth, of music happily spaced.

Who would ever have suspected that musicians had little dodges for the snatching of rest. The rest must be the two seconds of respite that a jockey may give a horse at a critical point in a race. Jockeys say that even two seconds will make a difference: perhaps *the* difference: but there, perhaps, it is the jockey that makes the real difference. Thank you for taking all that world of kind trouble for me.

Please, is there any trace now in Manchester of the Gaiety Theatre, that Miss Horniman[1] made into a Repertory Theatre nearly 50 years ago? It may, of course, be famous, but I have not heard of it lately: & so many theatres have been turned into cinemas.

I do not know much of Shaw's criticism, but he had a phrase about the Fr playwright Victorien Sardou.[2] He spoke of some of his work as "Sardoodledoo", but of course in France all the arts use a flaming rhetoric, that is of the essence of French nature. All late nineteenth century criticism was very full: the artists of that time were noticed. I remember an American critic writing of a tenor: "Every time he got to his high note, he fell off backwards"; but usually the critics had a knowledge and belonged to a camp or clique: & you would hear artists telling their supporters to see that so and so got a knife between the ribs, or some arsenic in his soup, or a bat on the head in a dark lane, so to speak. I write figuratively. The medicine was often given in the next number.

Though the assassin tried to kill, & the clansmen tried to exalt, the work in question, the work remained where it was.

Now my blessings on you, as always. (You get good nights & good mornings always.)

You must be very frank and tell me when you have had enough.

Bless you and thank you
John Masefield

[1] Annie Horniman (1860–1937) founded the Manchester Repertory Theatre at the Gaiety, Manchester, in 1908. She also put up the funds to enable the Irish National Theatre to settle permanently at the Abbey Theatre, Dublin.

[2] Victorien Sardou (1831–1908) wrote comedies and historical dramas. Puccini based his opera on Sardou's melodrama *La Tosca*.

54

. . . Friendship is very rare, my dear, & very precious, & grows rarer & more precious in old age, so do not ever think that if the head becomes stupider the heart is deader.

55

My grateful thanks for your so kind, so welcome long letter, letting me share all your joy . . . you share so much with me. You are always breaking off a piece of yourself & giving me, as it were, first bite . . .

. . . Certainly your concert . . . must have been a big experience . . . to smooth out all the personal wrinkle into the unity that is one with Unity, & perceives truth, & knows it for beauty & the undying: what else is Life in life?

56

Alas, in this life the heart clings dearly to friends, & each friend's passing kills some of the life of the heart.

. . . In my own belief, in this life we meet & are helped or hurt by all that we have helped or hurt in other human lives, and that we shall meet all again until we touch perfection.

57

Reyna dearest

You ask about the *Martian*[1] book. I did not read it till many years after its publication. It came later than the other two. Much of it is an account of du M's schooldays, & also of his misery when one of his eyes failed (later) & he seemed to be going blind. All of this is probably true record; & some of it very well felt & told.

The celestial part: Perhaps he was at all times conscious of some beneficent sacred feminine influence watching over him & guarding him.

That lively sentimental thug, the Fr poet Verlaine, had a similar feeling.

"I often have that strange penetrating dream of an unknown woman, whom I love and who loves me . . .

For she understands me; and my transparent heart for her alone, alas, ceases to be a problem . . ."

In the day of his full mature power he (du M) sets this image down supremely in *Peter Ibbetson*. It is possible that in the *Martian* he tried to tell an actual personal influence that came to him in recurrent dreams at a critical and dreadful time in his life.

Who can doubt that benign spirits do sometimes bless us thus, or that the dead who have loved us are allowed to help us thus?

At all times, du M was deeply sensitive to the beauty & goodness of women: & his best work must have made thousands of men more reverent of them & tenderer to their claims of being equal sharers.

Later schools suggest perhaps that women would prefer to be knocked on the head with a club & dragged away to the cave in the wild wood.

When du M wrote, telescopes had revealed markings on Mars, and people were wondering whether the Martians were trying to signal to us, or might descend upon us, or even come and (as it were) select pets from among us to look after & guide, from some superior instinctive wisdom. All this must have been common talk and speculation then, in all thinking & reading circles. Intercourse with Mars (the nearest likely planet) seemed, then, not impossible; and to a man like du M, possibly beneficent.

However, the school of the romantic was passing: & the school of the realists coming into vogue. Wells must have published his tale only a very few months or years after du M's death: if not even before it.

. . . The Duck verses[2] are about Great Hampden Common in Buckinghamshire. There used to be a duck farm on the hill there, and every night the wild duck used to come over (I know not whence) & cry to the tame ducks to up & come along, & all the tame ducks were in a great twitter & trouble at it. The wild duck came in great waves (I suppose migrations getting ready).

No-one could forget the incident of September dusk and the wild flights in the air putting madness of excitement & terror into the myriad ducks in the pens. They wanted to come but dared not & could not, and the wild ones could not understand, and came again & again to call them—a strange wonder.

[1] George du Maurier (1834–96) wrote *Trilby* and *Peter Ibbetson*. His third work *The Martian* was published posthumously in 1896.

[2] JM's poem "The Wild Duck" which first appeared in his third published work, *Ballads and Poems* (1910).

58

Dear

My grateful thanks for your letter about *your* wild duck, written in such a difficult busy week too. Thank you for it.

And thank you, also, for your thought of sending me the little Ruskin book. (I have it, thank you.)

I do not like his remarks, nor his drawing, concerning the collier's rig. He is not dealing with a top, as he claims, but with a cross-trees, a much slighter structure, & in drawing this he does not know which things are important, nor what each thing does, nor even if it does anything. He leaves out much, as he says, & puts in what is not or should not be there. He says that the sail is reefed, when it is furled, and furled abominably in a manner impossible to that time.

I do not know much of Stanfield's painting,[1] but I have seen wonderful prints from him, and these have been precious to me, for they have shown me certain points of now obsolete rigging, of great interest to me. From these, *model riggers* could have rigged models, or re-rigged broken old models.

I will not say anything about the cross-trees that JR [Ruskin] produces from Stanfield. I do not know the original, and not much can be said in its favour. But CS [Stanfield] *was* a sailor, a pressed man, too, and did know ships & their movements as a sailor does, and often painted with a truth delightful to us.

Turner's big *Trafalgar* picture is a fine display, but rubbish as a rendering of any moment of the battle or of the *Victory* at sea at any time.

Huggins could not have painted the fine display, by any possibility, but at a lesser theme, such as the famous *Falcon*, he gives any old sailor (& any model-rigger) intense joy.

Turner (in some of his Liber[2] things) & in his engravings of the Ports of England, and in some of the wonderful sketches in the Nat Gal collection of his drawings, is precious indeed, but not in his big display sea-paintings; not even in his famous *Victory in Three Positions*.

In *Trafalgar*, Turner's theme was a *Resolve* Triumphant, and he did it triumphantly, but Ruskin's guide to it was a naval pensioner who knew ships (& may well have been in the battle) and knew very well that no ship & no battle ever looked like that.

I will look up Stanfield's book and prints.

[1] William Clarkson Stanfield (1793–1867). He began life as a sailor, and attracted the attention of Captain Marryat, who was the first person to recommend him to take up art as a profession.

[2] *Liber Studiorum: Illustrative of Landscape Compositions, viz. Historical, Mountainous, Pastoral, Marine, and Architectural . . .*: a collection Turner compiled of compositions drawn, and partly engraved, by himself, to illustrate landscape types.

59

Dear

You may have forgotten mentioning the Ruskin allusion to a design by C. Stanfield?

It raised an interesting point, which has given me some delight, for which my thanks now go to you, with other thanks for a dear letter and dear likeness, both gladly had this Tues. morn.

The Stanfield design is called "The Semaphore. Portsmouth". It shows the old Semaphore Signal Station (off to the Right) and in the centre what Ruskin calls "a frigate running into Portsmouth Harb".

Now, to begin with, she is not a frigate, nor running, but a sizeable ship of war, beating-in, and plainly about to anchor. She puzzled me and interested me a good deal, for she was so old in design for a book published in 1836 (with a dedication to the Huggins lover, W the 4th.)

She had evidently puzzled the engraver too. But JR is wrong to object to the cross-trees engraving. He should have seen that what he takes to be topmast rigging is mainly staysail halliards; (on the left) a rightly placed topgallant and royal backstays on the right; with the fore-topgallant brace pendants, hitched there momentarily, the yard being down on deck in the cross-trees themselves, between the two arrays.

Now the scale of the engraving is very minute. The foreyard is one inch and one quarter of an inch long. The yard cannot be less than an 80 foot built spar, which means that each quarter inch of engraving has to represent 15 feet or so. You will judge from this the engraver's difficulty at points where small ropes seem to cross. Some of the foreshortened hull is misleadingly engraved, but remember, it had to be cut in reverse on metal.

Not being at ease, and feeling that the strange ship might be easy to trace . . . . *Lo, she had been rather Cunningly Conveyed* (Convey, the wise call it) *from a Fine Engraving* by N. Pocock,[1] *The Pride and Glory of Bristol.*

So many thanks, for all this fun.

Bless you.

PS In the engraving, the ship, foreshortened somewhat, is one-inch & one half inch *extreme length*. In her original being, her length of keel would have been perhaps about 140-150 feet, & her length overall (figurehead to taffrail extreme length) nearly another 30 feet.

The engraver had to portray a broadside extreme length, with its rigging-gear, guns, ports etc in 1 inch & a half, by about one quarter of an inch.

Please, remember, that my suggestion of the fore topgallant brace pendants is all that I can suggest at present. Even with spectacles & a magnifying glass I cannot be certain of all my guesses. If I can find a clear print of the Pocock I shall see at once what the original was.

[1] Nicholas Pocock: see Letter 18.

60

. . . You asked me about Ruskin.

Please, that is a big subject. He was *the* great influence for righteous feeling between 1850 & 1900. He had a mind of much beauty & generosity; the beauty perhaps a shade inhuman and the generosity beyond all bounds.

Those who read at all then were moved by him in their youth: moved to the marrow; & those who heard him speak got up & followed him, for he had a persuasion that altered peoples' lives.

There were 3 movers of men, then, urging for a great change in the structure of society: Carlisle [*sic*], who wished to have an autocrat employing force: JR who wished all educated people to know what enlightened rule had been & might be: & saw the loveliness of Nature & the power of sweet persuasion: & Morris, who felt that all depended on love & work, love of mankind & of life, and love of work & delight in work.

JR had the greatest influence of the 3, but fell under a cloud, and is now little read perhaps. He was often not quite sane late in life, & lived out of the world rather.

He gave away, in lovely schemes, & in gentle personal kindnesses, all his personal fortune of £200,000.

His father was Agent here for the great vineyard of Domecq, in the sherry country near Cadiz, & being an upright eager man, fond of art, he went to many noblemen in England to sell the unique sherries that that vineyard grows. The wine was much drunken then, & the costly toxin made him very rich, & Ruskin the boy, going with his father, saw all the art collections in England at a very early age.

He was a careful & feeling copyist of works of art, but I have not seen any work by him in colour: only pencil drawings of buildings & of sprays of leaves.

As a lad, I loved his writing.

Millais painted his portrait in a fine thing called *The Trout Stream*, JR beside a Scotch brook.

61

. . . The arts at the moment are what cattlemen used to call "milling".

When cattle roved or ran in any direction and were headed off by obstacles—rocks, river, jungle, or riding cowboys—they "milled", or went in big circles, till a new direction appeared, or was shown: then they ran or roved in that new direction.

try, & perhaps in music, minds are rebelling against what has been lately done, mocking the doers, and feeling that the world is beginning again, & that only the young, beginning with it, have any perception of what is important to that world. In a way, they are right.

The young, now, are in a new society, not yet stable, not yet safe, with the old society in ruins, the old culture gone, the old leisure gone, the old forgotten, & the new classes suddenly powerful, vocal & finding their feet. Many young men are writing or making music where early homes had no music, no books. They begin the arts again, & naturally loathe the art that was before them.

Being young, they have much energy, being un-disciplined they rebel: being often from rude quarters in camps, or cities, in wars or factories, they often talk without restraint, without law & order, even without decency: and feeling that art is freedom, in which one word, or one note, is as good as another, & one subject is as good as another. Being young & full of energy, in a world charged with an atmosphere that seeks to explode, sometimes the atmosphere takes them, & uses them, & then flings them by.

Presently, one such explosion will clear a direction, & the milling herd will move off in that direction, & a new Movement will be apparent, & great things be done again.

62

... You ask about Burton's great book.[1] It is hardly one to read through, but read *in*. I have read it through, but read in it often: all must love to read in it, and to get ideas & fables from it: marvellous tales, wonderful subjects. All poets love it. But the great theme demands that the lover should at one time read it through to grasp the power of the mind that had all that wealth of illustration.

... You ask what companions one would choose for the desert island. Well: surely if it were not too much of a desert, one would choose with Mr Whurr, the poet, "a polished female friend".[2] For books? on the whole, if alone, the *Iliad*, but if with the p.f.f. the *Odyssey*, and (with either) at least the Homeric Dictionary.

[1] *The Anatomy of Melancholy*—Robert Burton (1577–1640)—one of JM's favourite books. It was published in 1621 and went through five editions during Burton's lifetime, the last appearing in 1638.

"What lasting joys the man attend
Who has a polished female friend."

63

. . . Did you ever hear the Moslem proverb (attributed to Mahomet and to many other eminent Ms)?

"He is a fool, who asks a woman's advice, but he who doesn't take it is a madman."

. . . Please, will you consider whether you wd like a tiny course on seamanship: the rig of masts, the simpler gear, the different sails? You probably know most of these things already . . . . I would love to write to you on these topics of rig & gear. I love your interest in ships; for all your interest in them is so much like mine; or am I all wrong? And then, your interest in them is so real & so genuine, that I would love to share what I have of all this with you, if I may.

But you must sing out Avast and Belay, & so forth, when I have the unhappiness of being a bore to you.

Rig & gear are fundamentally *simple*: a few essential things are repeated over & over again in the same way in varying sizes.

In a big ship there is much gear, but it is the gear used in small ships & arranged in the same way, & led to the same places, so that even on a dark night one can go without hesitation to the right pin. Ropes that carry a strain are also stiff from the strain, & show at once that they are dangerous by the feel.

Probably the last 100 years of the sailing-ship, 1795–1895, caused the loveliest of all the marine paintings, and certainly the most remarkable sailing-ships ever known in the world.

. . . Do you usually write on a rocking-chair with a sort of blotter on your knees? What a seaman you are!

64

Reyna mia

My grateful thanks for your gentle kind letter. All good wishes to you for the new season at the Hallé, & all prosperity to the move at the end of the month. I hope that all will go smoothly as you move in, and that the concerts during that fortnight will not be too exhausting nor too distant. All happy fortune to you, & may all blessings crown the move.

You ask (or suggested that I should answer) about the Blackball ships.

The first Blackball Line was an American firm of clipper packets sailing regularly (once a month, or once a fortnight) between New York & Liverpool. The House-flag was a red burgee with a black ball in it: the black ball was changed to a White Star by the White Star firm.

About 100 years ago, a Liverpool man called James Baines acquired the house-flag & (perhaps) some of the packet-ships as well. He ran a very famous Black Ball Line to Australia under this house-flag. I am not certain, but I think that the ships of both lines often bore a big black ball painted on the foot of the fore-topsail. The ships in this line made some wonderful passages. They were mostly wooden American-built clippers, carrying passengers, emigrants, freight & the mails, but the wooden ships had only a short life: & steam, & iron construction came into swift competition, and James Baines met with other disasters, & went out of business. It must have been then that the White Star people began a new line with the changed house-flag.

James Baines was much talked of in Liverpool when I was there: & one heard a good deal of his famous ships, some of them the very famous works of the American, Donald McKay.

All wooden ships, no matter how well they are coppered, work themselves loose, and sop up water. These famous ships were driven by pretty hard cases, and strained to the utmost.

. . . The Black Ball was a name to my youth. I knew a man who had sailed in 2 of their clippers, the *Red Jacket* and the *James Baines*, and had seen some stirring scenes in them (mostly under water, for they were driven half under all the time).

65

. . . I am grateful for your tale of the Guide at the Albert Hall,[1] & for your account of the latest male & female fashions. The sleeved Georgian waistcoat is a good thing in cold weather, but green eyelashes I have not yet seen. Have you tried them yet? How do you do them? And please do you green the eyebrows, too? I do hope that you haven't done those yet, for I loved them so.

The elms at Kensington [The Broadwalk] were getting dangerous. At a certain age, elm-roots get down to London clay, which disagrees, or keeps them from what does agree, & then the heavy tree limbs become brittle and may snap off without warning.

You ask about *Ziggurats*.

There used to be a Colloque Archéologique: *Journalist*: Pray, tell me, Sir, what dig you're at? *Archaeologist*: I'm digging out a Ziggurat.

There are countless mounds in Persia, Babylonia, and Assyria which are the remains of Ziggurats.

The land there is (I suppose) mainly flat. When the Kings wished to build a palace or temple, they built it up high according to their power.

The Ziggurat or Zikkerat is usually a stepped pyramid, such as you will have seen in Egypt. No doubt the Tower of Babel was such a one; but unusually big & splendid. The things were built of mud brick, but the perpendicular outer casing was glazed tile, & often the glazed tiles had superbly decorative raised reliefs on them. The effect must often have been very grand. The shrine or palace was at the top. In this form, of the stepped pyramid, I think one passed from step to step by stairs: but there is another form in which you walk up in a winding corkscrew road, no doubt suitable for chariots, & this must have been an improvement. The mud brick has disintegrated with time, so that they appear now as mounds: often vast. In some strange way, Dante must have imagined something of the two kinds, blent into one, for his Mount of Purgatory; & made of that something so startlingly beautiful that one can but wonder.

A few of these Ziggurats have been dug, & the writings of some of the tablets in them have been deciphered.

They seem to be mainly "My name is Ozymandias, King of Kings", or "I am the King", or "three Ardebs of Oil of Spikenard", "Two orims of blue zighal", "I am the only King", etc; boastful utterance, or accounts.

You ask about the seals.[2] Long ago, it was easy to have seals made from ancient seals or coins in the British & other museums. The work was done by specialists in the Museums, & very well, & very cheaply, at a few shillings each, & the results would last for ever & give beautiful impressions to thousands. Unfortunately, few took the opportunity, & no museum does the work now (nor anybody else), the engraver has gone, and the Museum "formateur", or caster, who used to do these things, is no longer employed. My favourite seals were made from Greek coins, or from seals made by Greek artists in ancient Persia. I have a few others of different sorts.

Probably few seals of beauty are now designed anywhere; & the formal commercial seals, or the end of a thimble, the head of a nail, a screw, or keyhandle, suffice for the registered package, even if adhesive paper will not.

Formerly, of course, there were no gummed envelopes, and you had to fold & seal your letters, and with a seal that people knew to be yours, carried on your person . . . .

. . . P.S. Of course, if you MUST do your eyebrows green, or be, more or less, done-for socially, so be it: but could you do them at intervals, say, one now, and perhaps the other at Christmas, and so, as it were, kind of break it gently.

[1] A guide (in a coach passing the Albert Hall) said: "Ladies and Gentlemen, on our left is the Memorial to Albert 'All, and on the right is the Kensington Gasworks." I had this story from William Reed, Elgar's friend. ANS.

[2] JM used to seal his letters with varied and beautiful designs in the wax. ANS.

66

. . . I will write later about the fish question. It was widely believed by sailors that if you boiled a piece of silver, say a sixpence, with any unknown fish, the fish could be safely eaten, if in the boiling the silver did not turn black. I heard of this often, & will try to get you written instances.

But I cannot understand why modern whalers should have done this with dolphin meat. Dolphins have been eaten for centuries, & were a great delicacy in the Middle Ages.

A sailor told me long ago that dolphin meat reminded him of veal.

But remember: sea-cooks usually *boiled*, rarely baked, and perhaps never fried. You will know the old jape, that a sea-cook couldn't boil plain water without burning it. I daresay he would have made any meat, dolphin or other, liker leather or old wet velveteen than veal.

Possibly, the silver had a cross scratched on it.

In Ireland, they used to shoot at ghosts with crumpled-up sixpences marked with crosses. I heard of one man, who was supposed (with some justification) to be the Devil, who was potted at with such a sixpence, but it lodged in his watch or pocket-book (I forget which) & he wore it, later, on his watch-chain as a charm.

But sailors seldom can catch fish at sea: & the edible fishes are now pretty well known. The buccaneers—pirates, who were often on tropical islands, & had lots of stolen silver—were often made ill by poisonous fish.

But of this later, I trust.

67

. . . There is a book by a French doctor (Bompard)[1] who sailed a rubber dinghy from Monte Carlo to Barbados, to show that a castaway can live for weeks on sea-water & fish (no other thing save some rain & a little plankton, the minute stuff that whales eat). He did it: but nearly died. He ate his fish raw & squeezed their juices in a lemon-squeezer & drank those. His point is, that you must not let your body get too dry at first: drink a little sea-water at a time, at once, & catch & squeeze your fish soon . . . .

It impressed me very much: & it has made its mark among both sailors and doctors, so that he must know that his heroic sacrifice has been worth while, and may be certain to save the lives of men & women . . .

[1] Dr Alain Bompard, a house surgeon in a hospital, was called out to a shipwreck in 1951: the appalling horror of it caused him to put all his efforts into investigating the possibility that a person could survive at sea, on the products of the sea and nothing else. He sailed alone across the Atlantic in 1952, in a rubber dinghy taking sealed-up emergency rations, which he never opened. He was at sea sixty-five days, living on fish, juice squeezed from fish (which contained some fresh water) and sea-water. He came ashore alive, but a very sick man.

68

. . . I hope that you, too, will be ever so happy during these next days, in the Sunny South, where, even if it be not very sunny, people eat Cornish cream with meat (or did, long since); & creeks of the sea run far inland; and schooners & barquentines could sometimes be seen tied up in green country alongside an apple orchard: loading cyder, I hope, for people who wd otherwise sup beer (or sorrow).

69

. . . So many grateful thanks for your rousing letter from the West, all about your being drenched, & blown speechless . . . . You ask: how did sailors see what to do in the tougher blasts. Well—the eyes to some extent adapt themselves: & to some extent are less necessary than you might suppose. The things to be done are all simple, & have to be done in restricted space. Even a big sail offers only about a yard of roaring devil to each man at a time. All the man has to do is to beat down Satan under his chest, & beat down another yard before the first gets loose again. In the old days, when men were always reefing, it must have been very hard to know when the points could be knotted, but if the sails were split the burden did not fall on the hands: they had to shift the ruins, but did not pay the damages. I knew an Atlantic mail boat officer who was in the NY to Liverpool service for years. He said that often in the winter gales he only knew that it was raining when the wet streaming down his face had ceased to be salt. When it was salt again he knew that the rain had stopped. As soon as it struck bitter cold he knew that the Centre had been passed, & that the trouble was due. But one good gale will teach all this: they do not differ much, one from another.

70

Reyna mia,

Many thanks for another very charming kind letter.

. . . You ask about Dr Johnson: was he a fiddler? No: he was not in any way musical. He made some remarks about music—"Women have a great advantage, that they can take up little things without disgracing themselves: a man cannot, except with fiddling."

—"I once bought me a flageolet, but I never made out a tune."

—"I might as well have played on the violoncello as another, *but I should have done nothing else.*"

Dr Burney (a Dr of Music) says that late in life Dr J "listened very attentively to the harpsichord". He called out, "Sir, I believe we shall make a musician of you at last." Dr J replied, "Sir, I shall be glad to have a new sense given to me."

Late in life (near the end) Dr J asked Dr Burney to teach him "the scale of Music . . . . Teach me at least the alphabet of your language."

Late in life, he was, I expect, somewhat deaf.

Perhaps the underlined remark is the essential one: that it might have become a rival art, and kept him from what Nature urged on him as the Law of his Being. There is a (?) proverb: "No angel is given two messages", and his was certainly the message of pronouncing on words, on books, on men. He was ever prone to what he calls "idleness", & shrank from what might have become of great enjoyment to him.

. . . PS In the porch of Wolverhampton Church, there used to be a marble to a fiddler (Phillips, I think) with an Epitaph that Dr Johnson re-wrote or re-made, greatly improving it, but the marble was not changed.

71

My grateful thanks for your most charming kind nice letter.

I fear I must have written un-clearly about the Epitaph at

Wolverhampton. It was written by a Dr Wilkes & probably remains there as written. Garrick recited it to Dr Johnson, & Dr J felt that it could be improved, & at once made a great improvement, but this improvement is only printed in Boswell: I don't think that it was ever used on the stone itself.

You should have little trouble in (roughly) dating your ships. Most of our sea-paintings are from shall we say 1750–1950, the 1st 100 years are of wooden ships, with straight sheers, & big single, square topsails (the second sail from the deck).

The second 100 years are of mostly iron ships, with curving sheers, & usually double topsails, with a small-depth sail, the lower topsail, as the second sail from the deck. This is a rough test: very rough: but a guide.

... Please, be very careful about bathwater on painting.[1] You may so easily take off all the glaze, & come upon old soluble paint that will come off too. Even a fine feather brush may mar the glaze or crack it.

A very soft "face" sponge with a very little tepid water will clean the frame, but if you value the painting I would advise an expert hand, for you will be dealing with a tricky, & very variable, material often very delicately laid on. Dreadful things can be done so easily—and then: "Wake Duncan with thy knocking: I would thou couldst."

I am not surprised that a wise man remembers your face and Christian name (and lovely Christian eyebrows) and voice and ways. I am not at all surprised. Do not you find this a frequent happening? Is it not sometimes even something of an embarrassment??

May all lovely happy blessings gladden your days.

John Masefield

Gumption used to be a dreadful mixture of paraffin & bathbrick; there is now a stuff called Gumption, sold in tins at iron-mongers.

[1] An artist friend had told me he cleaned (roughly) old oil paintings by putting them in his bath! ANS.

72

... The Bristol photograph[1] shows a wooden brigantine, of a once familiar coastal type, using a spare gaff as a derrick for hoisting in or out cargo from a lighter. I call her a coastal type, but of course she could have gone anywhere; & very likely often went to Newfoundland for salted codfish, & then took the fish to S. America, or the Mediterrⁿ in time for Lent in the RC countries.

The Teignmouth photograph shows many wooden coastal types: a wooden brig (I expect French) drying sails on her main-mast, and at least 2 barquentines beyond. The distant ones may be schooners: I cannot see. One always saw barquentines in Teignmouth, but I never saw a brig there. If the brig were English, she must have been the last English brig, for the type was obsolete here: too costly to equip & to run: but some owners just scrapped the main yards & ran the vessels as brigantines, or topsail schooners.

Teignmouth used to import coal, & ship potter's clay & granite, among other things. She had a brisk sea trade, coastal & other but the stuff now goes by road, or rail, or to the big ports, and I think that all these small vessels from 60 tons to 250 or so tons, that once gave her harbour such grace, are gone.

[1] I had sent two photographs taken by my father at the turn of the century. ANS.

73

. . . The painter Spurling[1] did some remarkable ship paintings knowing very well the later types of sailing ships & making very good shots at the 1860–1880 type. He did the jacket picture of the *Wanderer* for me: a pretty thing, but not like the *Wanderer*, whom he never saw. . . . He was especially good at painting the famous ships of the Australian passenger & wool trades. He may well have painted the *Hesperus*,[2] one of the most famous of these.

She was a big full-rigged ship, with a long topgallant fo'c'sle, a great deck-house just abaft the foremast, and a long poop coming (perhaps) 20 feet foreward of the mizen mast. She carried a lot of passengers at a go, & I suppose had a 'tween-decks laid mainly for passengers. This was in the 1875–1890 time, before she was a training-ship in Devitt-Moore's scheme. She was 1777 tons; she had every care in fitting: and her sails were miracles of cutting and filling: double topsails on all three [masts], double topgallants on fore & main, a deep single topgallant on the mizen: royals on all 3 and great topgallant masts on all 3 on which sky-sails could easily be set above the royals: but all sails were cut with the care with which yachts' sails are cut.

. . . There is now (I hear) only one sailing vessel, without an engine, making a living under sail [1954]. She is a Portuguese barquentine, engaged in the Banks of Greenland codfish trade.

Don't you go fishing in her, whatever you do: it is cold work done from small open boats.

[1] John Robert Spurling (1870–1933) went to sea at the age of sixteen when he had a bad fall from aloft. He served some time on the *Sabraon* and the *Hesperus*, but never fully recovered from his accident, and eventually took up a full-time artistic career. He illustrated the sea and ships magazine, *Blue Peter*, and a jacket for JM's *Wanderer*.

[2] Not to be confused with the schooner *Hesperus* of Longfellow's famous ballad. A Blackwall passenger ship, this *Hesperus* was launched in 1873; she was never wrecked.

74

. . .My thanks again for a vivid interesting letter, full of strange & lively personalities. It is jolly to know that Russia still cares for great things & that France is still enjoying. Nations do survive their rulers, somehow.

You ask about a catspaw, as a sign of wind. You will often have seen in a river or puddle a sudden ruffle of the surface caused by a gust of wind. It is a little scurrying surface ruffle. You can make it by pouring tea into a saucer & blowing on it to cool it. It is a pretty effect.

Often, in a calm, it is the 1st sign that wind is about to come. You will see this running scuffle darkening a little of the surface, and then dying away.

Sailors (long ago) used to whistle when they saw such ruffles, thinking to call the wind. Later, they got clumped on the head if they ever whistled on board, "because no-one but a——fool would do such a thing".

But some used to go to the nearest backstay & scratch it with a fingernail, for just the same reason, & yet were never clumped on the head.

In the Medit. Sea, & on any coast near mountains, one watches for a catspaw very closely, for gusts of violence come from the glens, & the squall comes down without clouds, & the catspaw is the only warning.

. . . Catspaw: the name. Possibly, because the effect is a little as though the still surface of the sea had been hurried over & marked by myriads of cats' paws.

. . . All blessings & thanks to you. It is 2 years today since you first wrote to me.

John Masefield

PS You will not need to go to sea to see catspaws. You will see gusts ruffle water-surface anywhere on any stillish, uncertain day.

75

. . . Whistling seems to be a dangerous habit—perhaps it is a part of man's wholesome belief that pride goes before a fall, that one must never exult, nor seem safe, nor presume, for that at one's side, or just behind, is that which never sleeps, that which does the justice, and restores the balance, and puts the lily in the dust it grew from.

. . . Alas, I do not know much of Camden,[1] except the *Britannia*. He was one of the great ones of our great times: & great in his life, too. He saw what the young Ben Jonson might become & helped him to become it: and has that praise from Ben Jonson later, that is indeed a praise.

"Camden, most reverend Head, to whom I owe all that I am in Arts, all that I know."

This is no small tribute from one esteemed as the greatest poet and scholar of his time, to one, as it were, already crowned.

Camden was a scholar & a herald, holding some post, & usually a Master at Westminster School (Head of it at the end, I think). He is buried in the Abbey, like his adoring disciple, Ben Jonson. But Ben was buried standing. I think Camden lies at full length.

They dug up Ben about 110 years ago, & found him standing up in the Nave there, not the Poets' Corner, where the stone is. He had red hair, they say.

There is a tale, very likely true, that Ben asked K. James the 1st for a boon—"eighteen inches of England". The K. said he might go so far & not be ruined; so Ben asked for a plot in the Abbey, in which he might be buried standing: so there he was put.

Qy. Possibly Ben, to avoid a tight fit, asked for 2 feet, or even a yard???

. . . You may have heard of the Admiral who said ,"I wish this war would end; then we could get the men back to battle-practice."

What is called Christmas[2] always reminds me of this tale.

. . . *Reynard*. Chaucer's tale comes from a French source. There are many animal tales in old French, Dutch, German: and Reynard the Fox is in many of them, in the 12th, 13th & 14th centuries, some satirical, some just animal-tales, but very popular everywhere.

Your nurse read to you *Uncle Remus*, by Leland,[3] who heard his tales of Brer Fox and Brer Rabbit from an old negro in one of the Southern states. In nearly all these tales Brer Rabbit outwits Brer Fox and Brer Bear, but is far from being a faultless character. The book is now scarce, but very delightful. There is a nice negro proverb quoted:

"Mighty poor nigger don't hear de dinner-horn."

I liked your Epitaph on the Puritan. I read a late 17th cent. one some time ago but forget the victim's name (my own would fit the metre).

> The Lord is pleased when Mortals cease from Sin.
> The Devil is pleased when hee a Soul doth win.
> The world is pleased when any Scoundrell dyes
> So all are pleased, for here —— —— —— lyes.

May blessings attend you always

John Masefield

PS Forgive, please, if you know this one:

Brother Elephant: Why weepest thou?
Brother Rabbit: From Terror, brother.
Brother E: What terrifies thee?
Brother R: The All-Highest orders that all giraffes shall lose their heads.
Brother E: Why weep at that? thou art not a giraffe.
Brother R: No: but how can I prove it?

[1] William Camden (1551–1623), antiquary and historian, was headmaster of Westminster School in 1593. He made tours of investigation into heraldic and other matters throughout England, and published his *Britannia* (in Latin) in 1586. This was translated into English by Philemon Holland in 1610.

[2] It was Christmas 1954.

[3] One of JM's rare mistakes. *Uncle Remus* is by Joel Chandler Harris, not Leland who wrote *Hans Breitmann's Party*.

76

. . . In the picture,[1] she [the *Hesperus*] is running with a fair wind that is very rapidly increasing, so that she is burying her bow, & having to shorten sail, but she has still far too much after sail on her, and is probably steering as wild as a hawk, with 2 men at the wheel, having all that they can do, & every bit of gear strained to the utmost. Her hands at the moment are snugging-up the lower fore & upper main tgs, before hopping up to furl them, but why they do not do more, I cannot think. The flying and outer jibs have just come down but are not yet stowed. Probably the gale has suddenly increased; & the next sails stowed will not have quite such fancy furls as you see up aloft. All hands will be called on deck within 2 minutes.

[1] I had sent JM a postcard reproduction of Spurling's painting. ANS. (See Letter 73.)

77

... By happy chance I have found 2 packets of Spurling ships.

He was a good seaman, & had a lively eye for a ship; and it is a marvel to me (and to the foreigner) that he wasn't paid to paint great fleets of clippers at speed, in friezes, all round Lloyds, and the Exchanges in Lon, Lpl and Manch, and in every city hall.

The poor foreigner does not know how foreign he is till he has been here some time . . . .

... In those days of Oregon pinetrees, she [the *Hesperus*] had a staggering jib-boom as well, poking out ahead like an endless fishing-rod. She was sold to the Russians about 1920 (perhaps earlier) & as she was very strongly built she may still be afloat (or made into bombs).[1]

I doubt if JS ever saw her,[2] and I don't much like the way he avoided showing this: he buries her bow in water & foreshortens all her counter from recognition.

... Ships often had *figure-heads*, not faces, and in olden days *Knight-heads* with faces, & *cat-heads*, each with a cat's face, but you spoke of her forward space, the bows, as "the eyes of her". All 3 heads were in the eyes of her.

[1] She was sold to the Russians in 1900—for £9,000—and renamed *Grand Duchess Maria Nikolaevna*. After complications arising from the Russian Revolution, she came back to Britain, and was once again renamed—this time *Silvana*. She was broken up in Genoa in 1923. ANS.

[2] Spurling, in fact, served some of his time in the ship. ANS.

78

... The *Cutty Sark*, though very fast, was never much for looks. No ship looks well when in ballast: she looks well only when down to her marks on her waterline. Then the slants & curves & straights all balance & charm, and she is a thing of great beauty. I doubt if the *CS* was ever that: but in early days, with big crews, she was sometimes wonderfully kept. When she was bought from the Portuguese, rigged as a barquentine, I saw her in Falmouth: a sad figure of fun. Later, she was re-rigged, and looked better, & when she was with the *Worcester* in the Thames they kept her tidy.

I hope that they will keep her really smart & shiny & clean, with colours and House Flag always flying, now that she has come ashore.

79

. . . To go back for a moment to Mr Spurling's *Hesperus*. He may not have seen her: & could not have seen some others of the ships he drew, but knew that there were prickly survivors who knew them all & would pounce on any mis-statement. He had to go carefully at the points the sailor looks at, the sheer, the bow, the counter, the trim, the rake, the rig, the order . . . . And he may have met some survivor who told him some lively yarn of how they shortened down etc, and what so and so said and what old so & so did. Your picture may well be a record of that half hour, the first half of it, just after they had called all hands, yet before all hands were on deck. She was probably well under-manned, even with her cadets, and put sorely to it, to shorten-down in a hurry.

It is so strange & so touching that you should like to read all this blether of 60 or 70 years back miles from anywhere, & of things long obsolete.

> She was the clipper *Hesperus*
> She sailed th' Australian sea
> Her half-deck pinched a pawn-broker's sign
> And hung it on the main-mast tree.

80

. . . In the Spring, if your Robin nests & hatches young, you can easily tame him to come for currants. They are fond of currants, & will soon learn to come onto your hand for them; and then if you will shut your eyes & keep very still they will take them from your lips. It is a gentle experience, to feel the little thing flutter at your mouth, & gently take the fruit.

. . . Thank you for your true tale of the Bowery Boy.[1]

The Bowery used to be kind of tough: & in my young days it had a pretty tough theatre, where they did real plays with the meaning of death in them.

A friend of mine went there once on a Saturday, to see a play in which the hero was seized by the villain's gang & tied down to a railway line just outside a tunnel-mouth. Then you heard the train in the tunnel: then saw the head-lights, & heard the roar & the whistle: and then of course, in the nick, the heroine dashed up, cut the bonds, & flung the hero clear as the train roared across the stage. Well, on this Saturday, the lady was late on her cue, or the silly hero mizzled his tip, & the train ran into him *and upset*. My man said he saw this. I hope he did.

Steve Brodie's was the real centre in the Bowery then. SB was a politician who jumped from the Brooklyn Bridge for a bet: a good jump.

[1] On a voyage to New Zealand in 1942, a voyage during which the ships before and behind mine were both torpedoed, I had a day or two in New York, when I visited the Bowery and saw some alarming characters. ANS.

1955

Reyna mia

My thanks for your most kind welcome letter. I fear that this will have to be a tiny letter but it may just answer your question about the *Adventurer*. It was, as you guess, a periodical of the kind of the *Spectator*. It began when Dr Johnson stopped the *Rambler*, and ran (perhaps with some of the *Rambler* writers always) for a long time (140 numbers). I suppose it was a weekly.

It was run by Dr John Hawkesworth,[1] a very able writer, who kept a school. He was made Dr on account of its (the paper's) improving tone. Dr Johnson wrote for it: & as Dr H wrote in the manner of Dr J, some doubt who wrote which.

Hawkesworth was given all the journals & papers of Capt Cook's First Voyage to the South Seas, to edit & order for publication. This he did with enormous success, that is, the book succeeded, but no doubt the originals were vivid, interesting papers to begin with.

He published a big edition of Swift, with a Life. Dr J refers to this, & says of JH that he was "a man capable of dignifying his narration with (so) much elegance of language and force of sentiment."

I fear that I cannot do as much in this brief note, but I must add that Dr H had some detractors. He was too able & too successful not to have roused jealousies. Someone says that he was utterly spoiled by success: but surely that may be better and less frequent than being utterly spoiled by failure. Another says that he became latterly "a coxcomb in his dress" but leaves us ignorant of the details, fancy-waistcoats, choice stuffs, queer cuts, or shoe buckles??? Gainsborough might have welcomed such variety: & so should we, after a dose of 18th cent. portraits. Alas, after some late unhappiness he exchanged his gay costume for a shroud.

"Odious, in *woollens*, t'would a Saint provoke."
Forgive this scrap
John Masefield

Hawkesworth was responsible for a collection of voyages, in a big folio edition, and put into it some odd, out-of-the-way papers very interesting (to me).

[1] John Hawkesworth (1715?–73), edited *The Adventurer* 1752–4.

82

. . . You asked about Swinburne. Very likely, he would mean nothing to you: things & aims are so changed. He was an unusually skilful metrist. Tennyson said, or wrote, of him something like this: "He is a reed, through which all things blow to music."

He was passionately fond of literature and generous beyond all known men in praise of poets whom he liked and friends who were anything to him. In praise of understanding of life he was less happy: you might be disappointed in his subjects: & his success as a metrist is less likely to be liked now than wondered at then.

It was said that Adah Menken's[1] death was more than a sorrow to him: a blow or stroke from which he never recovered really. *This is but hearsay.*

Watts-Dunton, a Lawyer and writer (not a bad poet) took the ruins of him (nearly extinct, the little body was) & guarded & kept it for about 20 or 30 happy years at Putney.

O the jealous rage of those excluded from that Paradise, & the knaveries uttered by them against W-D.

But for W-D, S would have died in misery & sorrow. W-D kept him, & spruced him up, & encouraged him to go on, & was a guardian angel to him.

He (S) wrote much vehement support of poets little known. Rossetti turned him to the study of William Blake: & his study of Blake was the first really searching study, bringing light.

Adah Menken was a very lovely circus-rider (& dancer). She wrote poems, & was much in the circles of Rossetti, ACS & other writers. The verse is clever, the content no special shakes, but she herself was lovely & her life-experience unusual & rather grand. She died (I think very suddenly) in 1868: much mourned. I read her verse once, but forget it now & it may be much better than I say: she was adored everywhere, for her cleverness & her niceness, as well as her beauty.

You must not bother what people write now of ACS. Like other poets, he had his limitations. Unlike many other poets, he had amazing powers of generosity, of perception, & exquisite achievements, of kinds then precious to the writers, beyond pearls, beyond rubies, beyond I will not say wisdom but certainly common sense.

[1] Adah Isaacs Menken (born Adelaide McCord, 1835–68) Actress, circus-performer and writer; friend of Swinburne, Dickens, Charles Reade and, in France, of Dumas and Gautier. She is buried in Père Lachaise cemetery, Paris.

83

... For some years before he died, Thomas Hardy worked with his 2nd wife, Florence Hardy,[1] at a life of himself, in 2 vols. I judge that he wrote most of Vol I himself, but much less of Vol II. This is the best life, probably: & all future lives must be based on it.

[1] Hardy married Florence Dugdale in 1914, when he was seventy-three and she thirty-five.

84

... [Swinburne] was not an expounder of human life. He had some passions & generosities (more than most) & was a master of verse. These are great qualities.

ACS loathed Thomas Carlyle. I do not know all his reasons: but like Andrew Aguecheek, he had reasons good enough. TC liked Prussianism & hated France; liked force and thrift, & disliked beauty and splendour. ACS wrote outrageous things about TC, during TC's life & later: partly because TC disliked [Charles] Lamb. ACS fell often foul of Carlyle & hit him some jabs. Next to the last Napoleon, the Roman church, a writer named Buchanan, and in 1 or 2 other darknesses, he hated political repressions, & anyone who disliked [Victor] Hugo and Lamb. He got Carlyle as it were with both barrels here ...

85

... I am glad that you liked [Swinburne's] *By the Sea*. You will probably know that he describes the coast south of Southwold,

Suffolk, Dunwich etc, especially the Dunwich bit, where there were great collapses 80–60 years ago. A great church tower still stood when I was there 50 years ago, & may stand still, but all the graveyards of the city were washed away in ACS's time, & countless bones strewed the beach. Medical students used to go there to get such helpful chunks of man as they stood in need of at the time.

Lesbia Brandon is in such a mess from the people who have dished it up that it is not worth the trouble given to it. What it was to have been, and may once have been, it certainly is not now. Too many cooks seem to have dealt with that particular broth. The thing is nothing.

No one could write a real book of ACS in less than 7 years. He is buried too deep in a long dead century: & the coming to know that century is now more difficult than it would have been before the second war. And who would read such a book now?

. . . No doubt the ACS verse tires you after a time. It is so often lovely, but he is not one to lift into wider life (as a rule) . . .

. . . You asked me about [Oscar] Wilde. Alas, on that topic I cannot be helpful at all. I do not care about any of his work, & never did. Probably I have the wrong shaped head, or something.

Claude Vernet[1] was the grandfather Vernet. He was employed by the Louis XV–XVI in painting the great French sea-ports (& thereby suggesting something of the kind to Turner & Wm Danielli). He was for a long time at Marseilles, where a lively good school of marine painting existed. We have no painting by him at Greenwich, I fear, but I shall be able to see engravings of his work in a little while. Some of the Marseilles painters were admirable.

Claude's son was Horace, who painted the young & the mature Napoleon with varied glory & vain-glory. Horace's son was also a famous painter.

[1] Claude-Joseph Vernet (1714–89) a celebrated French landscape and marine painter.

86

. . . It is supposed that the plan of using Vernet to paint the sea-ports of France was made by the Marquise de Pompadour, at that time the acting Queen of France, in some (vain) hope of causing Louis XV to take some pride (or interest) in France, her Navy & her commerce. Her brother became Director of Fine Arts in France. It was he who arranged it with Vernet, but some third hand, no doubt a sailor or one well-versed in Coast Defence in sea-affairs, gave wise suggestions, which V often ignored.

The pictures were the King's. He is said to have looked at them with the cynical remark that these ships of M. Vernet's were the only Fleet France had.

... I do not know the Scotch play, the *3 Estates*,[1] but was interested in bits of it quoted at the time. Scotland shines more in the song & the story than in the play. The stage used was very much that of the Elizabethan ...

I am so glad that you have enjoyed *Chastelard*[2] ... I cannot believe that M[ary] was in any way guilty of the Darnley murder.

They have (or had) the mummy of Bothwell on view in a place in Denmark: the very body of the ruffian, & I might have seen him once, or would have, if I had liked him better, but there he is, if you ever want, & are there. (He may now be buried.)

[1] *Ane Pleasant Satyre of the Thrie Estatis* by Sir David Lindsay (1490–1555), a morality play in verse.

[2] *Chastelard*, a tragedy by Algernon Charles Swinburne, published 1865, concerning the love of Chastelard, a grandson of Bayard (the "chevalier sans peur et sans reproche"), for Mary Queen of Scots, which love leads to his death.

87

... About the engravings. Collectors of prints seek out the rare states of many engravings. An engraver, when he has done, say, a third, or a half, of his plate, may print a proof from it, to see how it looks & how it should be changed. He does this at intervals, taking a few pulls each time, till the plate is ready & finished. These proofs are called *States* and are numbered 1st, 2nd etc and, being rare, may become very precious.

You have engraved descriptions under yours, have you not? The early states have no descriptions under them, such as "A view of Clifton, showing the Bridge", & are sometimes called *Proofs before letters*. Yours are *Proofs after letters*; the copies issued in the books.

As yours are clear in detail, they are probably fairly early copies, before the plates got worn. The plates can be touched up a bit in this case & slightly changed in the process. Early states are often very simple and fine, & not marred with any fussy finish.

... The anxieties of Confirmation; I see no way of making them less real to the young. It is a time of perplexity to many of the young, many of whom are beginning to rebel against parental control, & to question all the beliefs of childhood, just as they also have every incentive to strike out for themselves, & exercise some authority in a school. Perhaps the Confirmation time comes a little too early, or at a moment when most people are somewhat upset by the worries and strains of growth. I was confirmed while on the *Conway*, with a lot of other men. The Bishop asked for a holiday for us, & some of the confirmees painted Liverpool bright red to mark the occasion.

88

Reyna mia

So many thanks for your letter, ever kind & forbearing.

I think that Kirk of Field[1] must remain a mystery, even if Holmes should come with Watson & take a lot of cocaine, & get you to play the fiddle to him. Too many traitors were at work, in too many dirty ways, forging papers, destroying evidence, spreading lies, bribing witnesses & if necessary, killing them, by the justice of the party.

There seems to be no doubt that a fierce Catholic party, backed by Spain, Rome & (a little) France, wished to be rid of Mary, to make Darnley the King, and then rule Scotland through Darnley & the Catholic lords.

Darnley wished to be King & seems to have been willing to get rid of Mary. It is hard (otherwise) to understand his share in the killing of Rizzio.

The Protestant Scotch Lords were eager to get rid of Darnley, possibly willing to get rid of Mary, & certainly afraid of Catholic forces coming into Scotland from Europe.

England, who had several fingers & a lot of secret service money in this very evil pie, was afraid of Catholic intervention, afraid of a quiet Scotland, & of a Catholic Reformation there. She was backing the Protestant Lords against Mary & the Catholics and was very well informed of all that was being plotted. Mary was ill, but shrewdly aware of all these main purposes at work around her.

In all the main plots, there were many master-skunks who would gladly double-cross their friends for value received. Mary was never a plotter nor killer. She was sorely beset; ill; among foreigners, among traitors, and in a land full to the brim with old bitter blood feuds & savageries, of which she (& we) knew and know nothing.

Bothwell was (seemingly) never a plotter nor killer, but a rough and tough Borderer, something (shall we say) like a good cavalry officer under the young Napoleon: a man of quick action: & not likely to get along with men of craft: he seems to have been hated by such: but Mary had found him to be of swift action & (to her) till then, honest.

Now, there is no doubt (it is said) in all this doubtful devilry, that

Sir James Balfour, a Catholic lawyer, owned & lived in a big new house a few yards (150??) from Kirk of Field House, and had bought a lot of gun-powder a few days before the deed.

It is thought that he & some of the Cath party caused this powder, 250 or 300 lbs of it, to be put in K of F House under the Q's bedroom which was under Darnley's bedroom, meaning (it is said) to blow up the Queen as soon as Darnley was clear of the building.

On the night of the explosion (a moonless winter night) the Q did not sleep there, but went rather suddenly back to Holyrood (800 yards away). Bothwell was with her, as Captain of the Guard.

I think that there can be no doubt that both knew that danger was threatening both Darnley and Mary, either singly or together.

Bothwell, as Captain of the Guard, left the Q at Holyrood & presently, after talk with her, went back to K of F & then to bed.

At about 2 a.m. K of F was blown up.

Darnley was not in the house. He was not blown up. He & his servant were scared in the night, ran out of doors in night clothes, were there (seemingly) promptly strangled by people waiting for the purpose.

Some suppose that Darnley knew all about the powder, having designed it for Mary.

Some suppose that the Prot Lords also knew all about it, & resolved to use it for Darnley: & lured or scared D out of the house, with some cry of Fire, strangled him & his servant in the garden & then touched off the mine.

Then, what so good as to accuse Mary & Bothwell of the crime, thus discrediting and ruining both, serving the Protestant cause, delighting England & blasting the Catholic cause?

They caught a lot of Bothwell's men, tortured them into making statements, distorted or falsified these, & killed the men.

It is impossible to get at the truth.

Who touched off the powder and who strangled the 2 in the garden (if they were strangled)?

It is not the work of a man like Bothwell: & impossible for the Q: but in its results it was made so to seem their work that all their later actions become explicable, & unavoidable.

To one interested in fiction, it seems possible that on a pitch dark winter night both plots worked, or might have worked. The (silent) Prots might have lured D out & strangled him quietly, half an hour before the (noisy) others touched off the mine. In the dark, a faithful friend might well have told the miners that D was out of the house and in the garden; & that the house could go up when they chose.

Balfour was away from Edinb at the time.

But now, a long weary talk about a weary theme. As SH might have said, "A difficult problem, my dear Watson. It reminds me of what Hafiz said in his immortal ode:

'The heart of man, O gazelle-eyed, can be a considerable conundrum.'"

It is now claimed that the Casket Letters are either forged, or not Mary's.

Bless you
John Masefield

I am so glad that you have found ACS's *Blake*. This brings you up to D. G. Rossetti, from whom we all derive. DGR was a friend of Gilchrist,[2] who died suddenly. DGR finished the Blake book for Mrs Gilchrist & the children. It was he who turned the set to Blake, and Morris to art. It was he who put ACS to Blake and encouraged the young man to those early poems & tales.

I am so touched that you should like these early Morris things, in spite of the wars and the times. It wd be hard to say what the *Hollow Land* & the *Church* & the *Guenevere* book were to me when I was young. The shadow of the joy is still with me when I read them.

[1] The house where Lord Darnley, husband of Mary Queen of Scots, was murdered in 1567. Kirk O'Field was a collegiate church in Edinburgh, founded in 1510, but in ruins before Darnley's death in a house built on the site.

[2] Alexander Gilchrist (1828–61). His *Life of Blake* was published in 1863.

89

. . . Jowett was Master of Balliol where ACS [Swinburne] was a somewhat unusual undergraduate. He asked ACS to read a play that he had written. This was *Bothwell*, which ACS read through in (about) 5½ hours of rapturous eloquence. At the end ACS asked what he thought of it. J (in the tale) said that it was this, and then that it was that, but that on the whole, perhaps, might it not be considered long? ACS is said to have said, "Perhaps you're right."

During what was left of the night J is said to have reflected that he was dealing with a very impulsive young man, & ought to have spoken with a greater tact, & more emphatic generosity. So he bade ACS come to breakfast, and said, "Thinking over your play—to me it is not a breath too long. I ought not to have made that comment."

ACS is said to have looked a little blank, & to have said, "I'm sorry about that. You see . . . I've burned it."

Then J looked a little blank, but ACS at once said, "O, it doesn't matter. I can easily write it again."

90

. . . Your tale of the Sark fisherman[1] reminds me of a tale told of a pilot (a black pilot) on the Niger. As the ship went upstream a lady asked this pilot:

"I suppose you know where all the rocks are?"

"All de rocks? O *no*, ma'am."

"Then how can you pilot if you don't know where all the rocks are?"

"'Cos I know where de water is."

. . . The D[uchess] of M[arlborough] was the wife of the famous D[uke], the soldier. The D was a forceful woman, and a great friend at one time (a long time) of Q Anne, but the time ended, on political & religious grounds: Q Anne being for the Hanoverians & Protestants, & the D of M for the other side.

No doubt the D, like most important office holders then, thought that writers were of no account, & could always be bought, but that cards were the occupation of rank, & that skill at cards shewed both birth and upbringing. To dislike cards perhaps shewed a tendency towards the puritanisms that in the 17th century had made a civil war. The Cavalier party affected the cavalier manner, though both parties still had very frequently a want of any good manners.

Perhaps I should say that the friendship of the D with Q Anne was in the years before A became Queen. As Queen, Q Anne had to keep her consecration vow, to stand by the Protestant religion, linking Holland, Germany & England, & keep away from the wiles of Catholicisms, France & Spain.

[1] This fisherman told me that, when out fishing, he never observed the surface of the water, but all the time "saw" the shapes, patterns and positions of the rocks on the bottom of the sea. ANS.

91

. . . The young blackbird will probably expect food every 20 minutes, for the growth is very swift & has to be helped by constant food. I have blackbirds here, in the nesting times: & can always tame them (if I wish) then, for the young are mad for food all the day long. Indeed you can readily tame English birds with younglings by offering constant food. They will come to your hand, and take food from your lips if you keep quiet (and shut your eyes) . . .

92

. . . Thank you for your lively study of the woman from Donegal. You will find many such in the Catholic parts of Ireland: often fierce, like yours, often queenly in all ways, manner, look & bearing: & sometimes of an utterly haunting shattering beauty, unearthly in every way, though they live in a cabin, with a mud floor, into which the pigs and the poultry stray: the cattle, too.

. . . What fun that ACS [Swinburne] should have given you so much interest & excitement.

I feel that all ACS's mysticism came from DGR [Rossetti] without whom ACS might never have bothered about Blake.

The [Blake] illustrations to Gray were reproduced *only in monochrome* by the Oxford University Press about 30 years ago. It is a costly book, but the big Manchr libraries might (& should) have it. WB never finished it: & I know not where the original now is. (It seems to have slept unnoticed for some years at least on a shelf in Ledbury.) WB was doing it for the Fuselis, for whom he had a great admiration. You may find some odd doggerel about Fuseli[1] in WB's poems—something like this:

> Of all the men I ever knew
> Who did not ——

But I will not write it from memory, as that may make it worse than it really is.[2] F was a competent painter & like Shakespeare "had the Phantsie very strong". But even if you see the monochrome reproduction it will give you not the least faint sense of some of the imaginative possession of Gray's thought: esp in the "Long Story", which helped to begin the Romantic Movement.

Some child of Belial has snaked my Blake: & I cannot give you the text of the doggerel.

(I err: the child of Belial, presumably myself, has snaked it back from where the silly ass stuck it.)

But I will not give you the text of the doggerel, for WB wrote nobler things of Fuseli: "Such an artist as Fuseli is invulnerable; he needs not my defence." HF was a Swiss, who came to England as a young man & attained a good deal of fame, as painter & writer. I will try to read some of his works: for he must have meant much to WB as man, thinker, & painter. I have seen few of his pictures; and remember only that they shewed a phantasy.

¹ Henry Fuseli, or Johann Heinrich Füssli (1741–1825), native of Zurich. He came to London in 1765, was encouraged by Reynolds, and was elected Professor of Painting at the Royal Academy of which he became Keeper in 1804. His paintings tended towards the horrifying, the fantastic and the sinister. (A century after his death his work was to be much admired by the Surrealists.) Among his pupils were Etty, Haydon, Landseer and Constable.

² See, however, Letter 363.

93

. . . You ask me if [Swinburne] liked Gray? I believe "not very much", at any rate, much less than he liked Collins, a contemporary of Gray, of even slighter output, & far sadder history.

You may remember Dr Johnson's outburst against:

"Weave the warp, and weave the woof"?

. . . "It is by crossing the woof with the warp that men weave the web . . . He has, however, no other line as bad." *(Life of Gray)*

Those who like a poet have in them something of that poet, & are in a sense, his kin & of his mental clan or household. This can be, and is, a happiness to them.

It is not necessary, though it is usual, for them to attack other poets not of their kin. All poets endeavour to make a kind of poetry: if one likes some kinds, one can leave the rest alone. Heaven is vast: stars are many: all have some light: all much, seen close.

William Blake, on the whole, seems to have been more of a marvel to meet than to know. Perhaps all who met him felt that they had met a man who had been in Paradise, but those who knew him well seem to have . . . well . . . what can one say . . . supposed that a touch had touched . . . or a screw unscrewed . . . or a bat got in the belfry . . .? You see . . . meeting him once, you might have heard him say: "Voltaire denied the Holy Spirit . . . & he shall be saved. But they shall NOT be saved who deny the Holy Spirit in Voltaire." But, knowing him well, you might have heard him read to you: "Hampstead, Highgate, Finchley, Hendon, Muswell Hill rage loud Before Bromion's iron Tongs and glowing poker . . ." and been just a little put to it, what to say when he stopped.

94

... *Evelina* was a very famous book by 1808; as famous, say, as *Adam Bede* was in 1908. Every reader (and there were many readers then) knew that *Evelina* was by Miss Burney.

I have never read it, & tho' I have it, I cannot. I have read some of her *Diary*, which is entertaining, & all that Boswell says of her friendship with Dr J is "they were great friends, she and the Dr".

Her brother was with Capt. Cook in the South Seas, and an Editor of Voyages thither: a very able man.

There is or was, a Wm Burney: I know not what relation (if any) who enlarged Wm Falconer's *Marine Dictionary* and made it a most useful (& much better) book, though Falconer's book is well enough for about 1760.

Did you ever read Falconer's "Shipwreck", a poem?[1]

... About R. Savage.[2] The general feeling *now* is that he was a blackmailer. Probably the truth cannot now be determined, but I always feel that the Inns of Court might have great fun trying the case at one of their mock trials, with what evidence there is. Johnson loved the man, & that is much in his favour, & loved him after such trials as he described. Alas, alas, charm is a kind of poetry, & many worthless poets have had it in themselves, & though they have been no good, & done harm, this charm has redeemed them in some people's eyes, for years even. Savage's verse now seems nothing. "The best water is the newest" & that is no longer new . . . However, Dr J found good in him, & that is very much.

[1] William Falconer (1732–69) wrote a long poem, "The Shipwreck", about a ship wrecked on the coast of Greece. He was later drowned at sea.

[2] Richard Savage, who received sympathetic treatment in Johnson's *Lives of the Poets*, claimed to be the illegitimate son of a nobleman. His poem "The Bastard", a tirade against his supposed mother, contains one famous line: "No tenth transmitter of a foolish face".

95

... Our old *Conway* model, wh we made for the King, used to be in South Kensington Art Section. I suggested it only, about 25 years ago [*c.* 1930]. I made none of it: the 250 lads of the moment made her, & it did not take long with so many duplicating what has to be so frequently used in a model, a block or dead-eye or screw-eye, or delicate eye-splice or whipping. An old Naval instructor directed them. She is a creditable effort.

. . . Were you ever interested at all in Napoleon? Did you ever read the kind of address he wrote to his armies from time to time?

"Soldiers.

"In 3 days you have destroyed the Enemy, swum the Atlantic, climbed the Alps, crossed the Equator and broken the Eliptic.

"The Emperor is content with you.

"But much more remains to be done." etc. I always boast, that I have met a lady, who had met a lady, who had met Napoleon. I asked the lady who had met the lady what the lady thought of him. She said that the lady "did not like Napoleon; he talked such bad French".

When I was young, a good many veterans of that age were still alive, you must remember . . .

96

. . . Somebody wrote of Napoleon (someone who knew him) that he was "as great as man can be without morality".

Remember, though, that he was born at the Revolutionary time, & was a young soldier when France boiled over in blood & massacre; & that then, by courage, craft, genius & desperate plunges into danger he got all the slaughterers by the scruff & shook them back into order: a staggering feat; & done in youth: with that calm beauty of face that the younger Vernet painted.

Later, of course, he was not left alone, & there were bloodfeuds, & vengeances, & endless intrigues against him. He was not one to accept these lightly & did frightful things: awful things: that Life, callous as she seems, never endures for long from anyone. No-one could believe him: no-one could trust him: tho' many would have if they could have: for who else could hold Revolutionary France?

You must not pity Napoleon at St Helena. The English saved his life by sending him there. The Germans and Russians wanted him killed, the Italians would have murdered him, & the Spaniards wanted to tear him into little fragments. I say nothing of ½ the French people & the Austrians. The man had become a curse to humanity. It was our humanity that caused him to be sent to Elba in 1814; when St Helena was first proposed Elba proved a mistake.

By that time Napoleon was utterly false; & he passed his time at St Helena writing lying memoirs to show that Waterloo was lost by faults of *Ney & Grouchy*.[1] This isn't so. Ney & Grouchy both acted to his own direct recorded orders: both were fine soldiers of very fine but different qualities, & both would have been sacked & degraded if they had failed to obey him. N lost the Waterloo campaign by detaching Ney on the 16th June, and Grouchy on the 17th June. With one on the 16th he would have beaten Blücher; & with Grouchy on the 18th he must have separated us from the Prussians. He detached them & fought without them. Blücher fell back on the 17th, & came forward again on the 18th, and N was scuppered as a result. Ney fought like a hero on the 18th, & Grouchy saved his army of 30,000 men by a most masterly retreat. Remember, that N had sent him with this 30,000 men with precise orders. Grouchy had obeyed these orders admirably, with the result that when Grouchy heard the Waterloo battle begin (at about 11.30 on the 18th) he was at least 10 miles from any part of the battle, in a wild countryside without any paved road, all brooks flooded, mud a foot deep everywhere, his men without food, the enemy in his front & already between him & Napoleon's staff, to say (in short) "the Emperor is content with you". He therefore attacked the enemy in his front according to orders, & did not march to the battle. Soldiers reckon that had he marched to the battle, *in that mud*, he would have arrived about 9 p.m. after the French army had fled.

Even if he had been present on the French R on the 18th at noon, the utmost of the French success would have been a drawing back of the English left, & the utter destruction of the French army on the 19th.

It is curious that we are blamed by all parties for the cruel shutting up of the Eagle in St Helena. But for us, he would have been handed to others who wd have scragged him, Sir H[udson] Lowe had a horrid job & a horrid prisoner: & kept him, at least, from afflicting mankind henceforth.

He was not then the beautiful young genius that Vernet painted, but a false, lying, scruffy scoundrel, who had played a wicked game & crashed.

This is the verdict, not of me, but of the world, surely. On the whole, the world says this.

It is a strange fact, and shows what mud was about, but Grouchy, 10 miles from Waterloo battle, did not hear of the defeat till 10.30 next morning, when a cavalry major came in. They thought at first he was mad or drunk. Grouchy must have felt like "The poor, lonesome cowboy, a long way from home", but he saved his army and brought it back intact to France, pretty well intact, that is.

¹ Michel Ney (1769–1815) the most famous of Napoleon's Marshals, and the one best-liked by the armies. And Emmanuel, Marquis de Grouchy (1766–1847), Marshal of France. An aristocrat who believed in the Revolution, he was employed by Napoleon from 1801 in military and political positions of importance. His conduct at Waterloo has always been the subject of controversy. He was held up by the Prussian

rearguard while the Prussians and English united to crush Napoleon. In spite of his later success in getting what was left of the French army back to Paris, he was disgraced and very nearly condemned to death.

97

. . . A Blue Nose is a Nova Scotian. They are supposed to have blue noses because of the cold, or perhaps because they raise a kind of sweet potato of that name: but the term is given to Newfoundlanders also.

98

. . . About the Thomas Hardy model.[1] It is a dreadful thing: but in talk once TH said that as a little boy he had longed for a model & had never had one; so I asked if I might try to make him one; so I tried to make "The *Triumph*, the new-rigged ship", of the old song he quotes somewhere (in a poem). It looked quite gay when new, but I was a wretched hand at tools at the best. I blush to see it now, but I think TH was pleased: & that is much to remember.

[1] JM made a model of a ship for Thomas Hardy; it is now in the Dorset County Museum, Dorchester.

99

. . . Your Clifton book is just a little too early to bring in the Graces, with whom modern Bristol reached her utmost Victorian fame. In my youth it shone bright, with WG & EM; WG at the age of 10, a skinny boy, playing against E Gloucestershire, and smiting them hither & yon, like somebody did the Amalekites.

You may not credit it, but once I opened a door for WG & might even have touched him, had I dared. I was within a foot of his right arm.

. . . When I was at Norwich, I used to think of the stone for the Cathedral, coming from Caen in Normandy, a 300-odd mile sail, in small loads, 50 tons at a time, poling up the Bure or the Yare perhaps, & making cunning use of every tide, every current, every slant of wind: & taking how long each time, even at the best? One sail in the ship: a week's journey even at the best. And how many loads of stone in the Cathedral, & what gear had they to sway it aloft by?

The Caen ships must have been something like the ship in the Bayeux tapestry, only bigger, higher in the side &, as the 12th century passed, more completely decked. The usual sailing wherry or barge is much bigger, lower in the water when loaded. I fear I over-estimate the average Caen ship's cargo. They might have carried 10–15 tons & later 20 tons or 30.

100

... About Besant's book.[1] You may not know, but he founded the Society of Authors, to rid Authors of the kind of harpy the book describes. There *were* such people then, & they often caught writers young & ate their lives out.

Besant was also fond of founding Clubs, mostly dining & lunching clubs, meeting once a month or so. He is said to have founded 14.

"Sir: they promoted kindness."

... I loved your Paris letter. I have been much in Paris, first & last, & knew it once pretty well.

All Frenchmen fish in any water there is. You should see the thousands with rods leaving Paris on a Sunday morning to fish in the Seine, the Oise, & even the canals.

[1] *Armorel of Lyonesse* by Sir Walter Besant (1836–1901), author and philanthropist.

1956

101

... Perhaps in your reading of old Naval books you have come across the name of John Mitford, who wrote *Johnny Newcome* as "Alfred Burton" about the years 1815–20.

He had served in the Navy in the Napoleonic Wars, & had commanded a cutter.

It is said that on retirement he lived in a shack in a gravel pit near London, & had a fixed income of 1/- a day & an uncertain income from journalism. It is said he spent his fixed income thus:

Red herrings	1d
Bread	1d
Onions	1d
Gin	9d

& his uncertain income got him clothes & did his washing & fuelling. He went mad after a time, & so an end.

All this may be the invention of rival poets, or journalists; it may be quite false.

Anyhow, I believe that he knew the Navy, & wrote from this knowledge this *Johnny Newcome* book, which I send, all coarse as it is, for the truth that the man's nature will not attempt to conceal. It is perhaps a prologue better read before beginning Marryat's *Midshipman Easy*, which shall follow.

102

... I cannot say what [William] Morris was to me when I first really read him. Long afterwards I knew his daughter a little & she said to me once, "You always remind me of my Father": & when I went out I wept. I often went to his grave at Kelmscott to say what was said over Lancelot's grave.

"Now there thou rest, Sir Lancelot, that never wast matched by mortal man."

. . . I sent you last week a copy of The Pardoner's Tale, & in the flyleaf I stuck a card of the Middle Ages, that is really a card of Chaucer's mind; that clearness, gaiety, childishness & infinite perception of colour & charm. We have nothing of that spirit. We live in gloom & know nothing of the Middle Ages; only of its violence. The real life was so intense, so unlike anything now.

But read The Pardoner's Tale before trying *Troilus*. It is a flawless tale, & may have been Chaucer's own invention. Do read it, dear, & see if you cannot like it, in spite of the Pardoner who so often intrudes on the story.

Did you ever read Blake's account of Chaucer, or see his picture of the Pilgrims??

I do dearly long for you to like Chaucer; so if I can help, will you always just do me the honour of asking? Little enough that I can do to help wise you. Troilus is a bit slow on his feet, & Pandarus is a shade long-winded, but they are both of the 14th century.

I want you to accept from me this clean copy of the Knight's & Nun Priest's tales. Please will you read both these at once. Some of his very best. The Knight's esp. I shall always think the dream in the NP a masterpiece of art: & in the K, all the wonderful praying at the shrine.

I do long for you to love these.

103

O yonge dere blisful mayden swete[1]
That go[th] so winsome on thy litel fete
And art so dere thou puttest al in tune
As is the nightingale in the May moon.

How shall I thank thy yonge kinde hart
So loving gentle to me as thou art
How bless thy kindness, goodness, to this man,
Making ech day a 20th of Jan.
My yonge swete dere Reyna kind
Al lovely womanhede and dainty mind.

My yongë brightë fresshë mayden dere
That fiddleth so that joy it is to here,
Swete gentil-hart Reyna, yow I mene
(As thesë wysë Spaniards clepen Quene)
I cannot at the moment wreten mo
For wit ye wel, Fortunë axeth so
My heddë ake for very bisinesse
And eke the post is going as I gesse.

[1] A "Chaucerian-style" courtly poem to Reyna, 20th January being the anniversary of JM's first meeting with ANS, in 1953

104

Dear one,

Please read *T & C* [*Troilus and Criseyde*] through. It is long: but it is by a Master; tho' he is still immature, he is often charming or very charming, & if not he is his Time speaking, & his City is there, too, tho' he calls it Troy: but most of all I long for you to feel the full tide of the tale sweeping you up into the ecstasy of the end.

I have some other Chaucer for you presently.

Of course much of it is immature and long-winded: an imperfect artist's butting at a great stone wall, feeling that if he butts on hard eno & long eno he will come thro to a green country & see the stars.

He jolly well did, in the end.

But long before the end he said some memorable things:

"As proude Bayard 'ginneth for to skippe".

105

. . . What fun for you, to see it in the shop,[1] and to forget the move, the misery & the cold . . . & then bravely & boldly to plunge . . . .

It is a 4 volume book, is it not?

I know not who Henry Bunbury was.[2] I think a Sir C Bunbury was one of the Club, who was at Johnson's funeral. (When I spoke at the Abbey in 1954 on Keats & Shelley I had one foot on Garrick's grave and the other on Dr J's.)

It is a marvellous book of knowledge, wit, wisdom (& understanding of 5 generations of poetry that Dr J considered as poetry). I have the 4 vols too. It is one of my favourite books. It is a masterpiece of writing.

How could anyone now write a history of the 80 or so significant poets of the 150 years, Gray to 1914? Who would try it? What a mess he would make of it.

Yet consider Dr J's mastery of all the foundations of his 150 years; the Cowley, Waller, Denham; then the supreme flowering of it in Dryden and Pope, the man of power & the man of art, the contrast of these, amid the schemers & triflers; then the decadence of the school; new aims beginning, the old aims failing, the revolt against the established canons shewing.

He was of the 150 years, & resented the new romantics, Gray and Mallett, but in his learning, wit, sense & delight in the great achievements of his school, he is radiant.

What a power in his contrast of Dryden & Pope; what a revelation of the time, in Savage; what sly wit, in the Smith, of the ale "too delicious to be resisted" & in phrases like "the smallpox destroyed the pleasing anticipation" (in wh life I forget).

Of course, a lot of the poets & artists of any time are only the breathers of an air then blowing over the world. They have a place in that fabric, but perish with it. Only a few get something from somewhere else, and leave it forever: it may be only a few words.

¹ I had bought a first edition of Samuel Johnson's *Lives of the Poets*. ANS.

² On the flyleaf of the book was inscribed "The gift of Henry Bunbury, Esq." Henry Bunbury may have been the caricaturist and author of comic books on riding and racing, which he illustrated himself (1750–1811). The Bunbury mentioned by JM could have been Sr Thomas Bunbury, owner of the first Derby winner, who died in 1820.

106

. . . The Milton is one of Dr J's best. He had in M a scholar better than himself, as pious, tho in a very different way, and a poet (in all ways serious) outstanding. He did not care for the romantic side of M, reared on John Fletcher & Shakespeare, so he is not up to much on some of the early work, nor the exquisite early verse, the gracious things in *Comus* imitated from John Fletcher, & the noble rhythm of "Christ's Nativity", the survey of the structure of *Par. Lost* is masterly, this view of JM the man is inimitable: the fact that he was a rebel dog just always showing through the fact that he was a thing of glory.

. . . It is a solemn thought that of Dr J's 50-odd lives, only about 5 are much-read poets today, & only about 10 more reasonably familiar. Indeed, I wrote last week of 80 poets between Gray and

1914—The Venturer would hardly select more than 30 for a series of
Lives, & what a swamp the Venturer would find himself stuck in.

. . . You ask what tree to plant for me? How sweet a kindness to
think of for me. What will grow well in Manchester? Would a spindle
grow? Would a red hawthorn grow? Or an ordinary white hawthorn?

Or a wild cherry?

"Loveliest of trees, the cherry now . . ."

Or an evergreen bay: or would a white Laurustine grow? I would
love that, if it would do.

"The flower that smells of sunrise and the sea, White Laurustine"

I could send cuttings if they would take: but would they?

107

. . . My dere swete, no, I never could write a Lives of the Poets of the
Romantic School. I am too far from books now, & the research
needed would be very great, & the school, too, how utterly out of
favour. No-one now wants to read them, tho many would love to
read how 1 poet killed his father & another bit his sister & another
poisoned his rival & 17 others lived in incest & other desperate
ways, & most of them drank, & ran away with the trust-money: they
would like to know all this perhaps . . .

. . . You delight me with your joy in *Troilus*. I am so very, very
glad that it took your gentle heart so utterly. I hoped it would.

Is it not strange to see him butting against the wall, page after
page, book after book, in the faith that he will get thro to somewhere,
& that somewhere will be an Earthly Paradise of Beauty & Power.
Then, after a dreadful journey suddenly, he gets thro, & suddenly he
leaves Gower far behind on earth, and gets into a Realm of Beauty &
Power, & is the first Englishman ever to get there: he is a poet of
power as soon as Diomede speaks, & then goes on & on & into that
starry beauty of the end from "And whan that he was slain in the
mancre" & that sublime sweet song at the end: "O yongë fresshë
folkës, he and she".

What a lovely end: and how lovely for you to know it for the first
time.

108

. . . My thanks for your kind letter: & for the tidings of your great
happiness in the Bach. Sometimes players and sympathisers, intent

and loving enough, do enter the undying mood into which the maker had entered: and live in that light and touch Eternity.

. . . You will find the Knight's Tale, in the main, a translation from a long poem by Boccaccio, but GC is at his freshest & loveliest in it, & writes with poetry, from poetry, not as a translator at all, but as a man who has been in April and meant to bring April to England, & then did it, dew & primroses & wild daffodils & young men in love with womanhood.

It is masterly told.

❦

109

. . . One authority for the Life of John Mitford[1] says that he only had 1/- a day for 43 days.

A publisher gave him 1/- a day while he wrote *Johnny Newcome*, & it is said that during that time he lived in the fields at Bayswater, in the open, on bread, cheese, an onion or 2, & a lot of gin, sleeping on "grass & nettles" & sometimes washing his shirt & stockings in a local pond.

I judge that he was all right in the Navy: life was ordered for him there: but he was scrapped at the peace, 1815 or so, & did not settle down. He slept out of doors about half of each week, & in a 3d doss-house the other half, and died in a London workhouse. He was often violent when drunk, and was mixed up in one (no doubt) serious crime, but was acquitted. What this was, I hope by & by to discover. He was of a good family and had talent. He was some relation of the Miss Mitford who wrote *Our Village*.

[1] See Letter 101, also Letter 112.

❦

110

. . . You may care to add the enclosed Topsail Schooner *Balclutha* to your collection. The *B* was just an old carrier of whom I know nothing save what the paper tells: but Topsail Schooners used to throng our coasts; & I must have seen hundreds of them; & they were often truly remarkable, pretty fast, & often crossing the Atlantic to Newfoundland, loading cod there for Brazil, & back from Brazil with (I suppose) Nuts, & Piaçaba fibre that brooms are made with; the tough hard brooms, stable brooms & the like. The one in the old print, no doubt, could set studding sails if the wind were fair

& she wished to hurry. These schooners were a joy to watch in the Mersey as you may suppose.

... Piaçaba fibre is from 2 or 3 sorts of palm-trees, growing in Brazil, near the coasts. It is taken from the leaf-stalks, & is very gristly stuff; it looks like wire, or whale-bone, & (it is said) you can make needles of it. The Americans made a very strong rope from it, for special purposes, at one time. I know not what the purposes were: but it must have been like wire to work. This rope is not the common coir rope made of the husks fibre of coco-nuts. Anyhow, piaçaba is the bristliest stuff going. Perhaps they stuff mattresses with it in hotels ...

111

... You ask about my landscapes. There's glory for me!

Landscapes: she actually sees that they were meant as such. O frabjous day.

When I go out into the country I see quite a lot of things, & when I come home I try to put some of them down on a card with a brush: & then wonder that the thing looked so different in the open air.

112

... The case of J. Mitford[1] seems to have been a charge of perjury brought against him by Viscount & Lady Perceval in 1814. I cannot learn more of it at the moment except that he was acquitted, & that the trial made some stir, & was printed. It is a pity that I did not set about this 50 years ago, when all these old Naval Records were so easy to consult: & all the old logs were there, to give compass bearings, & courses, & wind-directions & strengths, the orders from the Flag & the comments, if any, of the professional seaman. All were there, often with astonishing little side-lights into the life on board, in the days when, as Dr Johnson said, "A ship was worse than a jail: when there was, in a jail, better air, better company, better conveniency of every kind, and when a ship had the additional disadvantage of being in danger."

[1] See Letters 101 and 109.

113

. . . About the yellow hair:[1]

Chaucer drew his art from Italian & French poets. Now, he was deeply impressed by the *Romance of the Rose*, in which the lovely creatures, *Idleness* & *Beauty* (among others) have yellow hair: that is, the lovely are blondes. Some spiritual creatures, like *Courtesy*, are brown-haired.

It has been told to me that people usually dark, like the Italians & the Romanised Gauls, greatly admire blondes: the Spaniards do, & the Red Indians did. The Venetian painters certainly did. I must look up Dante, Petrarch & Boccaccio about the point presently.

But GC lived in the 14th century in the fervour of a great power of art. It may well be that one of the essentials of art then was a brightness, a glory. It was said that the inside of dingy shabby old Westm'r Abbey used to *shine* with brightness.

GC usually calls a good, or good-looking person, a bright person. It is his sort of Homeric epithet for such. Homer often calls a nice island or townlet "charming", GC might usually call them "brighte". Often his heroines have just washed their faces.

I suppose that he himself was brighte: a kind of radiant being, just out of an illumination.

These scattered suggestions may provoke some scathing sarcasm, if you deign to notice them.

But the 14th century created so much beauty that its sense of what belonged to beauty is worth the search.

Of course, many millions of men will ever prefer blondes; yet the great Friend & the great Foe will ever be of the native's colour, whichever that may be.

[1] See also Letter 38.

114

. . . Please, how much do you care about representations of ships?

Have you any books of these?

The books are *usually* very bad, for only sailors know what ships look like, & are doing in a picture, & know how they are fitted & how they behave. Only saiiors can paint them.

We have been great in sea affairs for 500 years, and it is appalling to me that so few books make it possible for our people to know what the ships of each century looked like.

We have a wealth of sea-painting, drawing, print & design done by men who were for years at sea: it is as great a wealth as our wealth in portraits & landscape.

How few of the lively drawings (to begin with) are known to people outside the Museums?

You could spend ½ an hour in the Print Room at the British Mus. & see more lively work than is in the books as yet: the same in the Print Rooms at Greenwich Mus. [The National Maritime Museum at Greenwich].

115

... In Ewelme Church near here, Chaucer's son, Thomas C is buried; & in a nearby, and even more splendid tomb, T's daughter, Chaucer's grand-daughter, Alice, Duchess of Suffolk, whose husband is in Shakespeare, is buried.

The effigy no doubt shows C's grand-daughter—she wears the Garter on her left wrist; in fact, she is the authority that prescribes this way of wearing it.

116

... In *Frank Mildmay*, if you read the fireship business in Aix Roads, you will read what Marryat himself saw & certainly shared in. His Captain (Lord Cochrane)[1] of *L'Impérieuse* was in charge of the advanced attack there, and was not backed up by the Fleet.

Cochrane was specially sent for by the Admiralty when he arrived in Plymouth, from a cruise, and was asked to command the fireship attack. You see, he had a great name for dashing, successful daring.

He demurred: saying that he was a very junior Captain, and that many of his seniors already at Aix would be furious. However, the Admiralty insisted: Cochrane undertook it: did it very well: put the French Fleet at our mercy: & then found his C in C did nothing to reap the victory.

Being an MP he said that his C in C failed: so there he was: with all his seniors his enemies: & the Admiralty & the Government compelled to back up the C in C against him. By ill-luck and some devilry they soon had a chance to sack him, which they did.

He then went to Chile, where he won Chile her liberty from Spain: so that the Chilean streets & ships are now often called *El Almirante Cochrane*. Later he was restored to our Navy & his honours.

You will find much about Cochrane and *L'Impérieuse* in *Peter Simple*, for C was Marryat's Captain in the Mediterranean and a very daring, dashing Captain, with an uncanny eye for prize-money, & a courage given to few.

Cochrane wrote his own story (about 1860) & I will tell you something of that before long, when I have looked at it again.

When he liberated Chile from Spain, he took the Spanish frigate *Esmeralda* in Valparaiso harbour, in his usual heroic style.

When I was on the *Conway* about 1893, 2 Chilean men-of-war that kept C in memory, the *Esmeralda* & the *Almirante Cochrane*, came to Liverpool. We dressed ship for them, & had the officers on board for an inspection. So Cochrane made even us idle dogs bestir ourselves for once, as a live spirit will.

[1] Lord Cochrane, later Earl of Dundonald (1775–1860) served in the Napoleonic Wars, was imprisoned in 1814 on a charge of fraud, and dismissed from the Navy. Eventually he went to South America and commanded the Chilean Navy (1817–22) and the Brazilian Navy (1823–25), during those countries' wars of independence. He was reinstated in the British Navy in 1832 and served as C-in-C in North America and the West Indies.

117

. . . Please, be very sure that no-one but poor you noticed the cough in the quiet space. Audiences & players were in the music (outside time somewhere) as they always are at such times.

I have seen dreadful things done on stages, while the audiences were rapt away, & neither knew or cared. I have heard actors (in the second act) give a cue from a fifth act, & lead all hands astray, & then lead them back to the 2nd act, no-one noticing in the least.

When I was very young, a young actor told me that when an audience is rapt, the cast might talk about the weather, & no-one would notice. He said that he was once touring *Othello*, with a very good Othello. He himself was Roderigo & 2nd gentleman & attendant, etc.

In Act III sc.4 Othello repeats thrice his request for the stolen handkerchief: it is one of the tense instants in the play.

Once, in this instant, with all the house rapt, a man in the audience cried: "—— the handkerchief, Governor, use your hand and get on with the play."

The audience and the actors, all tense in the mood, never noticed. My actor-friend, waiting in the wings, out of the mood, did notice.

☙

118

... Did you ever see T. Hughes' *The Scouring of the White Horse*?[1] They used to clean up the Horse every 10th year & celebrate the occasion with games & contests. Hughes saw the last of these games in 1836. If you know *Tom Brown* you will remember the Back-Sword-Play, or single-stick fighting (using forearm only).

This sport is now forgotten in the Vale.

I do not think the Teddington Lion is old. The old ones are surely 4:

The White Horse.

The Red Horse on Edge Hill—this was destroyed in 1798 but it *was* old, and re-cut on the (old) site.

The Long Man at Wilmington in Sussex Downs, Eastbourne way, a very tall figure, holding even taller spears.

The Giant at Cerne Abbas, supposed to be Herakles with his club (Dorchester way).

The white-leaved Cross, in Bucks, is under some suspicion of being 18th cent[y], and there are 3 or 4 White Horses (or ponies) on the Downs near Devizes, all modern: & lots of regimental badges on Salisbury Plain downs, genuine 20th century.

I have not seen the Long Man, nor the Giant, but have seen the others. The Giant must be a terrific fellow.

One of the wonders of W. Horse Hill is the Ridgeway, a prehistoric track running on the summit of the downs for many lonely miles between a slight bank (on each side) on which are scattered ancient hawthorns, wind-wizened, & looking wiser than old men. The way is about 20-odd feet broad, unpaven, & lonelier than a desert track. Here & there it helps out an existing road, & these bits may be macadamised, then the downs re-assume; and the effect of its being so lonely, & so made by man, & so old, & now as a rule only larks go there, all this effect is over-powering: it is Nature big and lonely, and if one went out there for long one would come back & tell the world it was all astray, & then would be put to death, & so an end.

[1] Thomas Hughes (1822–96), best known as the author of *Tom Brown's Schooldays*, published, in 1859, *The Scouring of the White Horse* (of White Horse Hill in Berkshire).

119

. . . About John Fletcher . . . . During the summer I may be able to send you something I wrote about him. I love his work dearly. He must have been with Shakespeare quite a lot for a year or more: & much of Henry VIIIth is by him.

He must have got along with WS but I judge that Beaumont did not.

He and Beaumont knew WS's plays pretty well by heart, but seem to have preferred Ben Jonson. They worked together for a few years & in the time worked out a technique very different from Ben's; & then Beaumont died.

After his death, a very rare strange high-priest quality went out of his plays: so that one is sure that a lofty pontifical poetic spirit passed with Beaumont. Fletcher then took up with Massinger[1] & wrote many plays with him; & some by himself. M had many merits, but I do not like the flavour of his mind, mixing with Fletcher's quality.

I am sending you a tiny Fletcher book to begin upon. Read the *Faithful S[hepherd]* first: it is a very lovely verse. It is written in ignorance of the theatre, yet with a ghastly fidelity to Ben Jonson's tedious manner, with no perception of Ben's knowledge of the theatre. It was played: & after about two acts leading nowhere the audience stopped it with a riot. But it is lovely verse & lovely inventions: do read it. JF did it alone.

JF uses marine and other expressions with what an American poetess calls "A lavishness born of completeness".

You must not blame him (or me) for these. He was a lovely poet & you will feel the loveliness if anyone can. I know that . . .

. . . P.S. If you look up B & F in the *Ency. Brit.* the article is by Swinburne, and very good.

[1] Philip Massinger (1583–1640), a famous playwright in his day; author of *The Duke of Milan, The Fatal Dowry*, among many other plays.

120

. . . I loved your phrase of the conductor: "hands so dull that they seem to empty the music of all beauty and interest".

There is the living artist speaking.

O how often I go to a poetical play, by WS or other famous hand, & find the living bread turned into tripe & the living water into dishwater.

But then, sometimes, even in the slough of the despond, one player will perceive & speak as he perceives (or she perceives) from the undying & the infinite.

121

... This little iron inlay was made as a sword-hilt in Japan, but probably never became one. Don't let it drag you down. Remember the *Royal George*. She got too much weight on 1 side &:

> Down went the *Royal George*
> With twice 400 men;

on payday too, with the rum just coming aboard.

These sword-hilts must have been made in thousands, for most men wore two swords; & then, after 1878, the old order was quashed: the swords forbidden: & Japan became a modern power.[1]

But the demand for Japanese trinkets was very great in Europe, & these sword-hilts were exported as paper-weights etc. etc. & are perhaps still made as objects for sale.

[1] Until the accession of the Meiji Emperor Mitsuhito in 1867, the feudal empire of Japan had been almost totally isolated. The country immediately began a swift process of Westernisation, modernisation and industrialisation, which met with some violent resistance; the most serious reactionary movement, the Satsuma Rebellion, was finally quashed in 1878.

122

... Not long since we were talking of the downland ... There is another track across the downs, crossing the Ridgeway & going on to the South into a great loneliness. There are few things for some miles: then one comes to a lonely spot where there are the barrows of the dead, incredibly moving: you come upon seven great graves, the Seven Barrows; & I doubt if any one could see them without a prayer.

You have seen no man, no house, for miles, and then you come thus upon death.

Men used to think that there had been a battle there, but men did not bury the dead in battle, then: "darkness was the burial of the dead"; darkness & kites & the roots of things. There is a spring there, & so there was an early settlement, & the barrows are the family tombs no doubt, for when the hearts had done with it.

The farm, the cottages, are at the spring, away from the graves & screened from them. The graves dominate the place, each a great round grassy swelling in the nothing of nowhere.

123

. . . I am so glad that you have liked the Fletcher. It is an astonishing breath of poetry. How did the young man attain that peak? Who encouraged him? What fired him?

And how did that spirit go willingly to bondage under Ben Jonson? How could he put such a poem into the fetters of a Ben Jonson play? But the poetry is a marvel. And don't you wish you had the little satyr in your garden under the laurustinus, to come to you for bread & milk & cherries?

124

. . . I mentioned the little place Badgeworth. It is 4 miles from Cheltenham, 2 miles beyond Leckhampton. If you do go . . . you must please look at the N. side . . .

You will know all about Piers Gaveston, Edward the Second's Gascon friend, who used to mock the nobles to such a point that they murdered him.

Edward II married him to his niece, Margaret (Margaret de Clare) who, later, after PG was murdered, married an Audley: a relation of that (Saint) Katharine Audley, the Recluse of Ledbury . . .

Piers Gaveston was the Ward of the Saint's property during the minority of her son.

Margaret Gaveston, being a Clare, had much property in that part of Glos.

Dere swete, this is but the prelude, I hope to come to the point by & by, bear with me yet a moment.

Edward II, being deposed by his wicked wife & her lover, & the ambitious son Edward III, was in Berkeley Castle, about to be murdered. According to history, he was shockingly murdered in Berkeley, and then given a glorious state funeral & state tomb in Gloucester Cathedral,[1] where you could (& perhaps still can) see the tomb; very fine indeed; and 1000s came to see it, fearing a judgement for murdering a king.

But there is a story, of the time, a story impossible to prove or disprove, that Edward II was not murdered, but killed his gaoler and got away (to die as a hermit in Italy) & that the body in the Glos. tomb is the gaoler.

I like to think that Margaret, the niece, contrived the escape, & that it was she who caused Edward II's portrait to be carved in Badgeworth church.

I am certain in my own mind that she, who caused the lovely St Margaret's Chapel to be made at Badgeworth, caused her lovely artists to go to Ledbury, to build the lovely St Katharine's Chapel over the site of the Recluse's house on the N side of Ledbury church.

[1] Edward II was buried in Gloucester Cathedral in 1327.

125

. . . You ask about Nelson, & Hardy.

I do not know Hardy's sea-service well, but I think I am right in saying that he was a promising officer some 7 or 8 years younger than Nelson,[1] whom Nelson wanted to have as his flag-captain for some fine qualities that he liked to have in his officers.

I do not know his service after Nelson's death. It was no doubt competent, but never unusual . . .

Nelson *was* unusual: all his service was unusual. When he was young (17–18?) he had a radiant experience or vision. In a glow of certainty, he saw "his king & country as his patron" & knew that if he staked his all on any venture, he would succeed in it. It was a revelation of what is eternally true, & could no more be disregarded than a bidding of an angel.

But before this, he was an unusual seaman. As a boy (14–16) he was competent to pilot any small ship from the Pool to the N. Foreland. Now this is no mean competence. Few officers of his time could have done it (and how many boys??).

He passed for Lieutenant after 7 years at sea, when he was not yet 19. He was made Lieutenant next day, & was a Post-Captain commanding a frigate when he was 21.

He made 2 line-of-battle ships famous as a Captain, later on, but while only 21 or 22 he was chosen by a great seaman (Adml Hood) to teach the Duke of Clarence (later, your old friend Give-me-Huggins, K. Williams the 4th)[2] "naval tactics": not the foolish tactics in use in our Navy at the time, but the new, enlightened devastating tactics of Clerk of Eldin,[3] then attracting the brighter young men.

These tactics he put into practice (on his own initiative) at the Battle of Cape St Vincent, where his wearing out of line was the first act of genius done by the Br. Navy since the greater years of Drake. Later he used them again at the Nile & at Tralfalgar.

There were fleet tactics: but of hand-to-hand tussle-tactics HN had a wide & successful experience: few men more.

In his general conduct of a fleet I judge from his dispatches that he was most unusual, and enlightened; with such care of his crews as Capt Cook would have shewn, and this at a time of unspeakable villainy, jobbery, robbery, & general devilry in every dockyard we owned.

But, for his seamanship, I would say that, as he was very thoroughly put through the mill in small ships, he was as fine a practical seaman as any man you could name.

That is *the* school for seamen . . .

He was a man of imaginative intelligence, on the spot like lightning in any instant needing decision. He was also a man of unbelievable winning charm that could persuade any timber-skulled Admiral in the service, & make all the fleet's Captains *shed tears.*

[1] Hardy was 11 years younger than Nelson.

[2] See Letter 13.

[3] John Clerk of Eldin (1728–1812). A merchant of Edinburgh who took a keen interest in naval affairs and whose *Essay on Naval Tactics* (1790) had great influence.

126

. . . I thank you for writing about the *2 N[oble] Kinsmen*, and the Fletcher (?) portrait. The *2NK* is really a profanation of a lovely theme: but yet: the lyrics & the line about Death being the market-place . . . golly!

Then, too, it was one of WS's very last works;[1] & done with John F, the brightest young man coming on: the only man really like WS in his mind, in his lesser degree. WS chose him as a fellow worker: & they must have been much together over the play, as over *Henry the 8*. Think of being with WS on equal terms, for a year and more: imagine it. Golly again.

Then, too, WS's use of the Messenger speech at the end: of the horse & the downfall—& his permitting JF to turn Ophelia into the Gaoler's Daughter for the sake of some clever treble boy who could sing her & act her.

It is a poor play of course: but the 2 men did it: variations on a theme by Chaucer (after Boccaccio) & one has to think of it.

[1] It is believed that Shakespeare collaborated with Fletcher in the writing of this play.

127

... I send you also a ship [painting] or 2. You will be so weary of these repeated ships. Alack. There was a prizefighter not long ago who grieved that you had only 2 hands to hit with, & could only hit an opponent in the head or on the body, wh got so dull after a time. So with the ships. They can only be going R or L; or towards, or away; & the sea can only be blue or green or dark, or else it will be mistaken for houses ...

... The dread of spiders may not be foolish. Many lands have fatal spiders still (terrible things: I have seen them) & also scorpions, not unlike in danger. It may well be that we had plenty of both in this land not long ago, & when they were here those that did not dread them died. Primitive men must have had an intense dread of all such small swiftly moving ways of death; and the instinct is in us all, to look out when they appear. Those that remain, like the asp, the adder, the karait, or the infected rat, etc, etc, are swift to move, & hard to see, & all may carry sudden death, giving only a second or two for escape or defence. These instincts show us what life was to man, *not so very long ago*. Do not be blaming yourself for having within you inherited wisdom.

128

... Castor & Pollux[1] were Helen's brothers. They were called the Dioscuri, or "the boys of Zeus". Zeus was supposed to be their father. They were both dead & buried in their native Sparta, before the Greeks went against Troy.

The Greek names of couplets are seldom easy for a little boy to pronounce—Zeus & Hera: Priam & Hecuba: Hector & Andromache: Odysseus & Penelope: Paris & Helen: Pericles & Aspasia: Agamemnon & Clytemnestra. C & P are comparatively easy.

[1] My nephew Timothy had two tortoises named Castor and Pollux. ANS.

129

... You were well quit of the *2 Noble Kinsmen* on Sunday. Nothing but the mind of a *rosse* mule[1] could have done such a thing, even in England, even in dealing with poetry. Hardened as I am, I hardly thought that they could have got to this: but they did ...

... English speech is often very, very bad: it comes from a shut mouth, & a terror of being overheard & a dread of being thought to be one like one of these foreigners ... the *2NK* people had (in addition) a natural hatred of poetry, & a determination to show that they wd have none of such nonsense. I cd not endure to listen for the K to appear, but turned it off.

I *have* heard exquisite speech, from English & Scotch speakers of verse: they exist: plenty: but if they go into theatres as actors, they seldom speak verse, & if they do, they are often under dreadful creatures called producers, who had no sympathy with such tosh.

But I have heard verse so marvellously spoken that even now the memory shakes me: Milton especially is glorious thus: all the best verse comes out best ....

[1] The exact meaning of this term is hard to trace; but since *rosse* in French means "ill-natured, objectionable", or, as a noun describing a horse, "a weak or broken-down animal"—and since, until 1914, France was a leading producer of mules, it seems reasonable to accept its derivation from the French; and certainly the combined meanings as applied here—objectionable, feeble, mulish—are appropriate.

130

... I send a few ship cuttings. The *Andrea* wreck is a frightful sight: but I did not like her looks when I saw her—she looked too like a cow with a hump.

The *Passat* was the last big 4 master that I saw under sail, in a big sea with a fair wind: going like billio ... golly, my beloved, she was jolly well hopping along, & I watched her for 2 hours bound "to Falmouth for orders", I saw her like a speck, & watched her till she was another speck, & O if you'd been there you wd have wept for sheer joy.

131

... Swinburne was a man of melody & could not have truly loved Ben Jonson, who has so little melody. I have great respect for much of Ben, but no great love. He wrote a most admirable poem about WS, the first good poem about WS, a lovely generous thing: noble praise.[1]

I have only seen 5 of his plays—& the 3 great comedies are outstanding.

The Alchemist much the best of the 3, about a rogue man-servant, pretending to be an Alchemist in his Master's absence. It is quite admirable.

The Fox or *Volpone*, too heartless for heart to endure, but a masterpiece of skill.

The Silent Woman, with some quite dead scenes that cannot now be made alive, is the funniest of the 3, but not so engaging in its characters as *The Alchemist*.

I have often wished to see his 2 Roman plays done, *Sejanus* & *Catiline*: & wd have produced them myself, if I had 20 men handy to be the Romans.

Then: a lot of his masques await the producer still. The Americans do some of them with great success. And we? Really, sometimes I am ashamed when I think of what English minds have made for us, and of what our national response is.

[1] "To the memory of my beloved, the Author Mr William Shakespeare: and what he has left us". Printed in the first folio of Shakespeare, 1623.

132

... I am glad that you have Dr Bompart's book.[1] It impressed me very much: & it made its mark among both sailors and doctors, so that he must know that his heroical sacrifice has been worthwhile, & may be certain to save the lives of men & women.

Some of his journal is deeply affecting: where he thinks he must be nearly across, & finds he has hardly started: and where the awful sea-creature looks at him & decides not to . . .

I have not heard of Dr Bompart's death: but few cd go thro what he endured & emerge unshattered. It is only too likely that he has died.

[1] Alain Bompard: see Letter 67.

133

. . . Thank you for telling me of your dream of the happy place you seemed to know.

Who can say what memories are wakened in dreams into overwhelming reality? Who can turn to sleep without wishing for dreams, even for "sick men's dreams—dreams out of the ivory gate, and visions before midnight"?

You will probably know a song by one Balfe—"I dreamed that I dwelt in marble halls".[1] A seaman parodied this for our delight long since.

> I dreamed I dwelt in marble halls
> Delightful to my soul.
> But I also dreamt (what pleased me more)
> That I found some rum in a bowl.
> I dreamed that my Naval Captain bold
> Stood forth that rum to claim,
> But I also dreamed (what pleased me more)
> That I wolfed it all the same.

[1] From *The Bohemian Girl*: music by Balfe, lyrics by Alfred Bunn. Produced in London 1843.

134

. . . It was a great game:[1] and if WG had been Captain . . . but he was not Captain.

It was not a friendly game, for in the Aust. 2nd innings, they resented an umpire's decision: and made their resentment felt for years afterwards. WG put down a wicket & the Umpire gave the batsman out. I think that he *was* out, but many there thought otherwise, & the bearings ran hot thence forward. It was a good thing that Australia won, for even so, *for 20 years or more*, our cricketers were asked: "Do you really think Sammy Jones was out that time?"

As it chanced, I saw the 2 Englishmen responsible, WG & Lyttleton: the only 2 I ever saw of that 22.

Murdoch, the Aust. Capt. was batting: & Sammy Jones was backing up, to snatch any possible run. Murdoch (a jolly good bat), snicked a ball to leg. S. Jones called to him to run.

Lyttleton, who was wicket-keeper, dashed at the ball, got it, & flung it left-handed, at the wicket. Murdoch darted back to his crease, the ball missed the wicket, & went to Grace, who, as Point, was, of course, up to the wicket by this time. Grace took the ball, said something to somebody, & then, seeing that SPJ was out of his ground, put down the wicket & appealed. SPJ was given Out, but the Australians thought that the ball was dead, & that he was not out. The case was wrangled over by the young & the eager for years: & many a black eye must have been earned & given over it.

WG was ever very swift at appealing, & I don't doubt that he scared some umpires now and then.

He was a great man. It is said of him that he once stayed all night with a difficult birth-case, till 6 a.m. when he handed over to his partner. He then went to Gloucester by an early train, went in first, for Gloucester: batted all day, made 220 not out, & then returned to his patient.

He had a strange intensity of watchfulness, a concentration of care: you will see this in his photographs sometimes: it is uncanny, and stamps him as a genius. His books do that, too.

[1] The Curator of the MCC suggests that this was the Test Match played against Australia at the Oval in August 1882 (JM would have been four at the time).

135

. . . I send more *Mayflower*[1] papers for you. Soon (I fear) there may be advertisements appearing:

"Come, all ye breezy Salts.
Come, play at pitch and toss with Neptune."

"Come to good old Boston
The Home of the Bean and the Cod."

"Only Ten weeks from Door to Door."

"All the ancient Inconveniences.
Concertinas! Sirens!! Bilges!!! Scurvy!!!!"

Think what the Poets say!

"Thou shalt swim as merry, I undertakey
As doth the whitey ducky with her drakey."

(Geoffrey Chaucer)

"Port after stormy seas,
Death (after such a trip) doth greatly please."

(Edm. Spenser)

I once met Capt. Villiers (about 30 years ago): but cannot claim to know him. He commanded an American sailing ship later, & fitted her with studding sails: the last ever to handle them, I suppose. I judge that he *joliment* knows his job sailorising.

But even so, dere swete, do not go West in the new *Mayflower* even if they offer to rate you 1st ship's fiddler: even if they pay you a dollar a watch: or a dollar a minute . . . .

[1] In early 1957 "a faithful facsimile of the *Mayflower* (*Mayflower II*), built of hand-hewn Devon Oak, fitted with hempen cordage, with sails cut according to the pattern of centuries past" was to sail from Plymouth to the USA, "the gift from the people of Britain to Her Majesty's former subjects". Naturally JM was interested in this project. Captain Villiers commanded the ship.

136

. . . Hazlitt's *The Fight*, a wonderful piece of journalism, is here for you.

For years I lived with men who talked mainly of pugilism, of which I know nothing, & at which I always get under the table, but all sorts of odds & ends of it are stuck like burrs on my coat, so please, dear, write to me about it, & you'll tap a spring . . . .

137

. . . I did not know that Mr Tunney[1] played the harp, but a man told me that he had heard him lecture (and well) on some aspects of Shakespeare. He must be a truly remarkable man. He decided (as a big young athlete) that pugilism gave him a good chance of making a swift fortune, so that he might read poetry ever after. So he took to pugilism, but felt he wasn't strong enough in arms & shoulders, so he went to lumber camps, felling timber, till he could about lift a cedar of Lebanon, then he felt he didn't bear pain well enough: so he got himself toughened up somewhat: this is the legend: I know not how he did it; but having done it, he did it: became a champion, & went in for poetry.

He was a lovely specimen I would say: but I never saw him, & only write from hearsay, & hope that it is true.

[1] Tunney, James Joseph ("Gene") 1898–1978. American boxer who defeated the late Jack Dempsey in 1926 for the world heavyweight title. Author of *A Man Must Fight* (1932) and an autobiography, *Arms for Living* (1941).

138

Reyna mia

My grateful thanks for a kind dear letter, & for the glad news that you had some times of quiet beauty by the sea.

Thank you, too, for the thought that the Hazlitt was with you there.

Did you ever go to Winterslow, 2 or 3 miles this side of Salisbury, high up on the chalk downland, where Hazlitt used to live? A marvellous fair place for views and skylarks?

While he was there (when at home) 140 years ago, in a moonless October night, the Exeter Mail coach, while drawing up there, was attacked by a lioness that had escaped from a travelling menagerie. She got hold of the off-leader and pulled him down, but was at this point herself attacked by a big dog, that chased her off: & tho she killed the dog, she was beaten into a shed & shut up.

Now & then one sees an old coloured print of the attack. You may have seen it in your visits to old curio shops. They used to have a painting of the scene at the Pheasant Inn at Winterslow, & may still have, if you ever go there. You may well play at Salisbury some time; & it is only 3 miles: & a rousing view from the top.

The Fight that WH [Hazlitt] saw took place in another place of singular beauty, on the Port Down just outside Hungerford, a great fair downland above the exquisite Kennet River & the lovely Kennet Canal (& less lovely Great Western Bristol line). It is still pretty much as when the fight was held.

I cannot say where (exactly where) the Ring was, but it must have been within a clear half mile. 20,000 people came to see the fight, & no doubt made that quiet scene pretty grim.

WH travelled (you will have read) with "Tom Turtell", the sporting promoter (George Borrow's friend) who was hung for murder some years later, at Hertford prison.

Please, some day, will you tell, if you know the works of George Borrow:[1] at any rate the two good ones, Lavengro and The Romany Rye: the rest are no special shakes.

I trust that you are well & happy: & that your Mother is better & that you are enjoying the music, & having (now & then) a thrill, as a new great conductor takes over?

All wonderful dear blessings to you
always my loving swete.
Jan

[1] George Borrow (1803–81). A great traveller and a remarkable linguist, whose other works include *The Zingali, or an account of the Gypsies in Spain*, *The Bible in Spain*, and *Wild Wales*. He studied the life of gypsies all over Europe. JM had a particular affection for him.

. . . Winterslow, or near to it, had a view of Figsbury Rings, an ancient earthworks, & of distant Old Sarum. It was a noble prospect on a windy fine day: but it may now be all derelict aerodromes: who can say?

But it must once have had men in it, for when I wrote to you I did not mention the manhood there. The coach had come in, no doubt to change horses, on a pitch dark night, & a lioness had pulled down a leader, and scared the other 3 of the team, & no doubt the relief team all ready to be put to. 7 terrified horses to begin with, all nervy thoroughbreds, squealing & kicking. No-one in the coach aware of what was happening: the driver as startled & staggered as a man can be, with his hands full of trouble, no proper light to see by, some great snarling beast out in the dark, a big dog going for it (a regular faithful Gelert) & the team in the shafts beginning to kick.

Then, evidently, dark or not, the men guessed or learned that it was a big beast of prey out loose, and at once with 2-prongs, brooms, pokers, whips & what not, they went for it in the dark & somehow beat it into a pen. I doubt if any dog, or any set of men, has ever been braver at shorter notice.

I fear that I cannot learn more about the event just yet, but it is a noble tale, & I will try to learn more.

I was first startled to it, long since, by seeing the old coaching print in a print-shop, & wondering what a lioness was doing after dark, pulling down the Western Mail . . . .

Port Down, where Hazlitt saw the fight is exquisitely lovely: but it was not chosen for the battle because of its beauty. None but the brave deserve the fair may be true enough, but the promoters of the battle thought more of security from interference by the magistrates. They no doubt thought that they had pretty well squared the Berkshire magistrates, but even so, over £100,000 had been betted on the event, & they wanted to reach a decision.

They therefore chose the Port Down, so that, if any Berkshire magistrate objected, they could duck him in the Kennet, or get him ducked, while they themselves walked over the near-by county line into Wiltshire, about ½ mile or so, to try the matter there. However, they were not put to this annoyance: but what the local people suffered from the presence of the flash gangs & rascality we cannot now know. One sees the race-train gangs of today: but they are Sunday School babes to the gangs of the Regency.

You may read about Tom Turtle by & by. Men showed me the scene of the murder he committed, as he drove back from some sporting event (soon after Hazlitt's fight).

Charles Lamb knew the clergyman who attended to him at his execution. There used to be a poem about his victim; it is (I believe) quite inexact, as poems may be, but it thrilled the young:

> They cut his throat from Ear to Ear,
> His Brains they battered in.
> His Name was Mr William Weare,
> He lived at Lyons Inn.

140

. . . The people of England always moved about a good deal in the drier half of the year, say April to Oct^r; and there was much water-passage along the coasts, Edinburgh, Newcastle, Hull to London & back. Liverpool to Belfast, Glasgow, Dublin, Bristol to Cork, & round the Welsh coast; a lively traffic. All probably pretty rough, but cheap. Boswell sometimes went to Edinburgh from London or Harwich by sea. "Get a smart sea-sickness, if you can," Dr J bade him, but I don't doubt that the N. Sea made it easy for him. Boswell was afraid he might "break some small things" inside him if *too* sick, but Dr J said "Sir, you will break no small things;" & he was right.

But ashore, all over England, from Tudor times, if not earlier, there were the Carrier's Vans, going once or twice or three times a week between important towns, taking some 15 to 20 miles in a day: very slow, but cheap, & taking people & goods at small cost. These halted at night at their regular inns.

In the great days of coaching, when the roads were good, on the four main lines W, NW, N & NE from London, the fast coaches cost about 5 pence a mile: but one could travel by the slower or very slow coaches, more like omnibuses of today, at about 1d a mile. If a rich man wished, he could travel all day by post-chaises, changing 2 horses every hour, at about 1/6d a mile, with tips at each change extra.

There is a bit about some old Carriers in *K. Henry IV* Part One. Quite early, in England, there were compulsory, regulated fares for the hired "post-horses", that could be had for hire on the greater roads. The fare was 2½d a mile for a public servant; 3d a mile for a private traveller; & 6d for the boy who brought back the horse at the end of the stage.

Many people, who had their own horses, rode 20 or 25 miles a day & put up at inns for the night.

"Riding post", carrying important news, men made wonderful time sometimes. Richard Boyle, in Jan. 1601–2, left Shandon (near Cork where the bells of Shandon rang) at 2 a.m. one Monday morning, sailed to Bristol (228 miles) & posted thence to London where he supped (no doubt very late) on Tuesday night. The road must have been unusually dry and sound for the depth of winter.

The ship must have been clean & swift, & quite desperately driven, with a fair westerly gale, & must have made a steady ten [knots], perhaps reaching Bristol at about 6 a.m. on the Tuesday; then to horse, to gallop 114 miles, 11 hours' gallop "gallop apace, my fiery-footed steeds": never mind food: an egg or two in milk & brandy, and then on. It was good going. The inns & posting-horses were often very good, & well-kept.

T. Chatterton, going from Bristol to London, in April 1770, drove, first *outside* to Bath, then went *inside* to near Newbury (Speen) for 7/-, breakfasted there, & then rode *outside* to London where he arrived at 5 p.m.; perhaps about a day for the 114 miles, but I cannot tell what the whole journey cost him.

Meyerstein, in his life of Chatterton, says that the Bristol coaches left the Rummer Tavern in Bristol every night (except Sat.) at 9 p.m., & left The Greyhound & Shakespeare Inn at Bath, at 11 p.m. The inside fare (all the way) was £1.10.0., the outside 15/- so I suppose TC paid in all 22/-.

He went inside on a wild wet night, then turning to snow.

141

. . . I have learned nothing more of the lioness at Winterslow.

Many years ago, I went to all the travelling shows that I could reach; and long long since, I saw a menagerie with some "performing lions" in it. They didn't do much except hop onto a chair & off it, while the tamer cracked a whip; but while they were quiet, a woman went into the cage, & the lion opened his mouth at her, & she put her head into his mouth, & then withdrew it, in about waltz time. Well: it was not a pleasant sight: but long afterwards I saw a similar menagerie, & in a cage by himself there was a kind of motheaten old lion, with the legend on his cage:

THE SAME LION WHAT ATE POOR MISS BAKER

It seems that a lady used to put *her* head into his mouth, & that once one of her curls tickled his throat, so that he could not keep from a convulsive cough.

Then there was the Polar Bear in the Circus who adored his

Keeper: & 1 day the keeper was washing him to make him white & polar for the performance; & by accident some of the soap went into the bear's eye, & the bear thought the keeper had done it on purpose; a fatal thought for the poor keeper: & the bear henceforth was like Eugene Aram in the poem "the poor bear walked remote apart, a melancholy wreck"!

Do you ever still read about pirates? And did I ever (or did any other ever) tell you of the *Flowery Land* pirates? It is sometimes called not piracy, but Murder on the High Seas; but the wise WS asks "What's in a name?" It was pretty savage crime anyway.

⚓

142

... I am always so very very happy to read that you have liked a book that I have sent: & I love your comments on them. What could be better? You note all the moving qualities: & share a deep joy with me. I love you to love A. E. Housman, for I have loved him dearly for 58 years now: & tho I did not often see him, I admired him deeply. (Hardy was of the 19th cent. & earlier.) AEH was a very fine fellow, but I never heard of his fiddling (nor, in spite of his noble poem about Abdon Burf) of his fifing: but he may have done both. (Hardy was both a singer & a musician; I think he cd play fiddle, flute, piano & serpent; & he knew an infinity of songs & hymns.)

Did you ever hear the Epitaph AEH wrote on a Salvation Army Lady Colonel that was run over by the Up Express?

> "Halle-lu-jah" was the only exclamation
> That escaped Lieutenant-Colonel Mary Jane
> When she fell from off the platform at the Station
> And was cut to little pieces by the train
> Halle-lu-jah, Halle-lu-jah,
> Mary Jane, the train is through yah
> But we'll gather up the pieces that remain.

... About the *Flowery Land*. I lived among sailors for all of 3 years, & often heard about her, for it shook the world (that event) only 30 years before, & it was in seamen's minds. The tale had crystallised in the telling, & *as told* it was much unlike the event; which was much as follows.

The *Flowery Land* was a small wooden ship, owned in London, & trading in the East. I am not sure if she had changed her rig to double topsails: I fancy not ... I do not know her tonnage nor carrying capacity, but suppose her to have been of about 400 tons, able to carry about 500 tons. She had a raised fo'c's'le & poop, a big deckhouse just abaft her foremast, & a flying light gangway by which one could walk all along her length on top of these superstructures, when her deck was awash with seas . . .

Her crew was as follows:

Captain, Mate & 2nd Mate, all English.

1 passenger, the Captain's brother, English

1 boy (13 or 14) English

1 carpenter, Norwegian. 1 cook, Chinese.

1 steward, Malay. 1 leading seaman, French.

1 nondescript "lamp-trimmer", by name Cassa, & 12 hands, 6 to a watch, nearly all Filippinos from Manila, & all un-English (tho 2 had English names). None talked English well, & they were not good seamen. Orders were given in Spanish or such lingo as they could understand.

The ship had a general cargo for Singapore: of iron pipes, bale goods, boots, shoes, clothing (cotton & cloth) bottled beer & champagne, with other merchandise, no doubt to be re-exported, to China or Australia or elsewhere.

She sailed from London on July 28th, 1863, & had fair winds & did well.

Her Captain was said to have been a little given to drink, but nothing out of the way. He called the hands opprobrious names sometimes, but nothing unusual. The Mate was strict, but none of the officers was what were called "bucko-boys" who ruled with belaying pins and slung-shot. The food & water were vile & scanty, but at sea this was usual . . . the ship & life were just normal & beastly, & the crew the normal nondescripts.

By 3 a.m. on the 10th September, 1863, the ship was somewhere off Rio de Janeiro, though well out at sea, having sailed some 5,500 miles.

The 2nd Mate had had the first watch, & was turned-in down in his cabin: the Mate was on deck, keeping the middle watch. He was forward somewhere, near the big deck-house, probably beginning to trim the yards a little.

Two of the Filippinos of his watch suddenly set upon him — he called to the English boy to run to call the Captain: & what with oaths & war-cries, there was a good deal of noise. The Mate was killed: the Captain's brother was killed: & then the Captain. Both watches of Filippinos were involved in this, but the worst men were in the Mate's watch.

The 2nd Mate roused by the noise, tried to reach the deck, but the hatch was now bolted against him, & the body of the Captain's brother lay on the companion steps.

As he felt that the ship had been seized, & that it wd be his turn next, he went back to his cabin & bolted himself in, expecting to be killed within a few minutes.

3 principal Filippinos came to tell him that they did not want to kill him, but would certainly do so if he did not navigate the ship to the River Plate, where they wd scuttle the ship & all go ashore.

He was a young fellow, about 21, and he agreed to do this, hoping that the luck would turn, but knowing that his life hung by a hair. Most of the pirates were for killing him, but one Lopez, (who may have been a Catalan, for that was his nickname) saved his life.

The ship was plundered: some bale goods were opened & pillaged, for clothes & shoes, the ship's petty cash (about £70) was divided, and "everybody that wanted champagne could have it".

"The deck exhibited a dreadful scene of debauchery", but nothing to what an English crew would have exhibited with such an opportunity.

The 2nd Mate was allowed to sew up the Captain & give him a decent sea burial, but the other 2 bodies were just hove over the side.

In the confusion, it seems likely that the ship's chronometer was not wound, for the 2nd Mate found it wanting. A ship called *The Friends* was sighted, & at the 2nd Mate's entreaty, hailed, so that he might correct his longitude. He was watched, during the hailing, with the blackest suspicion, & expected to be killed as *The Friends* drew away. But as he was their only navigator he was not killed: only made to feel his helplessness.

On October 2nd, he brought the ship within sight of land: and here again he was threatened, for "making the land in daylight". The ship stood off again till very early on Oct. 3rd, when she was not very far from the land, & the boats were made ready. They were somewhere to the East of Monte Video, a bit to the N. of the Plate.

The Carpenter, Anderson, was told to go into the hold to bore 4 auger-holes aft & 4 forward. He was a Norwegian, & had the wit to see that perhaps they would leave him to drown in the ship; so he prepared, & hid, beforehand, plenty of plugs in case they did. Leone, or Lyons, 1 of the pirates, told the others "If you want to kill the 2nd Mate & the Carpenter you may do it, but I won't." He talked better English than most of them, & had some authority. Anyhow they didn't kill the two.

They had the boats all ready; but not all went into them. They flung the steward overboard, & flung bottles at him till he sank. It is supposed that they tied the cook & the lamp-trimmer in the hold, to drown there . . . (they did not come in the boats, so these two may be held to have been murdered). The rest shoved off, saw the ship sink.

They reached the shore in the 2 boats at 4 a.m. on Oct. 3rd. Lopez gave orders that they were to say that they were the crew of an American ship bound with nitrate from Chile for Bordeaux, and sunk 500 miles out at sea. They came ashore & were received at a farm house of sorts.

Here the 2nd Mate & the French seaman, Candereau, got the farmer to drive them into the town of Rocha or Rochas, for the farmer said that there was a store-keeper near there who talked English.

It was a 21 mile drive, seemingly, and the drive was managed secretly somehow; the rest of the crew did not know they were going. They told the tale to the store-keeper, who (I suppose) telegraphed to Monte Video: troops were at once sent to round up the pirates: & the entire company was brought before what was called the Naval Court at Monte Video. The whole company was put under arrest, & shipped to England, where they were tried at the Old Bailey in January, 1864. Seven pirates were sentenced to be hung (all young foreigners), but 2 of the 7 were not hung. It may be that they were given life imprisonment, I do not know. One other man was given 10 years' penal servitude. No guilt was proved against the rest; who had really been brought to England as evidence.

It may be that the troops sent from Monte Video were Gaucho horse, for when they reached the scene of the boats' landing the pirates & others had scattered, & had to be rounded up.

It is not known to me what happened to the surviving 2nd Mate.

143

. . . Alas, I know no more about the 2nd mate of the *Flowery Land*. Perhaps he came ashore in Australia, and prospered there, like so many sailors. He was a Mr Willm Taffer.

But the execution of the pirates needs a word or two.

The executions were then public, outside Newgate Prison, at a side door opening onto the street called the Old Bailey. The prison then was like a long black coffin dominating that part of London with terror, as it dominated Dickens, in *Oliver Twist* & his wonderful tale of *Great Expectations*.

Both Dickens & Thackeray had written to protest against the appalling scenes at these executions, but Thackeray had just died & Dickens had been disregarded for 15 years, but the *Flowery Land* hangings made his words remembered.

The execution took place "amid scenes of abandoned depravity and rampant sin", dreadful even for that squalid place.

It is hard to believe: but many rich men paid £20 or £30 for a window with a view of the gallows, & passed the night of Sunday there, drinking & smoking till all was over. The window tariff was £4 a pane. (Part of the show was the building of the scaffold during the night.)

All the Old Bailey was crammed with people from 7 p.m. on the Sunday evening: & all through-traffic near the Old Bailey was blocked by traffic barriers on all sides. In the crowd were hawkers, with food, drink etc etc, many pick-pockets & their accomplices, organised religious bodies, coming to pray & sing hymns, & a multitude of scallywags coming to be turbulent. All through the night these people merged & milled. The accomplices of the thieves would begin imitation fights, during which pockets would be picked, & real fights ensue. When the religious sang or prayed, the turbulent sang indecent songs or shouted them down.

An old friend of mine, then a young man, had to cross London that Monday morning to get to London Bridge, & was jammed in the crowd there, & held fast so that he saw the man hanged. It was a wicked crowd: and at last roused London into protest. It was the last of the public executions in the land.[1]

When Newgate Prison was pulled down, some people were seen routing in the ruins: they said they had hoped to find "some bits of the pirates of the *Flowery Land*".

One case attracted some attention on the morning of the hanging. A drunken man, who had fought his way out of the crowd, was afterwards in a police court for cruelly beating his wife "because breakfast wasn't ready".

... P.S. Perhaps I should have told you that a sailing ship's steward was (almost always) unpopular.

He was the Captain's servant; & it fell to him to serve out the allowances, & to make certain that the best pieces of all the meat came to the officers, & that the men got the fat & the bone: & short allowance of all stores, & skimpy allowance of fresh water.

He was the real cause of much of the starvation that ensued: he was in league with the Captain.

The *Flowery Land* people were as hardly treated as any ordinary crew; not worse; I think; though they were a worse lot.

No doubt most of them believed the steward to be their foe.

[1] Following the Act of 1868, all executions in Britain took place within prison walls; only those members of the public with good reason to attend were permitted to see the execution.

144

... The early Holmes stories were complete in themselves. They came out 1 at a time in the first issues of the *Strand Magazine* (a new monthly paper): & O, to have been young, then; & to have to wait a month for the next. I have known nothing like it since.

An earlier generation was said to have waited thus, all a long & awful month, in suspense, to know if the hero of a novel would, after all, be allowed to be confirmed; and some clergymen are said to have rung the parish bells when at last the glad news came that he was to be confirmed. This was before my time, & I do not know the book's name, only the case; & how Gladstone came in one morning crying "Thank God—Edward (or whatever his name was) is to be confirmed." Dear, I did not know this anguish, but I did know the sickening wait for the next Adventure of SH . . . .

145

Lavengro is reckoned to be, in the main, a true account of Geo. Borrow's life, but the sequel, *The Romany Rye*, is supposed to be more mixed with fiction.[1] You must have this later.

He was a pretty good linguist, GB. Many years ago, I used to go to Oulton, where he died. He had lived in a house on the bank of Oulton Broad, where it is almost Waveney River. His house had been re-built, & I stayed in it sometimes, but it was not *his* house at all, all new. But near the water, there was an old octagonal summer house that he had used as a writing room. A man told me that when GB had it, he kept in it the Grammars & Dictionaries etc of the 29 languages that he knew. 29 is pretty well.

There was a big heronry across the water: & just beyond the boat-house the reeds began, lining the Waveney, and one could pull a boat into the reeds, & be out of the world, among bearded tits, kingfishers, & all manner of strangeness: & then, outside, loneliness, & vast expanse, & great churches, with no-one near, no sound, nor sight of man.

The drummer boy, Haggart, whom GB mentions at Edinburgh, was hanged in early life for murder. His book is a strange thing, as GB says.

The Oulton Broad is narrowish, & was then very lonely. At its W end, where I was, the real desolate Fenland began.

The Oulton people did not like GB, because he attracted many gypsies, who robbed roosts, orchards, growing crops, & hayricks; great thieves, then, they said, & verminous in their persons.

In the long run, a handful or two at a time, they could steal much.

About GB & his 29 languages. He knew more than that, I gather; only he liked the 29 specially; perhaps they were the first he ever knew, & those that he kept nearest to him in his writing shed; (as it were the photographs of his first loves).

When I was young, I once mentioned the 29 to an Anglo-Indian, who said, "In British India alone there are 323 different languages."

This kind of thing comes rather with a wallop on the young & may discourage a zest for languages. Please, let it not crush you at all in that way: I don't think it will, but please don't let me be the cause of grief to you thus, or in any other way.

¹ See also Letter 138.

1957

146

... I hope that the "visitation"[1] of your home has now ceased. There is a proverb "Every blow comes on the bruise"; & another "It never rains but it pours", & another to much the same effect which I do not quite remember. These visitations are but the effects of passing fortune, whatever that might be; but the poltergeist seems always to be associated, in some unexplained way, with a young person of about 18, of either sex, & the manifestations are only known while this youth is about, or present.

I have never seen such manifestations but I have read of a queer one, in Dublin, that would make a bed travel across a room with 3 people sitting on it. As the youth grew up, the troubles stopped. The deeds done by the power were inexplicable & meaningless.

... So many grateful thanks for your words about the waltz.

I loved dancing when I was young, which was the time of the imitators of Johann Strauss: & among the imitations were a few fine tunes. "Love's Golden Dream" was a poor waltz, but a popular song, & dancers often sang it as they danced. Metra's "Valse des Roses" is a poor tune, but it had its vogue once. Later in life, I loved the ballet; & in the Berlioz *Symphonie* & 1 or 2 other ballets I saw the waltzes divinely danced: the Berlioz especially: & in one of the *Tales of Hoffman* another. One of the Chopin waltzes delights me above most: Op 64, No 1;& another Op 70 No 2, both Hesitation Waltzes; & a third, No 42. And I love the 3 that Fokine used in the end of *Les Sylphides*. Ah, to be young & a dancer, & to be at a Hallé Ball, & to ask Reyna to dance the Berlioz with me: but of course her card would be full up long before. Still, I should be able to watch her.

[1] ANS had been having trouble with inanimate objects, and JM chose to believe that her house had been visited by a poltergeist.

147

... The Blake illustrations to Gray were in a big bound book of drawing paper, perhaps about 18 inches by 15 inches (& perhaps 50 pages?)[1] The book had been found in some neglected shelf or box (in Scotland, I fancy?).

The book had belonged to Blake, & had been used by Blake for illustrations to Gray's poems. The book, when finished, so I was told, was to be a gift to Mr & Mrs Fuseli. Fuseli was the painter of imaginative fantasy, of whom Blake wrote an execrable short poem of compliment, one of the worst of his worst kind; but the book was to be a compliment such as few kings have ever had: & few women, even from their lovers.

Blake bought a copy of *The Poems of Gray*, perhaps much such a copy as the little *Gray* that I gave you long ago.

He carefully cut out the pages from this book. He then carefully cut out the central square of the pages in the drawing book, & pasted into each square frame thus made one page of the Gray, so that each page of the drawing book showed a poem, or part of a poem, on each side of it.

In the margins left by the letter-press, WB wrought his illustrations to the poem according to the spirit moving in him.

The Gray book begins with the Odes, for which, on the whole, this time does not much care, but WB came to them when he was fresh, & poured out upon them a prodigality of imagined wonder, of colour, of invention, of delicate thought.

Now, I only saw the book once, long ago, for ½ an hour, with a man talking all the time at my side, and I cannot attempt to describe what is really indescribable.

The drawing paper was thick enough to take a design on both sides.

In my memory, the Odes & the "Eton College" were the superb, supreme achieved triumphs, finished & glowing & not to be described.

Then came "The Pensive Selina", less finished, but in monochrome or sepia-wash, & perfect in imagination.

To me, the wonders of Gray are the "Long Story" & the "Elegy": the one as a romantic imagining, the other as a masterly piece of verse, & in the quatrain, too, a glorious form of verse. Turning to these, I found, to my joy, that WB had been profoundly moved by the romance of the tale (no-one else had been, then), but the designs were unfinished; and alas, he had hardly begun upon the "Elegy".

There my knowledge, or memory, ends, but no words of mine can tell you in what sparkling sunny incredible world of Heaven the spirit of WB had moved in, & had made me move in. Why Blake gave up the task, I cannot tell: nor whether he ever gave it to the Fuselis.

. . . Please let me defer my words about Brueghel & his ships till another letter. He had, often, a ruthless, unblest, and disordered fantasy, but in his perception of the great moods of Nature, abundance, & withdrawal of abundances he was sublime & supreme.

He had 2 sons, one called "Hell" & the other "Velvet". One can only hope that between them they kept the platters clean.

. . . The seal about which you ask me is from a coin of Syracuse (silver) shewing the head of Arethusa, crowned with olive, & surrounded by dolphins. It is about 480 BC in date, & one of the finest coins ever made. The obverse of this coin I will seal this letter with. It is a chariot with a lion running alongside (hoping to sup on Pomegranate).[2]

[1] See Letter 92.

[2] Pomegranate was the name of the lead-horse of the Exeter coach attacked by a lioness (see Letters 138, 139).

148

. . . I was wrong about my Syracuse seal having the little lion under the horses. Some of the issues of the silver coins have the lion there, tiny but full of go, but the coin from which the seal was made is one of the smaller issue, & the lion is not there. These big Syracuse coins are of the very loveliest Greek splendour: divine works of Greek genius; & Cellini would have been the first to say that he was nothing beside such designers; just a common, coarse creature beside them.

Arethusa was a river nymph. The river was supposed to go underground in Greece & come up again near Syracuse, which had been founded by Greeks from near the river in Greece. Things put in the river in Greece are said to have come up near Syracuse: a pretty tale: I hope true.

. . . About the ships in the Peter Brueghel paintings.

These are important in the *Icarus*; *Tower of Babel*; the *Naples Harbour*, & in a wild study of a sea-storm. They are incidental in some other of the pictures.

They are of two types; the heavy northern high-sterned type, & the light one-masted galley-type, frequent in the Mediterranean.

I know little of PB's life, save that he knew Holland, France & Italy. In his paintings, he was apt to create a pastiche, or fantastic creation, from his memory or what his fancy prompted. He shows the southern galley-type in a northern setting, & vice versa. No doubt the sea-ports in summer shewed both types in the northern ports in the Mediterranean.

But it seems likely that PB did not know sea travel. I would suppose that he went overland into Italy. His ships are never his main theme, & never the scene of his imagined action. Had he known sea-life he might well have painted scenes from Jonah, or from the last voyage of St Paul; & perhaps wd have been likely to do so.

My own feeling is that he saw ships often in port; & may even have sailed about Naples harbour. This last he pretty certainly did.

In the *Naples*, ships are coming to the port from the NW & from the S, while others are leaving the port, which is for the moment empty. I cannot make out what the ships are doing. It may be a day of carnival or gala. The ships are flying streamers, & 1 or 2 seem to be firing small guns here & there. There seems to be a wreck in the left foreground, but it does not seem to be a battle . . .

Here, as in the other designs, one notices that the sails are not properly set, either not fully hoisted or not sheeted home.

This one might often see in a port, but not when making a passage, when sails have to be trimmed to the wind & sheeted home to a taut leech.

In the sea-storm, the ships are running before the gale under full course.

Now, perhaps this was marine custom then. Sails *may* have been ill-cut, ill-fitted, ill-trimmed; & ships may have run before a gale (to get a safe offing).

Possibly, too, a painter may have loved to show the contrast of a billowy sail with the straight lines of spars & rigging.

In the *Tower of Babel*, there is a populous little port at the foot of the tower. The ships have their yards lowered & sails furled: the rigging (as far as it can be seen) is accurately set down by one who observed closely & reported truly.

In the *Icarus*, the chief ship is (seemingly) just getting under way, with a light fair wind, for the sea port further on to the left. She has no footropes on her main yard, so that the man, casting it loose, has to bestride the yard; and runs a good chance of being flung alongside Icarus when the sail billows under him like the crazy loose foresail.

I cannot imagine what they are doing on board to leave the foresail as they do. There is only a light, crazy wind, & they are only just moving, & there is a wicked rock mighty near, yet the sail is not set, not sheeted, not trimmed, & the bowlines (if fitted) not tautened. I conclude that the Captain has been watching Icarus like the others. The shepherd ashore is looking up to see if any more poets are about to fall, for, if so, he will put his flock under cover. The fisherman has just got a bite: and the ploughman is so pleased with his scarlet sleeve that he doesn't care tuppence for anything else: how could he?

I seem to remember some Dutch engravings of PB's time, of various shipping, & at one time attributed to PB probably wrongly.

I'll just try to get information about these; for if they are not by PB they show the kind of ship that PB drew & may have been copied by him.

But, of course, the Dutch were great mariners, & great painters of ships, before we were.

PB was no doubt fascinated by the life & beauty of the foresail. It is painted with every subtlety of delicate feeling & every mastery of power.

Naples, in his day, was Spanish, & a very important port. Squadrons & fleets must have often arrived there from Spain: & perhaps the picture records the arrival of a Governor, or Prince, in the big ship in the middle distance. She may be about to enter harbour at the head of the fleet, & the outer ships may be just firing a salute or so, & letting their sheets fly in order.

Possibly some critic has already identified the occasion.

149

. . . Please, you must let me go on for a while about Brueghel & the ships.

His name is a place-name. He was born at a village then called Brueghel, not far from Antwerp (then a very great rich port). He soon moved, or was moved, to Antwerp, where he was employed by a Master Artist named Cork, who was a painter, engraver, & picture dealer, all in one, as well, no doubt, as a thoroughly good teacher of art in all forms.

PB went, or was sent, when between 20 & 25 years old, as a young man anyway, through France into Italy, where he went to Rome & to Naples. Antwerp was not then very Lutheran: he was well received as a young painter & engraver, & no doubt painted & engraved wherever he went, & made money; at least, he paid his way.

As far as I know, it was at Naples that he first drew ships, & made studies of them, careful drawings, & impressions of them, but never with a professional seaman's knowledge nor with a sailor's interest.

In the big Naples picture, the ships, that I thought had let fly their topsail sheets, have simply not sheeted their topsails home (as is usual among seamen); this is a characteristic of the Brueghel ships, & important to our knowledge.

In the Spring of this year we are going to sail a replica (?) of the *Mayflower*, pilgrim ship, to the US.[1]

Please remember this.

Now, when she goes, & arrives, her Captain, Villiers, who is a seaman of proof, will no doubt give his seaman's views of an old small wall-sided ship of the time, only 50 years or so later than Brueghel.

I want very much to read what he says about the trimming of the sails.

It may be that he will find it necessary to sail (whenever on a wind) with rather slack sheets.

Brueghel's mariners may have known this: it may have been wise sea-practice???

PB went to the Straits of Messina & there perhaps saw a fleet of galleys attacking some ships of burden. He drew this, & other marine details, including some wrecks, before he returned to Holland & his career.

He was not interested in ships. He was shaken to the core by Nature: the variety & terror & glory & beauty of mountain & river: the joy & life of summer: the death of winter: the gladness of abundance; the motives of crowds.

I don't believe he painted any ships after he was through with the *Icarus* except the wrecks in the autumnal scene.

But he had some studies of ships & galleys, carefully done; & about 1565 a *very good* engraver Frans Huys, a much better copyist than PB & fonder of ships, who saw a market for such things in Antwerp, engraved a set of eleven of them, & these are mostly signed thus: F. H. Bruegel—& are reproduced everywhere to this day (the best of them) as examples of Elizabethan ships.

They are marvels of engraving. FH must have had some choice Italian teacher of the Marc Antonio stamp; & they do show details very precious & very interesting, but not enough details to delight the sailor; & one or two details that show that the artist was not a sailor, & never had been.

I ought to have said in my last letter, that, of course, if a wind be fair, however violent, ships will run before it for as long as the seamen dare. It is a risky process in a small ship but PB would not have known that.

. . . PS I mentioned a PB wreck as in the autumnal picture. It is usually called a February scene, & some writers call it a March scene. It is a leafless wild scene, with men trimming trees & a mad sea below.

[1] See Letter 135.

150

. . . About 50 years since, the Spaniards built a replica of Columbus' ship, from the original drawings & specifications; & men of the Spanish Navy sailed her to Chicago (where I saw her.)

They said that they had not imagined it to be possible that a ship (by her movements) could make her crew so utterly miserable. I suppose she flung them about, & danced around, & pitched her head under, & soused all hands 10 times a day, & snapped her gear with jerks, & leaked like a sieve, & no-one could light a fire, so that they lived on biscuit (sodden) and the drinking water went rotten, & had a sort of rope in it, like slime, in all the good old ways.

. . . As to turning out: I was taught to jump to the order: & I rise, that is "I rouse & bitt", "rise & shine", "show a leg & put a stocking on it", or whatever you young seamen call it nowadays, when the instant comes.

As old Wally Blair on the *Conway* used to say, "There's no compulsion. Don't think there's any compulsion. But you MUST."

. . . I hope so much that you were not shaken or upset by the earth tremor [felt in England].

In the books of an American named Velikorsky (more or less) you will read of some tremors through which the Earth has passed in her exceedingly shady past. In these, splits, 1,000 miles long, occur in the dry land; the sea dries up 300 feet; the ice-cap melts, or thickens enormously & the earth tilts so that the sea wobbles. Then tidal waves come from the bulgy parts, the equator parts, & run, 1,000 ft high or so into the parts where there isn't room, so that up at the Poles there must be a sad mess. Well, then the Earth kind of shakes herself back into her orbit & goes on with re-adjustments & any maids left have to make new mops & get busy.

There was another writer not long since, who chilled my young blood (?) by saying that the mountains were wearing and would soon be too light to keep the earth's crust in place: presently volcanoes wd burst out everywhere; & 12 more or less blasted counties wd see the blaze again "on Malvern's lonely heights."

This kind of winter is a joy to newspaper writers . . .

151

. . . I, too, have known earth tremors, some in Ledbury, noticeably enough, & others in California, none bad enough to scare; but twice I have gone through ruined places only a few days after earthquakes had occurred; & these gave a terrible feeling of what a quake might do.

There was one awful deserted stretch in Northern Italy, in which there were no houses, & nothing growing, & the people not yet returned. It looked as if iron rollers a mile long had moved irresistibly about 6 feet below the surface, & had gone at speed for a mile or two & had flung up all the earth into a kind of mole-hill & plough-furrow, mixed. Golly my beloved, it looked too awful: for nothing had had time to grow, & no one had begun to re-cultivate.

Still, of course, it was nothing to Lisbon, of old, or Tokyo not long since . . .

152

. . . I do not know Moore's *Life of Byron*,[1] but have a respect for Moore, who is buried below one of the lesser White Horses (in the valley, far below) in Wiltshire.

There is a rousing poem by Lord B about the Lisbon Packet which a young mariner like you probably knows by heart.

I know not if you belong to a library. If you do, perhaps you might enjoy (and reading to your Mother) a reprint of a rare unfinished book, Hogg's *Life of Shelley*, so called: a dreadful book, about their days at Oxford (they were expelled together); I would say, too, that it is a lying book, but it is very amusing at a first reading, till one begins to question Hogg: then, alack,

> But the quincunx of Heaven runs low,
> & 'tis time to close the ports of knowledge.

[1] Thomas Moore (1779–1852), the Irish poet and author of *Lalla Rookh*, published his *Life of Lord Byron* in 1830.

153

. . . You ask about reading, & reading aloud.

It is always well to read with attention, but those who read much, or have to read much, will learn to skip, but will skip at his or her peril. The gem may be small, but will be a gem: & it is a shame to the reader to miss, & to learn, later, that he has missed.

In reading aloud, one must vary the tempo, & keep the threads & characters distinct.

In reading to one's self—one may be reading in order to perceive, feel & appreciate a particular style, a cadence, a use of metre, a sense of arrangement, the choice of words, the maintenance of a rhythm or balance. If so, one reads mentally, slowly, very slowly, bit by bit, with repetitions.

Do you not go over bits of music thus?

If you are reading a tale, the tale is the subject, descriptions of souls or sunsets are but digressions, & you are right to repeat the indignant remark of the sportsman who wanted to hear about the race: "O cut the cackle & get to the Horses."

Those who read tales aloud soon develop a fine sense of omission, from the look of the page.

Nowadays, many story-writers hope to have their tales filmed or broadcast: they therefore cut out digressions, & can often be read aloud almost unskipped.

When I was young, people wrote to be *read*. Readers were interested in writing, & read the descriptions & the analyses of the tormented souls: even read them with care & delight.

Latterly, looking through some novels of the nineties, this was made very clear to me. No-one could read the stuff now, but they read it then. Of course, I do not say that they read it aloud always; though sometimes they even went so far as that.

. . . You ask if I care for Byron's poetry?

No, I never did; but I always liked some of his things:

"So we'll go no more a roving"—

and you may remember how Peter Ibbetson & Mimsie used to love "The Island", with Neuha & Torquil? Well, I like "The Island" for their sake & for the sake of one vigorous couplet: and, I rather like the "Lisbon Packet": the rest, I don't fancy.

He had a bad physical inheritance & it poisoned his life. He suited a disordered time.

His effect on that time was very real: he meant much to it; but the time sorted itself out, and the sorted-out time turned to Wordsworth & to Tennyson, to Shelley & to Keats, beside none of whom could his work stand: no, not for a moment.

154

. . . My thanks for your dear marine questions. I will try to tell you about Dogger & Hoy.

The Dutch word for a kind of cod-fish is Dogger. They used to fish for this fish on a Shoal Bank in the North Sea, about 60 miles east from our NE coast. It is about 30 to 100 feet deep, this shoal, & the Dutch called it the Dogger Bank from the fish, & from the fishing boats they called Doggers.

We adopted the boat from the Dutch, & called our own boats Doggers too. They were wooden, bluff, strong things with a fore-mast, with 2 square sails & a tiny mizen, right aft, setting a spanker. They had a bowsprit to secure the foremast, & on their topmast stay they set a small jib. Under the bowsprit they had a spritsail yard, in case they wished to set one.

The Hoy is, or was, just practically a big, strong cutter (up to 150 tons) & able to set as much sail as a big cutter in case of need on one mast, 3 jibs, 3 square sails, gaff—mainsail & gaff topsail, but usually setting 2 jibs, 2 square sails & gaff mainsail. 1 mast only.

Hoys were much used in coastal services. They carried passengers from London to Margate (2 or 3 days) & to Deal, Hastings, Brighton in 1 or 2 more. Charles Lamb wrote about going to Margate in one of them. Pretty rough and ready. You may refer to *Johnny Newcome in the Navy* for Rowlandson's draught of the cabin of one such. They were roomy, strong vessels. I used to see the old, veteran hoys on the Mersey sometimes. I send hurried draughts of Hoy & Dogger for you

The Hoy is said to have been named Hoy, because if you saw one sailing, & wished to go in her, you shouted "Hoy", & then if she heard, or wished, she stopped & took you in.

155

. . . I will try to get a clear picture for you of Admiral John Byng,[1] the martyr, but I have few helpful accounts to hand. He was the younger son of *George* Byng (1st Lord Torrington) with whom you mix him. In a letter or two from now perhaps I'll be able to give you a just account.

I may have written to you about George Byng, not yet a Lord, when writing about Cloudeslie Shovell, for George was admiral (under Shovell's command) in the *Royal Anne*. He was "less than ½ a Mile to the Windward" (the Westward) of Sir Cloudeslie "when he saw the Breaches of the Sea, and soon after the Rocks, called 'The Bishop & his Clerks', upon which the Admiral (Sir C) struck, and in two Minutes there was nothing more of him, or his ship, seen."

"*The Royal Anne*, in which Sir George Byng bore his Flag, was saved by the Presence of Mind of the Officers & men, who in a Minute's time set her Top-sails, when she was within a Ship's length of the Rocks."

Reckoning in the overhangs & bowsprit & jib-boom this would have been just under 100 yards.

All hands were probably alert after a very anxious day, & no doubt the men were on the topsail yards, the sails loose, & the watch hoisting, in 20 seconds of time. The wind must have been to the N of West & freshening: even so, it was a close call.

. . . Thank you very much for your entrancing account of the coaching-horn.

I have seen and heard mail-coaches in my very young days. The guard would blow his warning, & folk would run to gates & doors: &, as he passed, he would pitch out his mail packets: & blow up a warning for the folk beyond.

I saw this: & heard this, for the Gloucester mail trains stopped at Gloucester, & the Ledbury-Hereford mail came on, in part, by mail-coach.

The horn was not called a horn, but "the yard of tin".—"Bright Harry blows his yard of tin."

. . . It is a dear joy, that you still read & love Chaucer. Thank you, too, for letting me mention the Wife of B[ath].

This is an interesting point: that Chaucer, the most perfect European poet, or shall we say Northern poet (for one must remember Dante) since the collapse of classic Rome a thousand years before or more, in his account of his society, makes her the outstanding female figure in that society.

Then, he calls her the Wife of Bath; not any Christian name; & he gives her the characteristics, or some of the supposed characteristics, of the W[hore] of Babylon. He does full justice to her power of intellect—

> In clothe making had she switch a haunt
> She passed hem of Ypres & of Gaunt.

—and to her daredevil courage—

> And thries she had been at Jerusalem.

1800 miles, this is, going overland, & over 3,000 by sea, in each direction: riding & walking over land; & at sea in ships that wd hardly do more than 70 miles in a day.

It does occur to some, that she, or someone like her, was married to Chaucer, who was not the ideal mate . . . she is the more puzzling, for her apparent lack of longing for children, or of maternal feeling.

But, then, was she not the usual type of woman who was not in religion yet went on a pilgrimage with gangs of pretty rough men? She had no children to mind, & no nicety of modesty to be shocked; & no-one could do the pilgrimage from Bath in less than a fortnight.

Chaucer was no doubt writing of one known to him, an unusual woman, amorous beyond most men, venturous, bold & able beyond most women. His sense of her is clear & precise.

The tale of her, as she tells it in her Prologue is less so. She runs 3 husbands almost into one, describes something of the 4th & 5th, & hints at a time of unbridled promiscuity.

It reads as though we have not the finished text of that prologue, but only what has come down to us. It suggests that at one time it was in C's mind to make her Tale the story of her own life from the beginning; & that he did a good deal of it; & went beyond all bounds, perhaps, & later repented (& burned it, perhaps).

It seems to me that the Prologue to her story is of different periods & moods, but that he had once certain character in mind, & that the W of Babylon was also a little in his mind, witness her scarlet stockings, & her sharp spurs.

There was in C's mind an image of devouring self-indulgence, & masterful lust.

Who could want sharp spurs, going jog-trot on pilgrimage?

The woman gives so much ready intimacy, with so little tenderness, so little reverent memory.

I do not doubt that GC had an enormous success, impersonating her, & telling her Prologue as a tale to the male friends of John of Gaunt: & I think that if we had the full version, the uttermost confession, the outrageous lady at her scarletest, we should say it ought not to be printed (but should do our best to procure a copy . . . .)

[1] John Byng, Admiral of the Blue, 1755. Went to the relief of the garrison at Minorca, which had been overrun by the French. After an indecisive action in which his small force was badly damaged, he decided to withdraw. He was court-martialled for neglect of duty, and found guilty, although not of cowardice. In spite of a strong recommendation to mercy he was shot on the quarter-deck of the *Monarque* in Portsmouth harbour, on 1st March 1757.

156

. . . Please will you forgive, if I cannot yet write, justly or clearly, about Admiral John Byng.

50 odd years ago, I knew about it (fairly) as I thought of writing about Byng. I felt that he had been murdered by the skunks in one of the skunkeries called ministries: & as I began to read for this, someone did a book on the theme, & I gave up my thought, for, indeed, it would have taken a year's hard reading in the Record Office alone, going through the Naval papers & logs, even before I started on the histories & newspapers of the time, at the British Museum.

I do not doubt that he was murdered by skunks in skunkeries.

In all Governments (so called) enormous power for doing & concealing evil is put into a few hands; & such power was as appalling in the mid 18th century as it is today. It is even possible that some of the skunks responsible for Byng's murder . . . But let me not go on thus; let the iniquity of oblivion blindly scatter her poppy over iniquity 2 centuries old.

157

. . . Will you forgive what must be a halting and faulty letter about the Gokstad ship, with nothing to report about the *Mayflower* yet.[1]

Gokstad is said to mean Cuckoo Farm. I believe that the Scots call cuckoos "Gowks" to this day, & no doubt many Scots families came from the North, near Gokstad.

It is a place on (or near) some branch of the long Oslo Fjord, in the S of Norway, but I have never seen the place. All that great Fjord is sea-bitten: & on the coasts & shores there are many great burial mounds of Kings; & a good many vast barrows where Kings are buried in ships.

The Gokstad mound was always known as the King's Mound.

It was dug open in 1880, & found to contain the remains of a fine ship (of about the year 900 AD?) in which the bones of a good-sized man, aged about 50, & rheumatic in his left knee, had been buried, with much of his property. The ship had been hauled ashore, stern-first, & buried in clay, with her bows out to seaward. Her mast had been cut off, at a few feet from her keel, & abaft this a sort of wooden tent had been built as a burial chamber. When the King and his gear had been laid down, on a bed, & all arranged, the ship was covered with the local blue clay, & then all was heaped over with twigs, moss & other earth, in a big barrow.

To get her out & moved to Oslo, they had to saw her in two, and proceed very tenderly (& restore much that was rotten or gone).

She is about as long as a cricket pitch, and has a noble sheer, & a great beam of 5 yards. She is clinker-built (that is, with over-lapping strakes) of good oak, with 17 ribs, to which the planks are *lashed* with withy.

The ship you saw must have been a re-fashioning, for after 900 years as a coffin & being sawn in two, etc, she was not up to the North Sea even in summer. But she *had been* a sea-going ship, able to row 16 oars to a side, one man to each oar, and she had a strong oak mast-step, for a mast that could be lowered stern-wards when not in use, & jammed secure by a wedge & a cross-beam when stepped for use.

The rudder was a big oar-blade, *on the right*, or *steer-board side*. It was moved by a tiller.

The ship had moveable fir floor-boards, that could be lifted up easily, for baling, or getting at a leak. She had a sort of rack, at the sides, for 64 shields, of which 25 were found: they were round fir-wood shields, about 2 feet 6 across, & painted alternately, black, then yellow, a nice chequerboard effect.

No doubt the great prow & stern piece were elaborately carved with the masterful & marvellous intertwisted runic decoration. Some such carver must have cut the decorations on little Kilpeck Church, near Ross-on-Wye, about 200 years later.

I have often had to commend your sense of beauty, & I hope have often done so, in a letter or two, but I must add one now to you for your swift perception of the essentials of these Viking ships. You say "her size and her lovely slim shape".

When I stood under the Gokstad ship: for she is raised about a foot, I judge, from the Museum floor, I was staggered by her size and by the appalling power of her grace. I cannot describe the great impression of her bow above me, and the power of her sheer. Alas, I cannot give you her height and depth at present; but she broke me up by her skill.

She was built by eye alone (probably), no tape-measures, no standard fittings turned out by machines, nothing but skill and adzes and axes. Shipwrights have told me that an adze is the Queen of all tools (only you nearly always half chop your foot off when you begin) and axe-men say that the adze is nothing to an axe, when you really get the hang of it.

These Norsemen *made their planks* with adzes and axes: strakes of oak for clinker-building. Golly, my beloved, if I could do that, or begin to do it, or be believed to be capable of learning to do it; and then to make that divine sweeping curving leaping glorious form, able to stand the sea . . . .

¹ See Letter 135.

. . . The Gokstad ship was surrounded by the King's horses (12) & his chief hounds (6), and his body was heaped with a lot of gear, including some *silk* with gold lace on it. The grave had been burgled, like so many tombs of Kings in Egypt, but possibly the burgling was not for profit so much as for consecrated things that could be used in the practice of magic.

In the Middle Ages, & doubtless earlier, the wicked used to dig into graves for things that were supposed to have magical powers, & they used these in magical practice, in spells etc.

Barrows were often thought to be fairy hills, you see.

Digging into barrows was called "hill-digging" and men "got it pretty hot" if they were caught at it; being probably burnt as witches. I am told that there is a statute of K Edward III against "hill-digging".

Starboard is steering-board or steering side from Viking times. Larboard, or port side, is supposed by some to be lading-board, or the loading side, the side that cargo could come in at, or a ship come alongside, without smashing the rudder. Others say that larboard was formerly Back Board, the side of the helmsman's back, & that Back Board got somehow changed to Larboard or to the Ba-board that the French still use: *"Bâbord la barre"* or "port your helm".

Others say that the side was called *Port* because the entry-port, by which men & gear came aboard, was always on that side, & that some always called it Port side, some Lading side.

The French Tribord, for starboard, was always unlike Baboard & led to no confusion. Steerboard, too, if properly pronounced, is quite unlike Larboard, but, in late times, as pronunciation worsened, confusion sometimes brought disaster.

. . . Sir George Byng had in his fleet a Captain Master, of the ship *Superbe*, 60 guns. This Captain had a cousin, a Colonel Turner, with whom he had a row "when they were both unhappily heated with wine". This means that they were not to be considered drunk but in something of the state described by Burns (who knew the state & symptoms):

> "They were na fu; they were na fu,
> But juist a drappie in their ee."

Anyhow they drew their swords & had a go at each other, & Captain Master gave Col Turner a jab between his eyes.

"Captain Master broke an inch and a quarter of his sword in Col Turner's forehead, between his eyes. It remained there eighteen years; and what is, perhaps, more extraordinary, the Colonel lived for 2 years after it was taken out by Small the surgeon. The piece of the sword is preserved as a curiosity by Edm Turner, esq, F.R.S."

One has heard of iron entering the soul, but not of iron entering the brain: yet how did this dodge the brain?

They seem to have wondered at the time.

But had Col Turner any brain? Why did he need a brain?

> "His not to reason why—
> His, but to do or die."

I forgot to say, of John Byng, that he was in the *Superbe*, 60 guns, under Captain Master, as a midshipman of 14, & was at the Messina battle, & may even have seen Col Turner with the sword-point in his skull.

It is easy to be wise & cocksure 200 years after events that I hesitate to write yet; I do not know enough; but I do know that skunks in power made him a scapegoat & murdered him for their own dirty skunkery & its results. It is a terrible tale: & it is terrible also to find, *in this century*, members of the guilty families writing deliberately lying books to clear their dirty forebears, who did not shrink from falsehood, forgery, theft & inconceivable baseness to hide their guilt & make Byng die for it.

159

... I am so glad that you met with the lovely Janet again.[1] Your description reminded me of what a woman once told me of Lily Langtry, the famous beauty of the 1880 time, when beauty was so rare & so precious. She was called "The Jersey Lily". You may possibly have heard of her. The woman told me that she had a face of ivory paleness, with marvellous "chestnut" hair, and an exquisitely made head. The effect she made (on men & women) was staggering.

> She need but lift a pearl-pale hand
> And all mens' hearts would burn & beat.

When she appeared in a London park, "Industry paused, & Commerce held her breath", as the Irish Circus advertisements used to put it. All present stood on chairs & benches to get a better view.

The woman who told me this, said that she was quite indescribably lovely (she was a girl when she saw her).

"When I came home, I fell on my knees and prayed, 'Oh God, do make me beautiful like Mrs Langtry'."

As far as I could tell the prayer was not actually granted, and Mrs Langtry for years had no real rival.

I saw Mrs Langtry long afterwards. She was acting in a piece, or in a charity matinee or something of the sort, in London, but in her make-up I saw nothing of what she must have been.

One of Rossetti's models, Mrs Steedman, was deeply admired then. She must have been exquisitely lovely, I never saw her, but saw her daughter once: a noble-looking creature.

. . . I loved your tale of the little fox in the park. There are few little things more entrancing than little foxes.

I met a man (about 25 years ago) who often kept foxes as pets. He said that they made charming pets at first, for a few months, when they were little, but that as they grew up, they became wilder & less friendly: the wildness drew them: they dreaded men & dogs & daylight, & longed for night, & some hot blood on their teeth. Then they would try to get away, & mope if they could not, & they then had to be let go, or they would die: or hurt themselves in trying to escape.

There is a pleasing tale in some book of Hunting Memories, of a rider in a hunt that checked after a gallop. The rider was aside, out of the way, watching the hounds casting & working, trying to make it out, but failing. Presently, to his amazement, he saw the hunted fox, right in the pack, apparently snuffing for the scent like one of the hounds, but cunningly always working back to the ground they had gone over & abandoned.

When he had worked clear into a piece they had cast across, he left the pack unobserved, & they cast forward & lost him.

The rider had the heart not to Holloa: if he had holloaed I would never have told you. He would have been like one of the skunks who shot John Byng.

[1] Janet Craxton, well-known oboist, daughter of Harold Craxton, pianist and composer.

160

. . . Please may I try to send some sort of answer to your question.

Ethelred the Unready would centre his life about the year 1,000 some centuries after the Sutton Hoo burial.

Pirate raids made life a misery here, at intervals, from about 425 to perhaps 600. Then came a time of reasonably firm rule with Kings strong enough to keep the pirates at bay. (The dates are very roughly given.) Then for some centuries, there were raids again, &

petty Kings snatching power & then being murdered, & this went on at intervals, whenever a really strong pirate got murdered, till about 1020.

Then, in 1066, a really strong pirate, the offspring of a wild stock of pirates, took the land & pretty well kept it. Things were steadier, but I won't say much happier. This is all very rough & crude, but does indicate the kind of chaos & sudden ruin that passed as life. It was a time rather like Texas in the proverb, "Good for men & dogs, but hell on women & oxen".

161

. . . I hope that you have seen the comet now.

I looked out for it for some nights but the sky to the N of this has the glare of Oxford & the sky to the NW of this the glare of Abingdon, till about 2 a.m.

I think that the National Union of Burglars compels the city to turn out much of this light at 2 a.m. or so, to give a poor fellow a chance; anyhow, the N & NW skies are darker then, & I saw the comet.

I sleep near a window, and my head usually lies about NE, northerly, while your dear head (if in bed at all) lies SW, southerly. So, looking out, I thought, "The Comet will be a shade to the West from Reyna's ankle" (which may all blessings ever bless) and there it was, a little as though some angel had trodden on the Pleiades, & rather pressed it pencilly, but the comet all right.

162

. . . About the fox story. It was told me about 40 years ago, in or near Farnham, as having happened near there. It may be in print somewhere.

Farnham 50 or 60 years ago would have been quite lovely hunting country: perhaps the tale dates from then: but possibly long before, in the great hunting days of Trollope, or even before *him*: Assheton Smith & Dick Christian.

Anyhow, a pack around there about Christmas time, put up a travelling dog-fox, a rogue of a lad, with a bite out of one ear, & ran him 7 miles, "licketty-split", as these inelegant prose writers put it,

& then, quite suddenly, lost him. No-one had viewed him: he had not gone to ground: but he was gone, "out Hangman's Stone way".

No-one knew what to do or say: they had had a great run, & scent had suddenly failed. They gave him up.

About the end of the season, they were drawing that same gorse or spinney & put up the same dog-fox, with a bite out of an ear; and again he ran, over the same seven miles, as no fox had ever run: and again, out Hangman's Stone way, he suddenly disappeared: he was gone: the hounds could make nothing of him: no-one had viewed him: so again they gave him up.

"A travelling fox," they said. "He doesn't belong to our country: but he's given us two runs beyond belief."

About next Christmas time, when travelling foxes travel, they thought they would try that out-lying gorse for a traveller once more, in the hope of having another great run.

But this time the Master of the pack got hold of a very bright boy.

"Bill, Bill," he said (or words to that effect). "Would you like to earn a silver sixpence?"

"Yes, please, Sir."

(Sixpence, then, would buy 24 good oranges, or 6 lbs of moist brown sugar, or 12 big half-penny currant buns.)

"Well, Bill, at noon tomorrow, you lie out at Hangman's Stone, & watch for a dog-fox with a bite out of one ear, & watch what he does, & where he goes, & then, when I come up, you tell me, & I'll give you a silver sixpence."

"O, thank you, Sir."

So, next day, Bill was at Hangman's Stone before noon, & the Hunt went to the gorse, & lo, there was the fox with the bite out of his ear, and away he went, over the same line, with a wet sheet & the sparks flying, and going as the devil went through Athlone "in standing lepps & no shinnannikin". Again he went for Hangman's Stone, and the hounds & the Hunt were bent on murder.

Near Hangman's Stone the hounds suddenly checked, & the Hunt came up at once, & there was Bill on the stone, & the Master rode at Bill.

"Bill, Bill, did you see the fox?"

"Yes, Sir."

"Where did he go, Boy? Where is he?"

"No, Sir," said Bill. "That wouldn't be fair to the fox."

Bill never told anyone, for all that they could do, & the Hunt never saw that travelling fox again. But when he married, Bill told his Beloved what the fox did. Near the Hangman's Stone he made a great leap to the top of a tall thick unlaid hedge & ran along the top of it for 50 yards, & then hopped into the hollow in the forks of a great tree.

Men may be this & that: they can be a sad lot in lots of ways, but a sex that produces a Bill cannot be altogether vile.

⚜

163

. . . A few days ago I had a short talk with a man who had seen the *Mayflower*[1] launched, & had been aboard her. He was not of a marine turn like you, & did not care much about such things, but said that when the great, high, as yet unballasted hollow shell first took the water, she shewed great tenderness, & seemed to be going over onto her starboard side (if any wind had been blowing on the port side she might have gone, all the way, but of course they would never have launched her in a high wind).

He could just stand up, in her between-decks, but could not wear his hat there: and taller men had to stoop. (He wd be about 5′10″.)

He said she had a crew of over 30 (or more than made the crews of big famous ships, 2,500 tons or more, of 70 years ago) and that in addition there were journalists, camera-men, & broadcasters, going all the way.

I asked if she was coppered, under water, against the sea-worm. He said, "No, certainly not coppered, but all *very white*." I suppose that all the under-water body had been *sheathed* with thin planks of fir thoroughly painted with lime-wash.

If you will look at the picture of the *Royal George* at Deptford, you will see the white of her lime-wash all along her water-line. It is a pretty good guard (in cold climate) against the sea-worm, but less lasting than copper, as a rule.

Some lime-washes, made of sea-shells powdered mixed with sand in a peculiar way, perhaps with other articles, make a thin, hard, very bright, white cement wash called Chunam, which is "as good as copper", or *was*, for now ships need no sheathing nor coppering, just anti-fouling paint sprayed on in dry dock . . . . By this time I expect all the *Mayflower* men have started quite promising beards, for lack of fresh water to shave with.

Or will the camera-men insist that they all shave?

. . . My thanks to you for telling me of the little seal, to go on your right little finger, the one you hold your bow with.

I have wondered whether you would ever think of a ring of mine (the only jewel, except for 1 stud & 1 tie-pin that I ever bought for vanity). I wore it for years, & gave it up long since, at a time when I was doing a lot of rough work, cutting & splitting some trees that came down. It would be a clumsy lump, I fear; (with a little pale-blue turquoise).

. . . The *Savoy* only issued 2 numbers, quarterly I fancy. It was rather before my time, but I believe that Beardsley & some writers cut themselves adrift from the *Yellow Book* & tried to launch an opposition.

But the Wilde trial had made all that tribe & school of art & writing suspect: and the *Savoy* went out with the copy I sent you (remarkable for Beardsley's story). I do not remember to have seen the first number, but probably I did (though years later, 2 or 3 more years, for it was while I was out of England.)

¹ See Letter 135.

164

. . . I was so very deeply touched by your telling me of your link with Sir Edward Elgar, & of your keeping his dahlia flower petals.

I have a tiny link with him, too. My young sister, at the age of about 8, began to learn the violin from him at Malvern, & was his pupil for several years, I think. I went early into the world, & saw little of my sister, who was 6 years or more younger than I.

Some long time later, about 1913, I think, she took me once to see the great man, somewhere in or near Hampstead I think it was, & he gave me tea; & I was grateful and admiring, but lost, for I didn't know any music, except the old song:

> Down went McGinty to the bottom of the sea
> Dressed in his best suit of clothes;

and the conversation gave me no chance to bring this in. However, musicians make more allowance than most, and one of his bright young friends has made more allowance than any, and lets me even write to her, & even writes the loveliest things to me.

. . . Sometime since, we were talking of the Seven Barrows. Well, last week, on a matchless day, I was there again, & came swerving West to the Barrows: & there, among the Barrows, was a string of race-horses, about a dozen, from one of the great training stables on the Downs there.

They had halted there, & the stable lads & girls had dismounted, & there they were, many in bright sweaters & queer rigs of cut & colour, holding their great lean lovely thoroughbreds, like the Britons of the Bronze Age come back. Some of the horses were nervy

& the boys & girls were not too happy at a car coming, but in a moment they were all at ease, & away again like a troop of Britons. I did so wish that you could have seen them: a troop of Arthur's riding to K Arthur's rampart here, to try to hold the line of the Thames: or the survivors returning, perhaps, to the peace after the battle at Badon: perhaps only a few miles S & E from there.

165

. . . I am so glad it[1] is back, & that it gives you pleasure.

Looking at the impressions thro a lens, I judge that you tend to press the seal while the wax is too hot (I do too) but if you pause a second or two, the wax begins to settle, & the impression then will remain true & firm: the wax will not blur & go runny when the seal is lifted.

Forgive me venturing to suggest this, please. The Americans say that the old are always putting one ear to the floor & then treading on it.

[1] JM's seal (Letter 163) had now been mounted upon a ring.

166

. . . How very dear of you to take all that time, & strength, & leisure to make me share your wonderful time & to show it to me out of all your joy . . . all the colour & the poetry . . . .[1]

But, O, ten hours in the heat of Rome, & wondering how you could get away.

Well, these things intensify the memories, & make a sort of frame or cover to them. Were you not quite desperately tired when you did at last arrive?—it is the one thing you have not told me, but I felt at the time that something was amiss.

And then, in the midst of it, you even wrote to me, with a little picture of a fore & aft schooner. I have painted her under sail for you, but I am not qualified to paint a Mediterranean blue (nor a Pacific green).

Ah, once, I saw in the horizon sky a green beyond praise; the reflection (somehow) of the lagoon of an atoll. All morning it grew greener, till, lo, we were in the lagoon, in the incredible emerald itself. It was the setting of life, that colour.

. . . I am the third child of six.[2]

1) A brother, who died many years ago.

2) A sister, whom I see about twice a year still—Ethel.

3) ——

4) A brother—Harry.

5) The brother who died on the night you first wrote to me—Charles.

6) The sister whom Elgar taught. I see her at rare intervals. I have never really known her well—Norah.

[1] A Festival of Music at Ravello, Italy.

[2] I had asked him about his family. ANS.

167

. . . I am so very glad that you liked the [Edinburgh] Festival. I was afraid that it might be a time of terrible strain, long long 6 hour rehearsals, perhaps some of the music not very rewarding, & Edinb so full that you might be sleeping on the floor somewhere, & perhaps the snow falling outside.

Then I thought that perhaps you had to do the "Edinburgh Concerto" by some great composer, a not very good work, but brought out from the dustbins from somewhere for the Festival, & that it was not scored for strings but for bagpipes, & that you, in tears perhaps, had to learn the bagpipes, & were all day hugging this kind of dead leather octopus (see *The Toilers of the Sea*)[1] in a row of 50 pigs being killed, & the Conductor quoting poetry to you:

> Hech, gather, Hech gather
> Hech gather aroun'
> And fill-a-yeir lugs with
> The exquisite soun'
> Sae bonny a piper
> There never was seen, etc.

(Though I expect you can play the bagpipes with anyone, & wear a kilt & tartan to the shattering of all male hearts . . . .)

[1] Victor Hugo, *Les Travailleurs de la Mer*, 1866 (see Letter 173).

168

. . . Do you remember my writing once about an escaped lioness that tried to pull down the near mail-leader, a horse called *Pomegranate*?[1]

Yesterday, by chance, I read that she belonged to a menagerie man named Ballard, and that she was an enormous attraction for 9 years afterwards, everywhere, & was then shown in London at St Bartholomew's Fair (a pleasure & hiring fair held every year, then, in Smithfield, and now abolished). Ballard is/was famous in his way, as one of the ancestors of the great travelling road troupe families.

I can find no more about Pomegranate, but I fear that he did not last as long as the lioness.

[1] Letters 138, 139.

169

. . . You ask me about Thackeray & *Vanity Fair*. I have never read *Vanity Fair*, beyond the 10th or 15th page (never could); nor very deeply in his other works. I think that he lived a brave life, for he had a terrible sorrow & strain; a wife quite mad and 2 little children to bring up, & writing his only means of living. The strain of all this . . . He died at about 50 or so, I believe.

He was extraordinarily dowered, gifted & equipped with a great reading of the 100 years before his time. He possessed all that century; and was masterly about it. *Esmond* is superb: *The Four Georges* brilliant: *Barry Lyndon* a rousing work. Of the later books I liked *Pendennis*; but could never read *The Newcomes*, or *Virginians*.

The Rose & The Ring is a jolly work, & Miss Sidgwick's dramatic version of it is a merry play.

He wrote a good deal of verse that I have liked; but now forget pretty much. Some translations from the French (Béranger) I liked "In the brave days when I was 21"; and the adaptation "There were 3 sailors of Bristol City", and "The Ballad of Bouillabaisse". There was a tale in verse, too, about some Monks & a Saint.

He was an accomplished draughtsman, & illustrated some of his lighter works. He did some burlesques of various modern writers, & these are very happy. He mocked Disraeli & Bulwer Lytton especially cleverly. *Esmond* seems to me the best I have seen of his, the best by far, but Destiny has a word to say in all readings that matter to one. Often the soul gets the book it needs, at the moment of the need: & that is happening to you now with *Vanity Fair*: so pay no heed to what I say: & never think that because I am not up to *Vanity Fair* that the book is the one at fault.

It has enchanted & moved many thousands, & no doubt will continue to do so.

It may be added, too, that the Late Victorians were apt to belong to 1 or 2 camps.

You liked Dickens	Or Thackeray
" " Tennyson	" Browning
" " Wallis	" Leighton
" " Meredith	" Hardy

Just as you liked your Church High or Low, or drank Tea or Coffee at breakfast. In conversation one wd say that there must be no disputing about tastes, & then one wd go away growling that the other fellow was a child of Belial, little (if any) better than an out & out paedo-Baptist (or Riper Years Immersionist) as the case might be.

You must never mind if you do not like books & pictures that others adore. You are you, & your Being has laws & likings that you must obey & follow.

Thackeray meant much to two generations of people: and that is a great achievement: very great: I do not feel that he will mean much again to many.

I never wished to read any book by him a second time (I doubt if I ever have), but I see his talent; & also feel for him: so much of his work done under a crying strain: so much was journalism, done for the day or the week, whether he felt like it or loathed it: his books make me feel, too, that he was pretty often pretty ill.

170

... Thank you so much for telling me of the dripping well. It is of course Knaresbo' that I was thinking of.

I did not know that it petrified as well as dripped.

Near Ledbury, about 1 mile S of the town, near the road that runs either to Glos. or Chelt, there is a brook that I wrote of in a tale once. It, too, in one short reach, petrified to some extent, that is, *it coated objects with lime.* We could peg old birds' nests in a quiet dimple & leave them three months or so, & then (if they were still there) retrieve them all lime-encrusted, & raise the wind on them, if lucky, by finding some mug of an elder who would give 1/- for one. Anyhow, one could always find twigs & oak-leaves quite covered with lime, & these we put into our private museums.

There used to be several such [brooks] on the S slopes of Bredon Hill.

It is very difficult to get a good petrified bird's nest. The nest is an old one to begin with, & it is not improved by being taken from its nook & pegged into a brook. Often it disintegrates within a fortnight, but if not, a sudden freshet may wash it all to shreds: forever & forever, farewell Cassius.

171

. . . Did you ever, as a child, fall under the spell of Victor Hugo's *Les Misérables*?

Did it (if ever you did) enliven in you a moving image of the Battle of Waterloo?

That battle does win some mention in *Vanity Fair* . . . .

It was, and is, nothing much of a battle now, and I doubt if English visitors to Brussels go much to the Field & drop a tear at the grave sacred to the memory of the Marquis of Anglesey's Leg.

When I was young many men who had fought in the Battle were still alive. I never met one, but saw one whose Father had been there.

Well . . . Victor Hugo gave to my generation an impressive clear print of the Battle: & all my generation thinks it was *the* battle. The Sayers & Heenan battle, that Thackeray wrote about, was nothing to it.

Perhaps you [became] a little stuck in *Les Misérables*?

Well, 1,000 pp about the miserables take a lot of reading, & if rammed down a young throat may rouse rebellion. You will, perhaps, sometime tell me, wiltow?

Not far from here there is chalk downland much as at Waterloo: & once, long since, a regiment that had been in the Battle was marching thro Berkshire & came suddenly upon a replica of the whole field, & began to cry out, as they marched, "Waterloo, Waterloo."

For a long time I thought I knew the place: but I have now found unmistakably the place . . . so curiously like, save that it has no buildings on it, no inn for Napoleon, no La Haye for the Germans, no Hougoumont for the Guards: & no "Horror breathing from the silent ground".

VH's description of it, in spite of much absurdity, is quite superb description.

172

. . . In the 1st war, I met a Naval officer, who told me of a Naval gunner who had once, at dawn, somewhere, spotted a German battalion of foot on parade on a beach, & had at once trained every gun on them & blown the lot into eternity.

His chiefs were much pleased by his readiness, & asked what they could do for him . . .

He said "Sirs, if it would not be too much, might I have 48 hours' leave? I *would* like to have a day's rabbiting."

173

. . . Ah, the *Count of Monte Cristo*. That is, indeed, a tale. Is there any tale that can compare with it? What a man [Dumas] was . . . & he wrote all the historical novels, too; & lots of plays, all meat & wine, & shudders & grand passions; O golly, golly . . . .

. . . I could never read V. Hugo's *Notre Dame* (I came to it too late). *The Toilers of the Sea* I liked, in a way, for though it is absurd, has no knowledge of the Toilers, it has an instinct & feeling for the sea, quite unique: the sea comes into it: it is all tidal & phosphorescent, and then, too, the 1st appearance, upon any stage, of the Octopus.

V. Hugo was an exile then, living in the Channel Islands; & beset by adoring English & Americans. V. Hugo didn't understand them. Two young American ladies came to see him one day, & VH said to his interpreter, "What say these Ladies?" The interpreter said, to the Ladies, that the Master wished to know what the Ladies wished to say.

The Ladies said that "they were just tickled to death to meet him".

VH still somewhat puzzled, asked again, "*What* say these ladies?"

The interpreter said, "Master, they say, that they salute the Eagle of the World."

After that, probably, all went well . . . .

. . . The book, *Les Misérables* is surely *the* great French novel. It is as long as all day, but it is a triumph of power. It held me breathless for all its thousand pages, & some of it I can read still, but I am not able to stand breathless for 1,000 pages now. It is an extraordinary feat of story-telling: often harrowing often almost unbearable: &

then at last quite shatteringly grand & healing. It is concerned, like all masterpieces, with the doing of Justice.

Reading through what I have said about Dumas & VH it wd seem that you may be puzzled. D is the story-teller, like the poet of the Odyssey, matchless as such.

VH is a novelist and social historian, working out some imagining of Justice & Destiny: not like the poet of the Iliad so much as the Tolstoy of *War & Peace* or *Anna Karenina*.

In *Trilby* in a chapter heading, you will see a quotation from VH's poem "Gastibelza". Did you ever read the poem? VH wrote it in 1 day of power: for he was a poet of power . . . in the old days it shook us all . . . there was nothing like it in the world; & now, 120 years later (or so) it remains a marvel (to me).

You must be weary of all this jargon of jargon . . . Why you put up with me I cannot think: it must be a frightful strain on any hot or cold day.

174

. . . *The Dynasts* [Thomas Hardy] is somewhat cumbrous but matures, & carries you along. It is unjust to Napoleon, I think, in that it does not even mention his great campaign before his abdication & Elba: and does not show the glory of the Hundred Days: the most amazing thing he ever did.

Please, will you be very kind & sure: & tell me what of the poems of TH you have? Have you a marvellous poem "The Revisitation"? What are your volumes of his poems? "The R" is in *Time's Laughing Stocks*.

I don't think you could easily carry about *The Dynasts* or the *Collected Poems*, they are cumbrous vols, but it wd be such a joy to me to know that you had a favourite poem sent to you by me. So . . . please . . .

I have twice seen acted versions of *The Dynasts*: some scenes are very fine: the retreat from Corunna or the Waterloo: esp. perhaps the Richmonds' ball at Brussels: & some of the Wellington bits in the battle.

Then as to TH & Napoleon—he is just to the ruffian's main character, that no prince could believe a word he said, but does not do justice to his incredible compact force in his last two years in command.

175

. . . About 30 years ago, being shocked at the appalling irreverence shown to dead men by writers & editors, I wrote a rhymed curse,[1] begging people not to write my life, nor to print my letters, & hoping that a curse might fall on any who did.

In writing to you about this question[2] I shall have to write with the utmost deep feeling of my heart for you, so be not offended, nor hurt, nor made sad.

Perhaps I may have to put a special clause in my Will about it.

Copyright in all letters belongs to the writers of the letters for the full term of copyright.

When a writer is old, he is very often out of fashion and disregarded.

When a writer dies, some say that he was a good chap but a poor artist, & others that he sometimes wrote interestingly but brought his parents to untimely sorrowful deaths, murdered his wife, ravished Jemima in the forest, & lived in sin with 3 choir boys & the curate.

Usually, after death, he is ignored for 5 or 7 years, & then some sons of Belial will think of writing his life, & will advertise for letters.

Some of these sons of Belial will advertise for letters before he dies.

Dear, beautiful Reyna, never send my letters to any one of these.

As Mrs Quickly so cheerfully said, "I hope it isn't time to think of God yet", but I want to write to you soon about my dying . . . .

[1]   "Sweet Friends"
Print not my life nor letters; put them by:
When I am dead let memory of me die.
Blessed be those who in their mercy heed
This heartfelt prayer of mine to Adam's Seed;
Blessed be they, but may a curse pursue
All who reject this living prayer, and do.

(Happily for the publishers, JM later came round to the idea.)

[2] ANS had asked if ever she might publish JM's letters.

176

. . . You may have heard the tale of Darwin in the Magellan Straits. He was there long ago in the usual stormy, snowy weather, & saw the huge Indians wearing almost no clothes at all, like my hard-case seaman. In the tale he asked one of these Indians if he felt cold?

The Indian asked him: Did his face feel cold? Darwin said, No, not to speak of.

The Indian said, "Me all face."

The Tale is probably made up, & you may have heard it at sea, where it, and the midshipman's pig, are almost, or were almost, the only tales told.

60 years & more ago many sailors suffered torments to become "hard-cases" to endure great cold & have an ear or so taken off by frost-bite. People would think that they were too poor to buy clothes, & would give them boots or woollens, & then they would sell these for tobacco, at sea, or in port, for rum, & hope that some other mug would have a similar weakness later.

177

. . . Do you always dread the usual book, as a weight likely to strain your playing muscles; & have I thoughtlessly tempted you into cramps by sending you great heavy gollops of books, such as WS's folio, Liddell & Scott's Greek Lexicon, & Fox's *Book of Martyrs* & similar invitations to sleep or study?

I fear you must often have shuddered, seeing a packet from me, & thought: "O, yet another 20 pounder: farewell my bow hand, welcome neuritis and the end."

. . . I am reading about how they blew up the wreck of the *Royal George*, at intervals, in the 60 years after her loss. They got up almost all her guns (& perhaps used them, for they were not out of date) & her coals, that "burnt very well", & some of her butter, which wasn't quite as fresh as some, but her candles were very good . . . . They found an engraved brass dog-collar. The dog had belonged to a Lieut. and was drowned with the ship, but the collar was returned to the owner, who was still in the Navy. They also found a stamp, for marking linen & so forth, belonging to another Lieut. This also was safely returned, but the Lieut. had become an Admiral (I think retired).

They found a lot of wine, still in corked bottles, but all quite unspeakably corrupt.

They found, too, that she did not perish from misadventure, but from absolute rottenness; a strain came on her heeling side, her beams broke & the side just fell away.

After they had salved & destroyed they raked the site by dragging anchors over the bottom of the sea, till they had made it nice & level again.

178

Reyna mia

In your kind letter about the Darwin tale, you ask about the midshipman's pig.

Can it be that this is now gone from the repertory?

Well: no doubt it has: It has almost gone from me: but it would have gone something like this.

Scene, the quarter-deck of a flagship in the Mediterranean "in 1800 and war-time". The Lieut. of the watch to windward; 2 quartermasters at the wheel; a marine sentry; etc etc. A hail from the maintop.

The Hail. On deck there, man overboard, Abaft all, Lee side.

Shouts. Man overboard.

Lieut. Let go the Life Buoy. (A splash off.)

Shouts. All gone the Life Buoy.

Enter the Yeoman of the Pigsties, dishevelled

Yeoman. O Sir, O Sir.

Lieut. What is it, Yeoman?

Yeoman. The Admiral's Pig, Sir.

Lieut. What of it?

Yeoman. Overboard, Sir.

Lieut. How?

Yeoman. As I was bathing of him, Sir.

Lieut. Holy Sailor.

Yeoman. O not my fault, Sir. It was his play, Sir. I never seen such a pig.

Lieut. Full for stays, quartermaster. Luff. Ease down the helm. Hands to stations for stays. Lively now. Bosun's mate, away all boats. Raise tacks & sheets. Lively now, cutters crews. Away, now, at the order. Lower your boats at the way stops. Stand by, all. Main top-sail haul. Main top there—do you still see him?

A hail. Yes, Sir, still swimming strong.

Lieut. Round she comes, my lads. We'll save him still. Let go and haul.

All hands. Hurray. Hurray.

Enter the Captain

Captain. Mr Osprey, what is all this, Sir?

Lieut. The Admiral's pig, Sir. Overboard, Sir.

Captain. Fore George, this will be a Court Martial for someone if he's not saved. Lively now, my lads. Carry on, Mr Osprey.

Lieut. What are you waiting for, port & starboard cutters?

1st cutter. Plug missing, Sir.

2nd cutter. Garboard strake bust, Sir.

All hands. Lively with the cutters or we'll skin the 2 crews of you.

Enter the Admiral

Admiral. What sort of Dover Court d'ye think you're holding here? Is this a ship of war or the bar of the Black Eyed Sue in Billingsgate?

Capt. It's your pig, Sir, overboard.

Admiral. Come on, my lads, five pounds for the boat that picks him up.

All hands. Hurray. Hurray.

1st cutter. I've put my handkerchief instead of the plug. Lower away 1st cutter.

2nd cutter. Bill's sitting on the busted strake. Lower away 2nd cutter.

Enter Yeoman of the Pigsties, dishevelled

Yeoman. O Sir, O sir.

Lieut. What is it, Yeoman?

Yeoman. It is not the Admiral's pig, sir.

Lieut. Not?

Yeoman. No, Sir.

Admiral. What is it, then? One of the topmen?

Yeoman. No, Sir, the midshipman's pig.

All hands. The midshipman's pig?

Yeoman. Yes, sir. What they call Little Pipsqueak.

All hands. O.

Lieut. Your pig is safe then, Sir.

Capt. Shall we carry on, Sir?

Admiral. For the midshipman's pig? No, Sir. Piggy must drown.

Lieut. All fast with the boats there.

Captain. Get her back to her course, Master.

Lieut. Pipe down there, Bosun's mate.

You must now be one of the few who can still pipe down, & do it really well: no mean feat.

I hope that this may safely reach you & find you all rested & sunburnt & seeing a ship or two, or even three.

179

Reyna mia

My thanks for your dear news of the Centenary playings & of your happiness in them.[1]

You ask me about Drinkwater.[2] I met him at rare intervals (about seven times, I think, but there may have been 1 or 2 more) I never knew him well.

He worked, as a young man, in Birmingham, I think, & helped to create an amateur body of players, to perform some of the great plays utterly neglected by our theatre of amusement. They did a good many of these (certainly *The Spanish Tragedy* & *The Two Noble Kinsmen*) & in good time a man built the Birmingham Repertory Theatre for them, which did many useful things: JD being a chief director, then. I think that they did his *Cophetua*, $X = O$, and *Abraham Lincoln* there. The *Lincoln*, of course, made him very famous.

He wrote a lively book on Swinburne, as I expect you know, & after his death there appeared a book on English poetry: brief, but good.

He must have been some years in Birmingham, which is a centre of the Pre-Raphaelite school. Burne-Jones was a native of Birmingham & did his best windows in the Church there. The Director of the Art Gallery there, Wallis, some 65 years ago, determined to make his Gallery *the* PRB[3] Gallery of the world: & by this determination made it so.

If you are playing in B, be sure to tauten up your rigging with your very best double Matthew Walkers[4] & go to the Gallery, & you will see the best Burne-Jones & Millais things in the world, with Morris' Holy Grail tapestries, too.

Among the later PRBs are some Southalls & Gaskins, & in one of these you will find a portrait of JD among the lively spirits of the town. (Southall, I think, but my memory is a sieve.)

Between 1850 & the 1st war D. G. Rossetti was *the* influence in poetry & painting. All the poets of my time were in no doubt of this: they were all moved by Rossetti: by the painting & the poetry too: moved to the core. Even now, some of the lines come into my head & take me away & away.

Forgive a brief note. Your letter came late again, as the posts here (Sat – Tues) are very odd indeed & grow odder.

Dear, blessings guard & gladden you & every sweet dream cheer & happy things delight you.

Jan.

[1] The Hallé Orchestra, founded in Manchester in 1857, was celebrating its centenary.

[2] John Drinkwater (1882–1937), poet and dramatist best remembered, perhaps, for his play *Abraham Lincoln*.

[3] PRB—The Pre-Raphaelite Brotherhood, consisting of Holman Hunt, Millais, D. G. Rossetti, W. M. Rossetti, Thomas Woolner, Frederick Stephens and James Collinson. Founded about 1849.

[4] "You ask about the Matthew Walker. I doubt if it be ever used by seamen now . . . it was once a very important useful knot." (JM to ANS.)

180

... So anchovies improve tinned salmon, do they?

Anchovies, the very word is wonderful. Doesn't it at once suggest munching, & loves, & a foreign land under the sun? There must be books somewhere: *Love Songs for the Viol*, by the Princess of Anchovia; *O Anchovy, ON, ON,* or War for Anchovia's Independence; *Mark Anchovy & Cleopatra*, or Life's Egyptian Relish.

Did you ever come across Botargos, the same sort of thing, but made out of the roes of tunny fish which the young bucks of Spain could not keep from hunting, though the Moorish pirates used to lie in wait for them, & eat the catch, & sell the bucks in the slave market.

This led to the phrase "Being a slave to one's appetites".

... The cutting you sent me must come from some English weekly of 1913. The house is my house in Well Walk, Hampstead, & the lane running up hill from the [drinking] trough runs into a lesser road called Well Road.

Keats & his brother Tom lodged for a time in Well Walk, & Tom died there. I believe that the house no longer stands. The Keats lodged with the local postman. (George Keats, the other brother, was there, too, till he married & went to America.)

After Tom died, John went to live with Brown, somewhat to the south, downhill from my house. [Their house is] now a Keats museum.

In May, 1914, as I lay awake (at midnight) a nightingale *nested* & sang in the tree just visible in the middle distance. Keats heard *his* nightingale only ¼ mile away.

181

... It is interesting to me to know that styles of playing will date a performer, so that you would know his approximate age by hearing him on a record or from behind a curtain. One can judge of verse thus, of course, & somewhat less readily, of prose: & we old ones are glad to have known the times of peace, when so many masters achieved, each master gladly saying, like Dürer, "I know very well that my achievement will be soon surpassed". But, alas, it was not so. We were dwelling on the slippery peak.

... Since you let me come into your heart to talk to you I will try to write now something of your sorrow & anxiety, & what must be to all loving hearts a misery, the watching of remediless ailments & the slow going of one beloved.[1]

There is no balm for this sorrow, nor for any real bereavement. A part of the life of the heart ceases, & there is no longer the loved face, the voice of love. For some 75 years now, I have felt sure that I have lived before, & shall live again; & that I have met in other forms, those whom I have loved & love, & that some of those, now dead, have often been near to me, as to others dear to them, & that the tenderness & guidance of those dead never cease, but are there, if we do not, in our despair, make it hard for them to minister.

But with this abiding tenderness there is also, to those dead, a great release from suffering, & a return to the gladness of childhood, & the over-whelming beauty of Paradise, into which we all pass, out of this old Hell, according to our power, according to our beauty, & to the mercy & gladness of rejoicing spirits who know our needs.

. . . About the storm that sank the *Pamir*.[2] At the moment, I am waiting for the daily charts of its wicked life, & have only the main outline of its course.

Storms are often like lives (or final outbursts) of homicidal maniacs. This one was an unusual storm, that did one of two unexpected things. You shall hear, when I have had a look at the daily charts.

I do not expect to hear any final verdict from the Germans: and the only account that I have had of the wreck is a French account, which I will send with my survey (perhaps next week). The survivors were not much in a state to know what happened: & the one who pulled thro was not a sailor, but the ship's baker.

So far I am puzzled about it. The ship was as strong as a ship can be & the Germans are good sailors, & all the certified sailors went down: five lads & a baker survived. Well . . . Destiny decided so: perhaps these six are to do great things, perhaps the other 74 or so are needed in eternity. We are in a vast universe, subject to an inscrutable rule of order, Beauty, power, giving to each a portion.

Please, will you tell me of your storm in the Atlantic, & what it was that scared you for a moment . . .

One of the many terrors of a cyclone is the confused sea that it rouses & leaves. As the wind shifts in the gyration of the thing's progress, the direction of the sea shifts, till at last appalling lumps & pyramids of water are running & clashing from every direction. It is a terrible thing in a very big ship, for any wave, from any point, may come over her 50 feet of freeboard, but it was unspeakably awful in the old sailing ships with only, say, 5 feet of freeboard.

When I was young, I was told of a French 2-decked man of war, perhaps an 80-gun ship, but described to me as a 74, which I don't think the French had. (I am wrong, it seems. The French had both types.) Well, this ship was in a cyclone, and the centre went over her (in the story) & all the crew, seeing the sea gone mad, went mad too.

I don't wonder: but I have never found out when & where this happened: so let us just, like Britons, proudly say, "Wasn't that like a lot of foreigners? A British crew would have smashed open the spirit-room & handed round the rum & gone down blind but merry." The freeboard of an 80-gun ship would have been about 17 feet; & a cyclone sea would run to 30 or a bit more, or indeed, now & then . . . to what, O my beloved, to what might it not run?

[1] ANS's mother was gravely ill at this time.

[2] The loss of the German sailing-ship, *Pamir*, puzzled JM greatly. He had learned about meteorology in his *Conway* days, and had had grim experience of weather at sea. He always studied the weather conditions of any marine battles or disasters.

182

. . . Please, may I say one thing. There are some people about, who make a living by begging to see personal letters of writers or painters, saying that the writers or painters have agreed (even in their life-times) that the beggar should write his official life or lives. One or two, perhaps working together, are trying to get letters or anecdotes (from me or about me) from anyone that they can hear of as knowing me. They have no warrant nor authority from me, but they have molested most of my known acquaintance; and I would like to warn you against them, if by some chance they should hear that you have letters . . . .

Perhaps, long hence, when I am forgotten, you may like to write something & print some of them . . . .[1]

[1] See Letter 175.

183

. . . I do thank you for your dear letter & for telling me of your knowledge of Trollope.

He wrote about 80 novels, of wh I have read 72 (I think): & *The Warden* is the best one to begin upon: so I will send that soon & you shall try. He drew the enormous upper middle class of the great Victorian time, & is the nearest we can come to Balzac, but is better, for he writes of a settled state sure of its ground, certain of its future.

May *The Warden* delight you, & welcome you into its wonderful successors.

. . . I am venturing to send you two curiosities in case you may like to have them: a proof copy & a prompt copy. The notes pasted into the prompt copy are written with my left hand.

From time to time, for the last 37 years or so I have had occasional writer's cramp. For some years I have had to write wholly with my left hand. Last week, after long freedom, I wrenched my arm, & the thing returned, but it is now much less painful, but please will you forgive this letter being a short one.

I believe that I miscall my arm-trouble as writer's cramp but it is true that I am a writer & that when it occurs, writing becomes difficult or almost impossible. It began as a strain, from carrying very heavy bags, & recurred the other day from my being a silly muggins with a corn-sack, so do not pity . . . . Its present pangs are yielding to infra-red rays, & I hope to be normal again next week, probably being a muggins in some new way.

184

. . . Shelton's *Don Quixote* is a jolly book.[1] Is your copy "The Tudor Translations"? No, but it may be a re-print from them. During the 1st War, I used to carry a Spanish *Don Q* everywhere, and found it almost the only book that I could read: and some of it I know almost by heart. I did so especially love the second part, which seemed so noble a statement of every fine thing in the Spanish mind of that Century . . .

Shelton was probably well known in his day as a Spanish scholar. I wish I knew if he knew WS [Shakespeare], for WS & John Fletcher seemed to have worked at a Cervantes plot, & *may* have had the script from Shelton. Who can tell? I wish I could tell. I judge that Fletcher introduced the script, & if so—O it opens up such surmises about all that dark age of marvellous poetry.

Was John Fletcher ever in Spain? Ever at sea?? "Ah, questioner," as Carlyle would have said.

Quevedo's prose is not known to me, but I know some of his verse: he did some terrible things: & some rather great.[2] For some years I read much of the history of that Spanish time, wherein he cut a great & somewhat sinister figure, knowing prison, poverty & hunger, like Cervantes, & having a good share of power & glory too. There was something savage in him (of the Dean Swift sort), with something of greater culture & profounder wisdom. He belonged to the Cervantes period: Swift to the Pope & Dryden period. He talked from a greater mood of the world's mind than Swift.

¹ Thomas Shelton made the first English translation of *Don Quixote* (1612–20).

² Francisco Gomez de Quevedo (1580–1645) author of *Pablo de Segovia*, a picaresque romance. His *Visions* were translated into English by Sir Roger L'Estrange in 1668.

185

... "The Tudor Translations" were an issue of the late Victorian times: most of the choice Elizabethan translations. They were the joy of the Victorian heart: or one of the joys: they brought some noble prose again.

I am posting to you a copy of *The Warden*, by the same post separately. It would be kind if you could have a sort of look-see, whether you can abide, or not abide: no hurry: but it is the first book of a series: & if you like the book & the people you may care to read of their later doings. So have a look, please, wiltow, dere swete, at your dear leisure, & then, in your heart's kindness, let me have a word?

Thank you for sending me the (very skilful) song about the Spring, hitherto unknown to me.¹

That sudden pert surprise is not easy to write: the poet has to be helped by the musician, or to *be* a musician, without which he cannot do one third part of what a poet should be master of. This I do broken-heartedly assure you of.

¹ ANS had written what she remembered of an old pantomime song:

> The Spring has gone, oh dear me,
> I hope it will not go far!
> We have to sit about all day—
> We can't sit on the sofa—
> The spring has gone.

186

... I am hoping that one or other of my notes may reach you for Christmas.

Very often, I agree with your Mrs S, that all this nightmare & nuisance might be put a stop to.

Seventy years ago (or so) I read a poem to that effect, in a paper that then gave me much delight. It was called *Ally Sloper's Half-Holiday* (a weekly, illustrated) & the poem went like this:

> Christmas is coming, is coming, my Dear.
> I, the dyspeptic one, know it.
> Ills again, pills again, Syrup of Squills again
> Hang it, confound it, & blow it.

Well, it has survived: people have preferred to keep it: & on these great issues the popular vote must be right: the Heart is for it; & as Dr Johnson so often said of one thing or another: "Sir, it promotes kindness."

187

. . . All the old music hall throve on that blend of poetry: and when I was about 10 I enjoyed the blend to a point of ecstasy. Much of the work was flippant, & mocking at death & grief . . . and those were the great days of poetry, remember, when great men were mourning in marvellous verse, never to be bettered.

There is a character in Disraeli's novel of *Lothair* who says, "I rather like bad wine, one gets so bored with good wine." Perhaps the flippant verse could flick one weary of perfection. There was an American novel, *Out of the Hurly Burly*, that had some most popular rhymes of the kind.

You may know John Synge's play of *The Playboy*.[1] A man in that play tells of a man he knew who "went killing horses a great while till he ate the insides of a clock and died after". (The Irish pronounce the word AYTE. We pronounce it ETT, as in the poem:

> He went, just for fun
> Dressed up as a BUN
> And was ETT by a dog in the hall.

In this *Hurly Burly* book a journalist tried to brighten up the Obituary Notices: & wrote a poem about a little boy called Willie who ate all a mercurial thermometer:

> At Willie's funeral, Willie's Mother
> Smartly said to Mrs Brown,
> 'Twas a chilly day for Willie
> When the mercury went down.

There were half a dozen others, irresistible to the young, like the heartless Gilbert ballad of the cannibal who ate the crew of the *Nancy* brig. (It was one of Gilbert's first; and *Punch* refused it: so it went to *Punch*'s rival *Fun*, where most of Gilbert's best ballads appeared.)

¹ John Millington Synge (1871–1909). His best-known play, *The Playboy of the Western World* was first performed in 1907.

188

. . . I have been reading Cervantes again, & hope to be able to read a lot of him this time.

It is strange: I do not feel the greatness of the plots & the power of the telling, as formerly, when they laid me low: but I feel more & more the greatness of the man & the power of his spirit: & the privilege & also, perhaps, a little of the terror, of being such a one.

Perhaps the terror is that of being brought into that time with him, when all men had seen men & women burned, when pestilences walked by noonday, & every alley hid its murder & every parish its gallows.

One of his best stories is of a lunatic of jealousy, whose household is beset by a young poet, supposedly one who really lived; & died by gallows.

Then, there is in Spain somewhere, a legal parchment or decree saying that one Myguel Zarbantes (whom some take to be Cervantes) is condemned (in his absence) to lose his right hand (with public shaming) for having given certain wounds to Antonio of Sigura (& perhaps for contempt of court): but as MZ was not there presumably he was not publicly shamed & kept his right hand.

Then it is certain that in his old age, Cervantes was living in Valladolid talking at night with a young priest indoors, when someone making music in the street was suddenly set upon (probably a lover serenading a lady) and there were oaths, cries, the clash of swords, then shouts & alarms, a groan, & flying footsteps. Miguel Cervantes, an old soldier, and the young priest, Don Luis de Garisbay went out to find Don Gaspar of Espeleta, a noble, wearing his page's mantle over his orders, lying dying in the street. The watch came up, & the dying Don Gaspar said that it was all his own fault, that he had begun it, & that the other fellow, his killer, had been a perfect gentleman . . .

189

... I never saw your trick of the ring & the letters:[1] but when I was little I used sometimes to hang a sixpence (if I ever had one or could borrow one) on a thread, & hold it suspended over an empty tumbler. For a while, the hanging 6d was still: but often, after a while, it would quiver, & would then, it really would then (sometimes) twitch against the glass & *strike the nearest hour*. It did this more often than not, but it was often a very laggardly beginner. It may be some faculty akin to "divining" for water with a hazel fork. I expect that you have done this. It works fairly well with me: & it is very queer, for one cannot control it, the hazel leaps in the hand.

[1] This was a fortune-telling game, in which letters of the alphabet were laid in a circle, and a ring held over them on a thread. As the ring moved, a message might be spelt out.

1958

190

... My grateful thanks again for telling me of your progress in *The Warden* & in *Don Quixote*.

The Warden is the first of the Barchester series: & one of the best of the Trollope novels, being such a perceptive study of a fine man. When you finish *The Warden*, the *next* is *Barchester Towers*, the most famous of them all; & the *Last Chronicles*. But I see that you will like Trollope and there are so many others that you will enjoy: some very good ones, indeed, just fringing on the Barchester society, & others of political life, of hunting people; of Irish life (some of these last superb & terrible) and studies of characters, men & women, admirably seen & understood, with a knowledge & a certainty & a range that all writers must respect.

One does not go to him for poetry or for passion, but for the virtues & failings of the great Victorian middle-class.

Barchester, the place, is said to be wholly imaginary; but its distance from London would suit Salisbury (or Winchester or Canterbury) and some have written that the whole clerical series was suggested by a visit to Salisbury.

I do not know the truth of the matter. He drew a map of the imagined district, I believe. No doubt he had a very clear picture of it all in his mind: and O how he wd have loved Reyna for longing to hug Mrs Grantly.

... Continue with Don Q: presently he will come back home from errantry, & go out again, leaving almost wholly the satirical mocking of the Middle Age & proceeding nobly, grandly & with triumphal beautiful power into the declaration of the splendour of the Renaissance mind that had employed Titian to the full, had created Cervantes and was even then about to mould Velasquez.

The latter half of *Don Q* . . . Golly, my beloved, think what it was to have written the first half, & then to have stridden forward into a paradise never trodden: as WS did when he flung away *Henry V* & away to *Twelfth Night, Julius Caesar, Macbeth*.

And golly again, my beloved, Cervantes was a slave for years, & could have been bought for money in a market place, & branded & burned, & gaunched upon a hook, & chained to a bench to row, and beaten & spat upon.

Cordoba is near much great grassy land, where many horses must of old have been bred, as cattle still are: but no doubt there are still mares enough to give Rozinante strange thoughts of youth.

In the grassy great high prairie there, white cranes of exquisite beauty come down from Heaven like birds of God, & again presently take wing for Heaven, like spirits of blessing. The incredible beauty of these.

In the city there is a great Moorish mosque, now the Cathedral, surely one of the wonders man has made.

✻

191

. . . My grateful thanks for your letter, & for the good news that DH[1] is now shelved, & out of harm's way.

There are always hawk-men, Bedouins, misfits, the world's defiants. Usually the world hangs them quite soon, but in old societies the world does not hang them: they take charge: & bring the old societies into ruin, & the cities into ashes.

This is happening now: little gangs of defiants have upset Russia, France, Italy, etc etc, & had a good hard try at Spain, where the valour of a few devoted men put a stop to them.

Rome, of old, was upset by such gangs of wild misfits, who attracted other misfits, & brought all that achieved majesty into the dust again. They filled these islands with murder, rapine, ignorance, & continual, petty war for about $7\frac{1}{2}$ consecutive centuries, during which nothing of permanence was created except the boundary of Offa's Dyke, which was much less remarkable than the Roman lines of 500 years before.

While DH was living by robbing hard-working men, Keats & Shelley (among others of near his age) were doing otherwise, & using the language differently, & coming thereby to other places in human hearts.

. . . Do you know the *Exemplary Novels*[2] by Cervantes? They are the same kind of late exquisite Renaissance imagination, done with such skill, power & tenderness, and in a prose beyond all dream.

Will you read "The Jealous Husband"? It seems to have happened thus in Seville, when C was often there, when it was the seaport for the Indies, & full of the misfits & defiants of all Spain. It will show you how stern a thing life in Spain might then be.

[1] *The Life of David Haggart*, Edinburgh, 1821. Haggart, "alias John Wilson, alias John Morrison, alias Barney McCoul, alias John McColgan, alias Daniel O'Brien, alias The Switcher", was a young man who led a life of varied crime and was eventually hanged. See Letter 145.

[2] A collection of twelve stories, some written much later than others, and of very uneven quality, but containing some of Cervantes' best work. It was published in 1613.

192

... It is a pity that the sun did not shine for you five years ago,[1] for then you would have seen the river shining, & far away (half a mile about) the site of the little Roman town, now under the grass, to the R of the winter sunset.

It is now 5 years since you were in the room here, or in the hall, looking for the Pyrate book. It is a happy memory, and that bulb, that lit you to the Pyrate book, is still giving light (being very seldom used) & I am going now to turn it on again, wishing that you were there to have the book.

I have now turned it on, and seen the books you saw the backs of, Stevenson, Galsworthy, & books of the sea . . . .

If you were here tonight, you should have another book of the sea: the best I have: & would look out on the great wide valley, once mostly under water, & now under the last of the light, under an array of cloud looking (to me) very like snow before morning.

... I never saw any of the Victorian dandies: they were gone before my time: but I have seen pictures of some of them: the men, plainly, wearing stays, & rings *outside their gloves*, & shoulder pads, and calf pads, & trowsers so tight that plainly they *had* to be lifted up by 2 valets, & dropped into them, while 2 other valets held them (the trowsers) open to catch them. Just after the first war, I saw two loathsome little men who wore stays. I'm afraid I do not know how the old dandies got out of their trowsers. I suppose the valets held them upside down till they dropped out . . .

There was an old novel, I forget which, in which a real buck was ordering trowsers at his tailor's, and saying "Mind, now, if I can get into them I'll send them back." (He meant "unaided".)

. . . The *Pamir* enquiry seems to have ended, as you will see[2] but I cannot (nor can anyone) know what happened, for the accounts carefully omit the course she was trying to steer, & the compass point of the wind (and the steadiness or shifting of the wind)— these are vital points, & supposedly we are not to have them: & therefore we have to wonder the more.

As to undermanned: she had 86 able-bodied lads & young men on board, more than twice the crew of a ship of her size 70 years ago.

[1] This letter was written on 20th January, the fifth anniversary of JM's meeting with ANS.

[2] JM enclosed with the letter a cutting from *The Times*, 6th January: "The official enquiry into the Pamir disaster opened in the 13th century Rathaus of Lübeck today. The four-masted barque, a training ship for merchant service cadets, sank in the South Atlantic last September in a hurricane. There were only six survivors. The six young survivors are among the 25 witnesses to be called."

193

. . . Thank you for telling me of your progress in the *Exemp. Nov.*[1] There are 12 or 15 of these (6 or 7 more than in your 2 little books) & I am now reading them in Spanish (for the first time.) "The Jealous Husband" is a Seville story: it is said to have occurred when Cervantes was often in Seville, & there is a book that tries to prove (but fails I wd say) that the Loaysa of the tale was a wild young poet who was hanged (at the age of 23) for murder there.

It is an appalling tale in a way: the man could buy white slaves and brand them in the face.

There is no such prose anywhere in the world. When C is really moved he is surpassing.

I keep thinking: was John Fletcher in Spain? Did he meet Cervantes? Did he tell WS about Cervantes? Was it he who suggested Cardenio[2] as a theme to WS? They wrote it together you know, & the play is lost; & what a loss.

Do read "Lady Cornelia", for Fletcher wrote a play on that, as he did on "The Deceitful Marriage", making *The Chances* out of one & *Rule a Wife & Have a Wife* of the other.

[1] See Letter 191.

[2] In *Don Quixote*: the lover who is driven mad by the loss of his beloved Lucinda.

194

. . . A man wrote in *The Times* the other day that Trollope's Publisher or Editor wrote to him about the MS of *Barchester Towers*, complaining that he, T, had described a clergyman as having a "great" or "big" stomach, & that such a phrase would seem disrespectful to the clergy; & that T had therefore changed the word to "a deep chest".

Did you come upon the phrase? Was it the Archdeacon, or the Bishop? It could not have been Arabin or Harding—& I have not found the passage.

195

. . . Did you, as a child, come upon the writings of one Hawley Smart?[1]

Perhaps he is now little known, but once, ah, once, 70 good years ago, when the Baronet was biting his fingers raw from anxiety, & Polly was white from terror as she clutched her father's arm, & the horses swept into the straight with the Rollinger colt shut in far back, & Blue Nose Bill with a look of triumph on his evil face, came away upon the favourite . . . & the roar of the assembled thousands yelled its ecstasy: "The favourite wins . . . the favourite for a monkey . . . the favourite w..w . . ."

But what was that, far back, that flash of chestnut, under a blue & white silk . . .?

What? What? What?

O can it be?

(Well, it generally was . . .)

Looking at the above, it occurs to me that long since, when someone told K George III that some eminent soldier had been killed in the War in America (the War of Independence) the K is said to have ejaculated: "What? What? What? Shot? Shot? Shot?"

But these tales of the great are usually invented by the Mocker, to divert the Idle, as I so often warn you.

[1] Hawley Smart, a once popular novelist who published twenty-five books between 1870 and 1890.

196

. . . Please let me thank you again for your wonderful account of the Centenary Concert.[1] I have been to something of the kind, & a part of the wonder, & the emotion, was the opening of parcels, left 100 years before to be opened by us, unknown, unborn, who were to celebrate the day. It was like your C note in your overture, it rather took one by the throat.

. . . People write much nonsense about the *Pamir*'s manning.[2] When I was young, every sailing ship we had was undermanned: the usual allowance was one fo'c's'le hand for every 100 tons on the register: & of those fo'c's'le hands only 1 or 2 would be really good: most would be Germans learning English, or Norwegians learning the sea, or a few hard-case packet-rats & escaping criminals, with 6 or 8 boys, under 17, as make-weights.

The old allowance for the *Pamir* would be 30 or 31 in the fo'c's'les, 2 sailmakers, 2 boatswains, 2 carpenters (2 wireless) 3 mates, 8 boys & a captain, & with this she would have been reckoned grossly overmanned & 5 or 6 would never have been shipped.

As it was she probably had all of these, a doctor, 2 stewards & 33 lads from 15–18, each a picked lad able to pull his weight on a rope & do a man's work; such a crew as no ship of the old days ever dreamed of having.

. . . Thank you for so kindly answering my question about T. Smollett.

He was never a sea-captain. As a boy of 15–17 he had some (considerable) training as a medical student in Glasgow University. Then he took to writing, came to London, aged about 18 or 19, I think, & found that London did not like his writing.

We were at war with Spain (Jenkin's Ear war, I think it was) & he got a berth as a surgeon's mate in a man of war, & went out to the unspeakable siege of Cartagena:[3] surely one of the very worst of the unspeakable wars in which our imbecility & complacency of callousness have been displayed to the utmost under the worst possible conditions. (On the Spanish Mainland, the N of S America.)

To myself, the best thing he ever wrote is a brief damnation of the wickedness & folly of the high command there: but he also later wrote something of the savage life on board ship, in one of his novels, & something of marine character in a second novel. The description in the one book, & these sea characters, give TS a high place in our marine literature, a real place, but the men are not pleasing & the life described is truly appalling: in some ways more evil than the life described by John Atkins in some of his *History of the Pyrates* of happy memory.

. . . I am reading an *Exem. Nov.* about 2 young thieves (Nooky Nick & Little Snip Snap) who are undergraduates in a thieves' university in Seville, & are present at the Company's concert, when the leading man & leading lady make peace after a disastrous quarrel. It reminds one (a very little) of the great tavern scenes in *Henry IV Part Two*; much the same power, but not the same spirit. I judge that the priests made Cervantes change some of it (like Trollope with the deep chest). But I judge, too, that John Fletcher knew the tale, & kept it in his mind for years.

[1] The Hallé's Centenary Concerts bridged the New Year.

[2] The very long letter (not printed here) which followed this one took the form of a detailed essay on the sinking of the *Pamir*, which may not be of general interest; it is illuminating, however, in that it shows to what great lengths JM's thirst for knowledge, knowledge of any kind, would lead him.

[3] Tobias Smollett (1721–71), the surgeon, novelist (and a translator of *Don Quixote*) was surgeon's mate to John Atkins—thought by JM to be the author of *The History of the Pyrates*—on the man-of-war, the *Chichester*. The attack on Cartagena took place in 1741.

197

... I have been trying to find out for you about the mares of Cordoba, that cause such excitement in *Don Quixote*.

In Cervantes' time, they were probably still the most wonderful horses in the world, "the Cordoba strain", supposedly a cross between Arab stallions from Arabia, with the native stock: itself probably a relic of the Arabian, or semi-Arabian, stock left by the Moors.

It is thought that the horse in Titian's great picture of *The Lances* & that ridden by Charles the Vth in Titian's great portrait, represent the horse of Cordoba as he was, a very beautiful, compact creature, full of nerve & fire & endurance: a tireless lovely thing, such as carried Cortes in Mexico.

The type is said to be extinct now.

The French invasion of Spain in 1808 may have been the cause, for it lasted for 6 years, during which any good horse was at once seized for one or other of the French armies; and the colts seized too young; the stallions very likely sent to France, & the brood-mares not cared for, save by cavalry commanders, who seem to have been more intent on making hay for themselves than for gathering hay for brood-mares (even if there were any hay).

As I write of these things, I remember what a race-horse owner told me, many years ago. A friend of his sent a good racing mare to a good, but not surpassing stallion thinking that the match would bring a noble colt.

In the mating, in the culminating instant, the stallion died from sudden heart failure, and fell from the mare dead, but from the life so flung the mare conceived and bore a colt, which men were then watching with interest and care.

I heard vaguely, later, that the colt though good was never greatly successful: but the tale is strange.

The poet, Ovid, wished to die like that, but, alas, I think he died broken-hearted in exile, away at the back of beyond in the Black Sea.

198

. . . I liked your tale of the famous musician being asked if he liked horses.

There is a living poet who, as a subaltern in the Army, was asked that question by a General: "What? Eh? Fond of horses, are you?"

"No, Sir," he replied. "But I adore giraffes."

You will have heard that old story I fear, as I fear you will have heard the tale of the Lady who, to her great joy, found herself sitting next to Tennyson at lunch somewhere, & thought "Ah, now I shall hear wisdom from his sacred lips: now I shall know Beauty of Soul, and hear something to remember for ever:

> To remember for years
> To remember with tears.

But the only thing T said to her was one comment on receiving a slice of mutton. He said:

"Mutton should be cut in HUNKS."

(It is one of the three sayings of T now remembered, of all his conversations.)

. . . You ask me in your gentle way, do I think of my readers? I think of you, & you are one, & I have known others, now gone, & I think of them still, but few writers know more than 2 or 3 of their readers, so most of them do little sums.

English reading people in the world	300,000,000
People who read me	3
People who write criticisms of me	4

You will see, that these sums tend to check the swelling of the head that men are prone to.

199

. . . I liked your tale of the pair of horses that leaped a harrow over a fence.

Did not the mad John Mytton,[1] while driving a pair horse conveyance, a chaise or whatever it was called, make the horses take a turnpike gate? I think he did: & the horses got over but the chaise didn't: so there they hung.

RBCG[2] had a horse for 35 years, I think, & surely two well over 20.

You will remember RBCG's story "A Hegira" about the Apaches in Mexico? The story, or some of it, happened, & he saw the prisoners before the escape, & the last man killed, & the poor little dog: all this long ago, of course, 80 years perhaps. But 3 of the men & the woman were not killed, but seem to have reached the Apache country safely.

But when RBCG wrote, he had seen much frontier life, where debased whites (on every frontier) were ousting primitive dwellers, just as now the primitive dwellers are ousting the debased whites.

He was on the side of the native dweller, though he had some close shaves (I judge) from being scalped or scuppered by him.

I do not doubt that the 3 Apaches who got away took toll of the frontiersmen thereafter, with tough effect . . . .

About 40 years back, I was in Waco [Texas] which had been (20 years before) a pretty wild cow-town, where the cowboys shot out the lights at night. Cowboys were gone like the Indians, and there is a big University, with a marvellous special museum in honour of an English poet, Robert Browning, his books, letters, portraits, MSS (it seemed). I cannot tell you how this touched me.

You may not have been in Waco. It rhymes with Awake O, & it is a Wide Awake O burg all right. It would make you sing Bach's "Sleepers Awake", even in the Summer.

And, please, when you sing, do you sing contralto? I hope that even in this cold you sing sometimes.

[1] "Mad Jack" Mytton—a renowned English eccentric.

[2] Robert Bontine Cunninghame Graham (1852–1936), among other things a writer and traveller. He knew especially well the remote corners of the interior of South America, and the life led by gauchos.

200

. . . I thought your voice would be mezzo [it is]. Why did you not sing to me?

When I drove cars (now forbidden) I used to sing on Roman Roads that I knew very well, straight roads with all the turns familiar, & a mile clear at a time. Then I would speed up to 40 or 45 & with the noise of the engine, no-one could hear, then, & then only, I would sing, O marvellous perished ditties, about

> Jousting at Aspramont & Asphodel,
> Mombasa & Quiloo & Melind,
> And proude Bayard ginning for to skyppe.

. . . Long since, I knew a man who was much with Red Indians in the Far West. He said that in the day times he could do things that the Indians couldn't, but that at night by the camp fires, the Indians would put their feet into the fires, pick up a blazing twig or so with their toes, & give him a light for his pipe. They used then to grin, & say, "You kain't do that, Boss."

. . . I send you some US stamps of Cranes, such as those divine birds on the great grass at Cordoba. They are almost extinct birds now in the US but people are now striving to preserve them there, & have hopes of this.

We, in England, some 30 years ago, tried to re-introduce Storks here: but it was done on a tiny scale, & then dropped. We have, however, preserved the Bittern & the Hoopoe as English breeding species.

. . . I also send you a magazine about [Oscar] Wilde, in case it should interest you. I think you like some of his work.

Men who knew OW have told me that the Du Maurier drawing of him in this paper is exactly OW as he then was. (G du M drew him in *Punch* several times.)

201

. . . A man who was up at Oxford with OW (though not in the same College, & not quite the same years) has described him as he was then (1873–1874?): ". . . leaning his large & flabby form against the door . . . conspicuous for something unusual in his dress, still more for his splendid head, his mass of black hair, his vivacious eyes, his poet's forehead, and a mouth like a shark's in formlessness & appetite."

An American described him to me as he was a year or two later when visiting the US: "I saw him walking up Broadway carrying a lily. He was a fine figure of a man, but I am told he has gone bloated since."

Another American, who saw him at this time, has also described him to me as "very handsome".

Like many men living in towns before the days of Sandow's exercisers, he became unwholesomely stout. Men have told me that the prison starvation made him more presentable: but he did not survive it for long.

It is hard to say where to begin about him: but perhaps this, of his outward appearance, may make a beginning.

You will probably have read more of him than I have, & have seen some of the many books about him. He has been vilely praised, vilely maligned, lied about, misquoted, outcast, adored. For years, the half & quarter wits of the gutter & the carrion press have forged tales of him & spread them abroad. These are repeated, like jests in his manner. Who can now tell what of truth they had? The wits have been busy, too, pointing such tales.

As to his failing. At that time it was supposed to affect (from birth) about 2 men in every 100 men. It was regarded with a savage horror then. Now, it is said to be more frequent & to be less savagely regarded.

In Nelson's Navy & for long afterwards, it was punished by death; but it could hardly have been practised in a ship, where the whole of life is lived in absolute publicity.

I read one Court Martial upon an old Warrant Officer (about 1800). He was condemned to be hanged for it, but it was clear to me that he was as mad as a hatter (& drunk, too, at the moment) & I could not suppose that an Admiral would have confirmed the sentence: but I could not be sure: the fleet may have needed an example.

Men have often told me of the scenes of devilish joy in London streets on the night of OW's sentence.

I was then in America, but there the righteous horror took the form of giving every publicity to the trial, & the casting out of all his books from every library. At the same time his works were cheaply printed, 2½d or 5 cents a volume.

I send some rough jottings about OW, on 4 sheets, numbered 1–8 (being written on both sides).

I think that you have summed him up very shrewdly in your very wise way.

It used to be told, very likely quite falsely, that a lady once said to him, "Mr Wilde, I do so deeply regret that the difference between our sexes makes everything but Platonic affection between us quite impossible."

Generally speaking, you are right as the Frenchman (de Buffon) in the vital point: "Le style est l'homme même"—"The style is the man himself speaking."

It is there, in every work of art, the very man, with all the weakness, the falsity, the power & the glory.

Generally the sex in an artist is his impulse to life, to beauty, to all generosities & givings & forgivings. It seems to have run in Shakespeare like a sea, in Keats like a river of the South, & in Shelley like a moonlight cataract.

※

202

... You asked me, in your last week's letter, how much does the body affect the mind. The mind can usually direct it, more or less, as it is the only direction the body has, save for Custom & Decree. Often, the body can poison, warp, distort, or nullify the mind. At its best, the body exalts & exults, to make the mind exultant & exalted. Where Custom is noble & Decree exalted the mind will then do glorious things. Where Custom & Decree are debased the mind may then denounce them & be destructive.

You ask, also, where does Good end? It does not end. Evil does not end, either, until it has been made good.

May I say, at this point, that in writing of OW I did not meet men who had known him till he was 5 or 6 years fallen (a few days before his death in fact).

All sorts of legends had sprung up in those years. All literature was under a cloud still, but at about that time, greatly daring, George Alexander began to revive the plays. It needed some daring: & was rewarded.

Those whom I knew (men & women) who had known him (about 14 I think) must (some of them) have known some vital points about the trial, but these were those whom I knew least & could not question.

It is clear that for years the failing was known & talked of in London. The evidence against him was to be had right & left. It may well be that his enemies had collected it before the downfall. (This has been said by some.)

I have heard (& it seems likely) that the aim of his enemies was to drive him out of England; nothing more; for no-one wanted the scandal of the criminal case. They thought that he would go to live in France: anyhow, out of England.

In your wise letter about him, you put your wise finger on the point.

There was an unreality: & up against a reality, a point of law, a matter of evidence, the unreality broke down.

One told me that his Counsel withdrew him from speech as much as possible at the trial, because he had so deplorable an effect upon the jury.

Perhaps 9 tenths of the gossip is false. I only heard gossip & memory: & some of the memory I cannot be too sure of, remember.

203

... Alas for the sadness.[1] Life begins & ends in a personal helplessness that can only exist by the mercy & sacrifice of others.

Destinies are ordained by a Justice, an Order, & a Power that we can only dimly apprehend: & to some life may seem hell, to others purgatory, to some a chance to touch Paradise, to enter Paradise, to clean all evil away with mercy, pity, peace, to give away one's very self, to be nothing, so that others may be something; and to hope on, & even find a cheer to give, even in heart-break house, even in death.

I can only give words; you are giving life, you are doing deeds, blessing, helping, saving. That is real life, that is living in the imagination, that is beauty, honour, glory. I've none of these, but I can praise them, seeing them in you.

Do not doubt that great spirits also see them, & are by you to help you, ever ever ever all about you.

[1] This letter concerns the long illness of ANS's mother.

204

... I am wondering whether you care at all for the writings of Benjamin Disraeli, the first Lord Beaconsfield. Please, some day, will you say?

Perhaps "Dizzy" is now somewhat forgotten (like so much of Victorian time) but, to the Victorian of the last years, he was a milestone, or post of honour, a man who was a Jew, yet took all England & ruled her: a politician who was yet a wit, a real wit; & a writer, who, after triumphing in affairs, triumphed as a writer, in a time of great writers; & was original, too, as a maker of new fiction, that was the social history of the age he had adorned.

Sometimes, men have thought that perhaps Oscar Wilde had him in mind as one to be imitated or exceeded: but I have never heard this from those who knew OW. One of those told me that the Emperor Nero was the model there . . . .

But always distrust these tales. What is known as Little London is often very little, & very full of idle & lying lips.

But tell me of Dizzy, please, will you, some day, when you have a moment & the mood. Perhaps, often, I may tempt you into morasses of writing wherein your nice mind flounders, & you wish I wouldn't.

. . . Many years ago, being in Normandy, I used to go to little lonely sea-coast churches. In nearly every one there would be votive model ships, made by sailors who had escaped from watery tombs in them.

Many of the models were very well made, but the ships undoubtedly vile, and the escape of the seamen marvellous. They might well be grateful to have escaped.

I used to look at these things, & try to date them, getting first the decade, then trying to get nearer to the year, by what I knew of the changes in the rigging. Sometimes the models had been repaired 20 years after the first hanging-up, & repaired with modern cottons & strings: & always made worse.

205

. . . My thanks to you for telling me of Disraeli, & for your story of him (quite new to me).

I want to send you a book by him: the best of him: when I can find it. He remained an Oriental figure to the end, I would suppose, but he was a very great Victorian; & one of our great novelists, with a reasoned, wide, considered sense of the directors of our (Victorian) societies, but from their point of view, that is now out-moded & indeed now unthinkable, but it was working then, though ferments were working in it.

. . . So you were in Lincoln's Inn . . . I, too, long since.

When I first went to London, I looked up many Dickens' sites. The Old Curiosity Shop[1] was near there: & some of the places in *Bleak House* & *Edwin Drood*.

And in Lincoln's Inn, there used to be Sir Hans Sloane's Museum,[2] with some Hogarth paintings, & the skeleton of the famous horse Eclipse, and the skull of Jonathan Wild,[3] the infamous dog about whom Fielding wrote the marvellous novel. Do you know the marvellous novel?

JW was (rightfully) hanged at Tyburn at long last & an unknown poet wrote a glad poem on the occasion.

"The bowmen that's out on the lay
They do rejoice now at this Day."

The bowmen were not archers, but just outdoor thieves, such as pick-pockets, & "on the lay" was simply "lying in wait", for what Sir F. Drake called "a little comfortable dew of Heaven".

Eclipse, the horse, was foaled on the Downs near here; & the strings of those stables often delight me, as I go by.

(The bowmen rejoiced, by the way, because JW had often informed on their friends, & caused them to be hanged: perhaps Dickens had a thought of JW, or Fielding's masterpiece, when he created Fagin.)

Close to the Inn, long since, were some appalling rookeries, now gone; & also such old bookshops as one dreams of still: the 18th century at a penny a vol; & little Rembrandt & Dürer engravings in the 2d box.

[1] In Portsmouth Street, London WC2, where it still may be seen.

[2] JM is here confusing Sir Hans Sloane (who owned much of Chelsea) with Sir John Soane, the English architect (of the Bank of England, among other buildings). The Soane Museum still stands in Lincoln's Inn, and is open to the public.

[3] Wild ran a large and well organised gang of thieves. He was hanged at Tyburn in 1725. See also Letter 338.

※
๏

206

. . . I thank you for so kindly adding a leaf to the celebration of your birthday.

I trust that some of it was fun to you, but I fear that the rush to London & a big concert in the evening could not have been peaceful.

So early in the month as the 2nd, not having the Hallé list by then, I knew not where to aim for you: so aimed at Manchester, & had the grave discourtesy of turning my back upon you, & my gentlest thoughts amiss.

I fear that you were having a dreadful time, going hurriedly to London on Cup Day with all Bolton & half Manchester in the train, all very friendly, no doubt, but too many on each seat, & all offering you a bun, a lollipop or a cigarette, perhaps all at once: *embarras de richesse.*

This day the Hallé list is here, & I can read of your Tour to Poland and back, & begin to imagine you driving all those unknown roads. "Eastward, ever Eastward, t'wards the rising of the sun".

With a right-hand drive on a left-hand road too . . . . You will be at Linz, a big, busy City on the (I hope) blue Danube: & you may be very tired, or very, very busy, or so excited & happy & glad & fêted that you will have no moment [to think of him on his birthday, 1st June].

You will be on Continental Time there, I suppose, a clear hour earlier than ours. In astronomical exact seaman's longitude time you would be about 52 minutes earlier than ours.

So let it not be a bother: only a prospect. My thought will be at your heart very often all the time you are away, & will be outside, understanding, when the doors are closed.

. . . You kindly said that you would take *Rod^k Random* abroad with you.

He is the work of a fairly tough & rough-mouthed man; but you may feel sure that the tough & rough-mouthed chapters about naval life (when you come to them) are true; & the abuses of power, & the incompetence of privileged but crazy persons, in authority, are shown as they were, & as they have been since.

Smollett is angry at what angers; & for 1 ounce of injured vanity of him, there is a power of righteous indignation. He saw a frightful thing, & said that it was frightful.

The Cartagena Campaign[1] was the kind of thing that makes one shudder: but it happened; & words cannot tell its greater horrors; but it has been repeated more than once "in our island's story", & similar horrors, on greater scales, have had more awful being.

[1] See Letter 196.

❦

207

You are a real writer, a lovely writer, with a live bright pair of eyes, & all that power of being quickly & deeply touched that make your impressions so true & dear . . . .

I thought your letter about it [the Hallé Orchestra's East European Tour] wonderful. Your account of the crowds, the tempers, the change of currencies, the children, the people, the old & new buildings & the Warsaw ruins, all the applause there, were all inimitably put there for me. Who cares where Chopin's heart lies? I am shocked unspeakably that, like Thomas Hardy's heart, it is not with his sacred ashes . . . But I was touched by your heart, & your swift living, loving response to the woman at Prague. If you should be in touch with her, do you think it would get her into trouble if books & papers went to her from England: if such would help her when she has to sweep roads? Books & papers might well be utter ruin to her. Both are here for her, if you should think it safe, & would send them . . .?

I was in Nazi Ger^y before the 2nd War, for a brief three visits: short spells in hell: there were telephone traps in my rooms then: & there were the damned trembling, the devils exulting, & on them that hoped, the death-camp.

One thing I know now, "The luck will alter, & the star will rise."

The wheel is forever turning: & the change comes:

> The end men looked for cometh not
> There is a path where no man sought

—for Zeus stewards many things in Olympus, & Justice never sleeps.

I was thinking this last night: how Robespierre at the Terror seemed established, as a part of France: all powerful all over France: he had but to say Death, & Death fell. Then, in one day, it was all over: he was gone, & his system was gone: his creatures down.

At the long last the cup brims: there comes the change.

208

. . . Please, will you tell me, do you care for Browning's poems? You cannot, of course, care for him as we did, but do you know a famous poem of his: *A Toccata of Galuppi's*? And do you play Galuppi ever? (I suppose a Venetian composer for the clavichord 1660–1750??)[1]

It is one of my favourite poems: & I find that I can still say it by heart, if I lie awake.

[1] Baldassare Galuppi, Venetian composer of operas and a noted harpsichordist. His dates are later than JM thought: 1706–85.

209

. . . The ones[1] taken out of doors were taken in March (I think) when the rooks were building. Rooks are indefatigable toilers when they build, & as pirates they rival Capts Teach & Roberts. They pounce on any unguarded nest for any nice twig that can be wrenched out & taken.

But I may have been looking at spotted woodpeckers great or small, for both sorts, both very beautiful, are frequent here.

. . . I am glad that you like the Pornic poem.[2] He [Browning] stayed at Pornic [Brittany] more than once, I believe) & did a 2nd tale (about its odd link with Voltaire) in his later days, very readable but less poetical.

You were right not to like the "Epilogue"[3] much, & right as your true good soul to like colour. All the excitement of Nature's year is in colour.

And you are right as your dear heart to trust your dear heart about poetry. If you don't like it, upon reading it, put it away: a mind knows what its food is & chooses with a personal direction, its wisdom, which is its guide in life.

RB was able to model, & paint, & play music, read music, & had a mine of odd knowledge in him; & had a knowledge, too, of all Italian history & art. He meant very much to us when we were young: & then, his verse had a roughness on the tongue irresistible after so much Tennyson & his people seemed real after so much tripe; anyhow they had brains.

[1] JM had sent ANS some fine photographs taken at Burcote, mostly in the garden.

[2] "The Pornic poem" is Browning's "Gold hair: a Story of Pornic".

[3] First published in a 3 volume collection of Browning's poems in 1863.

210

. . . What fun for you to meet old friends, "vingt ans après", & one who had known Brahms.

One sometimes met men who remembered the past great ones.

I met a man, who had met a lady, who had seen Shelley (he being then un-married).

"What would you do, Mr Shelley, if you had all these children?" This is rather a staggerer for a bachelor, but the poet in him rose upon glittering wings:

"Do with them?" he cried. "I'd shut them into a room, with tubs of water & bowls of oranges."

Then I met a man who had met 3 men who had known Keats, & had no new thing from any one of them; & I met a man (among several such) who had known Wm Morris and said, "It was a treat to hear him swear."

I once met a lady who had heard Dickens at one of his matchless readings. She said that nothing in her life could compare with it for frantic laughter & uncontrollable tears. Mr Marigold, Mrs Gamp, Bill Sykes doing his murder & trying to get away: I fear, too, Little Nell: & I hope, too, the School-boy's Story.

211

. . . When I wrote to you about those who had met the famous of old, I forgot one whom I saw frequently, long since, who had known, intimately, one who had known the Lambs, Hazlitt, Keats, the Hunts, even Coleridge; & had I then known, and asked, I might have been able to write to tell you about all of these, some little personal things that would make them seem real, more real than even the cleverest book. As a famous detective wrote (not our friend Mr Holmes), "A bad description is better than a good photograph."

212

. . . I remember that long ago a clever caricaturist who was always jotting down odd faces in pencil on his cuffs as he walked in London, jotted down a startled face one day, & remembered it, as it had had a look such as he had not seen. Next day, he read that a murder had been done near by the place where he had seen the face; & going to the police, he told his tale & showed his cuff, & the man was traced, & *was* the murderer.

I read (I hope it was true) that he received £100 reward, for his readiness & imagination. The rest of the tale was confirmed to me as strictly true.

Now, of course, men do not wear cuffs when walking about London, & murder is so frequent that it is not much regarded, but O when I was young, when clever men recited: "The dream of Eugene AHHRAMM"[1] (that is how it was pronounced).

We knew & were often reminded, how dread a thing murder is.

[1] Eugene Aram (nothing to do with the caricaturist's murderer) was a Yorkshire schoolmaster, who was tried and executed at York in 1759 for the murder of a man called Clarke. Thomas Hood's poem "The Dream of Eugene Aram" was printed in 1829, and in 1832 Bulwer-Lytton published his novel *Eugene Aram*.

213

. . . What a pity that the rain fell so heavily at Cheltenham: there are lovely places nearby, that I hoped you would be able to see & delight in.

I read that, not far away, some local lunatic drove at midnight taking pot-shots at people's windows with a shotgun & also a rifle. I trust he did not waken you. He did not kill anybody, but was sober enough to hit the windows.

Long ago, in some of the old cow-towns in Texas, the people told me how the cowboys, in their earlier days, 20 years before my visit, would ride thro the town at whiles, shooting at all the lights, so that it was wiser to sit on the floor, & in the dark, till the outfits had all left for camp.

⁂

214

. . . So many thanks to you for your charming letter about the Maori & the singing bones.[1]

When one lives (even for a short while) in primitive lands, one shrinks, to some extent, from the life of the modern town thenceforward. A greater, inner, more marvellous life (in some ways terrifying, in others glorifying) is made apparent. Certain eternal things move & speak & direct: is it not so?

There is a singing body (not bones only) in a barrow in one of the sagas: *Njala Saga.* A buried hero sings.

Alas, my Reyna, that you should think that "I know almost everything about you".

Men are not clever, and how few know.

I knew a seaman, with 30 years' experience, who was asked if he was up to all the dodges of the sea, ships & seamen. He said "No: but I'm learning."

In a dream once, I had a flash about something that hinted at the truth of something that had long been a puzzle to me . . . . The flash shewed me that the truth of the thing was quite inconceivably more glorious even than the glory I had imagined: an incredible glory: & I know now that all things must be incredibly more glorious than the unawakened mind supposes: & that sometimes, in life, whole centuries are in a kind of madness, awful on their bad side (as ours is) but in a wild quaking ecstasy on their good side (as ours mighty seldom is) and that then spirits walk & talk with men, & the bones sing, not only in the barrow or the bush, but in the intense live body.

About 10 miles from here there is a house where people used often to hear a little child crying. Some couldn't endure it, but others got used to it.

About 30 years ago, they were altering the house, & found that a little boy had been buried in the wall of a stair there: presumably after being murdered. After the bones had been buried [properly] the crying ceased.

It was thought that the murder must have taken place about 40 odd years before: (if it were murder).

Perhaps, even yet, before your holiday ends, you may have some sunshine, & be able to cook your nice person brown in the garden, lulled by the tick of your new clock.

I do not much mind rain, for it fills my well, but these westerly gales smite me good & solemn.

Alas, no, they don't for I am like Miss M. Fleming:[2] I may "Hope I will be religious again, but as for getting my character again I despare."

[1] In the far north of New Zealand, where there were few Europeans, ANS had heard of a Maori farmer who was having troubles on his farm. He appealed to his Chief, who came with the *Tohunga* (Medicine Man) and, on the farm, they found unburied human bones; and were able to find them because they *sang*. After the bones had been buried, the Maori had no further trouble.

[2] Marjory Fleming (1803–1811), a Scottish child prodigy known as "Pet Marjory". She wrote a diary (from which comes this quotation), a poem on Mary Queen of Scots, and some other verses.

215

... Please take my best wishes for the success of the new Hallé season.

Cheer up about the fiddle. Most people would give 2 fingers & 4 toes to be able to fiddle even the first 2 lines of "Alice Where art thou?" or "The Place where the old Horse Died." Do reflect that with a fiddle you could go into any wild haunt anywhere, & melt the maddest & the stoniest heart there in 17 seconds (less, in England) & I suppose 3 in Africa.

Surely you feel that power, don't you?

Please will you tell me *who* has been saying nice things about me on the wireless? I ought to thank. I have heard none of them.

I missed the North Pole talk: but a man came here last year who had lunched at the N Pole the day before. He was the first N Pole man I had met. He had found the dining room rather too warm, he said (or did I invent that?)—age is the deuce with memory.

Please tell me what you are wearing & reading, & thinking of. I am wearing my grey, & reading about Coast Erosion & thinking about you.

216

... My thanks for your most kind welcome letter, & for all your London news, of your happy times with Tim, & of your Concerts; (alas: I heard none of them: the week not being propitious); of the changes in the London scene; & of Sir John's[1] matchless handling of the audience in the Mozart.

The behaviour of audiences: the brutality: the imbecility, now one, then the other: then both: as the biggest beast or the silliest fool present takes charge (or unite for a moment).

Audiences perhaps are much the same as the political electorate, whose results are before us.

There is not much stirring in my addled brain that can yield delight to you this week, but O you will be shocked to hear that England is slowly tilting, as it were, on its axis, rising on its west side about an inch or even an inch & a ½ in a year, and sinking about the same on the east side.

You will be all right: don't worry: but here it is a different matter: in another 2,500 years, perhaps sooner, this will be under water, with the seamen heaving the lead on me.

But dry your natural tears, my swete, for in spite of this, it now seems certain that the Ice Cap is receding, not advancing, so that soon the polar bears will be getting darker, and the walrus thinner in the waist. This is itself much.

Then: although all America seems to be floating bodily westward it isn't going fast yet: the anchor still holds, & men need not range a spare cable yet.

So I can end on a hopeful note, dear loving beautiful friend, & feel that a rosy future waits you still, as all my old heart will ever hope for you, while it can beat.

All blessings, all joys, all gladness to you ever.

Jan

[1] Sir John Barbirolli, CH (1899–1970) was conductor of the Hallé Orchestra, Manchester, from 1943 to 1968; in the latter year, he was made Conductor Laureate for life.

217

... I was thrilled by your quick change at the rehearsal, but you had your Naval training: & I suppose you would change for Divisions, or such a matter, within a minute, from wash-deck-kit to Go Ashore togs.

It was a fine feat of yours to be there, all square by the lifts & braces, & the red side ropes rove, & the side manned: all in a minute, as "in the flash frigate, the frigate of fame".

I was a quick changer once: & could undress in 20 seconds, but my costume then was somewhat simpler.

Sir Henry Irving was the boy for a quick change. In *The Lyons Mail*, he had a great scene as the Villain, a fearful fellow, on the Actor's Right. He went off R into the wings, as a villain. He walked with a measured step round the back of the scene, passing 8 highly trained dressers, each of whom flung something off him or on to him or changed his make-up a little. He did not change his measured step, but walked on, and entered, Actor's Left, as the Innocent Man, a quiet gentleman, facially something like the Villain, but benign & well-dressed & lovable.

Now *all* the spectators would have sworn that he entered at the very instant that the Villain left. It was miraculous, HI was an impeccable artist; & that double part was unlike anything else I have ever seen in any play anywhere.

In real life, & in the original play (a French play) the benign man was sworn-to as the robber of the Mail, & was guillotined, but in the English play he was saved just in time, & the villain was guillotined instead.

The benign man was, facially, & in figure, something of the cut & build of the villain. I suppose, too, that he was subject to very summary justice.

Even in *Oliver Twist* (1838) Fagin is hanged six days after his arrest. The law did not delay in the cases of felony.

218

... Bohn died when I was young, & his work was of great benefit to me at the time & later. G. H. Bohn.[1]

He was an English publisher of German parentage, & brought up among books in that very booky time, from say, 1800–1884. I think that he collected rare books, when few were doing so, when you could find incunabula in every old attic, & rare quartos in every inn. Golly . . . a time & a half.

He used to collect these I think, & then hold auctions of them, & sell them himself. He printed catalogues of them, & I believe gave all the people at the sale lunch, tea, dinner & supper: & as only he knew the value of what he sold, or almost only he, he prospered, & began publishing the books that he felt were needed by the reading public; these publications were his "Library" or "Bohn's Classics"; an admirable choice of books, several hundreds on the list, 750 or so, 3/6 a vol. They were a cosmopolitan lot: Cellini, Commines, Ecclesiastical, Devout, Historical, Scientific, Literary, Geographical, Humanistic, Mediaeval: all sorts & times: and he was the first to do this. Arber, Dent, Penguin, were all followers in his steps. He did a great work in lifting Victorian England out of savagery.

Some of the many books are now superseded: others are no longer necessary: are dead now: but the bulk of them are standard works, & if you should see them in a shop, you will find the lists inside: & be astonished at their range & excellence. Some went up to 5/- a vol or even 7/6; & were in several vols: others were 2/6: 1/6: even 1/-.

I hope that he died rich, surrounded by rare books & works of art: I never met anyone who knew him.

. . . The *Gesta Romanorum*[2] is a Mediaeval Collection of tales added (rather late, I fancy) to Bohn's Antiquarian Section. A few of the stories are superb: & Bohn's re-printing of the book brought it back into favour.

[1] Bohn, Henry George (1796–1884), publisher of the "Guinea Catalogue" of old books, and of many "library" series, such as the "Standard", "Classical", "Scientific", "Antiquarian", etc.

[2] A collection of stories in Latin, romances of chivalry, legends of saints, not all relating to the Romans, but each carrying a moral, compiled in England and printed about 1472. An English translation was published some years later.

219

. . . My thanks for your gracious letter here on the 23rd.

I have been wondering, ever since it came, in what green fields you are now wandering, remote from posts, perhaps among pagans, still using woad instead of woollen, for I have not had a September Page of *Where to Hear the Hallé*. Either it is not printed, or it has not come; so here I am wondering: & you perhaps . . . .

Please, may I ask you to be so kind as to tell me beforehand, if you plunge again into the wilds for a week . . . or ten days . . . where you are going?

I would like to look the places out on a map & say ". . . yes, the Dry Tortugas on Wed^y, that's where she will be; then on the Thursday to Bowler Hat in the Indian Territory: & on Friday at Skunk's Misery; & so by coach across the Sage Brush to Cowboy's Amen." Then I could follow your path, & think of you on your way, & wish you all sorts of cooling drinks at the one, & ice creams at the other, & eau de cologne & cushions & swimming-pools & so forth elsewhere.

... Did you ever read a novel called *Lothair*, by the Earl of Beaconsfield, Benjamin Disraeli, sometime Prime Minister here, & usually called Dizzy?

In its way, it is the most grandly planned of all the English novels: it is on a great scale; & its subject is the conflict and the problem of power in the Europe of 1867–1869: America just beginning to be felt, Germany beginning to threaten, the populace restless, authority questioned.

The scale is vast, as in *Antony & Cleopatra*; & the fable, of Lothair, a young man, absorbing.

... I never saw Nijinski. I saw his drawings at a show in the Albany some 25 years ago; queer mad things: done in his madness, from which, I think, he had then recovered. He must have been a marvel: & fresh from the great unspoiled Marinski tradition, that had only been two seasons away from Russia. Western ways have changed the few survivors of that group. I have not seen the real existing Russian ballet: & I cannot endure what Western ballet has become: but when Fokine was directing, & Bakst & Benois design-ing, & Nijinski, Pavlova & Karsavina dancing . . . .

Well, one by one, they dropped out; but I was able to thank Fokine in person, & to praise some few of the last whom he had trained . . . & to see a few of the survivors from the past, a very few; & all the last good performances of the great period of the ballet.

The first Western flowering I hardly saw, being then excited by other matters; so I missed Nijinski; but heard tales of his great flying leap in *Le Spectre de la Rose*, though usually that ballet wins one by the girl.

⁂

220

... The places named in my previous letter really existed. They were in the Texan cow country & may have ceased with the cow industry. Cowboy's Amen was a nickname for a very tough burg where even the tough found it a little thick. I forget the real name. Bowler Hat & Skunk's Misery may now have been re-named, & the cowboys are gone; the trail cowboys anyway.

I was told that *Chicago* is an Indian word for Skunk's Lair, and this may be the fact. Chicago was at one time kind of tough, and had in it more murders in one month than Great Britain in any average year.

But when I was in Cleveland, Ohio, asking about this, they said "Hell . . . no . . . Chicago ain't tough. Cleveland's tough," and then told me how a few days before 2 desperadoes had driven slowly down the main avenue shooting people right & left as fortune bade & the targets offered. They also told me of a local lady who came out of her Club & got into a car, not hers, and the car drove off & she was never seen again. Her own chauffeur saw her go, but too late.

I judged that Cleveland had gotten a kind of perhaps momentary bulge on Chicago in the way of toughness.

221

. . . When I was with sailors, long since, none had a good word for whalers. There were a few still, from Peterhead & New Bedford, but the sperm whale was almost extinct, & the service was hard & (I gathered) very vile.

Later, it revived under better conditions, & they took to shooting whales (not only sperm whales) & dragging the shot whale into an inner tank, & using all of him, instead of wasting most of him, as in the old days.

. . . I have seen an old sailing whaler or two with crows' nests aloft; I hope that none is left now. Ugly as the modern tanker may be, those vile old hearses were uglier.

I would not care to see a whale being shot & cut up, nor any phase of the voyage: not even pay-day at the end.

You may have heard the answer of the American whaling captain, when asked what sort of a life his hands led.

He said, "All I ask of officers & men, Sir, is common servility, and that of the most dog-goned sort."

The hands were not paid so much a month, like other seamen, but by "a lay", or minute share, of the ship's takings (no whales, no money). They might be away 3 years before they had a full ship, and could return. In all that time they lived in starvation & squalor, at watch & watch, & saw the wonders of the deep. The ships were a byword for vile conditions.

I seem to remember that Melville, who describes New Bedford so finely in *Moby Dick*, describes some of the whaling life in *Omoo*. He was in a whaler, I think, when he kind of topped his boom from her to live among the cannibals (in *Typee*). This was much like the Italian who deserted from the Italian army, & being caught, as a deserter, confessed to a murder long before, so that he could be sent to be a galley-slave instead of going back to the Army.

Being a galley-slave was no rapturous kind of life. It offered neither Budge nor Blones (see Mr Haggart [Letter 191]); & you may have found some hints of what it meant in Cervantes, who himself had been a slave, in galleys & elsewhere.

There is a fine ballad about whaling, however.

> Speedicutt was our Captain's name,
> Our ship was the Lion bold,
> And we are gone to the North,
> > Brave boys,
> To face the storm & the cold.

(The *Lion* was American-built, but owned in Liverpool.)

A word or two more, Swete.

Perhaps Cervantes, having a bad hand-wound, would have done little galley-slavery. He often saw it, of course. Most of his slavery was ashore.

222

... The *Waterwitch* brig was done by Huggins (or after a sketch by Huggins). He knew his craft, did Huggins, & the King (up to a point) was right in saying what he did.[1]

The *Waterwitch* was really fast. It is said that she used to wait for a Naval Squadron to come out of port, & there she would lie, hove to, till they had passed her; & then, setting about ½ the sail they were under, she would sail all round them; not from vain-glory, but to suggest (to any one who might notice) that the Navy might, at any moment, need speed, and that (at the moment) the squadrons hadn't got it. Presently, the Navy bought her & (it is said) used her lines for others.

They did not spoil her by changing, or over-masting her: she remained fast: & of great use in checking slave-ships in the Gulf of Dead Ned[2] & elsewhere. Till she died a ship's death, being broken-up, her crew could have sung a triumphant song that much delighted my rebellious boyhood: a song with a chorus, that (just possibly) you may have heard some old has-been sing, for the coppers of charity, in the streets of old Bristol.

The song was called "Up I came with my little lot".

I forget what the song was about, but O the chorus: I sing it still at odd times. There are few such poems now, but then, in the time of song, real song, it shone like the lily of July. Queen of the garden.

f And Up I came with my little lot,
And the air went blue for miles
The trees all shook
The coppers slung their hook
And down came all the tiles.
The donkeys shied to t'other side of there,
They brayed as if their hearts would break;
ff I put 'em all to bed,
For everybody sed
fff That my lot took the cake.

Now darling dere, you are off to Ireland. May all good & lovely spirits guard you & bring you safely home. As the Irish used to say to me, long since, "May the sweet Jaysus & his blessed Ma have you in their holy keeping."

[1] "Give me Huggins." See Letter 13.

[2] The Bight of Benin.

✤

223

. . . Will you tell me if you are, or were, any the worse for being a [blood] donor, the other day? Did you have to be like the boxers of old before a battle, & have special diet?

They used to say:

Two eggs to improve my wind.
Then two beefsteaks to make me real savage.
Then a chirping Tot, & let me at him.

But, of course, if they were having to keep below a specified weight, they had to dine on the suck of a lemon and let the wind take its chance. (The life of a hero, besides being brief, was often painful. *Il faut souffrir pour être bellicose*).

. . . I hope that *Lothair*[1] does not read like ravings from an impossible world. It is a mid-Victorian book, written when we were the supreme people. It was still 40 years or so before the First War, which made as vast a change as (shall we say) the Railway to the England of 1830. The world was much as *Lothair* says, in all its upper crust. Down below . . . well . . . that, at the moment, was not his subject . . . his subject was what was to happen next . . . & under whom.

Disraeli was watching the old leaders, & the coming of the new forces. I do hope that the book may interest.

[1] See Letter 219.

224

. . . I am so glad that you being a donor was not an exhaustion, later.

I was wondering whether I ought to have sent you some cream, or other restorative, Dr Parish's Chemical Food, or a pot of Glaxo.

People were very great at "feeding up", in my young days: that is, people in years of discretion: they thought that the young needed checking, of course.

In the sporting papers, every week, until the First War, one would always see challenges of great eaters: so & so would eat pigeons, or winkles, or oysters, or hard-boiled, or soft-boiled eggs, or muffins, or crumpets, against all comers; & the eating challenges were often accepted, & the matches held. I never went to see one (I often might have), nor the more frequent drinking contests, beer or stout.

In the 18th century, a noble Lord, such as Lothair, might have a henchman who would eat against all comers. There is a story printed of 2 Lords who arranged such a match with their henchmen, who met & ate.

Someone, later, wrote to one of the Lords, to report. He said, "I cannot at this moment of writing send your Lor^P full particulars, but your Lor^P will be pleased to hear that your man was the Victor by a Pig & an Apple-Pye."

. . . I am delighted that *Lothair* gave you so much delight in the noisy room the other day.

I have been rapt away, with readings, in my time, but not on the *Conway*. There (if one read) it had to be in the Library or on one's [sea-] chest, & one had to keep an eye out for gangsters & an ear open for a pipe. If one missed a pipe the chances were that you would get a "week", of being mug-man, or mess-man, or somebody's hammock, or a pump of some kind: & these delights I never had given to me, so I am sure that I was never absorbed there. I know I wasn't. I felt there that reading was to be shut from me for ever; real reading.

I am so glad that you like the pretty tale of Daphnis & Chloe. You may like this other tale, of Cupid & Psyche.[1] Please, do you know the third old tale, "The Golden Asse" of Apuleius?

[1] Apuleius (*c.* AD 123: date of death uncertain). His *Metamorphoses*, better known as *The Golden Ass* is the only Latin novel to survive complete. It contains the tale of Cupid and Psyche.

225

. . . You must not think that the Pig in the contest story was full-grown.

No: probably it was a sucking-pig, of very tender years: or weeks.

When I was young (though I never ate such a thing myself) these tender things were supposedly a delicacy & were much in request at Christmas.

Perhaps the contestants each ate 2, but then the winner, drawing a deep breath, held out his plate for a third, amid cheers, while the other fellow left the ring weeping & had to be helped home.

The great contest was to eat 30 pigeons in 30 days, I believe.

I do not know how the umpires made sure that the things were eaten, but no doubt the scrutiny was strict.

The trouble about pigeons is said to be this: it takes 25 hours for any human frame to digest a pigeon, or all the meat on a pigeon.

In 23 days, the human frame is satiated with an over plus of pigeon: it loathes pigeon: it shrinks from pigeon: but still 7 more have to be won through, or ruin stares . . . .

"Klondike or Bust", as the gold-miners said.

Men ate pigeons a good deal in those days so that perhaps it was only the last 3 that really tried character; but I was told that the finish of such a match was a real test.

There was a story of a famous pot-boy, who ate against all comers in London some 70 years since.

His publican asked him to eat 2 dozen raw eggs against the Lambeth Ogre one afternoon. He refused. The publican pressed, & re-pressed, but still the lad refused. The publican said, "But Joe, I've backed you to do it. Why can't you do it?"

"Why, sir," Joe said, "I hate to seem disobliging, but I got to eat a calf at 1 o'clock against the Angel." (The calf was boiled. 1lb of meat was issued at a time to each eater, and any left (I suppose) was given to the cat.)

I once (or twice) saw a man finish a walk of 1,000 miles in 1,000 hours (or over 41 days). No great feat of walking, but this man was walking 1,000 miles round & round inside a small dry swimming bath: almost small enough to make him giddy.

(A band played him home with "The girl I left behind me".)

. . . Please let me thank you for your sweet words about the Cupid-Psyche story. It comes in the *Golden Asse* story, about which you also kindly wrote. It is one of the great stories: & the *Golden Asse* is also, in its way, a great story, or stream of stories, often very strange and often more than lively stories. You must let me send it soon: only promise that you will not be vexed at my sending it. In that great age writers wrote from a full joy in life, & in writing; & as I write to you, from a full joy in friendship, heart to heart, kindling speaker to loving listener—the book may be a joy shared heart to heart. I know that I could read it to you without offence. It is more beautiful than the *Pyrate* book of happy memory.

It comes from a society much unlike our own, & full of deep devotions no longer known here, & of the intellectual excitements that devotions bring: and these are often strange & the strangeness is often beautiful.

❧

226

. . . Crowds are queer things. Many years ago, I went to what was called An Assault at Arms. It was a mixed sort of grill: some wrestling: some Hop, Skip & Jump contests: some fencing with foil & single-stick; & some exploits with the sabre by the master sabreurs of the English cavalry. There may have been feats of strength, such as weight-lifting or poker-bending or tearing packs of cards in two, but I forget most of it.

Anyhow, the GREAT event was the master sabre sargeant of the world, an English Guardsman, who was going to chop the carcass of a sheep in two with one good swipe of his cavalry sabre.

They made the most of the preparation, bringing in & hanging up the carcass: an unlovely skinned "dem'd moist unpleasant body".

Then the great man appeared & took a long time deciding which sabre to use, & was it sharp enough & was the foothold sawdusty enough, & was his balance exactly right. Well, the show had to be spun out: perhaps he was fined if he did it too quickly.

At last, taking position, he fidgeted around, & gathered breath, & took aim, & then took aim again.

Then, with a rumbustious swoosh he smote: & the dangling carcass was divided plunk at the breeches-belt, and the lower half bit, as it were, the dust.

Instantly the whole audience within 10 yards of the stage burst out, as by inspiration, but perhaps in a pre-arranged claque or rag, with a whistling and humming (very ably done) of the Dead March from *Saul*.

The effect was very funny (to me) but I have often thought of it since, wondering what the crowd would have done had the blow suggested other blows, instead of the March.

A crowd is wickeder than anybody in it.

227

... Thank you for keeping on to the end with *Lothair*. How simple &
beautiful the end is ...

It was all 90 years ago (1867–8) & all those people are away; but
that was the varnish on the picture, then, that thought itself the
work of art. That sort of attempt upon the young was then being
made (as it still is), and the book seems to me a marvellous study of
one such unusual attempt.

In this letter I would like to write something about Apuleius the
man. He was left well-off by his parents, & spent much of his wealth
in seeking after wisdom: the natures of plants, fishes, creatures: the
nature of Nature; & the cults & mysteries of the gods. He was long
in Egypt, & long in Greece, seeking these things & receiving
initiation into the mysteries & meanings of many rituals. I would
not be sure that he did not go to Persia; even to India.

There is a beauty in his mind that only comes to a seeker; & there
is a fragment of his, praising Pythagoras, which makes me feel that
that was his spiritual Master (at any rate for long years) and his
ideal. A singularly lovely youth, given to music, who sought afar for
lovely guidance, for communion with the divine Natures, unseen,
yet to be approached, and from whom Wisdom may be vouchsafed
to man.

The Golden Asse is a tale of delivery from the bondage of the body
by the direct mercy of a divine wisdom. All the tale of the delivery is
exquisitely told.

As far as I can judge, he was a student of Nature & of Wisdom all
his days.

When he married the widow with 2 sons, one son, the younger,
liked him: the other loathed him: & this elder son seems to have
conspired with a vulgar lawyer to accuse A of effeminacy & magical
practices.

The effeminacy charge seems to have been, that he used a mirror:
a philosopher who used a mirror, instead of leaving self alone ....

The magical charges were that he was always buying fishes to
make love-philtres & that of course these love-philtres made the
widow love him. He replied that he always had studied & dissected
fishes, to find out about them, & that no man known had ever made
a love-philtre from fish; & that this was a well-known fact: ask any
maker of love-philtres.

Another count of effeminacy was that he had once made a pot
of African dentifrice, (substance unknown, but perhaps some
powdered nut or bean) & had sent it, with some verses, to a male
friend. A read the verses in court, & no doubt the papers next day

wrote "Loud and Prolonged Laughter". He seems to have won his case easily.

The widow seems to have been about 40 or so, not 60, as the lawyer maintained. She was rich, but no doubt much of her money was held in trust for the sons.

A's defence would have taken all a long day, for at intervals he called witnesses to prove his points. It is a well-marshalled case, very interesting, for the mental power of the defence & for the superstitions on which the charges rested: an odd contrast.

A made a neat point. "You say I have dissected dead raw fish. I ask the Judge if he has not dissected many cooked ones."

The verses about the tooth powder are trivial enough:

> I send you from the Sunny South
> White Teeth & Glory for your Mouth
> From Araby the Rich it comes
> To whiten teeth & soothe the gums,
> Lest cloying caramels defile
> And O the wonder when you smile.

. . .He seems to me to have been a great & strange man, speaking out of a wonderful knowledge of the great & strange in thought & Nature. He was not telling a fairy story, but dwelling on a mystery. The symbol of the Ass, the intense moments, some deeply & poignantly intense, & the rose-leaves that set free . . . .

He passed his days trying to learn the secret rites of many worships: & learned much that was, as it were, a cloak about him of a beauty not of this world, & all now mysterious.

Is it thus to you?

* * *

228

Reyna darling

This may (perhaps) reach you on Christmas Day, & be a little word to your heart, then, if there be room, in that crowded time & place.

All blessings to you.

Please, when peace is restored, if any of it be left, will you tell me what you know of Walthamstow Church? (Old Walthamstow Church, rather up the hill; north & a bit west from Hoe Street Station.) For some while I lived near the Church there. It had then a pretty bell-chime, mechanical & jerky, like an old musical box, tinny in tone, too, but yet pleasant. It played "There is nae luck aboot the hoose", which was unusual, surely.

I was so much touched by your delight in Victor Hugo's account of Waterloo. (I could think of nothing else for days, when I first read it [*Les Misérables*], being 10, then.) But I have since then studied the battle for many years, & have been over the field; & have to say this: that VH burned-up into a visionary ecstasy, & saw the splendid ghosts of the Napoleonic saga doing what they perhaps thought that they had done; or he thought they had.

All that superb charge & collapse of the Cuirassiers in the Sunken Road at Ohain—"Rider and horse, friend, foe, in one red burial blent"—is surely mainly tommy-rot.

The English accounts make it clear that those charges were not in line, but in column, until they were across that road; that the sunken part of the road was well to the east of their line of advance; & that at no time did the Cuirassiers threaten us gravely after D'Erlon's first attack a little after noon. Then, they reached the crest & were frightfully & suddenly shot down by the English line, & were then charged & scattered by our Heavy Cavalry.

After that, they attacked all day in small groups and squads, supported by skirmishers, but never broke a square & were picked off in dozens by our men at close quarters.

But now . . . all joy to you.

Jan.

P.S. This is the *Tom Jones* that I offer to you for Christmas or for Christmas-time, with my wishes for your happiness, & peace, & fulfilment in all that your heart seeks.

The book is not made for reading in a bus, nor a train, nor bed. I fear that it will need a table wherever you read it.

Perhaps it is a book to read *in*, rather than right through. Some bits in it do invite from time to time, but it is not my favourite Fielding book.

The bit that stays in my mind is the strange bit where he walks from Gloucester towards Upton upon Severn, & gets (seemingly) into the Malvern Hills & the (almost) Romantic Movement . . .

In fact, I do not quite know where he *does* get at that moment, but I think that he got into the Herefordshire Beacon somewhere, & that it knocked him a bit odd, as that place does.

You may have noticed something not quite normal in that sort of poet that I am always warning you against . . . well. . . those old dwellings, & graves in the moonlight, they play the devil with a fellow . . . .

229

. . . I have been wondering where Hugo got his ideas of Waterloo. He was there, all over the field, & impressed by it, before the Belgians built their great mound & lion on the vital point. He saw it pretty much as it had been: and nobody can dispute the beauty & power of his main tale.

But of the Cuirassiers coming *in line* on to the sunken road in a charge & being engulfed (like the wicked in a tract) the first come the quickest buried . . . .

The Ohain road *was* a sunken road here & there. It was sunken for about 100 yards just behind the farm of La Haye Sainte. Then further E, about where Picton was, it was sunken in bits, as all roads in a chalk country will be; but that was not where the thrusts came. And the Cuirassiers came up hill, not killing their horses by galloping, but walking in the mud, & not in line but in column; & not knowing in the least where nor how they would find the English, who were on the crest in dense smoke, as guns & gunners only, but withdrew as they, the French, advanced, to the infantry in square further back.

When they reached the crest, the French paused, to deploy into an attacking line, & to see where the English were.

Where the road *was* sunken, it had to be taken slowly by horse or man, friend or foe. It delayed the English cavalry, often during the day.

It was always the rule of the English to let the cavalry come within 20 yards of the squares before firing. Because of the appalling power of a musket-ball at such close quarters NO cavalry got into an English square on that day & the mortality near the squares was appalling, not from the sunken road, [but] by English musketry.

VH may have heard tales from survivors, who may well have "lied like troopers". Or he may have had some poetical dream or vision of the battle which seemed to him to be the final truth of the battle.

I think that not many French who reached the crest ever returned to say what happened on & in the English position.

The Waterloo Letters [edited H. T. Siborne] *must* have mentioned this ruin of the Cuirassiers had it happened as VH says. They do not. The nearest approach to it in these letters is as follows:

The Cuirassiers made their first & fiercest attack about noon in D'Erlon's attack. They came up west of La Haye (clear of the really sunken part) & topped the crest perhaps where the Mound now is. Here they were blown into disorder, charged by the English Life Guards, broken into ruin, & chased slantingly across the main road below La Haye, thro the French guns, into the main French army.

In doing this, the flying Cuirassiers & their pursuers came to sad grief in a hollow stretch of that main Brussels Road.

Major Waymouth, 2nd Life Guards, writes:

"We rode over everything opposed to us. The 1st Life Guards made great slaughter among the flying Cuirassiers who had choked the hollow way . . . its banks were then crowned by Chasseurs who fired down upon the Life Guards in return, killing great numbers of them . . . this road was quite blocked-up by dead."

It was in this charge that Corporal John Shaw, the famous English swordsman & pugilist, received the wounds from which he died that evening. There is, near here, a stretch of Down, the Midfield Down, quite curiously like the position at Waterloo. If I keep going there, & growing much older, I shall begin, like K George the 4th, to think that I was in command there and was responsible, & then to say so . . . .

The Duke of Wellington did not want a history of the battle written. He said "the history of a battle would be like the history of a Ball".

A four-masted barque.

1959

230

. . . *Les Misérables* is a great novel. To keep the fires burning, & the suspense acute through all that vast design, & to make so much of it poignant and even heart-quaking . . . & then some of the escapes . . . some of the almost-triumph of evil . . . none but a marvel of a man could do that. He could do what he liked with his Cuirassiers: capture Wellington if he chose, & beat the English out of Belgium . . . all would be forgiven him . . . .

I gather from the Waterloo books that the Cuirassiers did not like their cuirasses, & always flung them away when retreating in a hurry—I expect they could easily be cast loose or put on . . . . Anyhow, they *did* cast them away, & the English were very glad of them, for the front & back were both hollow, & could be used as cooking-pans, for the bold Briton to cook his bully-beef into a stew, or brew a hot jorum when the rum was there.

They gave no protection against shot: & did encumber the wearer. They look very fine on parade, of course.

It is said that by about 3 or 4 p.m. the English men in the squares used to say, whenever more cuirassiers appeared out of the smoke, "Here come those —— fools again!!"

When I was a very little child, I saw a sword & a helmet that had been at Waterloo & had later marched on to Paris. The son of the wearer shewed them to me.

Quite a lot of survivors of the battle were alive then, but I never met one, as far as I know. I am pretty old, my dear dear R, & when I was young the Indians said that there was still mammoths alive in Alaska . . . . In fact, I date from the last Glacial Era. My heart is not cold to you, though; I can still send loving blessings to you, & do.

231

... About Emma, Lady Hamilton: Many years ago, I read some French lady's *Mémoires* (Comtesse de Something—Boigne perhaps: I forget the name). She had known Lady H pretty well, & admired her for her great beauty, & grace, & talent. Emma used to appear in some simple costume, & then, with coloured shawls or muslins would transform herself into any famous heroine in 5 swift seconds, & would pass into any other in another five, in a way that was indescribably lovely.

She said that this gift was all exquisite art, but that Lady H was loveliness & grace itself, lovely in every line & limb; & with a gay merry manner when not acting thus: but lovely, lovely; as indeed the Romney portraits make us feel.

232

... It was dear of you to write me such a letter for the 20th & to wear the turquoise ring. Thank you.

Here, on this 20th there is no you, save in my heart, & a drenching rain is falling; & a new flood rising fast in the river outside (the old one ran out yesterday). By Thursday, this new flood should be 4′6″ above the winter norm, for the western water should be passing then; & there will be a lot to come.

Victor Hugo knew the old, awful Paris of the Middle Ages, the Revolution & the early 19th century. Du Maurier saw it: the old Gothic Paris, with cholera every summer, & water brought to each house by bucket; the Paris of the old Morgue, as etched by Meryon[1] & described by Browning. The last Napoleon cleaned it all up & laid on new pipes, & made the great boulevards. I suppose the siege & the Commune cleaned up any that Haussmann had left of the old nightmare place.

Now that we talk of Paris, please, may I ask if you know Alain-Fournier's book *Le Grand Meaulnes*?[2] It was published first about 35 years ago I think, & translated into English, under the name of *The Wanderer*, some 5 or 6 years later.

Did you come upon either version?

AF was the last of the romantics. He was killed in the first months of the 1st War; & wrote only this book. Some letters of his were later printed. Alas . . . he was sometimes in the Brit. Mus. Reading Room when I was there (so was Lenin) but tho I often saw Lenin, & marvelled who that extraordinary Being could be, I never noticed

AF. I may always have been in a different room when AF was in the British Museum. I always saw Lenin in the Rotunda but I may have been in the Large Room when AF was present; or even in the Mss Room, for I was often there.

I may not have noticed AF, for I think he was only a boy of 16–17–18 when there, but none with sight could fail to notice Lenin. He was one that one had never seen the like of. One could but wonder what he would do. Well . . . we now know . . . a little.

[1] Meryon, Charles (1821–68). French etcher. His group of twenty-two Paris etchings, entitled *Sur Paris*, contains *La Morgue*.

[2] *Le Grand Meaulnes* by Alain-Fournier (Henri Alban Fournier 1886–1914) published 1913. The first English translation entitled *The Wanderer* by Françoise Delisle came out in 1928.

233

. . . I have shuddered to think of dear you in the fog & the frost. We have had both, & still have, but have also had floods. The river has been ¼ mile broad here for days, but it is now fast falling. I send a sketch. If you hold it right side up, you will see the edge of my garden, invaded. If you hold it wrong side up you will see the Plain of Troy, looking towards the Hellespont, & the Greek Camp.

234

. . . You must not think my painting of the weeds "delicate". You get that effect with a hard dry bristled brush dabbed onto colour & then dabbed onto paper. You try it.

. . . The flood has been lovely to see, in the bright sunlight, for the sea-gulls have been here, but not in any number, as sometimes in wilder weather. In very wild storms, & shocking cold, they swarm here: & then we have even gannets & many Arctic skuas.

There used to be a weather rhyme about the gulls.

> Sea-gull, sea-gull, here on the sand
> It's never fine weather when you're on the land.

235

. . . Did you ever have a real try at the novels of Richardson?[1] *Clarissa Harlowe* etc: all in correspondence? [They] are signed in all sorts of amazing ways such as "your rightfully aggrieved Parent", "Your now heart-broken & repentent Sarah", etc. These examples are imagined, but the real ones are even better than these now & then. You may not like a tale told in letters. The method is somewhat out of fashion now, but when unusual talent uses *any* method he makes it compelling, & Richardson compelled his time; a reading & native time, when England led the world in things she is good at, marine affairs, domestic comfort, decency, honesty, political imbecility etc.

(In justice, one should add gin, beer, woollen goods & horses.)

[1] Samuel Richardson (1689–1761) had a printing business and was, at one time, printer to the House of Commons. He produced his first novel in letters, *Pamela*, 2 vols, in 1740, 1741. This was followed by *Clarissa Harlowe*, his best-known work, and *Sir Charles Grandison.*

236

. . . Please let me thank you for your kindling lines about the conductors.

Now & then, one sees theatrical producers, but I have only seen one man produce a poetical play with a sense of what it was about, the fundamental sense. The others may have a lively sense of scene, & momentary effect, & can be invaluable to the company & its individuals, but that is a different thing. Sometimes, in the past, the Russian Ballets that came here were run by inspired men, such as Fokine: & then; ah, then, the horns blew.

. . . I am grateful to you for mentioning the Smollett. I felt that you ought to meet Commodore Trunnion,[1] that imp of fame, a sort of promoted boatswain of the old make: "Rough as a bear and drunken as a Gosport Fiddler."

The name, too, Trunnion (the side supports of the old cannon)—[there followed a drawing in ink]—I have drawn it cockeyed, alas, but the trunnions rested on the wings of the carriage & supported the gun.

Trunnion, too, is such a help to those asked to write a Nature Poem about an *onion*.

"All Hail, salubrious Plant whose pungent Scent . . ."

It is always easy to begin, but how to go on from there? How could anyone go on from there, with any hope, without the knowledge that he could always (somehow) finish off with a rousing bang & the word trunnion. It wouldn't be easy to bring trunnion in but poetry isn't easy, & the job is to bring trunnion in & stun all criticism with it.

[1] Commodore Hawser Trunnion, in Smollett's *Peregrine Pickle*.

237

... As Miss Nightingale is said to have said: "Those who visit the sick, or question the Nurses, should return an hour later and contemplate the damage they have done."[1]

... I send with this some prints of East Indiamen in dock, from which you will see the clumsiness & overcrowding: the want of clear-headed foresight, & imaginative direction, that beset our sea-affairs for so long. You will also see some of the gear in use, & the length of the lower studding-sail boom, & the size of the hemp shrouds.

I add to these some papers about life in one of the late 4-masted barques (with a photograph of her), rather a lovely type, of which there were hundreds & of which you may have seen 1 or 2 or even 3, but cannot now see. With these is some account of a film ship. You will know about Israel Hands, the original, as well as Stevenson's imagining.

RLS was a good natural sailor: but I am much puzzled by the *Hispaniola*—a schooner, 1750 or so, with a mizen mast. He meant her to be a schooner: the film people wronged him; but he did not allow for the smallness. Life in a schooner is more public than a town pump: & a word spoken aboard *must* be heard by somebody.

You may know that the incident of Jim in the apple-barrel over-hearing the real Silver occurred to one of the engineer Stevensons, in a small vessel in which he was examining the need for lights on the Scots coasts & among the islands. The Stevenson *was* in an apple-barrel, &, like other listeners, heard small good.

[1] JM, ever sensitive, did not want to trouble ANS by forever asking after her mother who was seriously ill.

238

... Voltaire ... I do not know him much, except *Candide*, & I always think of Dr Young's lines about him. Dr Young knew him when he was over here, & was startled by the extravagance of his impropriety. He wrote:

> Thou art so witty, profligate and thin
> At once we think thee Satan, Death & Sin.[1]

It is a neat couplet, but it ought to be better. Pope would have done it better.

I read his verse to Frederick the Great (pretty scandalous, but written at a safe distance from F's claws); and then, long ago, when I was about 20, when the 18th century was of no account I often found, for a penny a vol, the little English editions of his books: pretty scandalous these: but printed here, & smuggled into France, because they might have caused his being burnt alive had they appeared openly there. (Really & truly burnt, not just branded: totally erased, in fact.)

I couldn't care for these at all, but they are all glittery, savage, witty & outrageous.

Candide is all these things too, but do you know *Candide*?

[1] This should be ". . . we think thee, Milton, Death and Sin." Edward Young (1683–1765), a clergyman, wrote plays and satirical pieces, but is chiefly remembered for his *Night Thoughts on Life, Death and Immortality* (1742–5).

239

. . . I have begun to search for a little old *Candide*, but these things (once in every penny box) are now not easy to find. Still — courage.

Voltaire lived to a good old age: I don't think that he was a weakling or ill, but always very fit & dead on the target. He went for royalty & church, for those two governed France, & were unfit for the job. The one thought that the deluge would not come in their lifetime: the other refused all change till a deluge showed: they could, and did, burn & kill people for heresy. They owned about ½ France & refused to pay taxes.

They were supported by such an aristocracy as the world has seldom seen.

V was clear-sighted beyond most; and an expert financier of the adroitest. He knew pretty well what would certainly happen, that a few city mobs would upset the regime.

About the time of his death, clever scroundrels had begun to organise the Paris mobs, by paying vile journalists to utter vile lies.

The journalists were an unspeakable scum writing for an unthinkable gutter, which gutter presently cut off the heads of the journalists & the scoundrels who had organised them.

Presently Napoleon beat the gutter into a drilled force, with which he plunged Europe into about 20 years of massacre, blood and pillage, until, in fact, the survivors realised that V had been right, *that it is necessary to cultivate one's garden.*

The clear, horrible, Satanic wit had been right.

There is a vivid account, in some French lady's *Mémoires*, of V's last visit to Paris shortly before the Revolution. He was old & frail & glittering & Satanic: and all Paris bowed before him & waited on his lightest word.

240

... I was delighted with your tale of the Irish composer receiving his tribute.

Long since, I heard of an Irish writer, who, some 60 or 70 years ago, was said to have been called before a curtain on some stage to receive applause & perhaps bouquets .... He, too, had been priming himself for the mental strain of the occasion. He did not want to go on, nor did he see why he should, but at last he was there, blinking at the audience, who were all shouting *Speech, speech.*

After glaring at them a while, not knowing in the least where he was, he spoke:

> I don't care for anny of you.
> I don't care for anny of you.
> Me only friends now is the Planutts,
> Vaynus, & Adonis . . . and Jupiter.

He then moved sideways off the stage.

I have utterly forgotten who the writer was, & perhaps the world has too. Anyhow, it is almost certain to be a made-up, or embellished, story, for I have never failed to find inexactitude in the tales that reached me from that source.

Story-telling, when it becomes an art, ceases to be history.

... & this, my dere sweet, leads me to Voltaire, whose books I have been trying to re-read. I have read 3 or 4 of his tales this week, including *Candide*, & I find them curiously old, dull, & wandering. They are scandalous enough, frank, brutal & savage: attacking all the brutal, savage and outrageous follies of a corrupt & heartless society, abusing all its autocratic power. The effect is (to me) that of a collection of the French wire-tinsel imitation flowers with which the French used to heap the graves in their cemeteries. They make a dusty deathly show, but there is nothing lovely, nothing living, nothing of human feeling in them.

He is blamed for attacking Christianity. Well, he often writes appalling, coarse things about certain beliefs, but what he *did* most attack was, not Christianity, but the abuse of power by the Order of the Jesuits, who were burning people for heresy only 190 years ago (when Dr Johnson was an old man & Wm Wordsworth hardly born, & Wm Blake a little boy).

"*Ecrasez l'infâme*", he wrote: & righteously. As for his wit . . . well . . . "The best water is the newest".

In the book about the Huron Indian, the hero, the Indian, tells how an Indian girl had loved him.

"She would love me still, but she was eaten by a bear. I punished the bear, and wore his skin for a long time, but I am not consoled."

I seem to remember a word of his, or ascribed to him, that once pleased:

"They must be men, because they are fighting: & they must be civilised, because they are doing it so savagely."

One must think mostly now, of his courage in fighting the *infâme*: he ran much risk: & must often have been in great danger. All witty intellects make enemies: he was also very rich: & bringing him down might bring booty.

241

. . . I know not how many times, my dear Watson, I have warned you against these literary fellows. *They are no good.* It is true, one or two, now & then, have written of some imagined event in a way that has deceived a multitude old enough to be wiser: but what is this but fraud on a big scale, blinding the public to truer views of life??

Take now this scandalous Voltaire, the arch-type of all such: the one they would (nearly) all be if they could.

There he was, a public scandal, living with a lady scandal, a lady who knew Geometry, spoke Latin & English, & was always translating the works of Sir Isaac Newton into French.

He had built a kind of palace for her, filled with the most exquisite paintings, prints, porcelains, tapestries, grotesques from China, silks, stuffs, lacquers: the rooms all pale blue or pale yellow, the marvellous stands all heaped with snuffboxes, of gold, of gold & enamel, of crystal, of precious stones, of silver gemmed & silver chased: then there were collections of rings—all the jewels of east & west—& such clocks & machines & screens as never were. In this palace of sin, the lady in command would sing complete operas most exquisitely to her harpsichord: & he, a perfect host, would be inimitably winning to each guest, telling with an enchanting archness the most exquisitely indecent tales, or reading diabolic satires, or taking part in scandalous theatricals, or melting all hearts with this new tragedy, or bright romance.

His courage was sometimes heroical, as when he helped the poor Calas family.[1]

Then there was "The Abbé Desfontaines, a man, who, having a gentle leaning for the pleasures of Sodom & of Gomorrah, had been condemned to the gallows for having seduced poor little sweepers, and who was only snatched from the hangman's hands by the 'burning, indefatigable zeal & generous cares of Voltaire.'"

He was twice in the Bastille, & more than once exiled. A clear head & courage were his great gifts.

Desfontaines was a Jesuit writer: & perhaps the charge against him was unfounded: just the malice of an enemy: but the hangman, in his case, if allowed to proceed, would have burned him alive, just N of the Seine there, just W of the Louvre Gardens. Burning was the penalty for that "gentle leaning", that "doux penchant": and 2 years after his escape a man *was* burned for it there, not having any Voltaire.

Carlyle mentions Desfontaines as one of V's enemies lately dead. "Desfontaines is dead, and down in Sodom."

Now, my Reyna, forgive all this. We can talk of these things as friends, as we can talk of all things.

No Jesuit could have kept friendship with V.

Bless your dear eyes & heart.

Jan

---

[1] Jean Calas, a Protestant, was executed at Toulouse in 1762 on a false charge that he had murdered his son for threatening to turn Roman Catholic. In fact the son had committed suicide. Suicide then being a crime, Calas claimed that his son had been assassinated. Church and State combined to interrogate, and finally kill, Calas with extreme brutality. The Calas family moved to Geneva, where Voltaire took up their case, and pursued it so fiercely that in 1756 Calas's innocence was established, and the murder verdict annulled.

242

. . . I fear that this can only be a brief word: I have to go out: & then have a week of "recording" which is hard work even to young you: so judge what it is to the aged aged ruin.

At over 80, men are forced to ask: what am I to the watching world now?

Am I, perchance, a BUFFER, a breezy being, like a retired Admiral?

Or am I that more usual thing, only a CODGER, an old Codger.

Or can it be that I have sunk & sunk, not knowing, and am now an OLD GEEZER?.

O Say not that I am become a Geezer (the G is hard, as in Gout or Gander).

. . . It was in my mind to send you a novel by a man called "Hugh Conway",[1] a novel called *Called Back*, very famous once, & very good in its way. HC was one of the original "Conways", a 100 years ago this summer; & a promising able story writer who died very young. He never went to sea, but took to writing early. 100 years ago he lived near Bristol & played cricket with the Grace boys & their famous Dog.

His tale was dramatised with great success, & parodied & burlesqued. One of the burlesques was called *The Scalded Back*.

I still recall old joy in re-reading books that once delighted me; [they] do at least raise the ghost of old joy.

Amongst these the very first (in mature ways) at the age of 7, was *The War Trail* by Capt. Mayne Reid,[2] a romantic soldier of fortune & writer of wonders, upon whose living form I did, as I believe, once gaze, as he attractively halted his team of greys, long long since, at the Ledbury Cross Roads. He was halted at the Post Office, perhaps buying a stamp (1d) perhaps toying with the prose of an impassioned telegram. Now this book gave me intenser joy than I can well tell, but you are over 7 this birthday.

Then there is Thomas Love Peacock,[3] his novels, his poetry, so often a dear joy to me when greater men fail me. Is he much to you, or would you try him if I offered??

> The bowl goes trim, the moon doth shine,
> And our ballast is old wine.

---

[1] "Hugh Conway", pen-name of F. J. Fargus. See Letter 37.

[2] Thomas Mayne Reid, (1818–1883). Novelist; author of *The Rifle Rangers* (1850), *The Scalp Hunters* (1851), etc.

[3] Thomas Love Peacock, (1785–1866). Novelist and poet, author of romantic/satirical novels. *Crotchet Castle* was published in 1831.

243

. . . I send you a tiny Peacock book. The tale, *Crotchet Castle*, is one of
his very best, but in the last 70 years I have read all his books several
times & am reading them all again now, greatly enjoying them,
prose & verse.

He was a friend of young Shelley: & later was Shelley's executor.

He was secretary to the Admiral commanding in the Walcheren
expedition: & saw the full horror of Naval life & Army incompetence. He lived to a good old age loved & admired. He is unlike
anybody else.

In *CC* he touches off Byron & Coleridge very gaily, as Cypress &
Flosky.

244

. . . *Maid Marian*, by Peacock is no special shakes, but has some wit,
& some rather jolly songs. I suppose it was in some way prompted
by Scott's *Ivanhoe*, but it seems to stand the weather better after all
the years.

His long poem *Rhododaphne*, suggests Scott in some ways, but
there, too, is something that stands the weather better: a deeper,
more fundamental culture: though, of course, nothing like Scott's
instinct for life.

. . . I am so glad that you could get into the wild at Newt[n]
[Newtown Powis], & to think that we share yet another link, in
curlews. They come over here, now & then, not often, from some of
the wilder downlands; and never without raising a deep mood.

You may not know the downland, that lone wilderness, miles &
miles of it, with its thorns, as old as it, and the skylarks, & the lonely
wide un-trodden ancient trackways, rutted & hooft, with no-one
passing, & leading nowhere, but going on for miles, & gleaming now
& then with chalk, but no one on it, no house, no sheep even:

> Never a daisy in that mighty meadow,
> Never a tree.

(For the thorns are all crouched from the wind, & all else the rabbits
crop.)

I was out on the lonely downland: the really lonely: where the
sarsens lie still, like giants after a battle: perhaps 5 miles of lonely
grass, with the great stones prone. Glaciers left them there, perhaps,
what other force could?

But there is a dead copse on it, every stunted twig dead: & on any summer sunny day the place is marvellous with rare butterflies: the very rare.

If there were only bog, there would be curlews, too, & all the air haunted.

In one place, one surveys downland all about; 3 miles in every way, yet only one visible house: only downland & the skylarks.

No water there now, for stock or people.

245

. . . Alas, I fear that you have an anxious sad sad life at present. Love brings grief thus, alas.

But though there is change & rechange, there is a life, & a purpose & a fulfilment. The stars set, & re-rise: the stars vanish but re-form: even in their dust they are re-forming.

It is very vast & very splendid. One can atone, one can do better; one can pay back & win forgiveness: & meet again.

246

. . . Southwark Cathedral, some of it, stood near the Globe theatre. WS must have often past it, going to the theatre or the bear-baiting: John Fletcher must be buried near it, in some great pit of the plague.

"Souls of poets, dead & gone", or, as I would now quote: "Roses, their sharp spines being gone."

Pepys was more N of the River, where he lived near Billingsgate & London Pool. Wapping, where they hung the pirates, lies away down the River: & Ratcliff High, once a pretty tough sailor-town, was also down-stream: and along all that grimy stretch what pressing of poor men, what shanghai-ing, what slipping of Micky Finns, what scores of nameless robbed, unclaimed Found Drowned, what infamy of theft, pickery & reset of pickery.

247

. . . Many thanks for your kind nice letter about the Cathedral, & then of your lucky time in Leicester.

Ah to go browsing in markets & old stores with an eye for things that are (somehow) out of fashion, but are of the utmost joy to the inmost heart.

There is a text in Proverbs: "'It is naught: it is naught,"' saith the Buyer but, when he is gone his way, *then* he boasteth."

What fun that THEN is.

London used to be full of such places, stalls, shops, even lines of shops, streets full of stalls on certain nights: & bargains on each stall; all the 18th century books (pretty nearly) at 1d a vol (or less): & old maps, & marine prints (and Rembrandt & Dürer etchings) for 2d a piece (or less)—incredible, isn't it? No: the not wanted is always cheap; and what any time has really wanted some other time will want again.

You must be getting to be a kind of Silver Queen.[1]

Athens used to be rich in silver, much as old Troy & old Mycenae were once rich in gold; but one of the many beauties of you is that you are not a bit stuck-up about it, & are friends with even writers, who are said to pinch any spoons going if you give them ½ a chance.

I was twice in Mycenae but didn't get any gold, only a bit of old pot from Clytemnestra's tomb (so called). Troy I never got to, but saw it, and later passed it at night, & was an hour near the beaches where the Greeks camped, & heard the rush of the current about the pier: it is often a rush of water there.

Troy is the one wonderful place I have seen, that and the Death Valley; & the Desert of Arizona. Golly, golly.

[1] ANS, in her rare leisure, sometimes sought and found bargains in old silver.

248

. . . Irving would have run your evening at the Palace Theatre[1] like a master mariner. If he had been there, everyone would have been in his or her place, keeping every gangway clear, or the lightning would have flashed & withered. I gather he was a dynamic force, whose very presence made order.

I once stood very near to him; & my golly, quiet as he was, that was clear to me. He was looking like Benedick, but Mercutio was there near the surface; & another spirit, too, of intellectual fire.

. . . No, there was no ceremony at my appointment [as Poet Laureate]. It came by letter: then I had to go to be received; & be asked some questions, wh mercifully I was mostly able to answer: quite simple: but the Censorship forbids me further. All was simple, simple:

Elementary, my dear Watson.

... You remember John Atkins who wrote the life of Mr Roberts?[2] A sea surgeon, he, and now I have his Sea Surgeon Book.

Let us thank our stars that we were not Sea Patients under him, nor his Roderick Random kin.

The Naval Surgeon book is a professional text book, by a man of much experience and much probity, much tried by the evils (many quite un-necessary) of insane regulation & of life at sea at that time, when men had not got very far towards mastery.

It is written in a medical jargon, to which one soon becomes used. Dr Johnson will have accustomed you to some of these Latin derivatives, and perhaps a little to that early 18th century view of Healing.

Dr Atkins comes out well, as a conscientious toiler giving his very best to the cases he considers.

Sometimes, one feels that the Surgeon was the one human and cultured man in the ship of the day.

Surgery now has anaesthetics, light, aseptic dressings, 200 years of advance. Here was an honest good man with a little rum, a few tallow candles, some not very clean rags & lints, in a rolling smelly, verminous cable-tier, with the cables close alongside, & the rats, roaches, ants etc all in search of food, all about.

If lucky, he had a little daylight from the hatches, but he could not have fresh air save from a wind sail wh could not always be set, & in calms (in the tropics) would not work.

I suppose that in the tiers, where he worked, his head would be just above the waterline. He ran some risk of a cannon ball coming thro as he operated; not much risk perhaps, but some.

He must have been forced to try delicate ops on head & heart, take up arteries, stop haemorrhage, etc, in uncertain light: tallow candles, when, often, there is no second to lose, & clear sight makes all the difference.

Then, later, his patients wd be in hammocks. Imagine doing dressings on a limb in a hammock.

Then, when the regulation weights & allowances of drugs & dressings were exhausted, as often, when most needed, what then?

> Many a man it gramy[d]
> When they began to fail.

At the end of the book, in the Guinea chapt[r], you will read of something that the ships endured in the settling of Mr Roberts.

[1] A command performance for HM Queen Elizabeth the Queen Mother.

[2] *The History of the Pyrates*, JM's first present to ANS. See Letter 4.

249

... You may wonder why Atkins makes no mention of scurvy, which was a fearful curse in his day, & for long afterwards.

Well: it is only a deficiency disease, & known to be that by him, & by many men of his day, & long before his day, but yet not treated as such by successive boards . . . .

It is a dreadful tale.

In the 16th century, *in 20 years*, an English seaman reckons that 10,000 seamen died of it.

30 years after JA saw the Pyrates hanged, in the mid 18th cent, the absolute, certain cure of the disease having been known for over a century, one reads: "The Channel Fleet often put on shore a thousand men miserably over-run with this disease, besides some hundreds who died in their cruises."

In my young days, I heard of instances in the ships of the nineties. The compulsory lime-juice ran out in the long voyage home, or got destroyed in some devastating sea. Now, I would say, it is conquered: but I suppose a million English seamen have died of it, first & last, either through the disease, or the use of wrong remedies; the figures can never be known.

Few living doctors can have seen a case.

JA brings home to one the horror of sea life as then lived. He did brain surgeries, & took up arteries, by tallow candle-light below the waterline: & had no possibility of clean abundant sterilised water, nor anything sterilised, nor anything but rum & wine as a tonic, nor anything but salt pork as a delicacy, nor anyone but perhaps a one-legged seaman as a nurse, nor any possibility of sheets clean or dirty nor any freedom from flies, & not too much freedom from lice (if any).

> There in the tiers lay ten Tom Bowlings
> The darlings of the crew
> The ship's bells never ceast from tollings
> The press-gangs pressed the new.

250

... Please, if it [scurvy] should appear in England, will you go to a chemist, and say, "Good Master Apothecary, please give me 3 pennyworth, either of the capsules or the tincture of the enol form of 2—Keto—L—gulono—lactone"?

And if he says, "I shall have to order that, Madam. Have you a Doctor's prescription?" You can say, "O never mind: an orange will do, or a lemon or better still some Fresh Black Currants."

Please, please do thus.

I think that the people of JA's time were proof against many things that we suffer from. To survive at all in 1730 demanded a toughness in the subject; about 9 out 10 children died young I judge, as in Tudor times; & the survivors were real live beings: you could hardly quiet them with a battle axe.

251

. . . Do I gather that you may be soon going to play in France?

If so, I hope it may be in some district glorious with stained glass, cathedrals, churches, in every style of gothic, & châteaux in every style of splendour, & also famous for the vital French fact, that "on mange bien", in all that district, for it does make a difference to the traveller, this last, after gazing too much on beauty.

"Gaze not on swans," as Pepys used to sing, at least, not too much; not as an occupation.

I was born into the decade that was opposed to [Oscar Wilde]; & never cared 2d for anything that he did, except some bits of *Salome*, where he worked for a prose that would have more colour than the usual stage, chess-board, black & white; the black black with age, & the white gone a bit yellow, from the same.

That kind of swan had been in the glass case, stuffed, too long; & few could gaze on her with patience.

I am so glad that JA [John Atkins] interests you still. The Guinea Coast is a sort of hell-place

> A place where the earth is worn so thin
> That hell comes leaking through.

JA off the Coast there, got the sea-breezes, but lived in the stench of the ship, below the water, in the reek of the bilges, putrid provisions, rotten water, & the reek of the 60 or 70 tallow candles that lit the orlop after dark, so that he could see his patients, & the other dwellers there.

> Welcome, stranger, to this place,
> Where joy doth sit on every bough.
>   Wm Blake

252

... I have been reading about Mr Saml Sutton, 1740–1780 or so, who devised a means of drawing the foul air from the bilges & lower holds into the ship's furnace & chimney, by a few simple pipes.

Bilge-water is nearly always rain-water that soaks in the timbers from the wooden topsides above the water. It rots at once, like the drinking water in the casks, & has an unutterable smell. I used often to pump it out, & sweep out the limbers[1] as it went. When the pumps began to suck, they screeched in an exacerbation of the smell. I called it "an ear-splitting smell", which describes it.

Mr Sutton heard of several cases of naval carpenters dying of the smell, which was, of course, made tenfold by the reek of tallow tapers, & the stench of some tons of rotting provisions, meat, oatmeal, ship's bread & Thames drinking water, all just above the bilges.

Mr S found much opposition from the seamen, of course. They took the line that he was a ———— ——— landsman, & that anyway the stench is what made the seamen the men they are. However, he prevailed, & the bilges were made sweet.

[1] Holes cut in the timbers on either side of the keel to allow the passage of water to the pump-well.

253

... I will try to answer your question about scent.

Any adequate nose has inside it a small patch (about an inch of it) of *very* sensitive mucous membrane from which many minute hairs of nerves lead to the brain (any adequate brain).

Now roses (and bilge water) and all other fragrant things, emit tiny particles, of unspeakable tinyness, that affect this mucous membrane instantly, & as soon as the membrane catches the suggestion, it at once sends the message to the brain, who at once says *good* or *foul*.

I called bilge water ear-splitting, & it was a good word, for the smell seemed to cleave between my brain & the skull: it really got to the brain & hit it pretty hard.

I don't think that anyone ever died from smelling a foul smell: but I have heard of men fainting from it. The sailors who died down in the bilges probably died of foul air, as in a gassy mine. But if a man fainted in the bilges, he might have knocked his head in falling, & fallen face down in the bilges, & been drowned in them. (There might be a foot or two of bilge water.) I used to hear country people say, "It was enough to give one typhoid of the nose," but typhoid is not had thus. Gaol-fever is typhus. Both typhus & plague are spread by the bites of the fleas of rats. The virulence of each infection may be quite inconceivably swift & fierce.

I like JA's tales of his cases. I like the one about the lad who came too near a big ship in a boat, & a big dog fell on his head & concussed his skull upon the gunwale.

I confess, however, that he is less piquant than Mr Daniel Rainwater who got into trouble in the (lion's) den. Mr Daniel Rainwater: what a name.

. . . P.S. I should have said that the rats get the plague from their fleas & die of it, & that then the fleas go & bite people.

A man from the East told me that the first signs of a coming plague epidemic are rats dying in the open.

254

Reyna mia,

Let me thank you for your friendship that told me, in all your agony of grief, with your brave heart broken.[1]

There was a very wise man not long since, who wrote:

> Since He has uttered Death
> Then, also, Death is well.

It is a part of the eternity in which we move: an eternity of change in the three divine progressions of Power, Order & Beauty, to which the stars are subject.

It may be agony of pain to the human heart from whom the beloved is sundered. The pain to the survivor all who who live have to know. But to the heart that has done with the body what release, what rest . . . .

Yet that freed heart has the consecrated affections, who shall say how old, how deep, how nurtured through Time? The freed heart (who can doubt) still loves, guards, blesses, helps, guides; may do all these things now, unfettered by an ailing body, seeing what we cannot see, prompting by ways we cannot know, and certain, now, of the eternity of all these powers of Power, Order & Beauty that give man's life all that it has of the abiding.

The feeling heart cannot but know the agony, all feeling hearts know it: it takes away a part of the life of the heart: but that life never dies.

[1] ANS's mother had died on 21st August 1959.

255

. . . You asked me about Sappho.[1]

I read a few scraps, long since, in the Greek: the famous thing about the apple on the high bough; & another bit or two.

Only scraps of her work remain: the works being routed out & burned, as not tending to propriety.

Swinburne's poem *Anactoria* perhaps suggests her fire & her quality.

No other woman poet can compare with her in these things for one half moment.

. . . She used often, what is now called Sapphic measure, though this was not her invention, the learned think, but a measure then used in Lesbos.

Thomas Campion tried an English version of the Latin version of the Sapphic:

> Faith's pure shield, the Christian Diana
> (Q. Eliz?)
> England's glory, crowned with all divineness,
> Live long with triumphs to bless thy people
> At thy sight triumphing.
> (1600–1603?)

[1] The Greek lyric poetess (born *c* 612 BC) of Eresus and Mytilene in the island of Lesbos.

256

. . . I am sorry to be so poor a help over Sappho. There are but two complete poems of hers, now known, both due to the admiration of men in ancient times, who quoted them in full.

Many bits have turned up in Egypt: & many of these with care & learning have been made plausible. Thousands more have been destroyed by religious people who disliked hymns to pagan deities & any mention of human affections.

One cannot know for what purpose of ceremonies her poems were made. The world that knew her best knew her to be a wonder. They credit her also with the invention of a little harp, to which she sang her work.

It is a sad fact, that poets are often assailed with much malignancy of spite & jealousy by less gifted or less successful poets; & another sad fact that the comedians on the world's stages enjoy mocking any popular figure for the sake of a momentary laugh; & yet a third sad fact that publishers will often utter, as by some famous hand, some gathered indecencies from the city gutters.

. . . As to the Russian writers, Count Tolstoy seems to me by far the best that I know: *Anna Karenina, The Cossacks*, and *War & Peace*: & some of the short (earlier) tales. I cannot read Dostoievski & do not care about Tourgeniev. There was a good sailor-writer called Semenoff or Semenyov: & liked the very early Gorki tales, but I don't think he developed later.

There was a marvellous tale (short) by Tolstoy, "In the Snow".

Alas, I cannot tell you of modern Russian fiction: I can read little now; & try to read mostly verse.

Knowing no Russian, I used to read the things (in French) a good deal, especially Tolstoy.

There was a late French book *Tolstoy intime*, his memories of Sebastopol (where he served as a subaltern in the Siege): as vivid & wonderful as *The Cossacks*.

257

. . . There are some dependable??? traditions about the appearance of Sappho, who lived 2,500 odd years ago remember.

She impressed her time, & all antiquity, as a Tenth Muse, a divine creature, & this divinity was accorded to her by the choicest genius of the world, the Greek genius. Ancient (really ancient) tradition says that she was not stalwart but utterly exquisite; dark, not fair: with a lovely voice & an exquisitely sweet singer, full of every refinement, choice in dress, garlanded, since she felt that the gods loved the garlanded (with violets in her hair etc).

She enchanted all youth to songs & dances.

She was married to a rich man; & may have lived to widowhood, & to have refused the love (then) of some young man. She may have had a Daughter (Kleis) but this may have been an adopted Daughter, or little girl of charm, & tender years. (Say 5 or 6, at a guess.)

She was an important figure in an important place, for Lesbos was large & very prosperous. She & her family & allies were twice exiled (to Syracuse) in political upheavals; & she was famous also in Syracuse. Long after her death a statue of her (said to have been utterly lovely) was in Syracuse till some ruffian stole it. (The statue was by one Silanion,[1] who lived long after her, but he may have had something to guide him, some carving or description.) As your friend Holmes wd have told you, "a good description is better than a bad photograph".

[1] Silanion, Greek sculptor of the 4th century BC. His statue of Sappho, taken from Syracuse, appeared later in Rome.

258

... To think that you have my Ossian tale.[1]

I loved the writing of it, & do not know how long it took: no time.

But the recording took 2 days I think: & they were long days, indeed.[2]

But my dere swete, it taught me again, for the thousandth time, that no poet ought to use only a voice. Music is needed, too; & I haven't it; & know no poet who has: but Sappho composed her music; & the Greeks had music for the hexameter; & Pindar was as glorious for his music as for his verse, & so were other poets, like Terpander.

[1] *The Story of Ossian* (1959).

[2] I believe this record to be the first time a poem appeared on tape before publication. ANS.

259

Reyna mia, dulce y querida,

You may be sad that you have only 1 little apple, but what is that to me, who have *no* apple, little or big.

Late frosts did for the blossom, & any fruit that formed fell from drought.

But last year was such a crop as none could remember: & so may next year be. Courage, dere harte, "amanecera Dios, y medraremos" (God will dawn & we shall prosper).

260

... You must not too deeply pity the French prisoners who made the models.[1] They were out of the war, & out of the appalling sea service of the time. Prison was hell enough, but it was Heaven to the war &

the sea service. They had a bad time, poor fellows, in the prison, & starved for love & freedom, but they could earn money, & buy drinks & dainties: & there may have been some means of getting letters home (I will try to find out about this).

In any case, under the conscription, none of them would have had any liberty under Napoleon.

Being without any kind of fun in the prisons, they gambled a good deal, for their allowances, clothing, shoes, & any money they earned. Lots of them were almost naked, & had to huddle together at night to try to keep warm. It is said that a dozen would sleep together, huddled together like spoons in a basket, all facing the same way & close up for warmth.

When the one position became unbearable, the leader would shout "Prepare to spoon . . . . Spoon!!" & then all the spoons would turn over & fit into each other facing the other way. I think that this was the case in many of the prisons: life went so, there.

¹ These particular models were of ships. The prisoners-of-war used to while away the time carving bones left over from their meals.

261

. . . At once, let me say, that I grieve not to have been more sympathetic about the prisoners of war. All prisoners & captives demand pity, for it is but hell, however well ordered, to be shut up, to be kept from liberty & love, from friends, hope, work, news, joy, amusement, fellowship, beauty, health; all that can possibly gladden, help growth, make life wiser.

We had, between 1797 & 1803 about 20,000 French prisoners, mostly seamen of all sorts, but some soldiers, too. They had about 5,000 of our men all told. After 1803, they had about 6,000 of our men, & 10,000 men, women & children who were in France when the peace of Amiens¹ ended. These 10,000 harmless tourists & business men were prisoners till 1814 (eleven years). We had in those 11 years about 50,000 French.

A *few* were able to work exchanges, not many, for Napoleon demanded that we should send back all our 50,000 for his 16,000; & we demurred, knowing that he would never send his 16,000, even if we sent our 50,000. So there they were; prisoners, in big prison-camps, or on parole of some kind in lodgings.

In all camps, armies & communities, there will be criminals, wild men, savages, with a good general level. Revolutionary fleets & armies were a pretty tough set, used to pillage & rapine as a way of life: but the conscripts were all the French people, very clever, orderly, thrifty men, quick at fun, very well able to make themselves comfortable, & naturally sensible & disciplined. The officers on parole broke their paroles a good deal (more than our men wd have done) but *on the whole* the prisoners were well behaved.

They were mostly young, & many of them tried to escape: a few got right away.

They were apt to fling stones at sentries, to fight among themselves, & to gamble, but they worked at jobs to make money, & some made a good deal thus, £100, £200, even £300, are sums mentioned. Our men were prone not to work, & very prone to get drunk if they possibly could.

Our prisoners in France could get, thro a British ministry, stuff for clothing & money for food.

Their prisoners here got nothing thus. We clothed & fed them, & the clothing we supplied was conspicuous red & yellow stuff, to help to prevent escape, for a man in bright yellow trowsers & a red cap was easily spotted anywhere.

In some camps, there were very evil sets of men, who gambled away all their possessions, lived on camp-garbage, stole, went naked, or almost naked, & slept naked on the floor all heaped together for warmth. These were the sort of scum that made the Revolution, the sansculottes, the Septembriseurs, the men of Marseilles etc. Any infamy that men can practise these men practised, & delighted in, & boasted of.

For the rest, prisoners have a low vitality, & are not prone to vice, other than drunkenness or drug-taking, when these are possible; for these blind men for hours together.

Besides, life in a prison, as in a ship, is as public as the town pump, & all except the wild savages were under observation the whole time.

What went on in the bare rooms of the savages when locked in for the night one had better not ask.

Except in epidemics, influenza, bronchitis & (in one case) typhoid(?) the prisons were clean & healthy. The English did run them humanely & well: but a lot of them were crowded: jammed together: so that in the big rooms there were usually 3 tiers of hammocks. I cannot decide which of the three sleepers in each partition had the best of it. I should vote for the lowest berth; which would you vote for?

Nothing could make a prison, when overcrowded, as all war-prisons are, anything but a hell. Consider this one passage from the Report of a Surveyor of Public Buildings 1813.

"The stewards are respectable men, & with their wives & children have only a common privy, to which all the French cooks have access, & the path to which is exposed to the whole of the prisoners.

Submit, that a small room & privy may be added to the stewards' accommodation."

(The state of things had endured for 10 years.)

Most of the inmates were young men half frantic with sex: & perhaps crazy, like Palamon & Arcite,[2] for some Emily seen passing outside the prison.

Letters did sometimes come to them from France, & money, & gifts even, but rarely & irregularly. What hells of longing, what aches of want.

> Art thou still there,
> My England, my country, my home?

[1] Treaty of Amiens (March 1802) between France, Britain, Spain and Holland, ending the first phase of the Napoleonic Wars. War began again in May 1803.

[2] From "The Knight's Tale" in Chaucer's *Canterbury Tales.*

262

... I am posting to you a photograph of a 5th cent. Greek Cup in the Brit. Mus: a cup decorated by a famous artist called Sotades.[1] It illustrates the poem of Sappho about the apple.[2] You will see the apple high up, the nice picker stretching unavailingly for it. Hold the photo in both hands before you, & bend the print a little. This will help you to see that it is a cup.

I also send casts of 2 Lesbian coins, one of Eresus, one of Mitylene, both cast about AD 120, under Antoninus Pius. I fear that the heads are done from different ladies, but both are meant for Sappho, some 7 or 800 years after her time.

... The painter Sotades, who did the cup, was a gifted elegant decorator of the most exquisite Greek period, 450–400 BC. The cup was found in Greece, & was probably made near Athens. The white glaze or wash inside the cup is said to have traces of a second figure to the left of the tree.

There were other, later, more decadent Greeks called Sotades. One of them was a scurrilous poet who made lampoons about the King of Egypt, the Greek Ptolemy Philadelphus, and went beyond all permitted bounds, as on many other occasions. He had to fly from Alexandria by sea, but was pursued & caught. His captor put him into a leaden box, & hove him overboard.

The Sotades who did the Sappho lady (the design on the cup) is fairly famous as a pottery designer: about half a dozen of his pots have survived: & there is one wonderful thing by him in Boston (of a grass-hopper raised on a white dish).

The handles of his cup are of a type of pottery called "wish-bone handles". They are stuck onto the body of the cup with an amazing glue which the Greeks had: and their glue can (I believe) be made now: & perhaps is. But we have never discovered how to make the marvellous black glaze of the great Greek "black figure pots" though the chemists have traced some of its constituents.

How movingly you write of Sappho. She wrote about 2,500 years ago: & it is 2,300 years ago since Sotades was moved by her poem to see this lovely, graceful woman exquisitely trying to reach an apple, with these lovely stretched ankles & appealing hand.

One of her inventions was a harp: perhaps the harp on the coin. That invention may, possibly, have survived in Lesbos.

There is another Sotades cup in the Brit. Mus; it must be a moving drawing: very delicate & dainty: yet it has somehow survived until now.

¹ Sotades, Athenian potter, at work about 460 BC. Known from his signatures on vases. Collaborated (or was possibly identical) with an anonymous vase-painter, who has been nicknamed "The Sotades painter". Three of the signed vases are in the British Museum.

² See Letter 255; also Letters 256, 257.

263

. . . About the musician who wants to write.

He has an abundant, strange experience to tell; that is half the battle.

So often a vivid, felt experience will tell itself. One has only to tell it by word of mouth: and there it will be.

Writing is made easier by practice, & by the study of quiet, good writing; the story of David, say, in (I think) Kings, in the Bible: then Defoe, Swift, Addison, Steele.

There are various slogans to bear in mind—

No flowers, by request.

Boil it down.

Nothing too much.

Thrift, thrift, Horatio—etc etc.

No little handbooks can help like those little slogans.

The best tale is simple, like the child's version of Elisha's story.

"Elisha was a very good man, and the bad boys called him names.
He said, 'If you call me names, I'll call a bear, and he'll eat you.'
    And they did, and he did, and it did."

264

. . . *Oblige* is a French derivative, & was (for centuries) both written
& pronounced obleege, obleige, etc.
    Prunes is a clipped modern version of a two-syllabled word.
Shakespeare wrote, & no doubt pronounced, it prewyns, and other
bold spirits wrote of pruans, pro-ines etc.
    Did not Dr Johnson write:

> Stew or triturate thy pru-ins
> Thus you lenify your chewins.

And Gray:

> Those that prune what pruins were
> Did old England's sepulchre.

Blake, surely, too:

> Those that prune the pleading pruin
> Slam the lid on Albion's ruin.

1960

265

... It is not easy to write of Wellington, knowing so little, but I come (on the whole) to this conclusion, that he was the product of the British noble order, of the French Revolutionary time, & that he had the hard indifference of his caste, but with the clear logical Irish mind, not the foggy & winey & senseless mind of the London Government. He was a man of intellect, employed by men with none, or with debased views of government; & living always on the brink of dismissal, keeping difficult lines with vile, untaught officers, & insufficient men, arms & money.

He had a few senior men whom he trusted & was just to. To his army he was . . . .

Well, he knew it, & he may be believed.

He was a gentleman: that is very much anywhere.

He was a practised soldier, used to run armies & governments in India.

He saw clearly, what no other man saw, that the French system of war *must* fail. They lived by plunder, & when that ceased they died.

He saw, too, that the French system of Battle must fail. The column was helpless against a steady line. No-one else saw this, but he shewed it, & ended Boney & his regime. His dispatches from Spain are masterly, with a sarcasm that (I fear) was wasted on the recipients.

In battle he was superb: in his arrangements out of battle I think the world blames him.

266

... Nelson & Wellington, in their so different ways, were men who carried their followers to success, the one by swift imagination & the instant pounce upon opportunity, & the other more by a perception of a better system than the enemy's.

Nelson had some winning qualities that Nosey disdained as too effusive.

I remember what a hunting man once said to me. "Hounds love the man who hunts them, not the man who feeds them."

It is very true, as I saw, when a boy.

Soldiers & sailors love the man who leads them to victory, & *does not waste them.* They respect the enemy leader who has this power, which is *the* power, being *imagination.*

Nelson, like Boney, was a little, compact & dangerous figure, Boney like a field-piece bullet, Nelson like a swift sword.

It is incredible that Nelson should have been so tiny, but go to see his little coat & pigtail at Greenwich. He was mainly spirit.

... Boney, Nosey & Nelson—they are all three a bit overlaid now, but they ruled the imagination when I was young. I knew people who remembered Waterloo, & the coaches coming with the news. I have talked with a lady who had talked with Boney: & I have seen 2 of the ships that were at Trafalgar, & the bullet that killed Nelson, & one of some of the real topmasts that carried the *Victory* into the scrum ... Like the chap in *Henry IV, Part 2*—"I cannot choose but be old."

Boney was the marvellous one.

Often I read the account of the Hundred Days, with amazement, that one man could have done it all; all that incredible adventure . . . .

O course, he was utterly worn out by the 96th day of it, but yet he thrust on to the 97th, had them all in his hand, the game his (one would say) till noon on the 98th. No man has done such a feat, ever, nor (I trust) ever will.

But his bolt was shot: he was exhausted.

Twenty minutes more of his fire would have carried him into Brussels on the 98th day, with Blücher a ruin, & Nosey a prisoner; & the oaths of Picton roaring somewhere to no-one; & the English Government up a gum-tree.

(This of course reckons the 100th day as Waterloo Day, 18th June, & this is not the usual reckoning, but let it be ours.)

Of course, apart from Boney's exhaustion, he had a raw army, with a staff all anyhow, & the horses, & dispatch riders, new to the work, & not knowing the ways. On the 98th day, he did not know

where his left wing was, & on the 100th day he did not know
(within 10 miles) where his right wing was, nor did the L & R
know very well where he (or the enemy) was.

Then the rain fell, & the army had no food, except what they
could steal.

I must write about Nosey & N at another time.

267

Reyna mia

Thank you so much for your delightful letter, & for telling me
about the silver, & about all your perils in the road-smash.

It is truly a marvel that you have lived that kind of risk, winter
after winter, ever since you first wrote to me, & yet never fail to
write to me, & write as though there was neither risk nor discomfort.

Did you know that (in a way) you are very like Nosey?

Not facially & nosily (though Nosey in his way was a very handsome fellow), & not for your power of taking peril in its stride,
but because "he was very fond of music, & played very well on the
fiddle".

How well you would have got along together.

His beauty was commanding & foreseeing (seeing sooner that
anyone else) as his marvellous portrait by Goya shows. (I am
trying to find a print of this for you.)

Goya painted him in Spain, during the Peninsular campaign
(the horrors of which Goya also saw & recorded). It is just about
the best portrait done in the 19th cent.

As to Boney's face: the Italian type: it had much beauty, as one
sees in the Vernet portraits, & the Death-mask. His eyes were like
fire, & one eye was said to be more terrible than the other: perhaps
the one in the better light.

Of the three men, Nosey's face seems to be the best all-round
face; but somehow he has not won, nor kept, so much love from
people; nor left such a mark on things & institutions. We have a
Nelson Day: not a Nosey Day, but even our Nelson Day is dimmer
than once.

This poor letter, alas, is all I can send.

My blessings to you, & may you keep out of these smashes &
find lovely coffee pots in the junk shops.

Jan.

268

. . . When I wrote, I could not answer you about Goya: nor can I tell you much about him now.

Alas, I do not know his big designs for tapestries: these (of the life of Spain) must be like the 2nd part of *Don Quixote*, very fine things.

I remember best the wonderful portraits of the Spanish Court (in the Prado, Madrid). These must be the very best portraits of that century.

I gather (from his own portrait, done by himself) that he was an explosive fellow; & as a youth he was involved, with others, in man-killings, & bull-fightings: many Spaniards are.

He saw the French in Spain, & the horrors done by and upon them: things fearful.

The French could not send a message safely with less than 20 men. "Yo lo vi," he wrote: "I saw it." Few, in Spain, could avoid seeing it.

There used to be a superb Goya portrait in the Nat. Gal. He put fire into some of his portraits, from the devil that was in himself. Some devilry of himself is in most of them.

I guess he was a tough guy.

His self-portrait has just a touch of resemblance to one of the portraits of Wm Blake, whose life was in the years of his life: tho Blake never saw the horrors of war, nor mixed in man-killings & bull-fights.

. . . I was reading Cowper's Letters a brief while past, & came upon the following, wh as a friend, devoted to you, & ever hoping for your welfare, I feel I must send to you. It was written to the Rev. John Newton, who was said to have been a slaver, if not a pyrat, in the Bight of Benin, before he became a Rev. (perhaps calumny).

Sept 9 1782.
He seems (he being a local clergyman) to have suffered considerably in his spiritual character by his attachment to music. The lawfulness of it (music), when used with moderation, & in its proper place, is unquestionable; but I believe that wine itself, though a man be guilty of habitual intoxication, does not more debauch & befool the natural understanding than music—always music, music in season & out of season—weakens & destroys the spiritual discernment!

Of course, Cowper was sometimes mad.

269

. . . In your letter about Nosey, not long since, you quoted a lady's book about him, that said he wd have liked Miss Jenny Lind "if only she did not sing".

Please: no doubt he said it: but what he meant was that Society did not recognise the professions. People who were Born did not toil, neither did they spin: a grateful country saw to that.

Then (& for a half a century more) Society did not admit the stage; that was outside the limits.

I do not know when, nor where, N heard Miss Lind sing. I judge that it was in her first London season in 1849, when she staggered all England by an exquisite voice, & an operatic manner fresh, direct, un-theatrical & compelling.

N was fond of music: & no doubt was enthralled by her.

But, then: she was on the stage: she appeared in public, painted, & impersonating. The basso wd threaten her, & the tenor (perhaps) clasp her. No: no: she ought not to do that kind of thing: it was not done.

If only she were not doing that kind of thing, one might meet her in Society, perhaps, & hear her in some drawing-room.

I saw Jenny Lind several times long since, & may have heard her voice, even (in Church).

I sat in the pew just behind her.

It is strange to think, now, that she was one who had talked with Nosey & (no doubt) the last Napoleon & the exquisite Eugénie.

270

. . . I venture to send you, for your friend, a copy of the Music verses. I forget when they were written: some time ago: but not very long. They were for a Christmas card, I think, or for some celebration, or for some sort of toothache that I had in my mind (so called).

I am so glad that you liked them. As a rule I fight kind of shy of this sort of O thou-y verse, having had a scunner of them, in mss, from strangers.

. . . There was a fearful yellow Indian who came to me with thou-y poems long since: truly an appalling man, with a sheaf of poems about thou. (Not *you*: no such luck.)

Golly, he was a terror.

This was his kind of thing:

O thou, whose theeness art my blank . . .
O thou
I, who am nothingness aware of theeness
I who am I, nothing more but thou
I impinging on the blank, for thou art thee.

There were 200 pages of this & he expected me to write a preface & get it printed for him. I tried to be tactful, but I was very firm. He left with a gloomy view of my thou-ness, & I have sorrowed ever since at odd times at not being more perceptive, & understanding; for, in a way, I could see what he was up to, & that he was not writing in his own tongue, & that in the yellow Indian tongue it might have been something.

. . . Thank you for telling me about your Wm Hone book;[1] I have never seen his collections of old matters; but he helped many people to know something of the Middle Ages, & thereby helped on the passion for mediaeval work that inspired nearly all lively minds from 1820–1900.

The contractions in the script you sent were to save writing. Many old mss are full of contractions. One saved writing & also saved quite a lot of expensive parchm[t]. If M. Ch'c'r had been writing to you he might perhaps have begun D'ing Reyna where I should put Darling Reyna, but no . . . GC would have begun his letter to you in verse.

O blisful Swete, dere Moone amid MY NIGHT,
O Grënë Cornë in my desert field
O to what Stranngers dostow bring Delight
Making the blackest Heaven starry ceiled?
I, the old withered apple wrinkle peeled
Salute thee, blisful Queen & ever pray
Joy may be thine, dere brightë fresshë May

Would it be a sad both[r] to you to write without conti'us, of y[r] p't thoughts & read'gs, so yt this link in us might still bring us tog'er, as cannot often hap in lyf?

. . . PS About the Class feeling that you so tellingly illustrated: GC was of the feudal time, in which there were marked classes, that were known, & observed, & accepted as divinely ordained. People were not to presume about them. Christ died for all, God watched over all, the Ghost comforted all, & Fortune did justice upon all.

Most members of the society worshipped & rode to Canterbury together: & the Knight told a story to all hands, & perhaps listened even to the Cook; certainly to the others.

Tempest[2] thee not al croked to redress
In trust of Hir that turneth like a ball.

¹ William Hone (1780–1842) was a bookseller who published his own satires, which were illustrated by Cruikshank. The book ANS told JM about was *Ancient Mysteries described, especially the Miracle plays* . . .

² Meaning "agitate, disturb".

271

. . . The word *Aroint* seems to be with us because WS uses it so effectively in *Macbeth* & in *K. Lear*.

It is (I say) the phrase still used all over the W. Midlands.. In Herefordsh. we used to say (or people used to say to me) Arr out the light, or Err out the door; meaning go, get, avoid, but meaning it meaningly.

272

. . . I can tell you now about Nosey & his fiddles. He was in India, at a very crucial time in India, when it was a toss-up if France or England were to command: (& to end the existing chaos).

Nosey & his brother saw that the Indians were deeply conscious of caste: & insisted that the kingly abstained from certain things. The French were insisting on equality & fraternity, & couping the gorges of people who objected.

N's brother (as I judge) told the young Nosey that he must insist on his rank & hold aloof. N therefore "burned his riddles" (that is the phrase) & became as exclusive as Royalty: or as his brother.

It gave both of them great prestige: & helped their quite outstanding marvellous triumphs.

> The strings that once in Delhi's halls
> The soul of music shed

were burned, & Nosey played no more.

273

> [Her feet beneath her petticoat
> Like little mice stole in & out
> As tho' they feared the light,

And O she danced in such a way
No Nun upon an Easter Day
Was half so brave a sight.][1]

The quotation that worries your dear head is from Sir John Suckling's "Ballad on a Wedding", which I enclose.

I do not know the real reading of the [fifth] line. This book[2] reads *Sun*, not *Nun*, & I think that Sun may be right; for Nuns wore their Habit, surely, & never dressed up specially, even for Easter.

Please keep the book: although I (or somebody) has cut a bit out of a page; perhaps in censorship, perhaps to save the trouble of copying a poem, wanted as a quotation.

The Wedding of the Ballad is said to be that of a Lord Broghill with a Lady Margaret Howard, both, I suppose, bright stars of the Court of Charles the First.

Please will you thank your Father for his kind comment on the Easter play of mine?[3] I heard some of it: & again, as ever, could have wept at my having no music, & no actor's singing voice: & in a verse-play a conductor, also, with a baton, in front of the stage, on whom all eyes must fix, & having a Sack for any luckless wight whose eyes aren't on him.

I asked a playwright once (I being very young then), "How do you feel, when you see your play performed?"

He said, "I sit in my Box and curse the Actors!"

I don't do that. I curse my own lacks that have made so many lacks in others to appear.

[1] ANS could not place these lines, learnt in early years at home, so asked JM who their author was.

[2] *The Oxford Book of Seventeenth Century Verse.*

[3] JM's *Easter: a Play for Singers* (1929)

274

. . . I hope that you will soon be having a happy study of Emma & Nelson.

I used to see Nelson's tiny little suit in a case at Greenwich; & the bullet, or slug, which laid him low. Then, elsewhere, I saw a sizeable chunk of the *Victory*'s mizen, or main, topmast, I forget which; & elsewhere, all the *Victory*; & a model of Trafalgar's battle without the smoke (only cotton wool); & somewhere or other a tricolor from the *Redoutable*.

Please, will you honour me with the grace & charm of your views of Emma? You are ever a wonderful letter writer, when the topic is pleasing to you: then the golden prose flows out of your heart, all sovereign in preciousness & honey to the thirsty palate! (Mine.)

. . . My thanks for this opening of another topic: the once Xtian King [Charles II].

I suppose that none wd call him the Father of his Country, but perhaps no English King has been the Father of so much of his Peerage.

I will look for the account of his escape from the Worcester Battle: I have it somewhere: & have, at odd times, gone over all the known route, but so long ago that it is now dim.

One of the very great things in his favour, & it is truly great, is that he remembered & rewarded, after 10 years of beggary & vagabondage, despised, & perhaps often hungry, *all* who helped him in his need, then, at the risk of ruin & death. This is a Royal thing: & it is (I believe) true, that those families still draw the royal bounty for their heroism & their sacrifice.

You may have been, not far (not very far) from Marlborough, to that Church of Manningford Bruce, where there is the tomb of Mrs Nicholas, who took the flying King as her servant, as she rode southward on a part of his journey. She wd infallibly have been hanged, or sold as a slave to merchants, had she been caught, but she did it; & had her reward, such as, I think, no other commoner has ever had; her family, that is, her Father's family, the Lanes, were granted the right "to bear the arms of England in a canton". You will see the arms on the shield there. Do go to see them. She was a brave soul.

The campaign of Worcester is interesting, but very dreadful. The royal army must have been 3 parts starved & shoeless & hopeless. I knew about the battle once, & went all over the field of it. Miss Strickland,[1] the Historian, wanted to know the battlefield (about 120 years ago, I think, perhaps somewhat less). A native said he could take her there; & did so; but she was much puzzled: & could not think that he was right. He said that he was right, for he had seen the battle with his own eyes. The battle that he had seen was a prize-fight, on the grass, between 2 old champions of the Ring.

. . . Now I have to go out, but I hope that you will enjoy the Flight stories.[2]

The Bridport close-call was the closest; & but for John Wesley's great (great) grandfather's dislike of being disturbed at prayers, he wd have been taken & killed, & where wd all our Peerage be, had that blow fallen?

How he escaped at all, with a face so memorable & his unusual height . . .

But what loyalty, what friends.

¹ Agnes Strickland (1796–1874) author, with her sister, of *Lives of the Queens of Scotland and English Princesses* (1850–9).

² *The Flight of the King* by Alan Fear, 1897; revised 1908.

275

... About Mr FH [Frank Harris]. He was (like OW [Oscar Wilde]) some years before my time, & tho I met a dozen who knew OW I only met one who knew FH; & remember that this man spoke of him as one of the cosmopolitan writers, living in the US, in Paris, London, & anywhere, with some streak of colour & of genius from each one.

I do not know his work at all well, but read 1 or 2 of his things in Reviews: all clever & good but I did not care for it as for those others whose work was all in all to me. Lately, I read 2 of his stories, once much admired, but it was too late then, for them: they belonged to the very late nineties.

He knew OW pretty well, I believe.

On the whole, I doubt every story told of OW. He was a city writer, moving in a glittery set, & the genius of the set. The reports by the set usually glitter a little, but are seldom genuine.

I do not know what FH wrote of him, but think that he touched the real OW, now & then, & gives some of the genius ... the one fragment that I have read suggests this.

I do not know.

But it used to be said that sometimes he & OW were really outstanding marvellous being together, outside the Café Royal (that is, at the back, away from the Regent Street side or front). Then, on lucky evenings, the two are said to have told amazing stories to each other, or against each other, each so picturesque, fantastic, witty, downright, searching, scented, coarse, with all the powers of their so different beings, that the hearers were spell-bound . . . .

I did not hear these ... but my adjectives (I hope) are not unjust. I put "scented, coarse", one for each of them, for these fundamentals came into the being.

I well remember the convulsion & tumult of the OW case.¹

That kind of thing was very rare, then, but 2 wars have changed man & his judgements. If he were tried today, the case would be dismissed on some medical plea that he needed treatment.

OW took a pleasure in showing that Sodom was his spiritual home, & FH could not avoid showing (on the contrary) that he was born in Gomorrah.

¹ See Letters 200–202.

276

... It is with great regret that I have to say that I cannot find my *Tartuffe*, & I feel sure that I own it both in French & English.

Tartuffe is/was a satirical study of Hypocrisy, religious & moral.

He is the chief person, a man, in Molière's Comedy of the name.

It is much acted in France, but, I should think, never here. Tartuffe makes clandestine love, you see; & advises ladies to be more careful not to expose too much temptation. He hands one his hankie, with the words, "*Couvrez, je* do beseech, *ces seins immodestes.*"

He wrote it about 1660–1664, perhaps, when Charles II was attempting to found a peerage single-handed.

It roused such a storm in Paris, it is said, that it could not be played nor printed, save in part, for a dozen years.

The devout looked upon it as an attack on all attempt to live religiously. They raised a real storm, & went to lengths of savagery, to discredit Molière, that have seldom been surpassed. M was a great success as a playwright, poet & actor.

They accused him of living incestuously with his own illegitimate daughter by his baggage.

This scandalous lie is now known & proven to be a lie.

It is never safe to believe a story about a writer.

The English never care for this type of the Molière play, being so often sickened by boredom after 5 minutes; but the French make it a trenchant thing (or did).

I like the lighter things of M: *The Forced Marriage* etc etc.

If I can find my *Tartuffe* it shall be sent to you, so that you may read it, & cry, with Tartuffe's friend, "O the poor man."

277

Reyna mia.

My thanks for your dear card, & most kind memory.

The two names are distinct, please.

The Clifton man is SYMONDS (like the Yat on the Wye).

The Blake man is SYMONS (a much younger man).

Both were highly cultivated men & discriminating critics: but the work of both has been neglected of late, like other precious Victorian contributions to life.

Symonds was passing out of favour when the century ended, and Symons was, perhaps, crushed out, by the first war. When the *Yellow Book* ceased, Symons started & kept going a periodical called *The Savoy*, for a brief while. He wrote an essay on Beardsley: & one on Dowson. He translated with an unusual swift exquisite perceptive skill, from the French & the Italian. (He knew France & Italy very well, I think.)

His translations from Verlaine, Baudelaire, D'Annunzio, are beyond praise. He also translated some of the tales of de Maupassant & Villiers de l'Isle Adam; & must have done much to bring the great French influence here. He had a sensitive instant response to places. When he wrote of a foreign scene, O golly.

He was said to have written all the last number of *The Savoy* by himself, using various pen-names. There is a prose story in this that made me wish he had written more stories. Possibly he did: but I only saw this one & some of his French translations.

O golly, he could translate: & for delicate verse & prose, also O golly.

Now I will golly you no more, but wish you all lovely glad blessings.

Jan.

278

. . . I do not know B [Charles Baudelaire] very well, but he is still much read in France, for his rebellion, & for his care for writing; a sort of newness of mind being the rebellion, however wrongful & disastrous; & a search for the word, a care, a tact, a distinction, that the French prize in writing, that he showed, in verse & prose.

He was a difficult lad to guide, I would judge; & having, as a youth, a taste for dandyism, he was apt to assume superior ways, perhaps.

His Father died when he was young; & his Mother married again; a Colonel something; shall we call him Le Colonel de Jones.[1] De Jones was a diplomat of high distinction, but CB told his Mother that "The Mothers of such as he (CB) do not re-marry."

In the revolutionary Paris of 1848, CB was seen walking alone with a banner among the revolutionaries. The banner bore the strange device: "Death to the Colonel de Jones."

However, de Jones (I believe) outlived CB.[2]

At the age of 25 or so, CB became overwhelmed by the writings of E. A. Poe, all of which he translated into French. This is his main life-work, I suppose. It was a sort of "possession". CB felt that he had known or written the words in another life or world.

In this life, the best comment on him is the superb poem "Ave Atque Vale", by Swinburne, which puts poetical truth instead of the coarse fact of literary gossip.

CB defied & was distinguished; & died mad at the age of about 46 or so.

He was much among the Painters of that time, Manet, Daumier etc.

[1] Baudelaire's stepfather was Colonel (later General) Aupick.

[2] Soon after, however, JM wrote: "But I was wrong about CB who wished 'Death to the Colonel de Jones'. Le Colonel pre-deceased him."

279

. . . CB was what the Americans used to call "a bit off his rocker". like many other interesting writers. He had a lady love,[1] whom his enemies describe as a "negress", but from his poems she seems to have been more copper-coloured: certainly not as black as some of these people paint her. Some people say she drank.

Well, poor soul, living in Paris after living in the tropics, & with a poet a bit off his rocker, I judge that she needed a dram or so, now & again. Presently, CB was quite altogether off his rocker, & "what could poor Robin do then, poor thing"?

I dare say that some painter of the circle painted her, but I have never seen her portrait. One or two of the poems give some suggestions, of an unusual beauty of form & prose:

"The hidden splendour and fatal beauty."

"The rude majesty of that straight firm form."

"She walks like a goddess and rests like a Sultana."

I think that she haunted all his off-rockery rockings, as a main figure in his more permanent nightmare.

1 About 1843 Baudelaire established a liaison with a mulatto actress called Jeanne Duval. She was certainly no Negress: Baudelaire speaks of "*cette peau couleur d'ambre*".

280

... As far as I can make out, the thing called a spittoon came from America, about 1840.

It was the custom of the manly sex (then & there) to chew tobacco, to an extent unusual. It was unusual over 50 years later, when I saw it practised to a degree that startled me. Many men, then, swallowed the juice, but most did not; and as there was no sea at hand as in a ship . . .

Indoors, the spittoons were of china, or brass, or of glass.

There was the story of a Middle Westerner who came to stay in the East. He, the wild son of freedom, raised on the prairie, had never seen a spittoon, and so, when his host kept moving the spittoon nearer to his guest with cautious feet, the guest exclaimed, "Say, friend, don't move them things any nearer; I guess I might spit on them."

All the American Railways, then, seemed to have a big advertisement, 10 feet x 10 feet, at every mile, with the legend:

RED MAN
The Mild Mellow Chew.

But 20 years later, such is the refining influence of woman, all this had gone; chewing seemed dead & forgotten, though 1 or 2 jaws still writhed a little on gum.

Superior people did not call the things spittoons but Cuspadores or Cuspidors, a Portuguese word, very superior, which means Spitters.

This was in use in the late 18th century, as a word & as a thing, being brought in, perhaps, by our traders with Portugal.

I wonder what the French for spittoon is?

A sort of war-cry, perhaps. Soldats de France. Ne soillez pas les jolis tapis de papa. Crachez dedans, etc.

281

... It was said that in the days of the fear of Napoleon's invasion, Br military genius dug a trench in Kent, 5 miles long, to bar his approach. I have such, marked in old maps, but forget where it was. Did you see it at all, or is it now ploughed-out, or was it all a myth, spread abroad to make N believe that we were ready?

We had a loyal toast:

> If the French come over
> We shall meet them at Dover.

So, no doubt, we should; but the meeters would have had no guns

I fear; & if they had guns, no powder; & if they had had both, no anything else.

It is always strange to me that N never tried it. The wind must often have been E for long periods during his command: & a permanent E wind means fine calm weather, when ships cannot sail to the E.

Well . . . N knew his power on land: & kept to the kind of war he knew he was good at, & to soldiers who could do his kind of war, or could be made to do it. The army might have landed & seized London; & then the Westerly gales might have set in for 2 months solid; & at the end of that time, he would have been done; somewhere on the way to Fordwich or to Sandwich or to Hythe, he & the Old Guard, eating broiled Marengo, and sending in a white flag to his brave cousin, K George the Third.

282

. . .Writers do not often work much together: but all young writers belong to a gang or clique. Youth demands this, I should judge, in all ages. The young men will meet in a newspaper or magazine office, & will form a lunching or dining club, with a meeting once a week or oftener: or they will lunch daily at some place, or dine, together, day after day, & discuss things & decide who must be followed & who must be condemned: & who could possibly get hold of some adored star & get him to come to a meal with the gang.

I always feel that someone in Burbage's company kept a gang together, & kept WS in it, all thro his active life . . . I do not know who it was: nobody does: but somebody did it, who yet didn't care two pence for poetry; & cut out 700 lines of *Macbeth*: and allowed the First Folio to appear as it did appear.

In Paris, it is warmer in summer, & the side walks are very broad, & the café tables jut out into the open & every café has a gang & the gang can get tick when hard-up there, & the café takes joy when one of the gang gets a red button, or has his picture hung, or his piece put on by the Comédie. This is a wonderful force, the café, in France. Something like it used to be in California, & in New York (perhaps more than now). Then, in addition to the gang, there may always be the *Master*: Zola with his *Causeries du Lundi*, [1] Yeats with his Monday evenings, Mallarmé, at his evenings, Rogers[2] at his Breakfasts.

An odd fancy, to gather people to breakfast. It seems like smothering the day in the cradle. Perhaps those who went to them never had any day to smother.

Rogers had Porson,[3] the Greek scholar, to dinner once: and P sat at his wine later: & drank all the wine: so Rogers foraged in the kitchen, all hands being in bed by that time, & found the kitchen brandy: so Porson drank all that; & even then cried out for more; but there was no more; so P drank all the inks in the ink-stand, & then said, "Rogers, will you see me home? I'm not very steady on my pins."

So Rogers, the good host, started to take him home, & when in the street Porson collapsed into the gutter.

This was a test of character I wd say.

[1] Not to be confused with the *Causeries du Lundi* (so called because they appeared in the press on Mondays) by Charles Augustin de Sainte-Beuve (1804–69).

[2] Samuel Rogers (1763–1855), "the banker poet", author of *The Pleasures of Memory*.

[3] Richard Porson (1759–1808), elected Regius Professor of Greek at Cambridge, 1792. He was famous for his love of wine.

283

. . .My thanks for your charming kind letter from the sea.

I hope that you are now safely at home again, all sun burned, & I hope not tattooed with a new anchor on either hand.

Did I tell you of the sailor I once met who had a Maltese Cross on his nose in blue? I met him in Greenwich Hospital, some 55 years ago, and truly, you never saw the like.

We had a long talk together, but I could not quite dare, on such short acquaintance, to ask how he had come by it, whether for love or from a sense of beauty or in some boyish frolic.

Once on, it was probably better to leave it, for it would have been agony to have it off, and bits of him, from elsewhere, grafted on instead.

I think that the charge in Liverpool would have been 2/6 at least for such a work on the nose. A flag, or a ring on the finger, could be had for 1/-, but no doubt prices are up now.

Many of my ancient companions plunged thus, and bitterly repented of it, but I never had the money myself, though, of course, I had the sense of beauty.

284

. . .I have been wondering about why my sailor had the Cross tattooed on his nose. I could not suppose that it was done from a religious sense, for his talk was far from pious; but skirmishing around, in the Virgilian Lots[1] way, lo, a clipping in *The Times*, about a man who put a tombstone on his coffee-bar, thinking that it gave the place a tone (clipping enclosed).

> That's what he did I sudden sed,
> And joybells rang inside my head.

He [the sailor] had it tattooed to give his face a tone, which otherwise it might have seemed somehow to kind of lack; but with it, lor lummy, they'd give him tick at Steve's.

He was a Mediterranean service man: & perhaps in some frolic at Malta . . .? Or was it the stamp of some Secret Society in Newfound-land, where seamen call everybody "a —— Blue Nose".[2]

. . . You mention the unspeakable ruffian, Jehu.

I do not know what horses they had then; but I suppose something smallish, with much of the Arab, with a good deal of fire & mettle, such, perhaps, as Assyrian bas-reliefs show, & Homer describes as at Troy, & the Egyptians cut & painted.

The ruffian drove furiously, on tracks & the wilderness, in light 2 wheeled chariots . . . how rimmed? How axled?

Had he iron? Is it not a lie? A propagandist lie, to make it apparent that he was a man of power, with divine guards?

His name is said to mean "Jehovah is He": but I do not know what the phrase means. Perhaps it is a sort of Babylonian boast about the god he worshipped. Shalmaneser might have said, "Baal is He. Baal is the Boy. Vote for good old Baal. Always a fresh surprise. Worship Baal, you fellows, & you'll come home with the booty: damsels for all: Baal is the He to bring you damsels." So then they voted for Baal.

But of all the beastly tales, Jehu's is about the vilest.

Now I cannot (after this long time) give you chapter & verse; but do you know, there is a portrait of Jehu?

Like the Abbot of Abingdon, "he got a knock from a King & incurable the wound".

Some King in the East got him by the scruff; and there is an inscribed Black Stone (it is in some Mus., perhaps the Brit. where I have seen it) telling of the event: and low down on it, lo, a little tiny Jehovah is He knocking his repulsive head in the dust to show that he will be a good boy, & pay up every ¼ day.

---

[1] "Virgilian Lots"—*Sortes Virgilianae*—a method of divination anciently practised by selecting passages at random from *The Aeneid*; more commonly done with the Bible in recent times.

[2] See also Letter 97.

285

. . .California, where your nephew Anthony is to live, is a friendly spot, but some of it is rather earthquakey & trembles (in parts) almost daily. When I was there once it was very trembly; every day, at some time a little joggle or threat: & one used to wonder, is this all, or is this only a prelude? You could see what it could do, when it went on, for there were ruins to be seen; but it never did more than joggle when I was there.

The troubles, the real ones, are often very brief, but they wreck the burg good & plenty, while they are at it. It is the fires, due to short circuits & gas & broken petrol tanks, that do the worst, for these fires go on for days, & no water in the mains.

286

. . .You talk of being a Nomad, but you have more variety than the Nomad & you go more quickly, & you have a lot more wonderful art, and then, usually, you find food & shelter & have not to watch your flocks all seated on the ground, & listen to the wolves drawing near & see their green eyes in the gloom with horrid warning gaped wide. No . . . you may even be at a Trafalgar Dinner[1] sipping Madeira, just like a Viscount in a Tale of High Life.

It is hard to imagine a blinder confusion than the battle of Trafalgar: an almost calm, with incredible smoke and roar & whizz & crash: & then after some hours of this, when 40 big ships were more or less knocked to shivers, a growing swell, with 3 days of storm on a lee shore . . .

[1] Sir John and Lady Barbirolli used to invite me to a little "Trafalgar Supper" each year, if it were possible to arrange it. ANS.

287

. . . If you should be in London for Christmas, it might be a happy jaunt to take your young nephew to the United Service Institution, to show him the peep shows.

There are about 20 of these, each about 3 feet by 2 feet. You go to them in a half darkness, & turn a switch, & lo, before you, at choice, will be now Julius Caesar's Landing; then, the battle of Ulundi; then, the Charge of the Light Brigade; one of the Squares at

Waterloo; Marston Moor; the taking of Quebec; the famous battle of Crécy; etc etc; while, up above, is the vast battle of Trafalgar; & all Waterloo, with Boney beginning to totter; & a lot of very fine ship models, & stands of arms.

In addition, Tim might show you about 500 lead (or tin) soldiers of all arms, painted & arrayed as in life at full size. These, mounted or un-mounted, expect attention from the female sex, but do not win it in their present place; & all, even the tallest Life Guards, only an inch and a half (boots & helmet measure).

288

. . . The feeling, when I was young, about the Whistler–Ruskin case, was that JR could not understand anything later than about 1860 or so; & would have disliked this American stranger, trained & taught in France of the Second Empire, in Satanic Paris where . . . where . . . O what . . . of sinny tinsel glittered.

But, come now, both men were extremes & angry & outcast. JR was an outcast, literally, without a caste, never to be admitted among the noblesse: his father was a wine-merchant; & yet spurning & loathing his trading England that had defiled & poisoned & starved & degraded all that it had the power to control. As a worker he was limited. He could copy faithfully & draw prettily. He did not draw figures much & I have never seen any work in colour by him. All his energies went into crying out against his time, in a rather shrill and (often) wordy way. Physically, he was limited, too, and was not a companionable being: but he was a pursuer of beauty, seeking for some gospel of beauty, & trying to state what he saw of this. Anyhow, he was generous past the time's belief, and learned beyond his world's knowledge, and sincere out of all reasonable experience; so that when he spoke, no listener had a chance before him. All who heard had to listen: & now & then, in his books, he wrote with this sincerity & experience & learning & generosity and golly my beloved he mopped the floor with the Dogs. But when the wicked have been reproved by one who is not in society, whose father only sold dry sherry; whose wife ran away with the dashing painter [Sir John Millais]; & who sometimes went mad up in the Lake District, the wicked recover their poise, repeating these things, & go off & sin some more.

Now, Whistler was an outcast of a different sort. He was an American, who, quite early, saw another society than the American. He saw Russia. Being put, quite early, to West Point Military

Academy, to become an officer in the US Army, he found that he could not . . . (Perhaps they found that he would not: I do not know.) I have heard that he tried for the US Navy, too, but am not sure how. (It may not be so.)

Anyhow, he went to Paris, to the studio that Du Maurier describes in *Trilby*. Du Maurier & Renoir were there with him.

In the Paris of that time, the ferment of Impressionism was at work, & this equipped him as an outcast against his teachers as thoroughly as instinct equipped him against society in America & in England.

He came to England, & found himself at once a foreigner, an alien, an artist, a pugnacious, superior, elaborate being in the England whose art made him squirm, & whose society would have none of him. Like other pugnacious, superior, elaborate beings, he mocked this society with a wit that they could not answer, with an elegance of mind that was new to the time, and an insolence as intolerable as Ruskin's outcry. Both men were eminent, both were widely loathed, & somehow they came thus to loggerheads through acting according to their lights, & declaring what they felt to be truth & beauty.

In a way, I think that the Law decided (no doubt at great cost) that both men were utterly right & completely wrong.

289

. . . I am glad that the M book[1] is proving to be such a find. One rarely finds a treasure of a book by chance; though it happens now & then. Hazlitt, in his inn at Alton, had Congreve's play in his pocket: it was not lying in the window-seat.

I wonder whether Shelley really found his bit about the Wandering Jew??? I would surmise that skyey dog wrote it himself in an airy moment; but the moment passed, & he never could get back to it, nor to him. (He being then but a beginner.)

Do you not dream of going to an inn in the wilds of Wales, and finding in an old Annual Register or *Pilgrim's Progress* a neat manuscript in the hand of Purcell, of *Quartettes for ye Fiddle, in hon^r of His Matie?* Or something of the kind by Arne would not be too bad.

But the great thing is always to keep a bright eye looking, so that when the thing is there the heart will be made glad.

[1] A work by Bysshe Molesworth. JM wrote: "I cannot find the name in my books of reference, and have never . . . read or heard of his work." The editor has had the same difficulty.

290

... The open field system went on until the Napoleonic war-time, but the Enclosures of the 18th century killed it.

The system may really well have been pre-historic, but the Normans certainly made it more feudal than it had been.

Piers Plowman[1] lived by it at one time, & I think that I know the very fields where he worked at it, & I did see before [it was] destroyed the cottage in which he may have lived (with his unmarried mother).

I am pretty sure, too, that I have drunk of the burn that he slept by, and that later miscreants, not knowing the crime they did, have put this divine water underground in some poisonous pipe of hell, where none can drink it, & probably wouldn't now, even if he could. Pipe water springing from a hill, now to quench no thirst of man or beast.

You will find there is not much to learn about some of the centuries you seek to know about. For about 500 years of dark ages, it is a time of dark deeds in murky little realms.

"King Wogga fought with King Pogga at the place called the Bloody Meadow. The next year was the Pestilence called Grim's Death, for Grim died." Cheerful tales for cheerful times you will find.

[1] William Langland, the creator of *Piers Plowman* is thought to have lived near Malvern, a few miles from JM's childhood home.

1961

291

. . . Quevedo.[1] I do not know his work well, but one of his sonnets seems to me splendid, & his Song about Money is effective, & his satires got him into prison, so they must have been good, or they wouldn't have bothered. Prison did for him, alas.

I have not looked (nor thought) of Q for 50 years. I meant once to study him, but I never did.

. . . About 1910, I was reading a lot of Spanish, having a plan of writing something that got shoved aside by another mood. I write about Q from a sort of speckled memory, & you must not take my verdict seriously. He was an important figure, a late Renaissance figure, speaking with the utterance & accent of a great time, so that anyone seeing a line of his would say, "Ah yes, school of Michael Angelo now run to seed"!!

Still, though overblown & run to seed, it is a great line & we have not that largeness now.

He was of very ancient noble family, & from early days moved in Court circles, in splendour & danger, amid ambitions & jealousies.

He was deformed in a way (crooked legs and too short) but enormously strong, swift in movement, & deadly with all weapons. At the age of 15 he did what no other poet has ever done, so far as I know. He qualified & was admitted as a Doctor of Theology. I suppose he could sign himself Q——DD.

But he was in the Court, not in Theology, & in the Court he fought a duel with another noble & nearly killed him. He had to leave Spain, & went to Naples where the Spanish Envoy used him in secret services of very strange kinds.

The Envoy got him a pardon in due course, but that was his life: secret service & diplomacy in high causes.

On returning to Spain, he was imprisoned (without trial) for 3 years, for supposed libel, but being proved innocent he was released.

He wrote, & was famous for, much prose & verse: the verse very fine, very varied, but a bit overblown:

> Healing, sweet Dream,
> By what so grim a fault
> Could I deserve so long a banishment
> That keeps from me thy mild forgetfulness
> So far, so far?

Presently he was flung into quod for a libel, & was there for nearly 2 years, till the great Olivares, the Chief Minister, came to his rescue: & lo, he had never written the libel. He had been wrongfully imprisoned, & as Spanish prisons were as bad as any of the time he died soon afterwards.

[1] See Letter 184.

292

... Voltaire[1] was much unlike Quevedo. .... He seems to have resembled Death the more as he drew nearer to it. The late descriptions all insist on it; he was a walking intellect, as lean as bright & as sharp as one of his couplets.

He was a kind of caustic glancing glitter, the caustic hurt, the glance saw whatever of profit was there to snatch, and the glitter always remained.

The Church wd have burned him, but didn't dare. He stood up alone against a lot of infamies, first and last. It is hard for us now to understand what danger he was in.

He stood up for the Calas family like an absolute hero. The noblesse, the Court and the Church would have scragged him any day; then he wd print a little book in England about any one of the three, & the one meant would writhe in agony; & he would reply, "What? ME? It is these terrible English: really they stick at nothing. The things they dare to print!"

He found France too dangerous at last, & went to the place near Geneva.

I should say that he was perfectly formed, but on the small side, & skinny to the observer's horror, as he glittered by.

He lived to be 84, and died in bed, much maligned & misunderstood. His genius was not to give light but shatter darkness.

[1] See also Letters 238–41.

293

. . . While you were away, I came across a paragraph in a book describing a young violinist's lessons in Berlin about 70 years ago. He was eager, but not good, tho almost so. His teacher was a man called Markees, who lived in the same house as Joachim.[1]

"Markees had got it into his head that I held my violin all wrong. In order to train my wrist, he used to make me play, or attempt to play, with my left arm thrust through the back of the chair on which I was sitting. If any young violinist wishes to improve his style, I advise him to try this method. But it will drive him almost crazy first."

Please, was this how you got there?

I'm afraid it won't be any good for writers, whose aim, I suppose, must always be to attain a mood in which the pen is only an interference.

Surely, it slues the player sideways, to his left, too much, doesn't it?

I do not recollect a sideways slue in the many orchestras I have watched.

Markees was a First Violinist in Berlin at that time: young & very promising.

The young man was Daniele Varé, an Italian, (with an English mother, I think) & a very clever writer, whom I once met, & wish I had met more. He is now dead.

He wrote a good deal: often with genius & always with charm, after being a Diplomat here & there, in a world now gone, almost un-imaginable.

[1] Joseph Joachim (1831–1907), a Hungarian-born violinist and composer who lived mainly in Germany. He was a friend of Mendelssohn and Brahms.

294

. . . J. M. Synge, whom I knew a little, was brought up as a fiddler, & was, for some vital years, intently eager; & up to all sorts of odd tricks for getting some sort of power into wrist & fingers. These I have now forgotten. Perhaps he had left them: for I never heard him play, or mention playing, except to say that, when in Aran, he sometimes played to the islanders. Even that he abandoned later I think: finding conjuring more popular with them.

. . . You ask me about Boswell.

I do not know his book about Corsica, nor his novel, nor his miscellaneous studies, such as that of the Douglas cause. I know the *Life of Johnson* & *The Tour of the Hebrides*; & these should suffice.

During the last 20 or 30 years some very scandalous personal memoirs have been published. These are diaries of his gaieties here & there. I have not read these, but have seen some of the reviews of them; & conclude from them that he was a pretty wild young rip, for the son of a judge, & a friend of Dr J.

But this young rip had social qualities of an unusual kind. People liked him, & he liked people, especially if they were people of genius able to appreciate such genius as was his. He had a very real genius for perceiving genius in people, and saying the right appreciative thing to it. Genius liked him; Rousseau & Voltaire saw this genius in him, Dr J saw, cultivated & guided it. Nearly all the clever people then living liked him; he was a Member of The Club,[1] with Burke, Paoli, Goldsmith, Reynolds, etc etc (& Burney) fellow-members.

Then, consider what it was to keep intimate with Dr J for 20 years, trace out that Life, & arrange it, tone down the fury & the savagery, avoid libel, avoid injustice, preserve all the wisdom, wit & piety.

He says, somewhere, that he was "not drunken, but intoxicated". Well, let it go at that, but being intoxicated is bad for a brain, & it was bad for his. At the end of the *Life*, he seems worn out. Drink is bad for writers; & it was bad for him.

But consider a young rip of 23, who wanted to enter the Guards, & cut a dash with many a gay Polly, standing up to the sage of 53, the Sage of the Dictionary, & by tact & love & real veneration winning that mighty heart, & making such a study of it. One will read it through, disliking the writer more & more, but it is a triumph. My Reyna mia, there is no book like it.

[1] Founded 1764.

295

. . . I am hoping to see the Boswell book on Corsica[1] fairly soon. Few people know Corsica; & B must have been there when Bonaparte's parents were alive, & perhaps the little N a babe in arms. But, no, N wasn't then born. B may well have seen the parents.

The book about Corsica was widely read for at that time there was in the spirit of the time that agitation for liberty called the Romantic Movement; the reaction from authority which led to the Fr Revol[n] & the freeing of Colonies from England & Spain. Corsica was rebelling against Genoa.

JB made himself sufficiently absurd, even so.

There is a picture of The Club somewhere, with JB standing at the left end of the table, behind Dr J who sits at that end. The

Members wear wigs, so that only those who are in profile look intelligent. JB is a bit dim, but Dr J. Burke & Goldsmith do really look as tho there were something in them.

It was Burke I think who wrote that Dr J was greater in JB than in real life. But in real life one did not see Dr J till about midnight by which time most men were drunk; & JB's life surveys the whole pageant, through the Dictionary to Westminster Abbey.

. . . I do not vouch for the truth of any tale told by writers about another writer. A tale told about JB says that on his return from Corsica he dressed up as a Corsican Chief, I suppose something between a wild Highlander & a junior Italian tenor in comic opera, & called on Ministers in London, urging them to support the cause of Liberty in Corsica against the Tyrants of Genoa.

The Ministers did not exactly fancy the job, & turned it down.

[1] James Boswell wrote *An Account of Corsica* (1768), and *Essays in Favour of the Brave Corsicans* (1769). It is probably the former to which JM refers. Boswell visited Corsica at the urging of Rousseau.

296

. . . We both live on an island, & argue that a big island is better than a small.

In those Hebridean islands, the winter storms may be terrific: no posts for days: the roofs blown off, in spite of the rocks piled on them; the boats smashed to bits, the poultry blown away: The Dr needed for 7 surgical cases, and the Chieftain having to amputate the worst of them with the family saw and his claymore; after making them good & drunk with the last of the whisky.

I suppose that when it moderates he may feel that he has re-lived the isle's romantic past.

(I once helped in an emergency amputation; but a Dr was in charge luckily, & all went well.)

On the island, I judge that things got like a cockpit in a British Naval Victory: 1780.

. . . Is there not a Text, that says: "Gin is a mocker: strong gin is raging"?

I am interested in your globular bottle. Of old, gin was often called square-face, because it came in square bottles, & soon made the drinker oblong or every which way.

297

. . . I have read JB [Boswell] on Corsica. It is a little book, clear & concise: a young man's simple story.

The essential points of JB. He was a martyr to the outstanding, the unusual, the notorious. He was overwhelmed by Voltaire, Rousseau, Wilkes, Liberty, Dr Johnson, Paoli the Corsican patriot, & no doubt by many a merry Sally who came out of her alley at him in her Saturday smirk.

He wrote an overwhelming letter to his overwhelmers, & pressed for interviews & had them: often more than one, for people like adoring youngsters & he was a very social lad, & was popular as a companion.

Remember he talked French & Italian fluently, played the flute somewhat; sang—more or less; had (when sober) the manners of the civilised; and always had this devotion to the overwhelming which was so marked a genius in him.

I don't think anyone would wish to read his *Corsica* a 2nd time. Paoli comes out well, but not overwhelmingly today. He served as a model, perhaps, till the lad could get at Dr J & really set-to.

JB made him a fine simple religious figure, but JB would have done better with George Washington; & much better with Garibaldi (a century later).

. . . Sometimes I wonder if JB ever really told Dr J the scope & intimacy of his intended revelations. JB must (at the beginning) have had qualms, was conscious that there are limits, that a friend trusts to affection, to right feeling, to reverence, and the sanctity that is in all intimacy.[1] Later, I think, he began to be pretty brazen and treacherous, if those words are not too strong: and swore, as it were, to set down all, and to blarney all his acquaintances into showing him every letter, & telling him every confidence. The last vol of the *Life* gives me this feeling. I don't think that JB improved as he matured: & wine does improve, but JB had no wine in himself— none; & the water of his spring had dried up.

[1] Any invasion of privacy or betrayal of confidence was a horror to JM.

298

. . . I thank you for your lovely letter, written in the anguish of your joy in the Passion Music.

It is a joy that is part of your Being, & will be moving in the Universe forever & forever & forever, as part of all Order & Beauty

& Power. Bach, & the lesser musics, most of them disciples of that spirit (his spirit) who entered Paradise through him, was (and they each were) one born to the seeking of that Paradise, & granted entrance to it, so that he became one in touch with all Order, Beauty and Power, one on fire with the fury of the suns, and in Spring, from fountains that cannot fail, and in Order by the law that all these millions & trillions of galaxies whirl in forever.

He was a little boy, a miller's son, who dared to take a book not his, to copy its scores by moonlight. Then, after tramping long miles to hear concerts, he sat, aching for food, outside an inn; someone flung him two herring-heads: & in each was a coin. That he took to heart & tramped off, not to food, but back in the dust to more music; & more & more longing for music, till he had all the power of a master, & could solace & inflame and enlighten all those on that path for nine generations (& for another 9 to come) and among them you are one, touched by him to his great purpose: a bringer of his light to others.

When young, men used to read Walt Whitman, a book called *Leaves of Grass*, with this poem:

> A child said "What is grass?" fetching it to me with full hands.
> How could I answer the child?

So, then, how shall one answer what is music? What are the arts?

Are they not all a striving to be out of a perishing self into an eternal universe of incalculable age & Order, Beauty & Power: & by the striving for any of these three does not one attain them all, in some measure, in accordance with the mortal capacity? Is not the striving atrocious, bitter, so blind, so fierce, so inhuman: & is not the Hope an atonement and is not the Attainment an ecstasy, to stand in the Heart of the Universe, perceiving infallibility, perhaps for one instant, to utter in that instant a few words, a few bars, some strain, some hewn line or drawn suggestion that will be a mark undying, to show the seeker that he is right, that he is on the way, that one who has been there has set this blaze on the trail, that you are on the way to the well at World's End, & it is there with the water running . . .

P.S. Some of the grammar in this letter seems to be a bit odd. Well, grammar ought to be odd now & then or the suicide ratio would go up.

299

. . . I ate a hot-cross bun with honey: and was glad to find the bun, tho costing six times what it used to cost, was much as in the distant past.

Later, I heard the chiff-chaff, which was very late this year, for often he comes early in March.

The birds that I love to hear are rarer now than they were; & some I have not heard for years. Some other lovely things disappeared here in the dreadful winter of 12 years ago, & have not been here since.

I suppose primitive man talked thus long ago. "We don't hear the pterodactyls at night now, as we used, when we settled in", or "I remember the last sabre-toothed tiger: he ate a lot of folks hereabouts first and last: an old dog he was, with only one eye. One misses these things now they're gone." etc. etc.

300

. . . I send this off on Tuesday, but I do not think that it will reach you, even if it reaches Berne, by Thursday evening.[1]

Still let me hope that it may, & that you are enjoying Switzerland, where you will hear the cuckoo-clock if not the cuckoo.

Good luck & a happy time to you.

I find the land too uppy & I like land to be rather down-y, like Berkshire just across the river here.

Still, as Boswell said of Scotland, the land has some "prodigious wild prospects" & some memorable waters; and although it tried Calvin, it did give asylum, later, to Voltaire.

Come home safely, & wrap up well before leaving the opera-houses.

[1] JM used to write to me in every place where I played abroad. This letter was sent to me in Switzerland. ANS

301

. . . I shall be relieved to hear that you are safely returned from that too jaggy land.

Are you all frost-bitten? Do count & be sure that you have 8 fingers, 2 thumbs, 2 ears.

The ears are very subject to go at the edges: do look to make sure.

Then, go to a good psychiatrist if you find you cannot sleep because the world is all changed to granite marline spikes each a mile high & frozen white, and that you are expected to climb these before the Orchestra can play . . .

One never knows what such a land may give as after-effects, & so, Reyna mia, please, let me have a reassuring word (if the ministering fingers are still on & can hold a pen).

But if you are well & hearty, please, may it be more than a word, for it will be ever so welcome to one who has thought of you all alone in the snow, perhaps being eaten by a St Bernard Dogg.

302

. . . I am so glad to hear that you enjoyed the Tour, though how you kept from collapse under such strains is not quite clear.

I expect you mariner girls are like the old seamen: "Every toe a marlin-spike, & the blood right good Stockholm Tar."

(Every finger a fish hook; every hair a rope-yarn . . . I forget the rest, but there used to be a lot, making the complete seaman a very marine figure.)

(Such as you don't meet often nowadays.)

303

. . . I thank you for your gracious kind letter about the old days of Texas, when they drove the cattle away up to Montana & Wyoming.

Those were the days.

But they were nearly over when I was born, and were less romantic to me than the still older days, when the Comanche rode all over Texas, & the Apache all over Arizona, & then withdrew into the unknown with what they had found.

Long since, I went all over those fabulous & marvellous lands; & saw some of the Indians, & the cowtowns, and the cowboys, but was never sure that what I saw was not a film outfit shooting a Western.

But I sympathise with your love of the Western, & I long to hear you sing to me of Jesse James . . .

> Jesse James was a man,
> A Friend to the Poor,
> He never let a Friend suffer Pain;
> And with his Brother Frank
> He robbed the Chicago Bank
> And stopped the Glendale Train.

Jesse James had a wife
Whom he loved as his Life,
3 children who were Brave,
But that dirty little coward
Who shot poor Mr Howard
Has laid poor Jesse in his Grave!!

"There were all too free with their guns," so people told me. "It really went too far, when they rode into town to wet their wads."

304

... Many years ago, I sometimes met a man who knew both the James Brothers.

They were Southerners, who were boys when the US Civil War began. They were in the war for Old Missourah, as devil-may-care sharpshooters & guerrillas. The South & the James were ruined in the war, so when peace came, they went in for revenge, & ran a very successful crime-gang, in the US & its frontiers. The gang held up trains & robbed banks & shot any critics who objected.

How many they shot will never be known but they are said to have shot a tidy few, for they wd shoot possible witnesses, to mak siccar [make sure], as well as open critics.

They were declared outlaws, with rewards of ten thousand dollars on their heads, dead or alive.

Two of the gang shot Jesse James in cold blood to get their reward.

I doubt if they got it: there is rather a lack in the tale here, but I believe that they were 2 brothers, who believed that Jesse was going to shoot them, doubting their faith to him. It may have been self-defence on their part.

The 2 brothers were named Ford: but one version of the song says that it was not the Fords,

But Mr Golly Howard
That dirty little coward
Has laid poor Jesse in his grave!!

Who Mr Howard was I do not know, but nobody who knew Jesse thanked him: & nobody wd give evidence against Frank, who lived to a ripe age, farming in Old Missourah.

My friend, who knew Jesse & Frank, knew them in the late 70s & early 80s (Jesse was laid low in 1882).

My friend knew Frank much better than Jesse, & liked him & trusted him, but said that Frank really did not understand that shooting a guy was anything wrong. It was what any guy did before the guy got you. He had done it since childhood, & seen it done almost daily all over the South: it was what any guy did. He described the Chicago Bank robbery by saying, "We went in and called for the wad . . . the cashiers stood up until they lay down." (Being by that time, shot.) Another version of the song says that it was Mr Robert Ford, to rhyme with Coward, who shot poor Jesse. The song has gone all over the world with wandering men, & the details vary.

305

. . . I have to thank you for a most dear charming letter about the birds. Nobody but you could have written such a letter; & nobody could have liked it more than unworthy me.

The curlews come over here at odd times, & formerly were frequent in the great wild field just across the river (& the jack snipe too) but I don't go down that way much now, & haven't heard them this Spring.

I may be up in the wilds tomorrow & may hear them there, with larks & some rarer birds that are better never mentioned, for in most parishes now:

> There is a little man
> & he has a little gun
> & his heart & his brains are of lead!

. . . We spoke of ACS [Swinburne]—his portraits. When he was in his marvellous staggering youth Rossetti painted him. The portrait is in Balliol. Genius perceived by a most perceptive genius: and the portrait is all wild fire & dreamy music & (I wd say) a Victorian Mother's terror for her Daughter's safety. Later, there was a photograph, very strange, not so wild, very facially like Paderewski, and suggesting not P so much as Chopin, in Scherzo no. 1, or the Sostenuto. Later, the shrunken elder that I saw, a queer galvanic bird with an odd hop; a marvellous head on a tiny withered little stalk; as deaf as a post; but with a big voice.

This was still the man Rossetti saw, that lived with Rossetti in Chelsea, & would insist on sliding naked down the bannisters till the Mother of the lovely ladies that came to be painted by Rossetti said that it just must not be: it simply was not done: poetical or not, however clever it might be, dear Ygraine must be painted at home, by someone who would come in by the day.

I have been told by 2 men who knew ACS fairly well in the early nineties, that he had (when in a room) an athletic sort of backward hop, onto a chair or sofa; & then a hop down, & then a restless hop elsewhere: a tiny little long-tailed-tit body, & a sort of burly bullfinch head: but the whole effect bird-like.

Generally, genius is misunderstood and frequently misreported. Don't believe all these yarns: they were all current, & I repeat them only as hearsay.

306

... About Swinburne—in the face, & in some of the portraits, there is a sort of something that warns not to mistake him for a bird, but to know that he was the son of an Admiral, and would tackle anyone twice his weight at any time.

He might have sung the old cowboy ditty:

> For I am a green-eyed rebel, that is what I am,
> And for Kings, Popes & heavyweights I care not a cent.

Swinburne's Hair (in youth) was famous for its quite extraordinary beauty.

... What bliss to have free days in Athens & Constantinople.[1]

While you are in the holy city of Byzantium do at all costs (and it used to cost only about 1/-—one shilling) go down into one of the amazing Water Lakes below the city: immense caves full of water (drinking water) on which you can boat in artificial light, and see the boats far off in the dim, & think you are coming to Elfinmere, or already there.

[1] Together with America, this was a part of the world in which JM was especially interested. He was particularly enthusiastic about ANS's prospective visit to Istanbul, amusing himself by using the city's earlier names of Constantinople (up to 1930) and Byzantium (up to 330 AD).

307

... I thank you for yet another delightful dear letter, and for all the charming account of your search for treasure in Tom Tiddler's Ground.

I never heard of the Portobello treasure field,[1] but I suppose it dates from 1739 & Capt[n] Jenkins's Ear. In my day, it used to be the old marvellous Caledonian Horse Market, just West from Pentonville Quod (see *Peter Ibbetson*) where you could buy horses "at a quid a corner" (or 4 quid the horse) on 2 days a week, and, on the other days, all the junk in London, among which you could get everything out of the moment's fashion, but nothing that the shops could get bigger prices for.

The Caledonian was a vast expanse, running up to the sky, & all the space a market of sorts, with harness, carts, the quid a corners and junk, & then say paper zinnias stuck round the booths, just as at the old Hiring Fairs.

Books were best looked for elsewhere, but one could get wonderful other things.

. . . I am so very glad that you are going to Byzantium. It is a staggering place. The walls & the Golden Gateway are superb, & the great Church of the Holy Wisdom is surely the greatest thing built by men; then the wisdom of the Greek mind, its beauty & power. You are *the* person to love it & be moved by it, *the* very one.

I am so glad you will remember the quinine. Mosquitoes can be a nightmare, but I expect your brother-in-law would know a modern dodge that daunts them. Even when I was a boy there was a thing called *Anti-Skeet*, which turned the boldest brazenest M quite pale, & there must be better things now. Only the female M bites, it seems.

[1] The street market in Portobello Road, London W11.

308

. . . I sadly fear that I never thanked you for the nice things you wrote about of *Ossian*.[1]

But you must not praise the frame. The main tale of the Fianna is an Irish creation, known & growing, for centuries, & known well to me, in translation, & from table talk in wild Ireland, for over 60 years. The Dermot & Grania episode is amazing (in the translation even) so I deserve little credit there.

You, however, the dear you, liked "The Country of the Young", that I did really toil at, and (I suppose) made a mess of, for it never really seemed to go.

For the end, of course, I had seen the place, & talked there with men who seemed to have been there, & seen the whole thing, St P [Patrick] and his young men, & poor old O an old crock fallen from Heaven, etc etc.

There will be no good narrative verse now, till the poet comes along with a power of music to make a chant that lifts like music, & thrills like music, & can go on an hour at a time enchanting hearers, & leading on the story as the *Iliad* does in the Greek & nobody else oes anywhere . . .

[1] See letter 258.

309

. . . I do want to urge you to expect quite hot days in Constantinople 75 or even 80, in an August day; but I am speaking from my own experience & from books, in saying that it is a city of sudden, very very sudden change, & that you may have a cold blast at almost no notice, & that you will have, probably, a cooling wind from the NE every night: the wind that gave Troy its name of Windy Troy.

So be prepared with a woolly something. You may not need it, but like the gun in the US proverb, "if you *do* need it, you'll need it so durn bad you'll be glad you packed one".

In Cyprus, I expect you will be on high land up to 600 feet, away from the plains, which can be *very* hot. There have been long troublous years in Cyprus, & the anti-malarial campaign may have been neglected, so mosquitoes may be a bother there. The plains are very hot: over 80 in August.

310

. . . You ask about Rabelais. I do not know him very well, but he was one of the great movers of the Renaissance in France; and he came from Touraine,[1] which is one of those parts of France that tend to make men glad with good living & drinking, glorious churches & châteaux, and a kind of festal prose & a poetry like certain wine, that fills the room with fragrance, & intoxicates the mind as well as the body.

He says somewhere: "the very shadow of an Abbey spire is fruitful". I think that a good many of his pages tend that way too. But that is part of what he meant. He had been a Friar, and also a Monk: and he had (I feel sure) come to see, or know, that "Abstinence sows sand all over . . ." and that Touraine is like Flanders a land of abundance, & that abundance is Nature's way &

a great way if rightly taken. Brueghel & Rabelais & Rubens ... & WS & Ronsard ...

"Hark the Dominant's persistence till it must be answered to."

He states Man's case. Here is an Animal in whom a giant impulse urges, & frightfully urges, to gorge, guzzle & beget, all on a gigantic scale.

Then he suggests some amazing schemes for teaching. These seem to be his main hope, but then, alas, he seems to see remedies of a kind that he does not explain, & perhaps means only that a man must seek explanations of all things, as the Man of Science seems now to be doing.

But, always, I think, when pressed, he sees something divine in Man's Case that must be sought to and clung to; so that all the clingers & seekers find & receive help as they always did in times past, & will in all time, without which (as I think he concludes), war will destroy him.

It is a book always somehow suggesting the *Anatomy of Melancholy*, which I can read in at all times anywhere with joy & comfort, but I can never read much of Rabelais. I do not like giants & dwarfs; and feel that man has acted from righteous feeling in omitting filthiness of speech, real foulness of speech, from conversation & from books.

About Rabelais's extravagance of speech.

He was one of the first *writers* writing to be *read* not spoken. All or nearly all the good writers, the abundant writers, felt the delight of doing extravagances, such as R's abundance, Marlowe's rumbustious line, Lyly's Euphuism, Gongora's Spanish abomination "Gongorism" etc etc. Now we say, "Thrift, thrift, Horatio", & try to practise it.

... The Thelemite motto *Do what you will*. That means Do the thing your nature urges you to do, follow the Law of your Being, *if it accord* with Divine & Human law

[1] François Rabelais (1494–1553) was born near Chinon.

311

... I must write later about Rabelais, whose work is really unfamiliar to me.

He seems a great figure at the peak of the Renaissance, when the Middle Ages reached the summit, & the great men saw that the summit had been achieved, & would lead men no further. They were at the top, & what was to come, now that they were kicking away the ladder that had brought them there, was unsure to them, but what was it to be to the multitude, "the mutable rank-scented many" who were all round them; a multitude of an intense wild ignorant vitality incredible to us: a vitality that had survived childhood in the Middle Ages? We can hardly imagine that vitality. It is the vitality, beastly & foul & immense, and worshipping gunpowder that was so like itself, that fills Rabelais's appalling people.

312

... I was wondering (while you were near me) what beauties of sound, recurring, expected, delayed, made more tempting, made almost unendurable, delighted that bright young head, & how many instruments had to combine to bring you your absolute perfection of music.

I knew, of course, that even if you told me I should not understand your description, nor the words of it: so I did not ask.

With writers, I suppose, the overwhelming instant may be only the use of one word (often only one): then, the happy image; then the line that is quoted, the proverb, the bit of wisdom that becomes the nation's wisdom.

To many, too, the measure used with an unusual mastery, or invented, or imported, is the darling thing: the couplet closed; the couplet not closed; the Rhyme Royal or Cressid Verse, the Spenser stanza, the Quatrain, as really used, the odds & ends of staggering things done & left to be discovered (so many Scotch things), and then amazing stanzas by Tennyson, Browning, Fitzgerald, Rossetti, Wm Morris, that people never use because the source would be known, & it wd be said that the user stole the measure because he could not invent one.

I have been passing my days lately devising stanzas. Probably they have all been used by someone, for the 19th cent. was a period of vast experiment, and many thousands of poets, often of great skill.

The usual poetry page will take about 36 lines, so that the stanza should not be more than 12 lines, so as to get 3 full stanzas onto a page.

The Spenser stanza has 9 lines, the 9th a long one, so that you would not get more than 3 full stanzas onto a page, & to put 3½ is monstrous but (of course) daily done: it is only poetry. What does the fellow expect?

313

Reyna darling

With these lines I am sending you the promised *Pamela*, whom the wicked Fielding called *Shamela*, and also the Wafer book,[1] with the picture of a Mosquito Indian, like Sir Toby B in the play, taking some malapert lady out of the boil, not knowing, till Wafer showed him, the Christian way of doing this.

Long since, I read a lot of these books, and (less long since) saw all that coast with the Samballoes, & Nombre de Dios, and Porto Bello, and the great rainy Darien, where so many thousands of our seamen are now in Dead Man's Bay:

> With their comrades,
> With their comrades all around.

About 57 years since, when I was in Manchester, writing for the *MG* [*Manchester Guardian*], I bought a copy of Wafer's old book, & the original Dampier book, for four shillings the lot; they being then not in favour.

I grieve that I have not these copies now, for if I had them they should come with these.

But will you graciously accept what I now send, with my every hope that they will please your dear heart that is so dear to me?

And (as one in Pamela might write),

Believe me to be,

Your gracious Being's
most obliged, most grateful
and devoted humble servant,
Jan.

[1] Lionel Wafer was, with William Dampier, accused of taking bribes, when Dampier appeared before the Council of Trade & Plantations in 1697. Both were sea-captains who wrote of their voyages as privateers.

314

... I am sending you yet another piratical book, remembering how these studies gave you a precious bias in my favour, long since, and longing still to keep it.

It is about a pirate of Spanish birth, called Little Gaspar. (Gasparillo).

He is supposed to have been a pirate in the Gulf of Mexico, between say, 1800–1835. He had a settlement near Charlotte Bay (well to the S of Tampa) on the SW end of Florida, in a lagoon called Bahia Gasparilla (as Bay being feminine in Spanish). The entrance to the Lagoon is called Boca Grande, or Big Mouth. The Bay & the Boca are still on the map, & are much frequented by tourists, who talk of the pirate now as Gasparilla (from the place).

All those coasts were much haunted by pirates: and 30-odd years ago there was an aged aged man there who used to tell the tourists that he had been a cabin boy under a pirate called Benito (the Blessed) the Terror of the Gulf.

He made pots of money thus, you may be sure. In the book you may read some odd marine events that I can neither follow nor swallow, but a mention of one Laffite, very famous in his day, not exactly a pirate, but a Receiver of Piratical Goods, of whom your reading may already have informed you. He, and his Lady Constanza, and a boy named Theodore, figured long ago in a romance of the Gulf; they kept a big settlement going at the mouth of the Mississippi, & made a lot of money, till the US Navy routed them out & policed the waters.

Laffite went to the Campeachy Coast (went alone, I hear) & was eaten there by wild pigs.

> Mourn, Britain, while I tell of it
> The Peccarees have ETT Laffite.[1]

The map that I send is just a bit S of Gasparilla Bay, but on the South West, near the left top corner, you will see the Captive Island where the ladies were stored for ransom. (Perhaps.)

[1] In a letter some weeks later JM wrote: "I have learned of late that there were *two* Laffites in the New Orleans piratical settlement near New Orleans, Jean et Pierre, French brothers, both of whom were scattered and ruined by the US Navy about 1814 or so. Jean seems to have been the lad the peccaries ate, but leave the matter open, will you, for it is an unusual fate & if it were Pierre he might be jealous."

315

. . . You asked me (long since) about John Ruskin.[1]

He was an influence on youth, when I had youth; but youth soon passes; but he championed causes that can never pass; and some of what he wrote cannot be neglected. You might like some of him a good deal (as I find I do); so may we consider together, presently, if this may be seen to?

There is a little pocket edition that would go readily into your hand-bag, for quiet reads in the bus, or in the waits at rehearsals.

He has a good deal of fun, here & there; and a rare talent for drawing, from the antique and from Nature.

He was consumptive in youth, and sometimes mad in his maturity, so that the curtain came down on his performance a good deal.

[1] See also Letters 41, 58, 60, 288.

316

. . . If this should reach you, it would be (perhaps) as you prepare to go to Constant.[1]

Many years ago I heard a poem about that city.

> A merry young Turk in Stamboul
> Tried to pull off the tail from a mule,
> The Turk was a charmer
> But didn't wear armour,
> They brought in the verdict Damphool.

Every minute you spend there will put this ditty further and further out of your mind, to your great advantage, but somehow Athens will stay with you as the more wondrous thing.

[1] Sent to ANS in Athens.

317

. . . Please, will you tell me if you care at all for ghost stories, of the kind written by the late M. James?[1]

Perhaps , with so many lonely midnight wanderings, these are not to be recommended, especially one or two that have remarkable drawings in illustration.

He was one of the most learned men in the world. I saw him sometimes, but never met him: and marvelled at him, he reminded me so strongly of Holbein's portrait of Sir Thomas More.

One who knew him told me that his memory was of a swiftness & certainty like photography. The page came into his memory at a glance, and remained in his mind thenceforward.

Men spoke of the danger of having such a man in any University, since he made youths feel that learning could be absorbed without labour.

Once or twice at the Brit. Mus. Catalogue, I turned over the pages that recorded his astounding achievement in Human Knowledge; and marvelled that such could be attained.

As for his Ghost Stories. Well . . .

"Macbeth does murder Sleep, the innocent Sleep".

MJ did not murder sleep; he was a Christian Scholar, he just scared Sleep out of the bed-room.

[1] Montague Rhodes James, (1826–1936), a mediaevalist, and Provost of Eton from 1918 until his death. Author of *Ghost Stories of an Antiquary*, etc.

318

. . . This is Monday the 14th, and I rejoice to read that you are at Istanbul,[1] having flown over the island where Rupert Brooke lies, and over Troy and Anzac & the Golden Gate, and are now in the Holy City of Byzantium; wonderful you, in a wonderful place.

I am sending this to Yugo-Slavia, for I doubt there being time to write again to Cyprus.

Some day, when you are at home & quiet, please will you tell me how to pronounce Dubrovnik?

Like *Treasure Island*, "it was a main place for pirates once", or at least Ragusa was; but then, I doubt if any safe harbour anywhere has not been that at some time.

Little inlets in our own moral land have seen some odd folks at times, the books say; and before the books, O dear.

I am wondering about this "open air theatre" at Byzantium. Can it be in the Seraglio Point area? I do hope it isn't flyey, mosquitoey, glarey, rainy, windy, dusty, or steamer-sirenny, nor even too Come all ye faithful & jolly well pray to Allah-ey; but exceedingly nice to play and hear in.

[1] *The Times*, Istanbul, 13th August 1961: "Sir John Barbirolli and the Hallé Orchestra have arrived to give a series of concerts in the open air.'

319

. . . It is a happiness to think that you are turned towards home, and that in a few days you may be again in England.

My next will be addressed to you at Turin, which will be only about a day away. Imagine what it was, when the little Ruskin went there with his Papa, in the family carriage, or when Sir Charles Grandison was carried over the Simplon, or Hannibal brought his army.

I hope that you have found intensely rapturous hearers wherever you have been. I hope, too, that when you are safely back, & have really slept in a real bed, you will have a restful day or two with no concert, no rehearsal, but just *rest*, and that then, perhaps, I may, after 8.30–8.40 in the morning, find a real word from real you.

I expect that (thinking of earlier returns) you are quoting the poem to yourself about another returner:

> We laid at last our wearied limbs in rapture
> Between the clean sheets of a Christian bed
> O, there are things I think we shall remember
> When we are dead.

Ah, when I have seen the Bishop's Light, or the Start, or Mersey Bar . . .

320

. . . What a lot you have already seen; Athens, Troy, Byzantium, Paphos, etc. etc.

Only yesterday, I was reading of an Iceland hero who killed "Grettir the Strong", an outlaw, lying ill on a rock off the Iceland coast. He took the outlaw's sword & cut off the outlaw's head with it, & in doing this notched the blade in a way that became talked-of. He then left Iceland, came to Byzantium, and entered a Viking Company, the Emperor's Varangian Guard, there.

But Grettir's Kinsman took up the feud, and went after him, though it was a far cry to Byzantium, and the trail hard to find.

He, too, reached the City at last, and then, after patient search, found the man and found him showing the notched sword and bragging of his deed. So then he (the Kinsman) mak'd siccar and cleared off the score; and lived, on the whole, fairly happily for a good while, which was much in a story of that time. "He lived happily ever after" was a little too much for hearers to believe.

321

... You are always surprising me by your knowledge of out-of-the-way books, poems, tales.

Perhaps, indeed, very likely, you will know a strange book about one *Mr John Decastro*, by one Mr Mathers??[1]

If you do know it, as you are just the sort of soul who *would*, perhaps you will tell me your theory of who the real writer really was??

Not Cobbett.

Cobbett could not have restrained himself so long; but then, if not Cobbett, who was it, and how comes it that he wrote no other book, and is not trumpeted abroad by silver trumpets, and serenaded by golden fiddlers at his well-pilgrimed shrine??

If there were a poem of poetical quality so great as the prose quality of this story, surely men would not rest till they knew the truth, who wrote it.

There is no such poem.

It must have taken the author a year or two to write. The writer was a man.

It was published just at about the time of Napoleon's leaving Elba; & in the fury of the Hundred Days & the fever of the peace & the frenzy of the next years, it passed unread, un-noticed almost.

"Oh Sherlock, is this elementary?' (Dr W.)

Within a few days, I may be able to say that I have at least a clue to follow, but you may already have a name to suggest.

[1] *The History of Mr John Decastro*, originally printed in London, 1815. ANS had an American reprint of *c* 1902, published in Pittsburgh, Pennsylvania, in two volumes. She writes: "John Mathers is merely a character in the novel. Real author still unknown. Cushing's *Anonyms* credits authorship to George Colman the younger (1762–1836). The American editor suggests William Cobbett (1762–1835)."

322

... There have been few happenings here. The rats have been rather a pest, but we have called in some assassins, & they say they will be here again in a day or two to make sure.

Then the pump went wrong, in a manner of some complexity, but it is now better than it has been. They think they'll "fix her by tonight".

There has been rather a lot of work, finishing some writing against time, but that has always a sporting zest about it: one likes to forestall the printer's devil.

You will be seeing the beginning of the vintage somewhere. Here it is plum time and the Summer apples are here: and a fair tomato crop. What a pity you cannot be here to share in these. Please, you must tell me if you would care to try some White Cherry Blossom honey, from the Middle Farm, to celebrate your Happy Return.

※

323

. . . Before you went East I promised to send you a little portable Browning. I send it with this.

66 years ago, I began to read eagerly: the young of then read Browning a lot, as they craved something rougher on their tongue and wider in the mind than Alfred Lord T, however different.

B will not mean so much now, but here is a pretty full collection of his main work (some of his mizen, too, I fear) and if you enjoy him ⅓ as much as we did, what fun that would be.

I sent you, I feel sure, a book by Richardson called by some such name as *Pamela*, or *Banns before Bedding*. Please when you have read to the awful escape of the Heroine from the wicked Mrs Jewkes and the unspeakable scoundrel, please will you tell me, for then you will read how clever Mr Henry Fielding responded to that stimulus.

He was a sprightly wit with a happy turn for satire, which he applied to the mockery of Sir Robert Walpole,[1] a successful minister, who governed, that is, passed laws, by buying votes when they were needed, knowing, almost to a guinea, what each Lord or Member would expect.

Such a figure, dealt with by the adroit HF & put upon a stage by an actor who had studied the original, became notorious in the London world.

Sir RW at last decided to stop Mr HF's happy game. He instituted the Censorship of Plays. *Every* play had to be submitted to a Censor, who had the power to prohibit, utterly and absolutely, any personal travesty or other outrageous matter.

In the language of youth, "the theatre has groaned under this tyranny ever since", & poor HF had to turn to other methods.

[1] Sir Robert Walpole (1676–1745), first Earl of Orford, father of Horace Walpole, and a successful minister and leader of the Whig party, who made extensive use of patronage. Fielding satirised him unmercifully, and as a riposte to Fielding's *Pasquin* and *The Historical Register for 1736*, Walpole passed the Licensing Act of 1737 which made the Lord Chamberlain licenser of theatres. The Lord Chamberlain, in turn, appointed an Examiner of Plays—in short a censor. Something like this arrangement continued until its abolition in 1968.

324

... It is so jolly to find that *Pamela* pleases you. I felt sure that your true delight in art would feel the power of the man in devising the plot & casting the net.

I think that the first piece published was but 2 vols long. 2 domestic vols (your vols 3 & 4 were added later).

Some folks object to a novel being told in the letters of imaginary characters.

All ways of telling a long tale must jar upon someone, as being "unreal". They are all, in some measure, unreal.

Milton has a line: "All *is*, if, I have Grace to use it so."
And Richardson's unusual gift was to tell tales most wonderfully in series of letters.

In my memory, *Clarissa Harlowe* stands out as better than *Pamela*. (It is twice as long.) In the third tale, *Sir Charles Grandison*, the hero loves an Italian lady but they shrink from each other because of their religious views. The lady is a kind of walking waterworks & is but damp company, but some people, perhaps more arid than I, admire this part of the tale as truly tragic.

Please tell me when you have reached the wicked Mrs Jewkes, and then you shall have Mr Fielding's reactions. It [*Shamela*] is a scandalous work but I think it *must* be by Henry Fielding, & one of his best, perhaps.

I thank you for what you say of Browning—and Ghost Stories.

M. James was a man of extraordinary knowledge of many extraordinary kinds. His ghost tales are the recreations of a great scholar, and are unlike anything else, but they have an uncanny power and suggestion, which might a little worry you, coming home in the mirk midnight, when the cat's in the waterbutt.

Browning. I only met 3 or 4 who knew him, & only talked of him with 2 of these.

He was a good musician. You will like "A Toccata of Galuppi's" (a long thing) & "Master Hugues of Saxe-Gotha", & "Abt Vogler". Nearly all the "Men & Women" & the "Dramatic Lyrics" are interesting & of his best.

The book that I sent contains much that I do not care for, but the young of my day were glad of a lot of these rocky crusts; and welcomed the quacking of a duck so wise after the bleating of the sheep that baa-ed all round us in the pen.

He was a wild duck who had flown in Italy, & in odd parts of France, & urged us to be up & on the wing.

325

. . . The other day I was reading some verse in a Church in aid of the Repair Fund: & was rather stumped for a marine subject when I remembered a case of a cargo of treacle that came adrift in a storm, & all the upper casks burst, & dripped crude treacle onto whatever was down below, & got down into the bilges, some hundreds of tons of it, & made about 2 feet of treacle in the well, and rose & rose.

They turned on the pumps to get it clear, but it jammed the pumps; & then things did not look at all rosy, for treacle will burn, & if it got into the furnaces it would burn like a Xtian martyr, or like billi-o.

They tried to clear the pumps (some of them) while others prepared the boats for abandon ship, & the rest, in Neptune's raging fury, blowing like Sin & all the ship dripping treacle, organised a chain of men with buckets, bucketing up the treacle from the bilges, hand to hand, & emptying it into the sea.

Now treacle does not go readily into a bucket, nor will it come readily out of a bucket, and if you fall into treacle it is hard to get up & if you get treacle in your eyes you can't see very well, & when your sea-boots are full of treacle you go kerlobsh kerlobsh like a parcels van in a thaw.

> But treacle treacle gentle friend,
> All was happy in the end.

326

. . . Over 60 years ago, one night when Yeats had just come back to London from Ireland, I heard him tell of an old Irish woman with whom he had been talking. He had been in the Irish wild west, a wild part, seeking out traces of pagan traditions, older than the Roman church, & alive under that covering at least in the old people. He asked her about the life of a spirit after bodily death, & the woman had given him various particulars then added: "But of course, Mothers always stay by their children, as long as any one of them can need her help . . . ." then she paused. "And after that," she said, "they go on."

She did not know to what they went, but was very sure that all went to something great.

327

. . . Thank you for telling me of your going flying.[1] I have only twice flown in tiny planes, both times over Texas, going high up, and lo, away, away to the S, a dark streak which I knew was the Gulf of Mexico, where Stout Cortez was particularly stout & F Drake by no means thin, & beyond wh, long afterwards, the Pyrate Laffite was eaten by pigs: a sad end to earthly fame.

You say that you came nearest to being a bird, in flying.

I have sailed (very fast) at times, but that is too busy a business for feeling like a bird. You have to feel like a very alert active seaman. I think that I came nearest to flying in skating, full tilt, on a real long stretch of ice; all hard & clear, making I know not how many m.p.h. (more than any ship I wd say).

. . . I hope that these scraps may reach you more frequently than those that went to the Levant for you.

Formerly the English post was a marvel to all the world. Men in Oxford would post (for instance) a letter to London at breakfast time (before 10 a.m., say) & receive an answer from London before 8 p.m. by letter post. Each letter would pay one penny postage.

No such speed nor cheapness exist now.

. . . There has been a rather glad late summer here, which I hope has cheered all your Western tour.

What a pity that you could not come again to these parts & share the only fruit I have this year, tomatoes.

They are nearly over now, but have been a delight.

I think that you are too wise & too well-read to dislike tomatoes, remembering Wordsworth's famous poem:

> Scorn not tomatoes, Cynic, thou hast scowled
> Mindless of all their merits; with this fruit
> Monks endure cells, however shaved & cowled;
> Seeing Eve bite one, Adam followed suit, etc

[1] ANS had told JM of flying in "a very small, old plane" in New Zealand, over the glaciers, during her stay there in 1942.

328

. . . The writer, M. R. James, was a man of marvellous memory. One of the games of his friends was to quote a line & say "which of Dickens's books is this from?" & he would answer at once correctly. On one occasion someone asked him this: " 'The traveller rose from the settle and walked to the window': Sir," he said, "which book is this from?"

The ghost-writer replied, "It isn't in Dickens."

This story delighted me: but perhaps you, as a woman, would say, "But that wasn't memory at all. Any woman would have known at once from the questioner's voice that he was up to some trick."

Well .... Mark Twain was once in a room with other men in India, & then an Indian pelted each & every man in the room with nuts (in no sort of order), & then after ½ an hour or so, he told each man how many nuts had hit, or missed, him, & where each nut had gone. I cannot tell you if they checked the matter in any way, or even counted the nuts. At a first breath the tale seems to show that memory was involved; & that if the memory had told the truth it must have been a pretty good memory, worthy of a better subject.

329

... I never saw a glass walking-stick. The sword-stick was frequent in my youth. You pressed a button near the handle & outsheathed a two-foot steel blade, with which one jab sufficed to slay the wicked garotter (so people said). The wicked garotter probably got his victim from behind, so perhaps the sword-stick laid out the brave man running to the rescue ....

Yet, often, the man in front of the victim was an accomplice, who had passed the victim at a rapid pace, whistling some gay tune of innocence, & only turned back as the garotter sprang out behind the victim.

I never heard of a glass walking-stick, but remember the Clouded Cane[1] in the "Rape of the Lock". This was (I believe) not of glass, but olive wood, or some tropical hard wood that polished to some fine effect, or had a queer grain in mottles.

[1] "The nice conduct of a clouded cane . . . ." (Alexander Pope).

330

... Thank you for telling me of *Mont Oriol.*

It is the best of his [Maupassant's] longer stories, I would say. I am reading it again now myself, & am, indeed, going through all his work for the first time for, perhaps, 50 years, or more, since days when he was reckoned one of the dozen leading masters studied by that time, so much more literary than this.

G de M had a valet & Man to run his bachelor's establishment: the "François" of the Lives of G de M.

One day at middle day François found at the door a smart dog-cart, with a most exquisitely smart young lady who said that she had been invited to lunch.

François had heard nothing about any lunch. G de M was becoming very forgetful (he was going mad) & had gone out to lunch elsewhere. He (F) explained this, & the lady asked might she, perhaps, leave a note for G de M.

F produced paper, & the lady wrote:

PIG

then climbed aboard the lugger & drove away.

Some of the best stories I see now to have been better than I ever thought them. But then how very good a good writer's best always is.

331

. . . G de M was one of the skilled & stirring writers that delighted England with his short stories 70-odd years ago. He was then *the* short-story writer, but since then, we have had Kipling, Sherlock Holmes [i.e. Conan Doyle], O. Henry, Crane, Arthur Morrison, Maugham, Stevenson, H. James, M. James . . . . quite a lot.

A German critic has said that 91 of G de M's heroines are blondes. I can well believe it. One reads the words "sa jolie tête blonde", & knows that on the next page there will be "les baisers frémissants et presque brutals d'amour"; & sure enough, there they are.

It has been said, that the blonde type is really rare now in France. Even the old Gaulish type described by Caesar, big-bodied, fair, very gay, bold, attractive people, is not often seen.

This rarity makes the blonde noticeable in France, & perhaps the blondes make the blondeness a little more noticeable by judicious touches.

There can be no doubt that *Mont Oriol* [1887] is his best long story or full-sized novel.

The best of his short stories are very very good indeed.

For a long time I think he supplied a paper or review with a story or study periodically. This led to trouble, for often his story was not enough for the space to be filled, & he had to invent a frame in which the short story could be told by one of a party.

Sometimes, even so, the dodge seems deplorable, & then one turns to the story that follows. In each of his collections of tales there will be 2 or 3 very good.

For the light, scandalous, gay French story he is unmatched. For some of the terrible extremes of French character he is unmatched. For the strangeness & wildness & nightmare of the brain going mad he is unmatched, especially in the phantasy that is just bearable.

He was brought up, I suppose, by Flaubert & Zola, who were, no doubt, a helpful father & righteous uncle to him.

332

. . . I am glad that the R [Richardson] books safely reached you.

I cannot like any one of the three great tales, but what an effort of will, to plan the three & carry them through to the end, what a masculine French mind, showing the way to Balzac & to Zola, yet using the method for his private views of morality, where Balzac saw the convulsions of French society in 30 years of revolution, & Zola the story of a family in his own time.

I cannot like R or his method. The views of the little gang to which I belonged were against any intrusion of morality into any study of living people. In our eyes, the themes of the writer were the overwhelmings, when morality neither bound nor helped, when hearts strayed & terrible things passed measure . . . .

333

. . . Long since, a man just back from one of the Bayreuth Festivals showed me a photo of Wagner.

IN TROWSERS OF CLOTH OF GOLD.

Now that is a costly stuff, & not at all durable, & I reckon out that *each leg* cost him thirty pounds, at least; & then all the rest (if he were elderly & a bit plump) a whole mint more. And then the buttons to match, probably gold coins specially bored, & then the rest of the suit to match or even to out-do such a foundation.

It is true, my darling R, that Strang[1] made me wear a cloak for my portrait. He had just been in Spain & had bought the cloak there, & told me that it took any man 7 years to learn how to put on a cloak. Women, of course, do it at the first go, & always right.

> How different from us
> Miss Beale & Miss Buss.

I never had a velvet smoking jacket.

You see, in the years after Wilde's fall, men had to be very careful what they wore. That kind of costume was supposed to be a part of the uniform of Sin, like long hair, hair-oil, scented hair, dyed flowers etc.

[1] William Strang, who painted JM's portrait in 1909.

334

... You ask, have I been in Texas? Yes, a good deal, long ago, in 3 or 4 different times, & over a lot of it. It is about as big as Africa to those who suddenly find themselves there.

I do not rank it as the South so much as the West. I look on the real South as the Carolinas, Virginia, Georgia, Alabama, Florida, Louisiana, Tennessee & Maryland.

All the Southerners in *these* States have the charming soft sweet speach you mention. I think they get it from the negroes, who look after so many white children there. "Yes, Suh, we-uns in the South, Suh, we speak, Suh, like the blue Taloosa."

Texas borders on Mexico, & of late years has made it a very friendly border, with a welcome to Mexican costume, music & dances.

When I was there this had not gone very far, & all middle-aged people whom I met there remembered the cowboys, the trails up into Montana & Wyoming & Nevada, the cattle ranches, & the shootings. All the old people remembered the "Indian trouble", too, & the Indian raids for scalps, & booty: these were the last raids of the Comanche & Apache braves.

I forget whether Billy the Kid was in Texas or further West. In the course of time there will be poems about Billy.

I had an old friend, long since, who went to live in Texas, but could not stand the tempo of the life.

As the proverb said:

Texas is all right for men & dogs,
But Hell on women & oxen.

He & his wife could not endure the daily & nightly shootings.

If there was a row it was Up & Up
And the first who Upped could bark
And then we toted the other guy
And planted him, out in the dark.

I went into a little old cow-town there, to wait for a train, & in a little old hotel there I sat in the bar, breakfasting delightfully, while the bar-tender talked to the customers.

"Say, Joe, we had a nice rain."

"Yes, Suh, sure we had."

"Say, Bill, did you ever see such a nice rain?"

"No, Suh, it was just a real nice rain."

"Gee, Suh, it was a nice rain."

"Yes Suh," etc etc "Gee, it was nice!"

"Gee, Suh, it was just a real nice rain!"

But here in England the rain is less rare than there, perhaps.

335

. . . I loved your letter of the fish & chips in the fog.

It is very hard to begin a fish & chip shop, for the fragrance is not that of Araby, & people protest against them. I used to know a painter, with whom I wandered into many odd parts of London, seeing queer things & places. He did 2 little London paintings:

"Fried fishshop in the morning/Is the Londoner's warning", shewing the Londoner, with a bit of a hangover, as it is now called, or, as we put it, showing that he had had some, slinking sicklily past the window, with averted eye and fearing the worst!

But beside it, there was the gay evening picture, "Fried fish shop at night/Is the Londoner's delight".

There all was Light & Joy. Beauty gazing & partaking, wit sparkled on the mind & half-pints sparkled on the counter. O, shepherd, pipe that song again, while Joe tells Alf what's going to win the three o'clock.

Outside, there were barrows with penn'orths of whelks & winkles, but he that had tuppence was all for the fish & chips, all hot out of newspaper. The poets of old used to go a good deal (for late suppers) to the cabman's shelters at the bigger London cab-ranks, but they were probably more costly than I could afford: & I never tried there. They belonged more to the *Yellow Book* time.

. . . I still wonder what Wagner's coat & waistcoat were, when he put on his cloth of gold trowsers. It is a maxim that the paler garments should be the lower ones: so perhaps his coat was crimson, with sable at cuffs & collar, & the waistcoat hidden (the coat buttoning up). You see he was probably aiming at a thunder & lightning effect, & the trowsers were the lightning. Black fur would have been rather fine, but then, what hat? A bowler? A topper? A Morny Cannon?[1]

[1] See note to Letter 28.

336

. . . When I was writing to you the other day, I forgot to mention a queer case mentioned some years ago. (We were discussing the fried fish shop at the time.) Well, the case was this, that a lady who was sensitive to printer's ink, taken internally, went to a fish & chippery for her lunch—this fragrant dainty was handed to her, done up in newspaper, as usual, but in this case some printer's ink came off onto the fish & chips, & then with them, into the lady.

Printer's ink is ink to which oil & varnish are added, with perhaps also some soap, in subtle ways which I do not know, & the mixture, like other mixtures, such as cocktails of some kinds, is more for men than poor delicate ladies unused to the rough & tumble of city life.

This mixture, thus, within the lady's system disagreed, so she brought a case against the fish & chippery.

I do not know more than this, for I missed the end-reports of the case. When I left off, I felt that she would not establish the case, but if she were very lovely, of course, the jury, or the judge, who knows? In a film the judge would have married her.

There used to be quick-lunch places in New York City, in which the men city workers used to post their lunches down their mouths like postcards: the complete lunch, with coffee, in 5 snaps, within 5 minutes of time. One used to suggest slogans for the counters:

> Why waste Time & Teeth
> Come—
> Dare Dyspeptic Death.
> Five Glorious Gulps then GO.

I remember a wonderful place in London, where, daily, men could choose from over 40 different kinds of sandwich,[1] each a triumph of skill & temptation, but perhaps the artists were made so rich that they retired early: it is not there now. No printer's ink came off from those things, no varnish, oil or soap.

Thinking over the case of the lady who thought herself harmed by the ink, I feel sure that it was the varnish in the ink, not the soap nor the oil, that did the harm: but then . . . there is the question . . . what oil? there is a thing called oil of vitriol, or used to be, which upset even the strongest.

Printer's ink might well become a habit, for it has a sort of warm spicey smell, rather alluring, a comfortable hot druggy kind of a possetty smell, a fragrance, the kind that does one good when one has a cold.

It smells like the stuff we used to smarten up the chain cables on board the *Conway*. It hung about the deck for the rest of the day & gave a sort of soothe to people.

. . . Please, will you, some day, be so very kind as to tell me if you, in your sea days used to sing a song about a lady called Meg? The song has a chorus:

> So blow ye winds, high yo.
> O blow ye winds, high yo.
> O clear away with the morning dew
> O blow ye winds, high yo.

The Lady Meg was the sort of lady that Mr Haggart used to call a *Blone* [blonde].

> She pincht a ticker from a man in liquor
> And was shippt to Botany Bay.
> So blow ye winds, high YO!

It is a wonderful song, from the Old Transportation Days, 1820–1840, the only good one among many such. I used to join in the chorus of it but forget most of the words now—but Meg's faithful lover followed her:

> I'll sail to Botany Bay
> Where the dancing dolphins play
> Where the whales & the sharks are having their larks
> Ten thousand miles away—
> So blow, etc . . . .

¹Probably Appenrodt's, at the southern end of Shaftesbury Avenue.

337

. . . I have been wondering whether you would let me cause Suttons to send you some things for the garden in which, like the poet Gray, "You plant and transplant, & are dirty and amused."

It is too late for plantings now, I suppose, but I wondered if, in March, you would care for some lavender plants, blue & white, to put in a bed well forward somewhere. Would they do with you?

You sent me a most charming kind card of anemones, for which I thank you. Would anemones, mixed St Bridgets, do with you? It might be possible to plant them now for next Spring: the lavenders would have to wait till about mid-March I expect (and need some care & watering in dry Springs).

Anyhow, mixed windflowers in flower are among the most adorable of all garden sights, & make the heart go pit-a-pat with joy, just as you do, as I am so well-qualified to say.

338

. . . Thank you for answering about the Hi-Yo song. It is so lively that I must try to find a text of it for you. The Brit. Mus. Music Dept. may be able to trace a good printed version.

It is one of the many transportation songs of 1820–1840, but much the best. Several of them I well remember as in the memory of seamen who sang them (with much sentiment).

> O I am a pore gell
> Misfortune I know
> I once went a courting
> A pore sailor boy.
> I courted him always
> By night and by day,
> But alas he's transported . . . (pause)
> And sent far away.

Then there was the very very popular:

> Now all you young ladies and gentlemen
> Pay attention to what I do say . . .
> If any of you takes what isn't hers or hisen
> They'll send you to Botany Bay,
> Singing torah li orral li oddity, etc.

This famous song you must have heard. Most of these seem to have been made by Irish convicts, and are revelations of broken hearts & homesickness, two things which are hostile to poetry in most natures.

I am glad that *Shamela* brought a smile. Mr Henry Fielding excelled in that vein, & must have had much fun having a cock-shy at such a target as Mrs Jewkes & her employer.

Please, some day, will you say if you would at all care for a *Tom Jones*, a rather big heavy single volume, but in good type? It would do for table-reading, but would be wrong for a bus or a train.

It is not quite up to *Shamela* & Mr J Wild [1] but is has some scenes: & also a touch of the early Romantic Movement, when he gets into my country beyond the Severn.

[1] *Jonathan Wild the Great.* A satire by Henry Fielding. Wild ran a large gang of thieves, in a highly orginal manner, opening offices in London where stuff stolen by his gang could be recovered at a price. He was hanged at Tyburn in 1725. See Letter 205.

339

. . . I wish you all glad success to your Bird Devices.

I used to saw coconuts in two for the tits & hang up the halves on wires. They were very popular, but I do not do this now, owing to the cat. I feed the birds with the poultry.

I found great eagerness for nesting-boxes if the tiny entrances faced South.

In those days, I wrote out of doors, & had birds all about me, some very tame, but not now.

You will find your boxes in request I feel sure.

. . . You ask me about Flaubert.

When I was young, most English writers were under French masters, and Flaubert was one of the adored masters, for his letters, his *Trois Contes* & the 3 big novels.

He was undoubtedly a big figure, a stylist, an artist, a searching critic, a most sound guide to young men, having probity and standards unusual in any intellect. While he lived, he was a precious guide & help to de Maupassant.

I do not feel that his writings have stood the convulsions of society. They belong to the [Second] Empire, are eminent among the ruins of the Empire, but the work is that of labour, not that of power. Compare it with Tolstoi.

340

Dearest Reyna

I was so glad to have your letter, & to think of your fun with Bruckner.

Now & then, every lover of art will be marvellously made akin to a marvellous mood of art to which some artist has been for a day or so admitted.

It is enough to know that that real world exists & is eternal, & is there, to be reached, where truth is, and joy is, and forgiveness of all sin, and understanding of all woe; & that this unlimited ecstasy is forever & forever & forever and that, in time, we shall all be in it forever & forever: not for just these moments, these flashes, but always . . . .

1962

341

... No-one ever makes more of my little gifts, & writes such adorable dear thanks, so infinitely more precious than the things they thank me for.

You are a dear to call the ship after my verses.[1]

I am glad you have liked these lines. I was about in despair, that I was dead, and somehow the lines seemed to suggest something . . . .

[1] Man with his burning soul
Has but an hour of breath
To build a ship of truth . . .

JM's poem "Truth" was published in *Philip the King and Other Poems* in 1914. He had given ANS a little ship of Dutch silver which, "having loved the poem and the present", she called "The Ship of truth".

342

... You may know an old book by Havelock Ellis,[1] a collection of facts & confessions, called *Studies in the Psychology of Sex*, in six vols.

I never met HE, but over 50 years ago I used to meet men who knew him, & helped (I believe) to suggest facts & to find confessions for parts of his work.

Some of the stories (life-histories) are strange: and seemingly true; and the result is something to read bits of, but always with the *Anatomy of Melancholy* at your side to read other bits of.

It is not a book like *Shamela*, that we can make merry over, & it is a long work, getting on for a million words long (eleven long novels long).

¹ Henry Havelock Ellis (1859–1939), author and scientist, brought a (to some) startlingly new approach to social problems. His *Studies in the Psychology of Sex* appeared 1907–10. The first volume, published in England, was the subject of a prosecution. Thereafter the volumes were published in America.

343

Reyna mia

I thank you for your kind letter from your frost-bound icy North. The appalling bleak tour, from ice-berg to glacier, now before you, and engulfing you, fills me with dismay for you, & bids me send, or try to send, a word of cheer.

I can only hope that at some gap in the ice-field there may be some brief comfort for you, say, a polar-bear sandwich, a little pemmican soup, or, at the least, a little blubber.

Often, at Christmas times, I send you a few shipping items that have come.

This year the *Victory*, in snow, is one of the best; but the best is surely the *Triton* frigate hove-to, by a backed fore-topsail & top-gallant, to pick up her channel pilot approaching in a lugger, to the R of the scene. This is by N. Pocock, a Bristol sea-captain, who beats everybody (I feel) at doing a single ship of this kind (in the 3 positions).

He must have seen Chatterton, I think at one time, for his ship carried C's friend to America & C came aboard to see him off.

Usually, one stopped a sailing-ship by opposing her main-topsail to the wind, *backing the main top-sail*. But pilots always stopped ships by backing the fore-topsails, because the ship renewed her way more quickly when this lesser barrier was removed, & pilots were too thrifty to lose, or risk losing, any slightest benefit.

. . . PS Do you, as a Bristol lady, at all care for Chatterton? Or do you say, with Dr Johnson, "Sir, the whelp must be acknowledged?"

344

. . . At Christmas, you very kindly sent me a green (Florentine) note-case of much distinction.

I am putting some writing paper into it (it will take some sheets 6″ × 4½″), & on these, I am going to do verses (I hope): & when I have some done, you shall see them, if they are not too grisly; & golly, you will say, O golly, what next.

This is what the poet says whenever he comes to a full● stop●

345

... I never wrote a word to you about Chatterton, yesterday. Please forgive.

Unfortunately, I do not count him as one of the moving figures in the early romantic movement. I never could like any of his work at all.

Meyerstein, who wrote the great *Life of TC* [1930], tried to show me my error, but he came too late, or I have the wrong kind of head or something.

The poor boy had a terrible life & death, & I have wished often that I could like Meyerstein's subject better: he gave 8 or 9 years to his book, & I count it a great book, but for TC's verse I cannot care; & for some verse of that time I have deep feelings, as for Gray, and ½ a dozen others, Mallet, Mason, Warton, Logan etc etc.

Even if you say, "Sir, the whelp must be acknowledged"; I must say, "Dearest, dear R, Meyerstein has acknowledged him, & nobly."

346

... I never heard Kreisler play, save by record; but I know what you feel about him (a little).

One should always try to hear the best of one's own time, but so seldom one can see the best at *their* best, and one can only remember the tales of the outstanding incredible ecstasies, of women flinging their jewels on the stages, men flinging their rings & watches & cigarette cases, anything, anything to give in return, for some momentary glimpse of paradise.

I have seen something a little like it, but never quite the extraordinary things of the legends.

... I have tried to remember what those who knew Havelock Ellis[1] told me of him, some 55 years ago.

My memory seems to say (& that is as far as I can go) that he was always so glad to find that some people recognised his wish to enlighten & to help; that he was deeply grateful for any confidence shown in him. I do not doubt that he was much misunderstood, &

quite possibly threatened with prosecution. You cannot possibly imagine the prudery of the late Victorians: the shock of the Wilde exposures; & the callous imbecility of those trusted with the care of the young. . . .

[1] See Letter 342.

347

. . . I thank you for your letter, & for the news of the ship's being now in order, & all square by the lifts & braces.

The big schooners, of which I sent you cards, were experimental sailing-ships of the American builders. I saw a good many of them, as of the other experimental ships, English, Scotch, French, & German; & on the whole, would say now, that the Scotch were the best-looking, & the Germans, by much, the best.

The big 7-masted Schooner in the card was a dangerous creature, I would say, at all times, like so many of them, whenever the cargo was out of her. A steamer carries a great weight of engines in her, as a perpetual ballast, but a big empty sailing vessel, she put her trust in de Lord, honey, & de Captain he sleep in de hotel!

She went over, & drowned all but one of her crew.

But all the same, she was a wonder, all steel, with steam-engines for all her heavy sails & anchors, & needing only 16 hands for 24 thundering big sails; & I suppose about 3 miles of running & standing rigging.

348

. . . I hope that the recent storm has not been very destructive to you in your few days of comparative peace. It was wild here, but did not bring any trees down, nor tiles off.

Here, in my reading, during the storm, I read of a big sea some 162 years ago, which came up against a big old man-of-war of 2 gun decks. The sea ran at her, tore her anchor from its bindings at the cat-head, lifted the anchor (weighing I suppose 3 or 4 tons) visibly high in air above the forecastle, and then let it drop (unkindly) on a lot of seamen there, with very terrible results.

It is always moving to find what wind & sea can really do when they get together.

Apart from this, I have been reading two French writers both of whom I expect you know. One was J. K. Huysmans,[1] who wrote about 1890–1905, & meant much to the young writers of that day. The other was François Villon,[2] the poet, who, also, was much read then, & perhaps still is.

He has been thoroughly annotated by pious Frenchmen so that he can be more easily read now. I think that he is the only recorded poet twice condemned to be hanged, who may quite possibly have been really hanged later, when he disappeared.

It is strange to think that some of the people, whom he saw & may have met, may, formerly, have seen Joan of Arc, on the one extreme, and the original Bluebeard, Gilles de Rais,[3] on the other. A lively time, that, to have known the three, & to have seen wolves in Paris streets eating people.

[1] Joris-Karl Huysmans (1848–1907), a novelist of Dutch descent who lived and died in Paris where for thirty years he worked for the French Sûreté. His novel *A Rebours* (1884), often cited as the supreme expression of the decadent spirit, is the exciting work referred to in Wilde's *The Picture of Dorian Gray* (1891).

[2] Villon, François (1431—after 1463), poet. Although twice exiled for being concerned in affrays, he was only once condemned to be hanged, against which sentence he successfully appealed. The horror of the experience produced his magnificent poem the "Ballade des Pendus".

[3] Rais, Gilles de, (now usually Gilles de Retz) 1396–1440. Fought with Joan of Arc against the English. He took to necromancy, kidnapped and murdered children, and was tried and executed.

349

. . . I hope that the *Black Death* book[1] may have some cheery moments in it. It was a very fierce infection, like the one in Athens, described by Thucydides, when even the birds were killed by it, almost instantaneously, & pigs (in the 1348–9 outbreak) seemed to die from it at once when they came near one dead of it: the poison must have been incredibly fierce & swift, I suppose paralysing the heart.

[1] *The Black Death: A Chronicle of the Plague compiled from Contemporary sources* by Johannes Nohl (1926).

350

. . . At the moment, I can find no trace of Mr Freme,[1] but it should not be too hard to get news of him, so the hunt shall begin. It will be some little while before I can hope for any result, but perhaps some little crumb may be found . . . .

[1] ANS had a silver tray of 1810, "presented to Wm Freme for his great service to the Commercial Docks". She asked JM if he could find out anything about Freme, and the letters contain the story of his successful detective-work.

351

. . . Commerce is usually harder to trace than Navy, for there are fewer public records . . . .

I have sent for books on England's Commercial Docks at Rotherhithe (the Redriff of Mr Lemuel Gulliver, Mariner); but I am prepared for either Bristol or Liverpool.

Docks began to be a major labour in all ports about 1790, for trade was increasing, & it was utterly impossible to discharge the many ships into lighters as they lay in river or harbour. The amounts lost by theft & fecklessness by this old method were truly appalling.

Imagine having to unload a ship, then having to load & unload her lighters, & then having to load various sheds into various carts and then . . . and then . . . . and then, and at each *then* someone had a chance to get some, and got.

There are some picturesque books about this; & who knows? Mr Freme may have written some.

352

. . . I grieve to have no news yet of Mr Freme, but I have begun the search & hope to find out (& expect to find out) something about him.

Really, you cannot imagine the squalid, dishonest, incompetent, criminal incapacity of the London shipping interests.

London lay on both sides of a tidal river, for some horrible muddy miles:

> With here & there a mouldy Church
> And here & there a gallows.

And on each side of the smoky, cess-pooly, Newgatey city-river was a double line of small ships each trying to discharge or load a cargo, into 1 or more lighters, or trying to get away to sea, or trying to get in to declare her cargo, or to have it examined, or searched or certified by the customs or Port authorities, or fighting some gang of thieves, or run into by a barge or other ship, or dragging her moorings into other ships or into London Bridge, or collapsing onto her side at low water & causing the ebb to heap her ballast into the shoals made by other ballasts, or being raided & unmanned by a naval press [-gang], or perhaps set fire to by someone eager to have some pickings; & no means (save the ebb) to get a fresh-water supply: & no power or pulley along the wharves for the use of a freighter carrying heavy goods & wanting to discharge them: & organised pirates everywhere, to get a cask or two of this or that, or a ton or so of coal slipped overboard, to be picked up at low water, & all hands, in all those miles, hindered from their tasks in every possible way by somebody's apathy, & nearly all hands drunk & all the drunk with a finger in the pie.

353

... Did we not once collogue together in old days about W. J. Huggins—Huggins the marine artist?[1]

Well, looking up the Dock question, I came on a reprod[n] of an engraving from a paint[g] by Huggins, 1828, showing the opening of St Katherine's Dock on the site of old St Katherine's Hospital near the Tower of London.

It showed some ships already in dock, & all dressed overall with flags, & yards squared, & all the yards manned, not like naval men, holding on to the life-line with both hands, but *each*

> EACH
> Man
> Waving 3 Hurrays & a Tiger[2]
> with
> his
> heroic
> Right Hand.

But not only that. On the summit of each mast a solitary seaman stood on the truck or plate of wood from 6 inches to a foot across. He too waved his right arm as the gun went off; I made out 7 trucks each with a solitary seaman on it, each waving his right hand.

The question of Mr Freme must now provoke a 2nd question: were these truck standers dummies?

The boy stood on the royal truck
With lovely views of all.
He said "I shall be out for duck
If I should chance to fall."

[1] See Letters 13, 22.

[2] A tiger was a shriek or howl (often the word "tiger") terminating a prolonged and enthusiastic cheer (US slang 1856 *OED*).

354

. . . I feel sure that all these men on the trucks are standing on pseudo-trucks or false royal-poles coming up perhaps to their shoulders & giving them absolute security as long as they do not play the fool.

But in my childhood the Navy had men who (just before my childhood) had been accustomed to a feat whenever their ship paid-off.

Before the money came aboard, at a sort of general "Hurray . . . Free . . . Free . . . for a good old drunk tonight . . . .", a man of the right top would run to the fore main or mizen truck, & would stand on it, with his arms folded, for one minute; & then, at a signal, would come down.

Now this was done as a matter of course & thought nothing of.

I never saw it done, but it *was* done, & sometimes men fell & were killed in doing it, but perhaps not always killed.

I have often wondered: how, if, suddenly, the stander wished to sneeze?? Or how he began to come down?

How would you begin to come down? I suppose the instinct is to sink down, so that the hands may catch the truck between the 2 feet; but the 2 feet fill the truck, & the truck is not secured too tightly, & on these festal occasions a flag is flying at it sometimes . . . Still, England expected.

355

. . . You will have heard of the Bisley boy??[1]

The story is that the Princess Elizabeth was a prisoner somewhere there while the Catholics wondered whether she should be allowed to live, she being (in their view) a heretic & illegitimate.

Whether they killed her, or let her die, varies the story, but the tale maintains that Somebody procured a Bisley boy, who looked kind of like the Princess, kind of tough & tart, & brought him up as the Princess, & that he *was* Queen Elizabeth the First, who swore so at Bishops & played off all the suitors, one against the other, & never told the truth, even when it suited her case to do so.

¹ In the mid-nineteenth century, at Bisley in Gloucestershire, a stone coffin was unearthed, containing the skeleton of a young girl. The coffin was probably mediaeval, but it inspired Canon Thomas Keble, the incumbent of Bisley (and brother of John Keble, the founder of the Oxford Movement in 1833) to invent a legend about it for the delectation of his friends. Princess Elizabeth, he said, while on a visit to her manor of Bisley, had died suddenly and been interred in Bisley churchyard; a village boy who closely resembled her was dressed in ruff and farthingale and sent forth to impersonate the Princess. The story took hold of the popular imagination, at least in that corner of Gloucestershire, and is believed by some to this day.

356

. . . I could not yesterday write in answer to your question about AB [Arnold Bennett].

I met him twice, but never knew him.

I met him first in the St James's Square: he was with a man whom I knew, & the man introduced me to him—& we both said something quietly polite, & then that was that.

After about 5 or 6 years, I met him again at a dinner-party; but had no talk with him. I do not remember any Mrs AB, but perhaps there was one.¹

This was the extent of our meeting, I do believe; & it was a long time ago, & I can only recollect that he was a well-built, well set-up, confident, capable sort of chap, rather good-looking, & very friendly & ready.

I never read much fiction, & at that time read very little, but I did greatly like 2 of his early books: *The Old Wives' Tale* (which you would like) & *The Grand Babylon Hotel*, though this was (if I remember—for once—correctly) but an extravaganza.

I have not read his later fiction, having never much time for reading, & always preferring verse, & things approximating to the poetical, ballads rather than plays in prose, & poetical plays rather than fiction. Then, too, I may read a book I really love 50 or 60 times, just as I write to one I love (such as you) 50 or 60 times a year.

¹ Enoch Arnold Bennett (1867–1931) married, in 1907, a Frenchwoman,
Marie-Marguerite Soulié, from whom he was legally separated in 1921.

357

... American men are deeply sensitive in many ways, much as English men were in earlier times, & still are in simple communities.

It is no disgrace to yield to deep feeling, but in the last 100 years or so, the schools, or shyness, or the two together, have made the English adopt an outward callousness that gives us a bad name abroad.

... Did you ever visit any old battle-field, in England or elsewhere, & try to imagine what the quiet [periods during a battle] was once like.

Usually, they are part of a story, & it is partly my task to consider them as such, & see if the story can be told or re-told; & yesterday I came upon the story of a soldier who had to report to his Commander in Chief, an Austrian Archduke, but was told that his story (of importance to thousands of men) would have to wait.

"His Imperial Highness is not to be disturbed: he is occupied in having a fit."

358

... I am writing now, dear sweet, to say a little about the Freames (as they seem to spell it in Lypiatt) who do not readily give any token of a William that will suit your tray.

It is an ancient family, known in the Lypiatt country from (anyhow) the 13th century, no doubt eminent dogs, as you may see from the enclosed [family tree].

But your real William Freme (or Freame), I do a little hear from London, as you shall hear.

His office was in Catherine Court, Tower Hill, a plain brick house now gone altogether. He was more of a *timber* than a *general* Russia merchant, & by timber we must suppose soft wood such as pine & fir, with pitch, tar, potash, & probably hemp & flax in addition (*from the Baltic when peace permitted* or convoy was possible).

Russia produced no hard wood, for ships of war.

1807. 18th Sept. Wm Freme, Esq. was at a meeting of the subscribers to the Commercial Dock, at the Old London Tavern, Bishopsgate Street, London, EC.

25th Sept. He was one of 13 Managers unanimously elected by ballot. After this he *usually* attended the Board meetings (every third week) conscientiously till:

1810 17th August, when he attended for the last time, or the last recorded time.

1808 8th April. He & another Manager were deputed to write a special letter to cause Danish ships that were prizes of war to dock in the Commercial Dock if necessary. This was a war-measure, and at once agreed to.

He was also appointed specially to a Committee for altering the Dock's warehouses.

1817. Some money seems to have been paid "To Freme & Walker", & perhaps William was the lucky Freme.

As a dweller in Catherine Court, he would have been a parishioner of All Hallows Church; & I hope to hear, but may not hear, if he were buried or married or excommunicated there.

It may well be that some of the stuffs be brought from Russia were gums used in varnish. I seem to have read somewhere that such things were: but it is more likely that he imported linseed oil, much used in the making of various varnishes.

In any case, he does emerge as one who was useful, loyal & conscientious in getting the Commercial Dock to be made to function.

After the truly appalling conditions of London River, with its organised piracy, theft, incompetence, danger, & widespread mess, with delay, waste & loss on a scale hardly now conceivable, he & a few others caused docks to come, where the ships lay safely, near winches & derricks, close to warehouses where their goods were safe, or factories where they could at once be used.

Your tray is the well-earned reward of virtue—& it is a joy, dear girl, to try to do something for you, of whom the very thought is ever a joy.

Jan.

PS I think that the Old London Tavern has long since gone. The London Tavern of later days was in Fenchurch Street, EC.

359

. . . I cannot remember if I sent you this photo card of the *Glaucus*, the famous Carmichael 4-masted barque, lying somewhere beneath your old haunts.

If I did, why, then, you will have two, & you will know some other Bristol person to whom it might bring a joy.

I add to it a card of a famous rarity, a 4-masted *ship*,[1] which I saw once long since (one of the experiments of the nineties). A man I knew sailed in her, but what happened to him I never heard.

She was (I have been told) *the* ship whose strange story I told in *The Bird of Dawning*. The Captain heard a Voice telling him to sink his ship and come away. He did his best to sink her, & got away with all hands in the boats, but when the boats reached (the Azores, I think?) lo, the ship had been salved & was there before them at anchor.

The Capt. recovered from the shock after a little rest.

The 4-masted ships came at a time of falling freights. They were too expensive to run as ships. The yards were usually removed from the jigger masts, which then set only 2 sails instead of 6, & this was a great saving in sails, yards, rope, gear & seamen: & I daresay made the vessels easier to steer, & perhaps quite as fast as formerly.

I saw 1 or 2 of them, long since, in Liverpool & Glasgow: & I had a letter once from a German sailor who sailed in the *Falls of Afton* in order to learn English.

The *Glaucus* I saw twice, at sea, in the N. Atlantic somewhere.

[1] A ship, by definition was a vessel having a bowsprit and three masts.

360

. . . In case these should please Tim [some ship pictures] I venture to send them to you, but perhaps modern youth prefers the space-ship, with re-fuelling balloons somewhere the other side of the moon.

The *Sovereign*'s hull is white, being lime-washed against the Worm, the Teredo-worm, that begins as a speck on the under-water plank, & eats in, growing as it eats, till it eats a smooth hole 2 inches across, & lets in the sea.

When this happens in 50 places at once, the ship sinks, and I suppose the happy worms just go on eating.

Presently men took to building ships of iron, which the worm did not have quite the teeth for, but the worms still have pier-piles & dock heads here & there & it is wondrous what they do . . . . It is incredible what they do.

361

. . . I went to Tewkesbury on my birthday [1st June], in lovely weather, & the hawthorn (a fortnight late) just beginning to be at its best.

Did you ever consider the Battle of Tewkesbury,[1] as something that once filled a morning there?

Just where the slaughter must once have been very awful, there is now (& it has been for 30 years) the ODTAA[2] Garage.

[1] The Battle of Tewkesbury, 4th May 1471. The decisive action of the Wars of the Roses, when Margaret of Anjou's Lancastrian forces were defeated by Edward IV's army, Queen Margaret's son Edward was killed and she herself taken prisoner.

[2] One Damn Thing After Another—*ODTAA* is the title of one of JMs novels.

362

. . . I have never read de Sade at all, & know nothing about him, but I now feel I must not languish thus in darkness, so I have sent for some books, & next week may be able to write of him. He was supposed to have been a bad influence; & one ought to know what to avoid.

For one said to have been brought up in an 18th century French army, & in criminal prisons, and madhouses, he seems to have kept an unusually clear head for cheerier ways.

Perhaps you will allow me to write later, when I know more, or at least know something.

I have heard, of course, the shocked tone of the Victorian elder.

363

. . . The things on view of Blake at the Tate were not all to my mind; for so many of his works are water-colours, & I suppose unable to stand much exposure. Probably the water-colours are only shown for brief special seasons each year. Thirty-odd years ago, the display was very splendid; today it is far less representative, & often forbidding.

I only really love his Chaucer outburst, & the Songs, & some of the little narrative water-colour drawings, such as the *River of Life*.

The reproductions to be had of him were few, and not representative; & for this I blame the management. His visionary heads of Poets, & his Canterbury Pilgrims ought to be obtainable: & an effort made to reproduce his astounding illustrations.

Ah, my lovely friend, thirty odd years ago I could have taken you to a marvellous room where you should have seen a marvellous book (I suppose about 18 inches by 12 inches) of *Gray's Poems* (say 7 inches by 5 inches) on each page taken from the published printed copies, & the rest of the page all marvellous illustrations by Wm Blake done by him for Mr & Mrs Fuseli, &, alas, never quite completed.[1]

Fuseli was a Swiss painter settled here. Blake wrote him a poem or two of a very unusual kind: one of them is this:

> The only Man that e'er I knew
> That did not make me almost spew
> Was Fuseli: he was both Turk & Jew
> And so, dear Christian Friends, how d'you do?

In the illustrations to Gray, my golly, my beloved, he must have been prophetically painting for Reyna, for all was inspiration & power & vision & ecstasy & forgiveness of sin.

There can be nothing like them save in the other Blake work.

I cannot describe them, but you, in a lovely dream, will have seen incredible beauty in incredible abundance & perfection, & known the extremity of heart's joy & soul's perception, & wakened knowing that this world exists for us, near us, & can at times be entered.

[1] See Letters 92, 147.

364

. . . I wonder if you struggled thro' to the end of *Mr John Decastro*, & have any theories as to who wrote it?[1]

When I first read it, nearly 60 years ago, it seemed to me a great work, summing-up, as it were, the sense, the religion, the practical goodness & rightness of the best of the late English 18th century, with the outer world of the romantic movement making its presence felt in imaginings of over-wickedness, mysterious dungeons, *Castle Spectres*, etc.

I thought that possibly Cobbett might have written it: but then, if C had written it, he would have told us so.

I suppose Combe, or some such, might have done it.

Did you ever read Monk Lewis,[2] or see his startling play of *The Castle Spectre*?

The time is ripe for a revival of interest in Monk Lewis. I do not think that he wrote *Mr JD* but he could have done work of such power, & was, moreover, a man of much generous goodness of mind. *The Monk*, which won him his nickname: didst ever read that, shepherd?

¹ See Letter 321

² Matthew Gregory Lewis (1775–1818), chiefly remembered for his novel *The Monk*, because of which he was often known as "Monk" Lewis.

365

. . . I wrote to the Lib for the de Sade books, but they write that the 3 for wh I asked are *all out*, but will be engaged for me.

Can it be, I wonder, that the Lib means to save me from temptation & pollution??

I have withstood, with success, the honeyed seductions described by Havelock Ellis & am I not to be trusted in the presence of de S?

They will probably send 1 of the books, the feeblest, next week; & I will write to you about it.

366

. . . As I feared, the Lib has not yet sent the de S books, not even the bowdlerised ones, so I am still (comparatively) unpolluted, & cannot (like the wicked young American in Matthew Arnold's Essay)— "Lower your moral tone any."

I still have but suspicion of what de S proclaimed or delighted in.

A lot of wits got loose in the late 18th century, & have been loose in the world ever since. As the Americans said, "There's a lot of crazy guys got off their rockers."

One of the causes of man's trouble seems to be this.

Most animals in this earth, away from men, & most men in primitive conditions, have a short mating season, when the food stimulus is greatest & most exciting—& a birth season when the food supply is most certain.

In birds, in this land, the seasons are close together; in men they are less close.

But men, in general, in what we call civilised nations (able to go fast & kill widely) have upset this order of sex indulgence. They mix, mate, & breed pretty much at will, so that the strain, urge, & nightmare of it is never out of men's thought, from say, the age of ten, onwards, as in Sonnet 129 by WS.¹

Then, city-life, however attractive & exhausting it may be, is more lonely than primitive life, & not delightful in its labour, like, say, farm or sea life, hunting life, forestry: it tires men & shuts them indoors.

¹ Shakespeare's Sonnet 129: "The expense of spirit in a waste of shame / Is lust in action."

367

Reyna darling

I thank you for your two lovely kind dear letters; & now send to your Harrogate Hotel the copy of *The Monk*.

Dearest, I read this against strictest orders some 77 years ago. I did not get much joy from it, except the joy of doing what I was forbidden, but I did see that it suggested powers or passions of much importance, & disobedience that brought disaster.

I thought it much more powerful than I think it now, but here it is for Reyna, & may she enjoy it.

About 25 years ago I saw his play *The Castle Spectre* acted. This is a much finer thing than *The Monk* but in both works there is (to me) the presence of an overwhelming uncritical Romantic Mood burning to get into Life &, as it were, ravishing any brain or pen that it could get into Life by. This Mood was (I feel) of an extreme wild power, & possessed Byron, Lewis, the boy Shelley, some of revolutionary France, & much of post-Napoleonic Europe, till it got itself civilised down by knowledge, religion, & years of peace.

The Mood swayed Lewis & possessed him. The only art in *The Monk* book is best seen in the verse, which always commands respect. Here & there in the tale there are gleams of power but I need not tell you that when I was 7 I did not note the absurdities.

For Lewis the man, I have high admiration: he was a noble fellow.

The Castle Spectre, with the enchanting "Perdita" singing the exquisite heroine's Song, & the clanking ghost, & the appalling villain, the blackest of black dogs, is a better work, but again, the Mood mastered him.

Indeed, men are often mastered by moods of witchery & devilry; & then, farewell, al is y-go.

368

. . . I write thus swiftly after the receipt of your letter to ask if you could let me try to arrange a day for you here, while you are in

London; or even (if an old friend might be allowed the privilege) of arranging some lonely billet for you on the river near here somewhere. You could be lonely enough there & "Kepen in solitariness", yet perhaps wd not mind coming to lunch or staying to tea here?

There used to be a song:

> This might be fun
> For Abra-ham
> But jolly poor show
> For Mary Ann.

369

... You write of threading amethysts on a string.

Will you be so very kind as to tell me, what string you use to thread them on?

I have often marvelled at the strings used by jewellers for this purpose, & would be glad to know if what you use be a special cord used by jewellers.

There are some nice strings made near here, such as your marine fingers would love to knot.

370

... I send a little of the string I wrote about. It is the smallest that I now have, & may be too coarse for jewels.

When I was trying to rig models I had smaller line than this, that I could splice & use for topmast shrouds & upper stays, but I have not any now so small.

All these good lines need to be stretched before use; & I would recommend you to hang a pack of books for a night or so on the line, from one of your clothes' or hat pegs.

I reckon that the string sent would bear a steady strain of one hundred pounds, but it would not do to trust it to bear you if you were lowering yourself out of the window.

Use it *double* for that, & be sure that your bowline-knot is hauled well-taut before you trust it. I know you will be safe with double: & remember, you are precious to me ...

371

... A great many years ago I read several translations of the Arabian 1001 Nights, & among them Lane's, Payne's & Burton's.

On the whole, I dislike the collection as the Devil is said to have disliked the Ten Commandments, as "a —— rum lot".

A lot of the tales are negligible, & a lot are just dirty & of the East; & I felt that Burton went out of his way to make the tales dirtier than he found them (which is often saying a good deal). Lane did not translate much of the book, but nobody can want much of it. I will try to find you a Lane [1839–41], but would recommend you not to bother about Burton.[1]

I liked the French translation, by a chap called Mardrus, but I am told that his version is really a re-writing not a translation.

Perhaps one fifteenth of the entire collection might be thought worth reading: one 15th at the outside.

One used to hear a lot about Burton, but I cannot care for any of his writing: not even for his journey to Mecca. Men used to say that a negro spotted him in the Holiest Place in Mecca, & that Burton scragged him dead with a knife, before he could cry, "Him a Christian".

I was told that he never denied the story, but I don't think that it can be true.

It was said that he translated an Arabian medical work about the direction of the sexual instincts: & that Lady B did not think that it could be a medical work, & so burned it.

This is quite likely to be true, for I don't suppose that B was interested in the medical side of the book, which yet was there.

I have never read the book, but gathered from a scholar that it takes the line that sex in Sodom should not be expected to be quite what it was in Cyprus; & that (in Blake's phrase) "One Law for Mrs Grundy and Messalina is oppression".

Please let me try to find you a Lane; & recommend against the RB. You would be so bored with such a lot of it.

Yesterday I received a queer advertisement from America, a de Maupassant tale, *La Maison Tellier*, wh I will post to you tomorrow, Wed.

It is a beautiful, strange, outrageous story; & somehow you must forgive me for sending it. It has all those elements of skill & understanding that Burton never has: & somehow a great beauty that I know you will see (& like me for sharing).

> My devoted love & blessing to you
> my darling,
> Jan.

¹ Sir Richard Francis Burton (1821–90). His other translations include the *Kama Sutra* and *The Perfumed Garden*.

372

Reyna mia

The posts are ever queer now & KL [King's Lynn] seems far away, but perhaps this may find you there, & I hope bring a little gleam into the gloom, if it be a gloom.

Do you ever read the detective stories of Simenon, the French writer?

I am now reading my third of his, but have only just come to the corpse, & am not yet even suspecting anybody of the crime, save the widow & the victim's son.

> All happiest blessings to you
> Jan.

373

... How sad to make the music for a Ballet & yet never to see the Ballet.¹

But you will answer, "We Make the Ballet. We *are* the Ballet. We create the Dance in the Dancers, & that creates the dance in the audience, & all the flowers that fall are really spiritual flowers flung from the Gardens of our Hearts."

I saw the Polish Ballet 25 years ago, but they were not then elegant (as I thought) but probably the inelegance was in me.

... About Degas, & his illustrations. As you know, he drew the French Ballet of his day; & I judge that the French B was not then very elegant, for France was overwhelmed when Diaghilev & Fokine brought the Russian B to them.

Degas was profoundly moved by the magic & grace of many swift movements. About 30 years ago I saw some hundreds of tiny studies in wax from his studio; all of swift sudden movements, horses jibbing, bulls lowering head for a charge, tennis players, men at an anvil, bell-ringers, bird preening, creatures drinking, children playing ... I know not what ... but all catching some sudden deathless exquisite poise that was gone before it was seen.

I saw also a swift drawing of his of Fred Archer, the jockey, going to the post somewhere (not racing).

Archer had an unmistakeable seat, that I cannot describe, & never saw, but would recognise everywhere, even now, from the many drawings in sporting papers seen in my childhood. I knew that the drawing was of Archer from the man's seat.

Fred Archer was a marvellous jockey: but always wasting & wasting, to make the weights demanded, he being really over-weight always, & this fearful life brought him to illness & suicide before he was 30.

De Maupassant had a marvellous youth, too, under the care of the great Flaubert: but he was a wild youth, never sated, & yet never happy in the attempt to sate himself. Men called him "The sad Town-Bull".

Well, men ought not to earn that sort of nick-name, I suppose; & it led to his madness & death.

Just before his mind became too terror-stricken, he wrote some marvellous uncanny tales; the best of their kind in the world.

[1] ANS was playing (in the orchestra pit) for the Polish Ballet then touring England.

374

. . . I thank you for your dear letter, & your stirring account of the Ballet.

O to be a part of the performance thus, in the joy of the poetic mood, in poetry & music & colour & paradise, all at one go.

And joy, too, to hear that the Poles have improved such a lot, & are now elegant as well as unusual.

I think that Degas wd have been about 25 when Archer was born, & about 52 or 53 when the poor fellow killed himself. He lived on after Archer's death a full 30 years or so.

Archer was I believe rather tall & big for a jockey, & was always wasting to make the weight, taking these fearful walks in 3 over-coats & a fur rug. He had a conquering kind of soul I gather, & wanted to be first or die.

Pavlova, I believe, had some frailty of the heart; & ballerinas put a lot of strain on the heart, intense strain at odd moments, & this led to her death (so a dancer told me).

Byron had some physical tendency to over-fatness. I have seen some terrible photographs of early portraits of him, showing [in] him a deplorable bloatiness. He took himself in charge & drank a lot of vinegar daily, & ate almost nothing, & then swam a lot, & drank a lot more vinegar, & by vinegar & starvation he made himself thin (& perhaps pretty savage) or so the stories say.

⚜

375

. . . I could not at once answer your question about Haroun al Rashid,[1] but I send you the following notes about him.

He began as a highly born Mahommedan Prince of the Abbasids, an Arabian dynasty in Persia, a dynasty descended from Mahommed's Uncle, & therefore highly important.

He first appears as a young Commander under the Caliph Mahdi (AD 774–784) leading armies westward from the new capital of Baghdad, & putting all Syria & Asia Minor more or less under Persian power. Two years after Mahdi's death, in 786 he became Caliph, perhaps by general vote (I do not know) & became famous for Justice, Peace, the Arts, & all sorts of wonderful things, that made Baghdad famous in the world. He corresponded with Charlemagne in France, just as King Offa, in England did, Offa of Offa's Dyke. It is a pleasing thought, that his envoy may have met Offa's Envoy at C's Court, & talked about the ways of Allah with him.

Haroun was an Eastern Caliph & took a very short way with Dissenters . . . .

"We cut zeir bl——ie trotes," as the Serb said to a friend of mine about the Germans in the 1st War.

But he is a legendary figure to this day.

In a vast roadless place like ancient Persia, lots of outlying tribes rebelled; & while marching to deal with the trotes in one such, Haroun died at a place called Tus, in Khorassam, in the year 808. He had had a long reign for an Eastern King.

Baghdad was called the Abode of Peace. It is on the Tigris River, & is crossed by many caravan routes. It is in a land of gardens of Eden, & was a famous market, for fruits, corn, silks, works of art, marvellous tiles, men of learning, poets, astronomers etc etc & all sorts of gazelle-eyed ladies wishing that they could only look a little like Reyna, but what chance of that was there?

[1] Haroun Al Rashid (766–809), second son of the third Abassid Caliph, Mahdi. Ascended the throne at the age of 22.

376

. . . I loved what you said about your time down the River.

I lived at Greenwich for some years, & knew the Hospital buildings & so many of the pictures & exhibits.

. . . I saw the *Cutty Sark*[1] when she came to Falmouth after the Portuguese sold her. She was then an old ruin barquentine (thrift, thrift, Horatio) & looked deplorable; but the Portuguese had kept her copper going, & the hull was in order. Later, we English re-rigged her as a ship; & I often saw her in Falmouth, & went over her mast-head (for the glory) about 40 years or so ago. Later, I flew over her (coming back from Holland, I think) when she was a part of HMS *Worcester* at Greenhithe.

She was very fast, in her prime, and made a name for herself: but we (of the 18 nineties) held out for the ships of our own time: as much bigger & more marvellous; & of these I suppose, we have no single survivor in British waters; not one.

Ah my darling loving girl with the joyous heart, you are welcome to my memories of the ships I knew.

I expect I have told you of the *Harbinger*, & the *Wanderer* & the *Dalgonar*: but you will not have seen the enclosed views each of which has its particular thrill.

The Australian port view shows you the sad end of a lot of ships, made into barques[2] for cheapness, & probably all soon to be sold cheap to the Norwegians, for about thirty shillings a ton.

They had a fine painting at Greenwich of Adml Vernon's squadron taking Porto Bello. Long after I saw it, I was able to blarney a ship's Capt. to stand right in to the Porto Bello mouth, so that I could see the scene; so I saw both it & Nombre de Dios, & thought of all the dead there, Drake's trumpeter & Hosier's crews.

> as in Porto Bello lying
> In the gently swelling flood.

[1] The *Cutty Sark*, now on dry land at Greenwich, was built in 1869 for the China tea trade. She once sailed 365 miles in one day.

[2] Barque or bark: a three-masted vessel with fore- and main-masts square-rigged, and mizen-mast fore-and-aft rigged. A barquentine: fore-mast square-rigged, main-and mizen-mast fore-and-aft rigged.

377

. . . I hope to include another press clipping about Ararat & Noah.[1]

The Religious folk there used to show Noah's vineyard somewhere there: a kind of scandalous place, I wd say: but it got all buried away in an earthquake, I believe, & now these old bones of the Ark are their only hope of a tourist season.

In the little print of the Ark, did you notice the little baggage at the door: one of N's daughters I fancy?

The adze is not like a plane, but a skilled adze-man can take off a shaving with it, though never, of course, a yard of shaving, like a good planer. The plane is *pushed from* the planer; the adze *hacks towards* the adzer.

30 or 40 years ago I met a lot of ship-builders who had served apprentice-ships in wooden building-slips, & had had to master the adze. They said that they had all *scars on their shins* to prove that they were real men. As the adze is a sort of battle axe with an edge like a razor, I marvel that they had any legs at all.

> Here, a sheer hulk, lies poor Tom Adzer,
> With whom none could compete.
> With one fell swipe (is it not sad, Sir?)
> He smote off both his feet.
> He who was once our liveliest prancer
> On penny-farthing bike . . . .
> And now I ask (and who can answer?)
> When shall we see his like?

[1] A newspaper cutting JM sent to ANS read "A small Anglo-American expedition has reported encouraging progress towards solving Ararat's riddle." Pieces of wood brought from a site 14,000 ft up the mountain (Mt Agri Dagi in Eastern Turkey) were believed to be part of a giant boat; scientific tests indicated that the wood was 3,500 years old.

378

. . . You will be going to Cheltenham, & not long ago, we wrote a little about Fred Archer, the jockey, who came from those parts, & was much about the place, at Prestbury, & at Andoversford, in his youth & brief life.[1] A. Lindsay Gordon[2] was there, too, at that time, & George Stevens, & Black Tom Oliver, 2 men whom he mentions in his poems: "'Ay, Squire,' said Stevens;" etc etc. But Fred Archer was one of the amazing men of the late Victorian era.

He died, by his own hand, in a wild hour during typhoid fever, when I was 7 or 8, & I only met one person who knew him—this one said he was "a blackguard", but yet asked him for a racing tip, at some meeting, & was given the tip.

When I was 7 or 8 I saw a photograph of his grave all heaped high with wreaths, & on one of the wreaths I read a label: *Gone, but not Forgotten*, & latterly I thought I would try to find out about him, for I distrusted that voice that said he was a blackguard, for I never knew any blackguard whose grave was heaped high with flowers. Something astounding is needed for that. There was nothing like that for Hardy. It was great for Hardy; but very different from that. With Hardy the great wheel had come full circle & the star had gone down beyond Swyre [Head, Dorset]. With Archer, the miracle had shone & had shattered, & what a miracle it had been.

[1] See Letter 373.

[2] Gordon, Adam Lindsay (1833–70), Australian poet, author of "How we beat the Favourite".

379

. . . I thank you for your list of the places [where the Hallé was to play]. Your letters generally come on Tues, & this coming on Tues, makes me miss Nottingham, but here I have a bash at W'hampton, & hope to catch you there.

60 years ago I shd have been there, in an office opposite the Gallery or in an old farm at Tettenhall, much delighting in a local poem by one who had returned from Niagara & had written a poem about it.

(The Volcano) They talked about the Vol—ca—no,
(The Volcano) And *IT'S* mighty, no doubt.
(Niagara)   But if *THIS* into *IT* did flow (the volcano)
(Niagara)   *IT* would soon put *IT* out (the volcano)

I have been several times to Niagara & to Vesuvius, & have always wondered whether IT would put IT out; & on the whole I don't think it would or could, for if the whole of N could be piped into the crater of V, there would no doubt be a local coolness & success, but in a very short time a head of steam would be generated, & all the top & base of V would go up in a bang like Krakatoa & N would find that the longer he went on the bashier V would be, & N is on a soft bit of rock, & N would collapse into a sort of a swoosh, & presently all the barrier that parts Ontario from Erie would cease to be; & there would be only one lake instead of two, with a blazing & bursting boiler exploding like billio on its margin, & heaving up who can say what new Rockies:

My gentle girl, remember this
Is nothing but a dream.

⚜

380

. . . Francis Beaumont, John Fletcher's great collaborator, came from near Leicester, & I have always meant to go to see the place, but never have, though Wordsworth mentions it in a moving phrase: "Forlorn Grace Dieu".

I suppose that the Beaumonts had some old monastic house (a nunnery I believe).[1]

Luckily the nuns would all have been safely pensioned off long before the poet was born.

[1] Grace Dieu Abbey, near Leicester.

⚜

381

. . . This should reach you on your return to Bristol, but the posts are odd, & grow very greatly queerer, like the railways.

Not long ago some iron railing standards, needed to repair a fence, took a fortnight to come 90 miles on a straight line. I could have wheeled them, by road, on a wheelbarrow, in less.

Last week, a letter of mine took four days to go ten miles. I had reckoned that it would take fourteen hours, from pillar box to recipient.

Still, I suppose some race-horses & athletes & so forth manage to get there quickly, as in the past: & these, for some reason, are important to England: & sometimes in my muddled head there comes a kind of a glimmer that it *is* so, & that if I could only grasp the fact I wd be ever so much wiser.

I hope that Bristol & the Gorge & Bridge remain pretty much as they were, & that old memories very happily revive.

Bristol, or its near-by haunts, were holy places to the young male in my childhood, for somewhere there the boy E. M. Grace & his more famous brother, WG, learned cricket in a sloping orchard, while a faithful Gelert of a DOGG fielded whatever balls went downhill.

There, too, the young "Hugh Conway"[1] began his career as a writer by going to the *Conway* & getting all the prizes, for Seamanship & Books alike.

There, too, the *Wanderer* lay, & later bore to safety a supposed murderer. As she towed out, a lady friend to this creature followed the ship on shore, as far as she could—" 'Farewell,' she cried, & waved her lily hand."

¹ F. J. Fargus: See Letter 37.

382

. . . Somewhere, not far from where you are, there is a place called Coberley; & somewhere not far from Coberley (I think, near the church) there is a kind of a pit out of which a spring gushes to feed the River Churn. Some people count this one of the sources of the Isis, that becomes the Thames near here (where the Thame River joins it.)

I have seen this pit, & all the other supposed sources of the Thames (there are 4 I believe) & it is the only one that is in the least worth the attention of the wise.

I was told a queer thing about it: & a queer thing is always a greater joy to the mind than the normal thing: that is where poets score so.

The queer thing is this. "That a scientist, or scientific body, analyses the water in the pit, & finds that the water is the primitive original Plynlimmon Spring water, the source of the Severn, & that this flows for a while as the Severn, & then goes under ground, right under the body of the lower Severn, & gushes up here in the pit near Coberley."

This pearl of strangeness is one of the few in my mind, & I fear, my beloved, that I must have told it to you long ere this, alas, "and what so tedious".

All the water there must come past this, on its way to the sea, & I see some of it as I write.

383

. . . I thank you for your gay letter about your party, which must have been one of the famous parties, & ought to have been put into verses like the others, of Hans Breitmann, & Grandfather McCarty.

The worst of parties is that they end, & then the morning comes so soon, & looks so cold, & one looks at the empty bottles & the cigarette ends, & begins the clearing up.

I hope to be away all day today out in the wilds on the Downs, where Prince Rupert fought a fight early in the Civil War.[1]

He was a wonderful son of a wonderful Queen, & how he could be grandson to K. James the First must be one of the problems for the Scientist.

Some spark of light was in him, & that was a rare product in our Civil War, & as it came early in the fray it was lost & mis-used & frustrated: so down came the crown; but early in the war, out on the Downs, he did his best against pig-headedness, & almost made his genius prevail.

I shall see the place, I hope, if it be not too foggy, & think of a valiant attempt, that almost . . . almost . . . Half an hour more, my gallant brave girl, & Charles might have had his crown on all the time, & died in a Christian bed, at Windsor.

[1] Rupert, Duke of Bavaria (1619–1682), was the third son of Elizabeth of Bohemia, daughter of James I of England, "The Winter Queen". He arrived in England in 1642 and Charles I at once put him in command of the Royalist Horse. The fight mentioned by JM took place at Aldbourne Chase, Berkshire, on 18th September 1643, when Rupert succeeded in heading off Lord Essex's troops, thus allowing the King's army to take up its position for the Battle of Newbury.

384

. . . Prince Rupert told the K what the enemy was doing, marching hot-foot to London. The staff did not believe (so the tale goes) being quite probably drunk (& very likely stupid as well, so I suppose) & when the King did at last believe Pr Rupert had not much time, but did ever valorously hurry, & flung himself on the enemy's flank & front out there in the wilds, where they have found a lot of bones & old burial. He delayed them, & the K did just occupy Newbury before them, but too late to seize the vital hill, & so lost first Newbury & the war & his crown.

385

. . . I am sorry: you asked me about Asser;[1] & I have not replied to your question.

He was (I believe) a Welsh monk whom King Alfred invited to court. He became a Bishop (of Sherborne) & wrote a book about the reign of K Alfred, which is (I suppose) our main authority for it.

In 1731 the book's MS authority was burned, & we do now have only an Elizabethan printed version which is supposed to be not quite free from additions.

I suppose that Asser pleased our respective childhoods by his tale of the burnt cakes, & of the candles that told the time by their rate of burning, & of the King collecting all the poems that were then reckoned any good.

There used to be a tale that there were 2 ancient historians, Bede & Asser, & that Bede was called Bede because he had Bees in his Bonnet, & Asser was called Asser, because he was more of an Ass than Bede, & that remembering this you would keep them apart & know that Bede came before Asser, B before A, don't forget . . .

Unfortunately I cannot find my life of Alfred, by Tom (Brown) Hughes, & therefore I had better not try to illumine you further, lest I lead you somehow into a kind of a nowhere: & I love you dearly & would hate to do that.

[1] Asser, or Asserius Menevensis (died *c* 910), a monk of St David's in Wales. His reputation for learning caused him to be invited to King Alfred's court. He agreed to spend six months of each year with the King. His *Annales Rerum Gestarum Alfredi Magni* was written about 893, and is a chronicle of English history from 849 to 887, and an account, written from personal knowledge, of Alfred's life.

386

. . . Last week, away in the fog, looking for a lone ruin, once beloved: & after 40 years of change I could not find the way to it. Trees had grown up & villas had been built, & the fog was so dense I had to give it up. I had put it in a poem, long since, & longed to see it again, but the place was so changed.

Well, I had seen it with my soul once, perhaps.

So away from fortune's malice presently the sun shone on a dream of wooded valley, just the sort to put on early English water colour by Girtin or young Turner . . . & there in the wild I never saw even England so beautiful: all in a dream & no-one on those roads, only a fox: & a stoat: & a pheasant, for miles; & no-one saw what must have been once a "beaver-meadow", I do believe, or perhaps not so, only a long lake with an England wetter than now; men being scarcer, to dig the channels . . . .

387

. . . When I was young, I thought the Monroe Doctrine, that denied the right of Europe, or the nations of Europe, to interfere (by might) with American affairs, to be a matter of pride, & of self-defence, very necessary to a collection of young republics.

Latterly I have been more & more anxious about the West Indian Islands, as possible causes of great evil in the world, having supposed, from the first, that a cynical war-like power, or power clever enough to plan & to possess great quantities of destructive missiles, might see what could be done there, quite secretly, in great tracts not known, not mapped, hardly inhabited, but so sited that from their secrecies hidden men might direct death upon half America, North & South, & all her central link, from Vera Cruz to Maracaibo.[1]

In my childhood (which lasted some 60 years, I think) I used to think of pirates of old, Benito, Geronimo, Laffitte, etc. living in some unknown creek in the greater islands, & sallying forth in a schooner, the rakish kind, with a long brass line, whenever the rum ran short or the harem needed new silks, but now one thinks of the possible pirates of today, lonely cynical trillionaires, owning an island, living in a mountain cave, perhaps on oysters & mangoes, & putting in a shot at Chicago at dawn, at the Canal al Panama at noon, & at Rio at tea-time: then turning on his television set to see the photographs of the results, while the local poets sing to their harps what a wonder he surely is.

Even if Cuba be made harmless in this present trouble, there are 5 or 6 major islands, & some thousands of lesser islands, where dangers could lurk: mortars to cast rockets of death; harbours to equip & re-equip submarines, with the certainty of wrecking the Canal, & keeping petrol from Europe.

Cuba is about 650 miles long (very jaggy miles) & 50 broad. She has a mongrel population of perhaps five millions, or, say the population of S. London, spread over her enormous length. The Americans have cleared away her yellow fever, malaria & smallpox, I believe; but lots of the islands must be trackless, roadless, craggy jungle or swamp, with the insect pests as before, & what else nobody knows.

She is subject to volcanic movements & cyclonic months: & is famous for multitudinous caves, great bats, cigars & disturbed politics.

When I was a boy in America, the cry was Cuba Libre, or Cuba Free. America has made her free: & this is now the 64th or 65th year of her freedom.

[1] This was written at the time of the Cuban Missiles Crisis.

388

. . . I have loved your letter with your vivid account of the Authority on the Silver Tray.[1] What a letter writer you are, my beloved, & what a joy to unworthy me to have all this vivid beauty of experience created for the UM aforesaid.

What fun to have knowledge. How one envies your Silver Authority & any other man with a special gift of the million ways of wisdom.

. . . Once, long ago, I saw 2 clowns in a music hall who came on & bowed: then went into the wings & brought on a tiny table 9 feet high, wh they put in mid stage. At this instant, stage hands brought in 2 chairs or rather very tall stools, 7 feet high, & put them one on each side of the table.

The 2 clowns bowed, & then marvellously hopped each on to a stool & bowed over the table.

They had a lot of little metal discs which they slowly spun on the table-top, & the metal discs as they spun made each a different magical note, for these sorcerers were playing a tune with them.

. . .You are in the sorcery line yourself, in a startling way, & it may be little to you, but O, as Wordsworth cries, "but O/ The difference to me."

[1] ANS had taken her George III silver tray—the one presented to Mr Freme—to be examined by an expert at Sotheby's.

389

Reyna mia

I thank you for your gracious letter.

I do not know much about Mr Fry. He is a poet with a good deal of theatrical skill, & as a poetical dramatist he lately won, & well deserved, the Queen's Medal for Poetry.

He came to tea here later, I was then rehearsing his play about Becket, & the King Henry II now running in London. It is a good subject: the two ways of law unable to be just to each other; & lots of men will tackle the theme. (I wanted to, myself, once, but did not like Becket enough & did not know Henry well enough; & could not write well enough anyway). I believe that he is having good success with his play.

March the 19th: only 20 weeks hence, 140 days, a Tuesday, like today.

Please, will you dearest Reyna mia, come to lunch & tea here, &

let me arrange the comings & goings; & stay the night if you can; my daughter being here to chaperone, & Katrina being still here to look after you?

?   ?   ?

What a beacon star already shining on the far side of the winter . . . .

390

. . . You asked me in your kind letter, what I found to like in Keats, in my re-reading.

Of course, I have read only the things that I most like in him: & these, of course, are among my favourite poems, & I admire them even more now, with a deeper sense of their quality, than I did at first, tho the special delight of new experience cannot be re-lived, & hardly remembered.

It is astounding that he should have attained such a maturity, with such a newness, at such a youth, with so slight experience; & that he, & the other boy, Shelley, should have been, both of them, the masters of a great century, which had produced Wordsworth. All the young of my time were his disciples & Shelley's. They were, both, the undoubted poets. Wordsworth & Coleridge were marvellous men, no doubt, but to the young, both were grown up. K & S spoke to the young, & had disciples, Arnold, Wm Morris, Yeats.

What is so splendid about both these young men is that both, in youth, tackled big subjects, leaped, as it were, at the flying star of Heaven, & got aboard, & went on into the eternal fields & skies, & were never mortal souls again.

I can hardly bear to read about Keats's last year of writing, 1819, when he did so many splendid things, & among them one that shows me that he, a doctor, knew that he was to die, like his brother, of consumption, & not marry Fanny Brawne.

Then his appalling voyage away in a foul little brigantine, the *Maria Crowther* . . . .

391

. . . As far as I know, the best Life of Keats is that by Sir Sidney Colvin, done about 30 years ago.[1]

He [Colvin] was one of the friends of R. L. Stevenson, & one of the most gifted of the late Victorians: his book was a work of love.

M. Arnold, in his *Essays in Criticism*, Second Series, has a brief, good study of Keats, with a page or two that might be omitted, quoting, with comment, a very private letter of JK that should never have been made public, being a love-letter written when JK was poisoned within by the seed that killed him.

Since Colvin's book appeared, no doubt others have added to the study of Keats.

R. Gittings made a profound study of Keats's great year of 1819; & made, also, a short study called *The Mask of Keats* (we have a Life Mask & a Death Mask of him).

In the study of 1819, Mr Gittings tells something about Mrs Isabella Jones, Colvin's "enigmatic Mrs Jones", who, apparently, told Keats of the 2 folk-lore beliefs of the Eves of St Agnes & St Mark, which JK wrote about.

Mrs J comes to life somewhat as a very clever beautiful woman, but then disappears, shortly after. reading of Keats's death from Severn's letter from Rome.

No doubt, she & Keats had written to each other, but the letters are gone. They had met on another 2 or 3 occasions.

She was much in Keats's London set, but never in London for long at a time. She wrote a formed but not clear hand-writing, & had a French seal of the setting Sun, with the motto:"Je reviendrai".

Perhaps she will come back into knowledge somehow as one who was much to the living Keats, in the last months of his real life.

If I were young, & had leisure, I would try to learn more of her; but learning about a woman last heard of, in London lodgings, 140 years ago is not now too easy.

Still, the search has its excitements, & its lucks, & many MSS are catalogued, many memoirs are indexed, many Registers of Wills, marriages & burials well-kept. More might still be found. Her miniature portrait might be found. It was in a Royal Academy show (with a miniature of Keats, too) & may still exist.

Forgive all this, but she helped Keats to two of his best things, remember.

¹ Colvin's *Life of Keats* appeared in 1917.

392

. . . Please will you, some day, if you can, tell me of this Club named after me (or after someone of my name)?

I have heard of a writer who was told that there was a Club named after him. The Club had an address, a note-paper, & published its proceedings in a little printed magazine written by the members (12 members, I think, all gifted writers).

The author received this magazine for some years & enjoyed it very much & felt that he knew all the 12 members as personal friends.

After a while the Club was disbanded, as Clubs will, & that was that.

But after some years the writer heard that the Club was fictitious.

A man in great sorrow had invented the whole thing to keep himself from going mad; he had written all the Club's proceedings & papers, after inventing the different members, & had kept himself sane all the time. He owned up to the writer, & it makes quite a pleasant story.

393

. . . I am reading about a French missionary who travelled in Tartary about 120 years ago, & got at last to Tibet. He lived in the cold, & his food was a little oatmeal boiled in tea with a little salt (when he had any tea, or salt, or oatmeal).

Once, in one of the wars, I asked in a restaurant what I could have for dinner, & the girl said I could have mushrooms & bacon, only there wasn't any bacon & the mushrooms only came once a week, on a Friday.

394

. . . I gather that from time to time you have great moments in out of the way shops & markets, of which all English towns hold some.

Please, will you tell me what books your eye looks out for with special gleam?

Long since, you quoted Beardsley's *Three Musicians* to me: & made me wonder if you sought out the 1890 books, *The Savoy* & the others: all now scarce; but once precious enough; & some still so.

When I was young, there was a German book-collector in business in London. He collected (especially) rare Bibles, & books of any extravagant indecency.

Once in London he came to an old odd shop of sorts, where he saw a Bible; & dissembled; & perhaps bought a Martin Tupper or so: but at last asked:

"How much you want for dis ole Bible?"

The shopman said: "I want thirty shilling for that old Bible."

The collector said, "I give you thirty shilling. You wrap him up."

The man wrapped up the Bible & was paid for it; & the collector went to the door, when the shopman said, "I tell you some tings. If you'd offered me 30 pence for that old Bible I would have took it."

The collector opened the door & said, "I tell you some tings. If you have asked me 30 pounds for this ole Bible I would have give it."

Then he went out & was away.

The collector left his things to the Brit. Mus., where I suppose most of his treasures are in the Secret Catalogue, of which I used to hear strange tales, but which I never explored. I used to hear dreadful tales of the difficulty of keeping it secret, & of the uselessness of trying, since such harvests of impropriety remained free to everybody.

Among the forbidden was the Arabic medical work that Burton translated, & Lady Burton burned.

395

. . . I worked on a farm in wild primitive country in New York State, when I was a boy, 67 years ago. The country is now all a vast NY suburbia, incredible, unrecognisable, where once I drove cows & fed multitudinous poultry, & blasted out rocks with dynamite, & planted fruit-trees that must long since have grown past bearing.

I shared a room with a man not quite sane, who used to sing a sort of song:

> Your delicate consti-tu-shion
> Won't stand the heavy marching,
> On the scorchy sandy deserts
> On the banks of the Nile.

(He called it Ni-yul. It seemed to have more go as Ni-yul.)

But he fell in love with a woman preacher & became homicidal about her, so authority rather kind of stepped in before her delicate constitution got stopped. I never heard what became of him.

He was pretty elderly then, for his Father & Brother had been in the Civil War: "Yes, sir, and they was shot: the both of them: they both got lead into 'em."

⚜

396

. . . I am still reading the French Missionaries in China & Tartary.[1] Huc, the writer, is somewhat long-winded, but a brave good soul, going in peril & discomfort into the unknown, into nomadic life, where the only settlements were Buddhist monasteries, & the only transport a pony, a mule & 2 camels.

On the way across the desert they came upon a huge crowd going to see a wonder.

They were going to see a Holy Bishop or Abbot open himself to the public with a sharp knife & then put the pieces back where they belonged, so that nobody could see them any more.

This (they said) they could only do in a state of great holiness, not only in themselves as Bish. or Abbot, but in all the spectators.

The two Missionaries determined to protest against such a show, & no doubt would have been murdered for doing so; but accidents forbade their presence; & the Bish. or Abbot did open up (with a cutlass, like brave Tom Bowling) in a state of tumultuous religious excitement, like a real revival in a Southern state.

Many devout Buddhists disliked this kind of show, would not have gone to see it. The sort of Cantuar or Ebor Buddhist Abbot would never have stooped to it. It was done by out of the way Abbots & Bishes, corresponding, perhaps, to the Dean of Zanzibar, or His Grace of Cape Coast cum Whyda.

There was another magical trick that these semi-savage Abbots did. They would display a Bucket or Basin, empty, in an open space, & then call aloud a spirit (not perhaps a very holy one) to fill it at once with water, & not to tarry, but fill it *muy pronto*.

Huc was told that if all present believed that this would be done, & if the Bish. were holy enough to compel the spirit, the Basin or Bucket would visibly fill with water, but he does not say if the water fell from above or bubbled up from within.

I have seen enough of the power of the imagination not to doubt this at all. It is queer reading.

Perhaps you will be interested in the fragment. Like Thomas à Becket both these brave missionaries developed "a blessed lousiness", but tell of a local cure for this, which wd have been a blessing in the First War.

¹ Evariste Régis Huc and J. Gabet, *Travels in Tartary, Thibet and China*, (English edition translated by W. Hazlitt, London 1928). See Letter 393.

397

. . . I am still plugging along at the Xtian Mishes in Tibet, & I think them very brave but mistaken. They have now reached Lhasa, but I expect soon to read that they were ordered to leave.

Some of their journey thither reads like the French memoirs of 1812: the retreat from Moscow . . . .

398

. . . For ten years now, the first letter I have written on Christmas morning has been to you, in thanks to you, & with tender thoughts of you.

This morning, the first thing I did, on coming downstairs in the dark, was to open the lovely packet from you (honestly kept till Christmas) & now (having fed the birds) I write to thank you for the beautiful copy of Swinburne's book of Roundels which Swinburne dedicated to Christina Rossetti, who is easily the best of our women poets. It used to be said that he was in love with her: & very likely he was; for he was ever swift to love people truly lovely & inspired.

A Roundel is a French form of verse, one of several that the poets of the 18 eighties were fond of trying (the triolet, villanelle, ballade, chant royal, sestina etc, etc.) As a boy, I longed to see Swinburne's book of Roundels: & tried to write in these forms, & now here it is, the book for me: published while my Mother was still living, & bound thus while I was on the *Conway*; & now mine . . . .

The feeling for French forms must have come from Rossetti originally. All the good things in the verse of my time sprang from Rossetti.

I spoke with Rossetti's Brother once, Christina's Brother, & saw the couch on which Shelley slept his last night's sleep before his death.

399

. . . This Thursday, the 27th, brought me your charming nice card of the *Cock*, with its darling note inside.

The Cock is a marvellous thing to me: & I always put a Cock somewhere into a book, or anyhow his crow, or his image (a weather-cock).[1]

You ask, is he Chaucer's Cock?

He has a bantamy slimness which suggests an early type, but I must look up Mediaeval poultry ... I do not know how far the bantam look had been bred away, in the centuries of Roman-Norman influence, & a Society almost entirely given to farming. Bantams are pretty birds, & lay well, but the eggs are small, & the birds will attack any birds near them, even ducks & geese. Few people keep them now. I *have* kept them, long since.

The reference to the Cock as a Christmas Bird is due to a (perhaps) 12th or 13th century Monk Latin poem about Christ's Birth in the stable.

The Cock in this Poem crows:

Christus Natus Est;

The Cow moos:

Ubi? (where?)

The sheep bleat:

In Baa-ethlehem.

There is more of it, which I cannot now remember, perhaps the Ass & the Shepherds. A few more voices anyhow.

[1] JM, as a child, was fascinated by the golden cock at the top of Ledbury's tall spire.

400

... About Beardsley. I had never heard of Wilde, till his trial, when I was in America.[1] I was then a boy of 17.

His trial & fall roused a fury against any unusual talent in an artist or writer, which lasted for many years: the fury cannot be exaggerated: it made life difficult or impossible for a good many, who only looked a little unusual, having talent.

The most promising talent in the youth of that time was Beardsley's. He was a lad such as could not appear oftener than once in a thousand years. On the appearance of such genius, at the time of Wilde's insolences, trial & fall, he was assailed by the maddened mob who hated intellect as an accomplice, a part of the poison, a limb of the accursed thing, offspring certainly of Gomorrah, with letters of credit to Sodom.

I heard of this in America; & returned to England just when the fury had driven Beardsley abroad, neglected, thwarted, misunderstood & ill, to die early in the year 1898. I never had the chance to see him.

But on my return to England in that year of 1897, I had the chance to see some of the books of just before the Wilde fall: & to recognise the extraordinary boy for the one intellect in the movement; & crude as I was, all raw & ill, I thought him the wonder of the time. I did not think it a great time; but it was a protest against a colossal blindness, & as such called on all generosity to lend a hand.

Just before the fall of Wilde, a publisher had started a Quarterly, called *The Yellow Book*,[2] with Beardsley as Art Editor, & a gifted story writer, Miss Ella D'Arcy, as Assistant Editor: all three unusual talents.

The Quarterly appeared as a Book, in yellow quarto boards. It was very well printed, & shaped, I think largely through the publisher's manager, Mr Frederick Chapman; a man famous in his profession, who had made the publisher a success.

Yielding to the rage of the mob, & orthodox idols of the mob, after Wilde's fall, the publishers sacked Beardsley, & tried to carry on without him. The result is rather like a ham sandwich without the ham: one misses a good deal: *The Yellow Book* grew paler & died.

Arthur Symons at once started an opposition, with Beardsley its leading figure: *The Savoy*.[2] It was always much better than the *YB* had been; but it, too, could not weather the fury & Beardsley was ill & dying; so *The Savoy* also died.

Now all this long preamble is to ask you, if you would care to have my *Yellow Book*?

I have all the 13 vols, some of them with the very fine designs of Beardsley on the covers; & I think all the original illustrations by various hands. These are not in a good state always; time & the methods of printing have marred them. And time has shewn up many of the writings rather cruelly. One feels that the only writers of much use in it, who bear the brunt of it, are Harland, Miss D'Arcy, Hubert Crackanthorpe & Mrs Leveson: the 2 first are always good: the third, unusual, & the 4th characteristic of the period. Dear Watson, you know my methods, & how much I love to share all my little old pots of honey with you. Would you care for the Yellow thirteen, that once roused such rage, & now seems so milky & so watery?

. . . Roundel. Reading your lovely book, I felt that I must write a *roundel*, so I have begun one.

Long since, we all wrote all these odd things for fun: & had some help from them: ease of movement, etc.

---

[1] See also Letters 201, 202, 275.

[2] See also Letters 45, 163, 277.

1963

401

... I have been reading about the navigation of the Mississippi, that I feel sure is known to you from Mark Twain's great book [*The Adventures of Huckleberry Finn*].

The writer lately read was talking with a negro roustabout, in one of the modern passenger steamers, on the popular negro topic of ghosts. A roustabout is a sort of river hand, who does some stoking & cargo shifting, handles baggage & takes soundings, washes decks, etc.

This negro was saying that many negro ghosts were always crying out for gin or for chews of tobacco: & that if you put out gin for them it always disappeared, & that if you put out chews for them, you could always see that the tobacco had been mumbled.

But . . . .

"You won't never see no tooth marks. Just gum marks. 'Cause there ain't no kind of ghost that's ever got teeth, not even the ghost of a dog. I was bit by a ghost once, on the arm. And it was like you was being chewed by a banana."

... You asked me last week how the roundel went.

I did one, but it has for the time got into other papers somewhere & I cannot find it. It was no special shakes, but it was a roundel. If I can find it you shall have it.

I suppose the ancient poets sang their roundels, & found the re-introductions of the refrains useful to mark different stresses upon the vital words of the poem. About 1875–1900 a lot of these old forms were revived. Rossetti perhaps began it, but Andrew Lang was the chief practiser of these things: he & the clever Nichols, father of Robert Nichols. Nichols's had much wit in them (Bowyer Nichols).

. . . A good long while ago, you asked me about John Ruskin. Now, today, I bought some rice to be a change for my hens, & the rice made me think that perhaps I never told you about what Ruskin called *Greedy Pudding* (& rightly called).

Now, when I wrote to you about Ruskin, I had some relics of a fair memory, & may have told you what part Rice played in it. Rice was in the greedy pudding, perhaps his Mother made him put some into it, to prevent his being too piggy: but what part the Rice played in it I cannot now recollect.

As a seaman, you may have eaten the rare sea-dainty known as Strike me Blind, which is rice boiled very dry with a few currants (tho raisins wd be better & strike one blinder).

So let us agree that a little rice boiled very dry was in the Greedy Pudding.

The rest had no reference to Mrs Ruskin, Senior. It was as follows.

Get some nice big bananas, 3 or 4 for each guest, peel them, scrape them till they are slippery, then split them longitudinally & stew them till you can wait no longer.

Then smear each split half banana with the very best strawberry jam (some prefer raspberry, but JR was for strawberry).

Lay them, thus anointed, on a white mattress of rice boiled very dry, & anoint further with Cornish or Devonshire cream.

It is no wonder that people liked going to lunch with Ruskin, & wrote charming letters to say how deep an experience it had been to them.

Perhaps the pudding would be better without the rice. Would short-bread be better?

. . . I have found (& send) the Roundel.

A Roundel for Reyna. January the 15th 1963

"Give way, my lads" the coxwains used to say,
Bossing the crew, and thinking themselves clever . . . .
"So toss her up, and splash me not with spray . . .
Give way."
    Then, out across the Sloyne or down the bay
    The cutter made the water-walls dissever.
    The sea-gulls mewed above us in their play.
All earthly ill surrenders to endeavour . . . .
Every tomorrow is another day . . .
All irons that seem barriers forever
Give way.

John Masefield

402

. . . I thank you for your dear kind letter, & grieve to think that the packet never reached you in time for the anniversary.

How it can have been delayed, alas who can wonder, & who knows, in weather like this?[1]

But the sleuths are out, & I do hope that they may soon cause it to reach you. Alas, they cannot cause a milder air-stream to mitigate life for a while.

But I can answer some of your doubts about the use of winter. It rests much vegetable nature: when severe, it breaks up the coarser clays, so that the ploughman and the corn have easier tasks: it stimulates the growth of fur upon the mink, so that the very rich may keep very warm till the burglar interferes: then, too, it assists the plumber to do very well in an otherwise unpleasing season . . . . You see, it has one side that may be considered.

[1] The winter of 1962–3 was extremely severe.

❧

403

. . . Here, one was sore beset last week, but since then it has melted a very little, & in 2 places I have even seen grass: otherwise it is all snow, re-freezing, & now also being snowed-on.

Near the house we can keep the tits fed, & I am responsible, always from the house, for some faithful blackbirds, robins & 2 cock pheasants, who know my methods & movements to the minute.

I have seen no rabbit since the snow fell 35 days ago, nor even any certain rabbit tracks, but some poor starving creatures are eating the bark from many small low lying boughs of shrubs. Many tree barks are probably poisonous to animals. They do not gnaw the trees.

The low boughs are gnawed white, & I am not sure that the pheasants do not do this, for we have a lively lot of pheasants here: they nest here every year & maintain themselves. I always find that a cock pheasant can beat a cat in any fair quarrel, so that the cat will not try again, when once he has been thrashed. The bird has spurs, & great wing power. He buffets the cat with wings, & leaps & spurs him.

404

. . . Today, instead of the cock pheasant there was only a hen, but I heard the cocks in the Wild wood. I daresay they were fighting for her, & she wisely ate their allowance while they were at it.

The winter is trying, for it is unusual, but it is but the ordinary continental winter. So when I growl, I tell myself to remember an appalling blizzard in Chicago, & the time I thought my ears were gone, & the time the thermometer fell 40° in (it seemed) 5 minutes, & the time the pipes froze on the 9th of March . . . .

So far it has not been nearly so cold here as in the 1947 winter, when the place was thronged with Chaucer's "frosty field fares" & some hundreds of Arctic skuas, & many gannets & lesser gulls, all pressed for food, but yet surviving somehow, as somehow seamen did in the old time, though there seemed no food at all in the salt & dust & decay served out to them.

. . .Please, what sort of tea do you drink? I never drink tea now, at any time, but in times past I have liked it.

Long since, I knew a tea merchant in a sea-port, & sometimes saw him tasting his particular blends, & even tried to come to his conclusions about them, but never could.

Once, too, I was asked to help taste a batch of Burgundies by some wine-merchants, but nobody agreed with my conclusions there, so I suppose my palate is faulty or my taste unsubtle.

There was an old country fellow at home long since. The Doctor asked him how much beer he could drink at a sitting. The old fellow thought a while, then said: "Sometimes I has a gallon. Sometimes I has two gallon. Then, sometimes, I has a lot."

405

. . . Thank you for telling me about the tea. I used to drink China tea, when I drank tea at all. A friend of mine said the other day that in a tea shop in London he asked for a pot of China Tea, & the girl called at the [speaking] tube, "Pot of weak Tea, please" (all teas being Indian, strong or weak). My brother, who is a tea planter, says that China Tea is usually Indian, but grown high up in mountain yards. But undoubtedly China Tea is a more delicate thing than the sort of soup "Red as blood" that Dr J used to drink (& then wonder that he could not sleep).

Please, if I were to send you what is called Lapsang Souchong Smoky Flavour China Tea, would you ever (when your Tea Pot comes home) brew some, & elegantlie sip it from your Silver Tray?

. . . I quake when I read of your journey in the snows, & the going adrift onto a wall top.

It made me think of the young (Admiral later) Lord Charles Beresford, who was out for a ride in Ireland, when his horse hopped from the road onto the balustrade of a river-bridge, & trotted across the balustrade as though he liked it. He gave the wilful beast his way.

Your ride on the wall-top beats that for danger, I would say.

I once met a merchant sailor who had met Lord Charles: & said, "I would die for Lord Charles, any day."

I asked him Why? He said "Years ago, at Alexandria, when he bombarded the forts there,[1] I was in a steamer in the harbour, & the Captain had a down on me for something (this I think likely to be true) & there I was, made to march up & down, on deck, in the sun, with a capstan bar on each shoulder. Lord Charles came on board to shift our ship out of her berth, and saw me marching up & down, & asked the Old Man what I'd been doing. The Old Man told him. 'Well,' Lord Charles said. 'It's very hot, doing that in the sun. Let him off, won't you? He'll never do it again.' So the Old Man let me off . . . ."

Lord C wrote a very good book of memoirs, but this little incident seems to suggest the man that the book reveals, a man who had the right instincts by nature: right & generous instincts, that made all sorts of rough & tough folk glad & grateful for ever.

[1] 11th July 1881, during the "Egyptian Crisis".

406

. . . Thank you for your letter, & for the news that I have written you 800 letters; of which I can only remember 2 or 3. Memory, in actors & writers, tends to fail in age, but somehow the letters have kept the bright friend who kindly began them.

You began them, too, by writing about *MH* [*Melloney Holtspur*], which no other has ever written to me about; & it happens to be something that meant much to me, & only you, dear darling, ever saw anything in it.

I meant, & hoped, to have this letter written some days ago, but could not manage this. Sometimes, I have a very great deal of writing to do: things to finish, or revise, or proofs to correct, as well as a great many letters that somehow must be answered, & by myself, for I have no secretary: & in this mess there were interruptions owing to weather, & chaps getting stuck in the snow here, & people wanting verses for this or that, & the telephone calling: so, in the end, I had to telegraph to you: perhaps the 1st telegram & this 801st letter.

I am asking for some smoky flavour China Tea to be sent to you from Portsmouth. I daresay it will have a sort of Naval dockyard twang: & I hope that your lovely tea pot¹ may soon be pouring an infusion from it for the favour of your elegant sip.

You call K William [IV] "Billy" or "Bill", in the Naval way. The Royal Billy:

> So "Long", we sing, "Live Billy the King
> For abating the tax upon Beer".

When he was but a Prince, he filled a lively page in Miss Burney's lively Diary,² for he came suddenly into the Maids of Honour at Dinner, & insisted on them all drinking the King's health in champagne, plainly wanting to make them all drunk, for the fun of the sight.

Providence, I need hardly say, protected the ladies from any such profanation.

As an American music-hall song put it, when I was in New York as a boy, "God will protect a working girl."

A parodist launched another song on the public there, & this, too, was sung everywhere.

"God will protect a millionaire."

I am sending you with this some marine scraps, not quite sure that these have not gone to you at some other time (one or two of them). The *Swiftsure* page shows the late Naval sailing-rig, marvellous in its smartness, & I like the tanker in the Bay of Biscay, by Mason.

I used to live at Greenwich, & was often at that palace, then, in part, a Museum of Naval things, & partly a naval college. The Marit. Mus. is now behind it, somewhat to the R, & somewhere there you will have seen the *Cutty Sark*, of which I send a wintry view.

I hope that it may be possible for you to come for a tea or a lunch in your brief stay in Oxford on the 19th. Hardly any snow has gone yet, since Christmas Day, a ghastly white glower under a whitish fog glower. But as the Chinese poet wrote:

> The enemy is marching in, with gongs & bongs.
> In less than 1,000 years they will be completely gone.
> Meanwhile, here comes the tea.

Jan

¹ An Irish silver tea-pot made in William IV's reign.

² Frances (Fanny) Burney, daughter of Dr Burney, historian of music and friend of Samuel Johnson. Her *Early Diary* (1768-78) was published in 1899. This story is from her *Diary and Letters* (1842-46), after she had retired from a post at Court.

407

. . . Billy the K was sometimes called Silly Billy, for he was often so nautical in his speech that landsmen could not understand what he said, but I think he was a competent sailor, & a CS cannot be silly.

. . . Feb 25th. It is still freezing every night, between 10° & 20°F, pretty cold, very dry.

> Spring, the sweet season.
> Can't come when its freezin,
> Poets lose their reason,
> The snow lies white.
> Frozen lies the daisy,
> Cows have naught to grazey
> But poets, being crazy
> They write: they write.

408

. . . I have been reading a life of Tchaka, the Zulu King, of late, & do not feel that he was quite quite; though he was said to have been a sort of poet, who made up poems to sing, & also practised divination, to find out if people should be killed.

One of his best poems, which he could listen to all day, ran like this (the whole Poem):

> What nations I have scattered.
> Who next shall be battered?

His divination was more subtle. He used to ask women: "Do you like cats?" and whether they said yes or no he killed them by some spiritual prompting, which died with him & cannot now be surmised. He was murdered later, but had a lively time while he lasted.

You have played divine music in lands where he once ruled, & perhaps all this is but an old tale to you, so forgive, as ever.

409

. . . I never met Mr Doughty,[1] but I read his *Arabia Deserta* long ago. We young men admired him much, but I was not one who got so far as to be admitted.

About 55 years ago, he let fly as a poet, with a long epic called *The Dawn in Britain*. I seem to remember that it was about the invasion of Britain by Claudius Caesar, whom he called "Totty-polled Claudius", meaning Claudius a little odd in the belfry.

It was an odd poem, followed by some much odder, & one, more or less religious, or solemn, which was not so odd, but what this one was called I cannot recollect.[2]

From the poems, I, personally, got the totty-polled notion that while in Arabia Deserta, Doughty got bitten by a camel, & got a sort of camelly virus into his poll, & was spiritually a kind of camel ever after, & always seemed to regard language as a kind of end of desert thorns that he would masticatedly chaw & again chaw, moaning in his wame all the while when the thorns were aspy; & gave him a frolic so to speak; but snarling & snapping if anybody poked a bit of sugar cane at him.

This method suits the prose, but it is not the method of any poetic master known to me; so I would say, stick to the Arabian book, which is unlike anything else, & avoid the poems, which are unlike poetry.

If I had written to him about the *Arabia* book, when he was in London in those years, it is possible that I might even have been allowed to see him: but I was shy, & thought it would be cheek to write, so did not.

Then, too, I had, a little, this feeling that the man had this camel-twang, to which I could not respond . . . so anyhow, I did not write.

Somehow, that expanse, from Libya east to the Persian Gulf, seems to me a fatal stretch, all inhuman:

"Where the heart shrivels & the spirit rots".

Only a few Greeks seem to have been able to make beauty there.

[1] Charles Montague Doughty (1843-1926), famous for his *Travels in Arabia Deserta* (1888). He also wrote poems, his 6-volume *The Dawn in Britain* appearing in 1906.

[2] "Adam Cast Forth" (1908).

410

. . . Liverpool used to be very full of tea merchants long ago, & sometimes, in the office of one of them, I saw him taste for his firm, he being a non-smoker & of a delicate palate (so he said). He (like you) tasted the new infusion with neither milk nor sugar, some 5 or 6 little cups, one after the other. He said I was without any sense of what a tea should be; & though I was young then I have not changed in this; & it is now a lot of years since I tasted tea at all.

Those Jesuits that I told you of [the missionaries in Tibet] used to have tea in China apparently made with boiling butter, & must have been quite shiny at the end of the meal.

You see what it is to travel.

411

. . .You ask me if horse-traffic on the roads made places noisy.

No, not very. In the city, one was conscious of a slow steady trotting noise, which seldom varied much. There were no motor-horns, blaring & screaming, & no lorries going fast & roaring. The present madness seems to become madder daily.

The cities, however, tho' less mad than now, & far less dangerous, all smelt like stables, instead of like garages, & London, all London, was very foul thus, in any summer weather.

I think that many cab & carriage wheels had some rubber covers, but the roads were certainly quieter than now.

I saw Oxford as a quiet little grey city beginning to have a noisome red rash all round it. I have not been to it for over 10 years.

Bristol in QE's [Elizabeth I's] time was a walled sea-port, & I suppose was pretty noisome in the summer, inside the walls, but still, the sea was near, & the ships & water moved about, & the winds did blow around.

Greenwich Palace was probably much less wonderful than the Wren buildings of the Hospital, which are very fine, & make the one superb water-front that London offers.

They have put the *Cutty Sark* in the picture I suppose, & if so I wish they had put some later & more impressive thing; a 4-master, like the *Wanderer* or the *California*, or the *Kate Thomas*, or like 50 others that now are all mingle mangle in my old memory, or something down in mud or coral somewhere.

. . . Winchester under King Alfred was probably only a hutty & sheddy kind of city, much in terror of a fire, & nearly all of wood & thatch.

I do not think that it was much to look at, & the place is down in a den (I always feel) squeezed down into the waters, & horribly rheumaticky & aguey, tho K Alf perhaps did not mind, while he read AS [Anglo-Saxon] poems & wondered what the devil the poet meant when he began with lines like:

Sea-flames' Daughter, Ragbert's Ransom,
What new wisdom from the wine bath?

& then, too, he could always be watching a candle burning against an hour-glass, & make up a sweepstake on which would win.

❧

412

. . . I wonder if you know at all these parts of England: the bend of the Thames to the south, from Dorchester-on-T to Reading; the Chilterns, to the east of this stretch of River; & the Berkshire Downs, coming near to the west of it?

From Dorchester-on-T to its source, the Thames runs very roughly west to east; the course, W, being at any of the shown sources near Cheltenham, being the Chelt, Corin & Kemble brooks (one of the best of them being said to come *under* the Severn from Wales, to bubble up near Wind Balloon Inn).

Away to the south of this stretch of Thames, there is the happy stretch of Berkshire, where some hundreds of race-horses go out in strings to gallop on the Downs, & raise hopes in people's hearts, but alas, not every horse can win. Destiny has her say in the matter.

But on the brink of Berkshire is Wiltshire, & on the very brink of this is the Inkpen Beacon, a hill, not as dear to writers as you would suppose from the name, but well worth a visit.

Do you know the Inkpen Beacon?

I used to go there a lot, hoping to see or hear curlews. It is a big strip of hill (chalk inside) & usually all gorsey, & in June & summer with many harebells, & larks & linnets, very lovely.

I was there the other day in the cold, but it was as bleak as the wild: no gorse in blossom anywhere, & a little snow falling in flakes, here & there, & no view, except a desolate hundred yards at a time.

To get to it, I had to cross the Battle Field.

Not Newbury, nor Donnington Castle, nor one of those of the Civil War, but *the* Battle Field, where the Gas-man fought Bill Neate before over 20,000 people for some 17 or 18 rounds of the old sort, with bare fists.

I expect you will know Wm Hazlitt's account of the Battle.[1] It is the best prose of the 19th century, pretty well . . . I can think of none better, except 2 other bits of Hazlitt.

But what WH does not mention is the extraordinary beauty of the Battle Field & the approach by which he went to it, by Denford Mill on the Kennet, and then up and on into a wild pasture with old hawthorns on it.

Inkpen has no associations with pen and ink. *Pen* is a British word meaning Hill, and *Ing* may be a corruption of some Anglo-Saxon name, such as Ina, or it may be an old word for Hill, so that the full name means Hill-Hill-unusually-Big-Hill (or may) just as Bredon Hill means Hill-Hill-Hill, and a little hill near Ledbury, Kilbre Tump or Kilbre Tump Hill, means Hill-Hill-Little-Hill-Hill, until somebody alters the name to Kilbre Tump Hillock.

[1] See Letters 136, 138, 139.

413

. . . I send a cheerful word about the Mississippi.

Sea folk, like you & I, take very kindly to water; even a canal isn't too bad, & even a puddle can be beautiful.

I have had various glimpses of the Mississippi, and there is no doubt that of all the moving wetness now going it holds the star place. What it will be when the US Engineers have finished with it, perhaps we will leave to the uncertainties of nuclear futures.

I saw it once in flood. They told me that the river was 64 miles broad just there, and was best left alone. I was going to leave it alone, anyway, for at an early age I was told (and believed) that *any bad water whatever is a great deal worse than it looks*.

. . . Memphis is an Egyptian city on the Nile. I have been there, too, but Memphis, Tennesse, beats it hollow. Memphis, that was once the capital of Egypt, is gone, but Memphis, Tennessee is a sort of Queen, throned high above the River. A stunning great city: once feared for yellow fever, but that has been long since conquered; and it is from somewhere near Memphis that white man first saw the Mississippi (de Soto, the Spaniard).

. . . Once, long since, you very graciously approved a little book by a young Mr Haggart, who came to a rather sudden end.[1]

Long ago, a boxer sent me a little book about his life.[2] I have read it many times, with admiration for his great qualities, and marvel at what life meant to him, in a sporting world in which very queer people did queer things.

I think that he is now dead. As I value the book & think well of the man, I wonder if you would give it a home? Do you think you could?

[1] See Letters 145, 191.

[2] *Reminiscences and Life of Jimmie Lowes* (born 1864).

414

. . . Please, you must not think that I knew the writer [Lowes]. I never saw him, but wrote to him 2 or 3 times, for he was fond of poetry (fondest of Shelley, I think, and that was much to me, and think what it would have been to Shelley).

I never had another such acquaintance, and am sorry I never met him.

I saw (several times) some of the sporting men whom he mentions; 3 or 4 of them were once very famous in their profession, where glory has to be struggled for and cannot last for long, even if won.

I saw (several times) the man whom he calls Jolly Jumbo, who weighed (so fame said) 22 stone. I remember a man telling me "they had to take the side of the house down to get his coffin out for the funeral", but I think that this is, or was, just the natural poetry of the English. He was to be seen driving a sporting turnout, one of the sights of London.

. . . One of Keats's friends wrote a poem about a boxer who was "Good with both hands, & only ten stone four". This one was good with both hands and only nine stone six, & has had no poem, perhaps because the rhymes to six are less helpful.

> He settled many a pitman in two ticks,
> Tho they were fifteen stone, he nine stone six.

415

. . . Presently you must let me add a book about a much more famous puncher of people (on jaw or nose usually) whom I never met, but did see punching (the Gymnastic Bag) late in his career several times.

This was the unique John L. Sullivan,[1] whose fame is still green, I am told, in sporting circles.

. . . I am glad that you liked the Randolph Caldecott[2] design of the Hunt escorting the Bridal party.

The Hunt seems rather soberer than it was like to have been perhaps, for liquor flowed at feasts, then, as I sometimes saw, & very clearly remember.

Men were men, then, and the ladies were good at snowballs, and had to be.

One of the men, then, one of the most remarkable in some ways, the best-known, most shocking, and most popular man alive, was the boxer John L Sullivan, better known as "John L" (just as the Graces were known as "EM" & "WG") of whom I asked you.

It is hard to say what makes a man immensely popular. Usually there is some touch of vulgarity (which will link him to most), sometimes he brings hope in despair, sometimes he voices a popular prejudice and can lead a cause, but always there is courage, something of dash, leadership and power to fascinate, something fiery & starry.

I had better send you a book about John L for I may otherwise fail to do justice to him, & he was rather a wonder, for even in training he weighed 15 stone, & was the strongest fighter ever in a ring, and, for a very heavy man, extremely swift, and at all times of unconquerable spirit.

So sometime next week, dearest darling R, you shall have his Life, with the portraits, and read how he knocked some heavyweight off a stage into the orchestra and broke three violins.

[1] A renowned boxer. American National Champion 1880-91.

[2] Randolph Caldecott, *Graphic Pictures*, 1883, and *More Graphic Pictures* 1887.

416

... I read of your visit to Scandinavia ... I suppose Denmark, Norway, Sweden and perhaps, Finland?[1]

If you go to Norway, you will see the Viking ships (near Oslo); &, if to Sweden, this salved 17th century ship, & the lovely Marine Museum at Gothenburg, & the 18th century theatre near Stockholm; & if to Finland, perhaps their sailing training ship, once a British ship.

And in Denmark, Copenhagen, you may see the grave of Hans Andersen. Dear, put some English flowers on it, if you go there, from you & me, take a tiny few specially. He wrote all those marvellous tales; & it cannot be a far cry from where you will be.

When you can, please, will you, most kindly, let me have your itinerary, with the dates, & the addresses.

When you went to the Levant, I wrote to all the places, but (I suppose) often too late. I did not then know that posts are *much* worse now than formerly, & that letters take longer to get anywhere.

I wd say that Scandinav is pleasanter, & cleaner & not so dangerous as the South & the Levant.

I took to the Finns & the Norwegians very kindly. There was a *marvellous* bookshop in Finland, in the capital there: Helsinki, which sounds so like swearing, but isn't so at all.

¹Between 13th May and 18th June the Hallé Orchestra's Scandinavian tour was to take them from Norway (Bergen and Odda) to Sweden (Gothenburg and Stockholm), Finland (Helsinki), back to Stockholm and thence to Denmark (Copenhagen and Esbjerg, from where they sailed back to England).

417

. . . I thank you for your kind promise about the tour to Scandinavia. I went by way of Germany, to Sweden, thence by sea to Finland, by sea to Sweden, by train to Norway, then (I think) by sea to Elsinore & Denmark; & ended up somewhere in France, after Holland & Belgium.

I expect you will be flying, will you not?

It was interesting to me to be in the Baltic, where my old ship, the *Conway*, had been (as HMS *Nile*) during the Crimea, and must have thrilled thro her heart of oak at her Admiral's still famous signal: "Sharpen your cutlasses, my lads, and the day is ours".

I suppose Sir J [Barbirolli] will say something of the kind as you embark.

Napoleon was very proud of the kind of thing that he gave out on these occasions.

"From the tops of the Pyramids, 50 centuries look down on you", etc etc, but Wellington kept pretty quiet till all was over; and then said a scathing word to a favoured few.

418

. . . With this, I send the account of the famous one [John L Sullivan] now slowly passing from memory, but once a light, a beacon, or a warning glare in most men's hearts.

When I was very little I heard, somehow, a popular song, which I think I sang at the age of about 4, to the horror of elders. It was called "Climbing up the Golden Stair"; I remember one bit of it only:

> You must tell the Jersey Lily
> There's a sight to knock her silly,
> Climbing up the Golden Stair.
> And tell John L. Sulli-Van
> He must be a better man
> If he wants to climb the Golden Stair.

Well, it was not prudent to give advice to JLS; and the Jersey Lily was an exquisitely lovely woman, such as I was little likely to see.

But I did see her, long afterwards. She was acting in London, & I daresay John L was in London too, acting or sort of (punching the gymnastic bag). There they both were, the rumbustious cross of a bull with a tiger, & she the loveliest woman of her decade.

People have told me of her: "She had an exquisite white face, with a mass of chestnut hair, there were always 1 or 2 hundred people waiting outside her London house, just to see her come out; and when she was in the Park women and men would climb on chairs & benches to get a better view of her; she was so incredibly lovely."

Beauty was rarer then, remember: there were only the three: Madame de Navarro, Mrs Stillman, and the Jersey Lily (with Mrs William Morris a close fourth in many minds).

I would have put Mrs WM the third, for Rossetti was always painting her: and I sometimes go to her grave now, & put flowers on it for Morris's & her sakes, & for her daughter's sake & Rossetti's sake, and for unforgettable lines in some of WM's poems: "The straw from the oxyard is blowing about".

As Wm Allingham wrote,

> What a little thing
> To remember for years.
> To remember with tears.

419

. . . I am afraid that I have no memory of what my friend told me (if she told me anything) of the Jersey Lily's eyes. I expect that they were dark, perhaps darker than her hair, and given greater value by the ivory of her face.

At that time, and for some dozen years more, make-up was almost unused. Probably the Court forbade it, during the reign of Queen Victoria, but I would say that the feeling of the time was against it, and perhaps evening lighting too dim, as a rule, to show faces clearly. Electric light was not yet everywhere: men had but gas or candles, the one too hot, if plentiful, and the other both smelly & drippy.

... You wrote to me some time ago to tell me of your going to the *Cutty Sark* at Greenwich, and O I grieved that I had not been there to go with you & tell you which was the chronometer and which was the starboard watch.

I thought: I will go where Reyna has gone.

I saw the ship, then a poor old broken down ghastly ghost of a battered barquentine (but plainly British built & a clipper) when she first came to Falmouth.

I went aboard her then, & several times later on, when Capt Downman had re-rigged her as a ship. Once, I went over her masthead, to see if I still could, and found that the knack remained.

And yesterday I went aboard her again, in her dry dock at Greenwich, and wished that you were there, but alas, no you.

But O what a change in the ship.

She was all dolled-up & re-done regardless, with all her brass like the rising sun, and her 'tween decks all laid & all clear sweep; and all her houses furnished and some of the bunks made up, and records of her & prints & books & photographs, and then on deck . . . .

I had not expected to see her with her rigging set up with dead-eyes, but it was, and so well done; and there was a skysail yard again, when I hadn't seen one for 25 years; and the old way of hoisting the upper topsail yard a couple of feet, instead of letting it come to the cap, right on the lower-topsail yard; as was the later way, when all was for thrift, & crews were kept down.

They had done her very well indeed, I thought.

I used to live at Greenwich, and could walk under the Thames to the other side by tunnel, when any very thrilling ship showed in the docks there. There was no *Cutty Sark* at G in those days, but there was a Naval ship-rigged training centre: not a ship, but an imitation water-line model, with real masts & yards, where boys trained for Naval service of some kind before going to sea in HM ships.

420

... This, I do hope may be a fine sunny day for you so that you may enjoy the beauty of the little port[1] to the full.

It must have been a wondrous sight in the old days when so many nations shipped their masts here, & I suppose used the old method that I so often saw as a boy.

They would cut a hole in the ship's bows, & by skilled arrays of pulleys get the end of a 70 foot pine into the hole, and then edge her along into the ship, as a python might perhaps swallow a crocodile, & then gradually bed the spar down in the hold, till there was room for another one, & so on till the ship was full. Then they would rebuild the ship's bows all good & tight, & so away for home:

"Pipe all hands to man the capstan,
See your cables run down clear."

as I hope you are doing at this moment.

[1] Of Gothenburg in Sweden, where JM sent this letter.

421

... Now you will be at the turn of the course, at the home of the musician Sibelius,[1] and the land of the *Kalevala*, which gave Longfellow the idea, and the measure, of *Hiawatha*.

It used also to be a city with the best bookshop in the world, and one of the best bookshops, for English books, that I have ever seen.

I hope that you will see it still flourishing like a green bay tree.

I spoke in Helsinki once, and was told (I hope truly told) that Sibelius was present.

... The people told me terrible things of the Russian army. It had invaded Finland during the 1st War, & tho it had been a peaceful invasion & the army well-behaved, it had terrified all hands, for nearly all the army were pock-marked from small-pox, & were nightmares to see.

Here, after being warm, it is again cold, but with a slightly lifting glass.

I do wonder much about the weather that you are having, whether you have cold to bear, as well as lack of regular food & rest, or whether

> All day long the great Sun rolls his fire
> Intol'rable in the dusty march of Heaven,

and food & rest become alike impossible.

May these things be ever kind to you, & your brave blithe heart beat on from delight to delight.

[1] Helsinki, Finland.

422

. . . How wonderful to have a word from you, & the news that 2 have
come to hand. This is the eleventh, and it comes with all my thanks
for your beautiful account of you at Bergen, & of all its beauties &
all your memories. I loved these.

And you have really seen an old wooden Norwegian barque, once
so frequent on the seas, for the Ns take to the sea, & built their ships
themselves, and when we sold off all our sailing ships they bought a
lot of them cheap at about £2 a ton, & rather gave up building in
wood.

They always flew what we called the Norwegian House-flag;
which was a *wind-mill*, that when adjusted to the wind and set going
would go round like a windmill and pump out any water that had
leaked in, for all wooden ships will leak: well I know it.

These little windmills could (I think) be moved about, to pump
sea water for washing-down decks.

I must have seen hundreds of such barques: they used to *sail* into
the Mersey daily, to save tugs etc, & one learned to admire them, for
their seamanship, & the skill in their rigging: all smart for port: one
cannot see such sights now: mattings, pointings: just the things that
would delight you.

❧

423

. . . I have been reading the *Iliad* for the last 3 or 4 months (after
about 30 years of reading none) and now I feel like someone in the
Greek camp having a letter from beyond the other side of Thessaly,
out Ithaca way, perhaps, saying that the country is looking lovely,
and that it looks like a good wine year, and the mackerel are in.

Here it is hot & thundery: & almost cuckooless; he has left this
district, and is now away for the year, I judge, so that I must wait till
May.

It is odd to look thro the old Caldecott pictures, of an England
utterly gone: & the men with mutton-chop whiskers, or beards, and
suits such as one cannot now see, & stiff white collars, and alcohol of
2 or 3 kinds at each manly meal, for none but the recklessly brave
could deserve (or think they did) such Fair as then blessed [the]
earth.

This I shall hope to post tomorrow, the 9th, & if an airmail letter
cannot make Helsinki by the 13th it deserves not to be called an
airmail.

424

. . . I have memories of some little paintings by Chardin, the French artist, at the Stockholm Galleries; and of a lot of early Gauguins at a Gallery in Copenhagen.[1] At the latter Gallery was, also, a Roman bronze of Pompey the Great, a man who gave me a couple of years of slavery long since (much to my advantage).[2] If you see the name in a guide book your marine heart may think it is a picture of Portsmouth,[3] but no such luck, he was a Roman, mentioned 2 or 3 times by Shakespeare, & quite curiously like Mr Asquith (that was) once our Prime Minister.

I was down in the West a few days ago, going over the battlefield of Tewkesbury, a field that is still mainly field, and a battle that I now begin to understand. (Time I did, some may mutter.)

They show, I believe, 3 houses as the house where Q. Margaret slept the night before the battle: and I saw the 4th house, where I believe she *did* sleep, if any sleep came to her, poor soul.

All that great field was once a roaring battle, with mad loose horses, & a thousand dead & perhaps 2000 hurt, and summary executions all next day.

[1] The Hallé was back in Stockholm, prior to going to Denmark.

[2] JM published his play *The Tragedy of Pompey the Great* in 1910.

[3] "Pompey" is the sailors' nickname for Portsmouth.

425

. . . I do not remember much about Copenhagen, but I remember asking to see Hans Andersen's grave, & finding myself not understood. At last, it dawned on them that I meant *Christian* Andersen, & then I was able to see it, & to lay some flowers on it, for, for long years of childhood his tales were supreme to me; & some still seem matchless, & unlike anything else.

426

. . . Sometimes, in Liverpool Docks, long since, one had the joy of seeing a fine ship, all smart for port, come into dock with her tug, and see the lines passed, & the crew heaving her in to a song that never varied:

> I think I hear the Old Man say
> Leave her, Johnny, leave her.
> I think I hear the Old Man say
> It's time for us to leave her.

And tomorrow I shall be singing this for you, for tomorrow perhaps you will be singing it to yourself, as you go to the Hook, or thereabouts, & then tomorrow anyway, you will be thinking of singing it as you approach Harwich, & home, in a few hours.

427

. . . Here, nothing much new has happened, except cold weather & a crop of weeds.

The fruit farmers have been hit with the early fruits but are still hopeful for the later kind, but there is much cold & wind, & all fruits will be late.

Perhaps you have not seen the cherry farms here. They are wonderful in the blossom time, with the hives of bees to cross fertilise the trees & gather the pale honey. But they are most wonderful in the cherry time, when the barns are stacked with cherries, black, scarlet, pale red & white, & of many different sizes & tastes.

The arrays of graded cherries remind me of an Oriental Jewel-shop I saw once in Ceylon, in which there were great drawers full of raw gems, of different colours, much as you will see drawers full of corn, lentils, oats, rice, bird-seed & so forth in a poultry-food store.

Some of the jewels were such as I had never seen or imagined, and some were very queer, & supposed to influence life; and some were of a most unusual sublety of beautiful colour.

428

. . . I am in a sort of chaos of work that doesn't get done, & of people who want to know what is meant by a word written in a book 60 years ago, when I forgot what the word meant 50 years ago, & cannot find it in the dictionary.

What am I to say to such . . .?

I can say, "It must be an obsolete marine expression, like 'spurling', or 'strike-me-blind', or 'Liverpool Button'."

429

. . . If this should ever reach you, & you should ever be free, at some later time, to answer questions, please, will you some day tell me, if, at Bexhill, there be any hill at all, and on it any Boxwood (trees or shrubs), once a treasured wood for small joinery.

If there be any Boxwood there, do look out for Bullfinches, which love to nest in box.

There have been bullfinches in the box here; & in Hereford, too, a gay delight of them, long since.

I do not know what the name for a lot of bullfinches would be.

One talks of a Quire of Ningtingales, A Threnody of Swans, a Lamentation of Curlews.

Would it be a Cow-lure of Bullfinches? Would it be a French Assent of Peewits (*O, oui oui*)?

There is a great charm in the slow call of the bullfinch & a singular beauty in the colour of the bird: a most lovely beauty.

430

. . . I do wish that you were here, for I am in a few minutes going off to a fruit farm, where the strawberry season is on . . . and I would love you to lunch, later, on some of the spoils; for as the old English bishop[1] so wisely said, "Doubtless God *could* have made a better berry, but, doubtless, He never did."

[1] Bishop William Butler (1535–1618), quoted in Walton's *Compleat Angler*.

431

. . . Special thanks for your last letter, with the question about the "Liverpool Button".[1]

I hope that no such thing exists, but it did once exist.

Liverpool was a great port for all Western sailings, & London kept pretty much to the East. The slops for sailors in Liverpool, oilskins, sea-boots, dungarees etc were often deplorably shoddy, & the seams of dungaree overalls & oilskins would come adrift (often at first wearing) & the buttons come off.

Sailors were often utterly destitute with no ditty bag nor house-wife for repairing clothes. They used to improvise fastenings of rope-yarn. They would tie one foot of rope-yarn in the button-hole; fix another where the button had been (boring a hole for it with a marlin) & then tie the two yards together in a bow. This was the Liverpool button proper. A bow-knot of rope-yarn. Sometimes, they made a more seaman-like fitting, using the existing button-hole as a becket, and working, on the button side, a little wooden toggle on a string, that would serve as a button. Sometimes you will meet such a fitting on men's pyjamas today. The toggle was made of a bit of firewood or splinter; it crosses the chasm & is buttoned into the becket.

[1] See Letter 428.

432

. . . The Brueghel will I hope long delight you. I must have delighted in it for 40 years.[1]

I have never seen the Vienna Bs (some of the best) but the Naples, Amsterdam ones I know, & the English Magi one, & the sublime *Corn Harvest* in New York (the best of all), 1 or 2 German ones, & 1 (in private hands) in Sweden.

There is a German *Carnival*, not in this book, & not one of the best. The Swedish one is not in this book either. (It is of the mad fantastic type.)

There must, at times, have been a mood of mad fantasy in B, like the mood of the mad painter Dodd (Francis, I think)[2] whose work is strange dream; & is appearing now in London.

FD is said to have made a list of all the painters better dead, beginning with his Father, who was an Academician. He killed his father, & was then put into Broadmoor, where he painted till he died. (That is the story.)

But the power & scope & splendour of B's work are only to be had in rapturous sanity.

Who but the marvel can be sane and rapturous?

[1] *Breugels Gemälde* (1932) by Gustav Glück, a superbly illustrated book on Brueghel's paintings.

[2] JM seems here to be confusing Francis Dodd, RA (1874–1949), among other things official war artist during the First World War, with Richard Dadd (1819–87) who murdered his father and ended his days in an asylum.

433

. . . You (my dear darling) came into my life at a sad moment,[1] with a word of praise for something that I had wrought with intensity that had not pleased. Y,et it had pleased you, & you had written what no other had written, & could not & would not have so written had you not been someone somehow intimately dearly near akin to me.

When I saw you later, on Jan. 20th, please, I knew you for this, if it be not presumptuous in me to say so: and I resolved to try to make you glad of me in your life, and have been glad of you as of few people in life, and have loved your dear noble bright beautiful spirit, and have felt that you understood in what depth & kind & thanksgiving this love was and is.

You will remember how Peter Ibbetson, the homicidal maniac, & general misfit, lived in chains & cells in Broadmoor, in the Paradise of the thought of Mary.

What short-comings have been in me in all this I beg you to forgive & forget.

All my letters & thoughts of you are but thanks for you: and very poor thanks, too, being no great shakes, & old with it, only you have made me glad & this is all I can do to say so. John Donne would have said, "He could have jolly well kept silent about it".

I bless you.
Jan.

[1] ANS's first letter to JM came on the day of his brother's death.

434

. . . I wonder whether you ever think of the place of friendship in life; what determines it; what it is; what it has of destiny, what it is of design; what of momentary nearness, and passing mood; what of eternity?

. . . I'd .say the *Corn Harvest* [Brueghel] at NY is the greatest utterance of Man about Nature. And there is a thundering other, of Winter & Twilight, with men & dogs coming home, a staggering thing.

435

. . . I thank you so very much for your kind telling me of your Brueghel favourites.

There is a lively shippy one of Naples harbour & coast (which I saw in such weather from the sea once)—very good: but I do not like the looks of early ships; except that bit of the bow of a Greek one on which the Winged Victory stands at the Louvre. That is a lovely bit of line: she must have been a beauty.

I dearly love, too, that feast in the B book where a man stretches to take a bun from a bun-bearer.

436

...I felt that perhaps Mr JLS[1] might prove agreeable reading to you.

I do not quite know when pugilists gave up fighting with bare fists. It must have been 1880–1888 sort of time, when prize-fighting was not very reputable, and society was prohibiting it unless done with gloves. The old London Prize Ring Rules were falling out of use, & the Q Rules coming in.[2]

I expect that JLS usually fought with gloves. He fought his fatal fight with Corbett with gloves, and not on a floor, but on a flat earthen grass patch, which must have needed a fearful effort of muscle in the heat of New Orleans.

In those days, many boxers had their photographs everywhere on view in sports shops, men's out-fitters etc & JLS & Mitchell were among the best known.

Mitchell was really a welter or middle weight, not a heavy weight. I remember photographs of his back, from his neck to his waist. It must have been sold by the 1000, for it was everywhere.

[1] John L. Sullivan: see Letters 415, 418

[2] The Queensberry Rules, framed in 1866.

437

... Coming from you on Friday,[1] at about mid-day between Maidenhead & Henley, I came to a road-block of many cars & many policemen.

They would not say what the trouble was (I supposed a road-smash). They said (evasively) that "it was very important", and slowly sorted out the road-block, and turned my end of it, to go back a mile or two & get into another road to Henley.

This I did, & presently came to another road-block with infinities of police, and another slow sorting out: and after a while I got along upon a small country road, past quite a lot of police to Henley Bridge.

Of course, by this time, I was thinking: "Can this be the Train Robbery?" & I expected to read that it was: but not a word yet to show what it was. It may have been a big collision, or it may have been romance, with the police about to catch the arch-crook with 1 million & ¾'s in decayed bank notes on his person. "Ah, Watson, had you been there: it would have been like those old days in Baker Street, or shall we say Dartmoor, in those days of youth & cocaine, before anybody had any method at all."

It was rather a queer romantic end to a romantic day; with the rain clearing to a bright yet evil sunset & a falling glass.

Perhaps during the week I may hear what the important trouble was. I wish that you had shared the suspicion of importance that the occasion roused.

¹ JM and ANS had visited the *Cutty Sark* together, at Greenwich, on 16th August 1963. On that day he gave her a Battersea enamel box with the inscription: "Sacred to Friendship".

438

. . . I was much interested in what you told me of your thoughts of going in the *Herzogin Cecilie*.¹

I send a paper about a model of her, with views of the model, which will show you the kind of thing she was, a big 4-masted barque, with a big midship house, & the usual rig, double top gallants, nothing above the royals, and the rigging probably all wire, even the running gear.

You may be able to see that the rigging is set up by screws. The shrouds come down *inside the bulwarks* to the waterways on the deck, so that hands could hop into the shrouds without having to rig Jacob's Ladders.

Now the Channel, either side of this island, is a beastly crowded, foggy, stormy, dangerous ships' graveyard, & you might have had a miserable long sail.

Long since, I heard of one who went that kind of cruise.

Of course, if she had been going into blue water, & landing you, at say, Funchal or Gibraltar, it might have been better fun; but then, as the Chinaman said of the toboggan run—"But walkee milee back."

Among the other press cuttings, I send a horrid one of an Italian training ship with her sails in the gear, perhaps drying, before being furled.

There are also some snaps of those big London barges that we used to call mud-flats. They were wonders of the deep, and I'm afraid that they have now quite come to an end, as going concerns.

. . . I judge from the prints of the *HC* that she was of the late type of 4 m.b., [4-masted barque] with a big mid-ship house and gangways from which all 4 masts' gear could be worked in safety.

You might therefore have had little danger in her, but the sea in these climes is uncertain & tidal, & sudden, & in any 4 m.b. *very near*. All 4 m.b.s were apt to scoop up 50 tons of sea at one dip & swoosh the seaman about in it, just to show him where he stood.

[1] ANS had considered joining the sailing-ship *Herzogin Cecilie*, whose owner offered short cruises from English ports.

⁂

439

. . . I have not had any light yet on the matter of the W. Indian banjo-strings, before the *Cutty Sark*'s grandfather brought them the English article.

I hope to have some news of them during the week, but I suppose that all who used banjos then were slaves, & what they used was not much regarded by those who were not slaves.

Monk Lewis, the author of *The Castle Spectre*, who owned slaves in (I think) Jamaica, may tell of them in his picturesque account of them.

The usual strings seem to be made of gut, of some kind (not catgut, but that of sheep—pigs?—donkeys, mules & horses) especially the guts of the lean, tough specimens.

The W. Indian negroes *may* have used any of these, or may have had some tropical liana that served the purpose.

There is an old song:

> Dey dance all night to de old banjo
> With a cornstalk fiddle and a shoe-string bow.

But I have no memory of any line about the strings used with the cornstalk fiddle, nor what gave the resonance. Perhaps the text should read: "With a shoe-strung fiddle & a cornstalk bow."

But then, what were shoe-strings made of? And again, a banjo is twanged with fingers, not by a bow.

It may be some while before I can find out about it, but I will try to find what the W.I. used. Possibly Monk Lewis tells.

※

440

. . . I think of the Naval Lieutenant in Q Victoria's great reign who wished the Captain "Good Morning" when the C came on deck at 7.55 a.m. As the C took no notice the NL repeated his remark, & the C took official notice.

"This is not the place for Good Mornings, we do not say them. This is the place for WORK."

※

441

. . .I do miss that little page of *Where to hear the Hallé*.[1] It was always cut out and stood on the ink-stand made for me out of a piece of the *Conway*'s starboard cable-bitts; & then I could see where you are.

With this I send a tiny MS poem, typed by me on one side. As somebody said about Sodom, I think, in the Bible, or, no, a suburb of Sodom called Zoar, "is it not a little one"?

Please, do you know the poems of AEH [Housman]? Probably you do: but they came, away back, just at the very time when they could be all the world to me: and for years they were. I have his poems on the table always, and as Ben Jonson said of WS "I loved the man . . . on this side idolatry."

Do you remember how some years ago you asked me about de Sade, the demi-rep, & I had never read him, & tried to get him, & the Library fearing, no doubt, lest I should be morally completely done for by him, never sent him?

Well . . . they sent him today, thinking that by this time, perhaps, I should be all morally done for anyway, so, why delay longer?

I tried to read him for about 10 minutes, but was too bored to read further. Perhaps it wasn't wicked enough: it wasn't sane enough. It was not of our time: & I could not imagine anybody being corrupted by it: only bored and vexed. It may be that *the* wicked MS in the Brit Mus, that none but the King & the Archbishop may ever look at, is a similar fraud.

[1] In the magazine *Hallé*, a periodical about Manchester's Hallé orchestra.

442

... By all means let Sir J [Barbirolli] see the views of Woburn
Buildings. They are turning all the block into a big hole, but
wish to keep W.B. Yeats's room, as a special place, & I hope they
will succeed, but the plaster in all that stretch of houses was
ruinous, & I daresay here & there very dangerous, & Willy's old
fireplace & kitchenette are gone, now, re-plastered over, for
safety's sake.

They may not approve, but I want to write some verses about
the Room, & all those dead men & women.

443

...From external evidence I judged that a kind and devoted Aunt
has helped me to receive a charming letter from Tim, who wrote
from the Nelson Country.

I have never seen that country.

I remember reading, many years ago, that the Father of N, the
Rector, was a man of rigid rule over himself: always sitting bolt
upright in any chair, never leaning back on a chair-back, nor
resting arms on chair-arms; and never pampering his eyes with
spectacles.

There is a relic of Nelson at Oxford, is there not, a flag of sorts,
somewhere? I forget.

If not, they have at Pewsey, in Wiltshire, not very far away, a
real relic, the Quarter Gallery, or a part of it, of the Spanish first-
rate *San Josef*, taken by Nelson off Cape St Vincent, in 1797.

This is in the Church; & I have seen it, as a railing somewhere
(I forget just where, but perhaps between the nave proper and the
Chancel.)

They used to have a few feet of the *Victory*'s old (mizen, I think)
topmast, in London, the one she had at Trafalgar, but the Services
Museum has now been dispersed & I know not where it is now.

They brought Nelson home in a rum cask to be buried in St
Paul's: and this brings me to the next head of my discourses which
may interest you, for it is about Lord Byron ...

Did I tell you all this?

Alas, I fear you will say, "Only twice, but I shall love to hear it
again."

444

. . .The Byron matter is, as follows, only I cannot do more than begin it in this note.

Some years ago (a good many years I fancy) the Byron Tomb was in disrepair, and a Committee of local people caused a complete repair & restoration to be made.

Not long ago I met one of the men engaged in this work . . .

Now, as an old journalist, I see that I must write

To be continued in our Next . . .

445

. . . If I may go on about Byron?

The tomb or vault was in a sad way, & the men found that the body of Byron had become exposed. He was removed from the shell in which he lay, and placed in a new coffin. My friend looked upon the real Byron, dead, I suppose, about a hundred years or more, yet well recognisable as the Byron of the portraits.

He was dressed in white, with some sort of black silk scarf coming from the throat to the waist.

They re-interred him at once: and all was done with right reverence.

Years ago, when there was a fire at St Mary's here, & the roof of the chancel smashed the chancel floor, I was one of a party that hoped to hold an inquest on Amy Robsart.

It was thought that Lord Leicester, her husband, had had her killed, so that he might marry Q Eliz: & her grave was under the chancel floor.

So I & the scientists & others attended, to open the traditional grave to learn the truth; and it was a strange experience. They came at once on Elizabethan brickwork but it had been disturbed about 100 years or more before, & there were graves of that time all across the chancel (above Amy Robsart); Cardinal Newman's Mother was there, so we at once gave up the search, & left the dead at peace.

446

. . . There are two or three enchanting little chalk streams in Wiltshire & valleys full of little villages well worth a visit.

The Saxon pirates who killed off the Ancient Britons settled and farmed these valleys. The A Brits had preferred the Downs up above.

The rivers are called Sem, & Nadder & Wylie, all 3 to the W & NW from Salisbury. I haven't seen them lately (nor for 40 years perhaps).

Further N from Salisbury there is the Avon with Amesbury where Q Guenevere was the Abbess (& Stonehenge near it). This used to be lovely, but it was all Camp in the war-times & may not have recovered.

But there is a wonderful stretch away more NW from Salisbury, south of Devizes, & to be reached from Devizes & Pewsey (N & E respectively) & stretching for about 20 miles from Upavon through Urchfont westward, to Market Lavington & Edington. This used to be a heavenly kingdom, with chalk downs above, & I've no doubt many little chalk streams to water the many little villages. I have not seen it for 30 years, but it is a place for archaeologists, with old camps above & holy wells & shrines below: & up in the downs all sorts of lost & forgotten holy places, & queer names like Gladiators Walk, Hag Hill, Cuckold's Green & Mental Hospital.

Further West & North there is the line of the Wansdyke wh runs from Inkpen west to near Bath: a great barrier made by K Arthur (I wd say).

. . .I do not know Wiltshire well, but it is full of lovely things & places.

There is a very good inn called the Ailesbury Arms, at Marlborough, & this is in the midst of beauty. Just outside, on this side of it, is Savernake Forest, which is still a forest with deer in it, & also a lovely reach of the Kennet River, with the site of Cunetio, a Roman city, which Sir J's ancestors[1] may have helped to found. Then, on the other side, are downlands amazing & wild & lonely, with Barbury Camp, that Sorley wrote the poem about, & all sorts of marks of primitive Brit settlements, fields, villages etc. Then by the Bath road you come to Silbury Hill, a giant tumulus, the biggest ever, I believe, and then the Avenue of great stones leading to Avebury, a Temple of vast stones, a wondrous site.

Then, going more to the S, you can see the tomb of the lady who piloted King Charles II to safety, & had the privilege of having the Royal Arms quartered on her scutcheon as the brave soul deserved; & there is a lovely drive, Pewsey to Devizes & back to Marlb.

But I think the Kennet valley is the loveliest thing, & all the downland N & NE from it, in Berkshire really, but so easy to divinely drive to from Marlb that I recommend it: the White Horse Hill, & the Seven Barrows, & so round Lambourne, & the place on the Kennet where Wild Darrell burned the baby, & so to Hungerford & Inkpen Beacon.

. . . There is a Roman road here, still visible but overgrown, going towards Otmoor, a narrow straight strip of jungle usually; but bulldozers are tearing it away now; & then it is ploughed into fields, where it is not left as hedge.

I used to read, as a child, of Roman roads, & wished that I could see one, but unknowingly I often was on a bit of one, for it was still a road leading from a Roman city to another Roman city; and later I drove all the way of it & saw both the cities, both much battered by Time.

You may be reading Housman's poem "When Uricon the City stood . . . ." Did you ever go to Uricon? There is a vast heap of basilica or forum wall in the midst of grass. The forum must once have been just about the measure of Birmingham Town Hall; & the city about a mile across; & the lovely brook once its drink & its bath now romping free to the Severn.

¹ Sir John Barbirolli was English born, but of Italian and French parents.

447

. . . It is a happiness to think of you only 50 miles or so away, actually in a house where I have sometimes stayed, long since, several times.¹

Much longer ago, I heard, or read, that a piece of K Arthur's Round Table was at Winchester, but when I did get there, hoping still, it seemed to have gotten mislaid.

If they have since found it, and shown it to you, perhaps you will some day tell me about it, but not till you have had a rest in your bed at home.

Keats was in Winchester in the best moments of his life; & must often have walked from the Cathedral to St Cross. He wrote the *Autumn* there, at about this time of year,² but with a higher barometer: and one may say that Autumn was never before so felt.

¹ Sent to ANS at the Hostel of God-begot in Winchester.

² John Keats composed his "Ode to Autumn" at Winchester in September 1819.

448

. . . I have been reading about the Wool Clippers in B. Lubbock's book.¹ I don't mean sheep-shearers, but fast full-rigged ships that took passengers to Australia & came back with wool & gold-dust & hides & tallow. They were rather before my time, but I saw some of them, tho London was more their port than Liverpool. The few that I saw were absolute corkers: fizzers of the sea: for the trade was very profitable for a time, & these sailing-ships beat the steamers there & back, there being so few big foreign coaling stations. Of course, the Suez Canal gradually killed their supremacy.

Wool is a deadly dangerous cargo: It is apt to ignite down in the hold, like a haystack stacked damp; & then alas for poor Tom Bowling.

[1] Basil Lubbock, author of *The Colonial Clippers* (1921) and *The Nitrate Clippers* (1932).

449

. . . You tell me that the day that may bring this letter to you will be spent mainly in Portsmouth.

I hope that it may be passed with leisure enough for you to see something of the Port, & the George, & the Blue Posts, & the other landmarks, as well as the Nelson Museum & the *Victory*.

The place always gives me a queer feeling that it is pre-historic, and is not, and cannot be, anything but something in eternity, with a great fire above it and a great strangeness in it: & all of England's destiny concerned in it.

When a poet gets into this kind of thought about anything, some say the bees are in his belfry, or ring for the hurry-up waggon from the local asylum; but the kind of thought, tho akin to madness, is akin to poetry, wh is all that a poet is ever any good at; (& he not always).

. . . I have just finished again an early book of Lubbock's about the Wool ships to Australia; & NZ, & most of them rather before my time, but the *Cutty Sark* comes into the book; & a few that I saw, right at the end, are there, & are in my memory.

There are many old photographs of them; & most of them show them in order, for they often earned great sums of money, from passengers, & from carrying English goods better & more quickly than the steamers of the time.

They were manned, too, by English sailors, & marked us as a seaman people: very good in a mess, very good at an art that most nations are less good at, and doing all this without help from any government, without thought of any future, without real sense, without generosity or mercy or supervision, but going into hell & out for what they could find there, & letting a captain, 2 mates, 20 men, a cook, a carpenter, a bosun, a sailmaker & 4 boys, be the ship's dockyard & equippers, all the way & back; & be sure that she would look smart when she did come back.

It is a strange story, though some of it is terrible, & some appalling. It will show you what the sea was then, to the ships & men of then, with the buckos & drink & the wastrels they fostered, & the records they broke.

450

. . . What fun to be writing to you in a place so linked to the 16th .[1]

Often in some vital months, coming away from Willy's old den, I would pass the end of Tavistock Place, with all manner of wild excitements of poetry & the arts all jumbled & fiery (and mighty smoky rather than lighty) in my skull . . . .

You pass much of your time in the perfect practice of great art. We at Willy's were all in the theories of our gang, and the hatreds that theories provoke. What a sad lot we were, but what an excitement it was, and how senseless going to bed seemed . . .

. . . WBY was there for 25 years, for about ½ of each year, & there on all the winter Mondays he discoursed wisdom to all comers, & induced something liker wisdom, in each, than had been there before.

There, too, came Synge, and . . . and . . . and . . . and . . . after 60 years I wonder if there will be anyone next week who was there then.

If there be a peep-hole in Paradise, what a flutter there will be at it, as they all crowd round it saying, "Willy's old room is all lit up, & they are all saying what wonders we were. By George the Great, we *were*: how right they are at last!!"

[1] The day of their visit to the *Cutty Sark*. JM had left ANS at the Avondale Hotel, in Tavistock Place, where she was staying.

451

. . . I never mentioned (yesterday) my admiration of your description of going to Salisbury from the west at sunrise & seeing the Cathedral, spire & all, with the dawn behind it. Lucky & sensitive you.

It is a splendid clump of invention, unique in being all of one design, which is not often the case; & such a design . . . .

I think that Salisbury must have been a main original for Trollope's "Barchester".

In the old days, I felt that Beauvais cathedral in France had never been built, but had been as it were a divine bubble blown by a divine Being. Sta Sophia in Constantinople gives the same effect.

Beauvais, alas, got blanged pretty well west in the last war. It is the greatest loss man had in the last war: a divine thing gone; a divine thing that all knew to be divine, that touched the divine in all.

❦

452

. . . I loved your dear letter this morning, & bless you for it, & must send instant thanks for it, and for the kind photograph of the Round Table that you so generously sought out for me.

Long since (I cannot think when) I saw this relic, & I shall put the card in my *Morte d'Arthur* that was the first book I bought in New York when I vowed that I wouldn't be so ignorant.

Dear beautiful girl, you give so generously & thank so exquisitely, & who could help loving you?

The Irish night-porter at the Avondale told you the truth:[1] he truly does: & it is a joy to know that you are back . . .

. . . May I deeply thank you for telling me of your time in Bristol & your walk with your Mother? I loved all that deep nearness to you, so beautifully felt and told.

My own Mother died when I was about 6½ and I think I then entered into hell fire.

There is a lyric by John Fletcher, in a great play that no-one ever acts: it ends thus (the lyric):

> Nor shall these souls be free from pains & fears
> Till women waft them over in their tears.

I have been writing an essay on John Fletcher, whom I judge is the nearest akin to me of all whom I read, tho an incredibly better writer than I can ever be, a man of the Renaissance, whom WS chose as a collaborator, & whom these dogs in theatres neglect, who wrote the marvellous line: "Like a ring of bells whose sound the wind still alters;" and the shattering couplet:

> This world's a City full of straying streets
> And Death's the Market-place where each one meets.

The couplet is carved on a tomb in Epping Forest, old Chingford Churchyard, where I used to go, just to see it, for no-one has honoured John Fletcher more deeply than he or she who put it there.

¹ One night after a concert (& much travelling) I arrived very late at my hotel, the Avondale, looking, no doubt, very tired. The night porter said: "Cheer up, miss, he still loves you!" ANS.

❦

453

. . . Perhaps I have already sent you this booklet. Please forgive it, if I have.

It contains a view of a part of the garden of my old home, with the Church beyond it.

Some of the trees have shot up since I was there, & some of the shrubs have gone: & my old home stood very close to the left side of where the photograph ceases.

The house still stands pretty much as it did: some of it late Tudor, I wd say, & some about 1630 & some (a good lot) built by my grand-father.

On the extreme R of the view is where we boys had a cricket-pitch & below this, at the very foot of the view on the R, I used to see glow-worms at night.

. . . *War & Peace* is a great book, isn't it?

Tolstoi knew war, for he was in Sebastopol while we & the French besieged it, in that mad war of the Crimea. He wrote some wonderful pages about his time there, or perhaps dictated them, as it was a late book.

Russia did lead the world then, in music & ballet & in literature; but now, what, since 1914, what, that speaks to the soul of man?

❦

454

. . . I am sending you a rather chaotic cutting about some branch of the Freme family, & am stirred by it to try to get a little nearer to fact about your Tray man.¹ I shall get a sleuth to have a try, anyhow. If the sleuth will really try, he will find something, for not all the Brit. Mus. was bombed to bits, anything like.

Fifty years ago, or so, when I was really working at the BM I learned how very much was to be found by any experienced searcher: & searching was fun, though exhausting fun. Excitement in fuggy air is a sort of double poison: one saw some queer specimens illustrating this: I was 1 of them.

. . . It is dear of you to ask about my childhood. I wd gladly tell you anything you ask, but perhaps could tell it best by word of mouth, rather than by writing.

It isn't a mystery at all, but it was a shadow, I wd judge: & made me the kind of night I am.

Anyhow, it was my lot & portion, & anything in any way different wasn't my lot & portion, and any different resultant wouldn't be me; however much better for all hands a different resultant might prove.

With it all, my golly, I have had a time, & been amid beauty & known great ports, & learned a little, & had some friends, and writing to one of the dearest of them all at this very moment . . .

. . . The piano-tuner is here, & I am writing this in the room where I unpacked your dear gift of the [ship] model, on the 20th Jan, that day, when you were first here. I am sitting where you sat.

The piano is never played now, but I keep it tuned.

I've been writing verse lately, out of your little blue Bristol ink-well; and when one writes verse one has to read a lot of verse; & then one cannot sleep, but lies awake making verses of unusual measures; & sometimes one falls asleep making marvellous poems in dream, & then wakes remembering perhaps half one amazing word, and then all day keep wondering was the word beginning with skinfull, or tinfull, or sinfull, or was it spindrell, or windrell or findrinny something (a kind of prehistoric Irish tinny something), which Yeats puts into a poem or two, but I never have put it into one yet, not knowing what it was like.

As the piano-tuner has now gone, I am back at this ink-well & think, as I read this, that you will consider that I am gone a bit barmy on the crumpet.

What is still good in me well knows your dearness & beauty & thanks you for it.

[1] William Freme: see Letters 350–2, 358

455
. . . I have been doing some verse this week.

Verse is a big garden, like music, and a lot of beauty is there, if one could only get well in, & pick, & get away with the spoil.

Please, did I ever send you the Beardsley book *Under the Hill?* There was a Satanic sort of garden that AB had the key to, & the book is the tale of the beginning of a visit to it.

456

... It is possible that I may hear a scrap or two more about the Freames. Was your man's name Wm F Freame? (I forget.)

I believe that in England one can take any name one likes, & that criminals frequently do so, actors sometimes, writers fairly often, & pugilists sometimes. But those who adopt new names may like the change to be formally made known and recognised. Generally, therefore, the change is licensed (with a fee, I think) and made public: and even so, it may be the cause of legal worry when property is transferred.

In most European countries, the changing of the name is made difficult. Victor Hugo says somewhere that a woman's real name is her Christian name, and this one knows to be generally true, but to me the woman's real name is what her lover calls her . . . .

... Long since, I used to go much to Cornwall, & wd get up very early, & go to wild lonely beaches when no-one was up: and on one beach, once, in Cornwall, in a winter dawn, lo an otter, the only one I have ever seen, getting things in the rock pools, perhaps minnowy things for a relish, or perhaps limpets, but perhaps only, like me, just enjoying the lonely beach & the dawn.

W. B. Yeats [when in Galway] once asked an old Irishman if there were badgers in that part of Galway.

The old man said, "No, but there's Authors in the Rivers."

I am to see WBY's old Rooms formally preserved on Nov. 20th.

I thank you for telling me of Sir JB's remark about the opening of *Tristan*. Browning wrote a fine thing about the miracle of music, in his poem "Abt Vogler":

And I know not, if, save in this, such gift be allowed to man,
That out of three sounds he frame, not a fourth sound, but a star.

I suppose you will have played lots of Vogler's[1] music, & have a musician's memory, & can re-create whole compositions at will from reams of it; star after star.

I get a lot of joy out of verse, but memory is not what it was. There are certain sudden momentary splendours that one cannot forget: amazing things, as when Charmian says "O Eastern Star" in *Ant & Cleo*.

One can think of that all day, & then all night.

[1] Vogler, Georg Joseph, known as Abbé or Abt Vogler (1749–1814). Organist, composer and teacher. Amongst his pupils were Weber and Meyerbeer.

457

. . . Did I mention the name of the other book that you mention, that was to follow the [Havelock] Ellis? I cannot think what it could have been, unless it was Pepys, which I have often thought of sending you, but have not, because in some ways he is a reference book of frequent use to me (who am too short of reference books), but who counts among the naval books, & will be with you sooner or later.

Unfortunately, his zeal for marine affairs was apt to lead him into temptations, to which, like other men, he was very yielding; & then would tell the world in odd jumbles of French, Spanish & Latin how yielding he had been.

Why he did this, when he had many enemies, who might at any time seize his scripts & read his shorthand I do not know; but he judged that they would not, and they did not, and after all, they are fewer (these amorous entries) than one would suppose; & do not take away from his righteous zeal for the King's Service except in 2 or 3 cases.

I do not like the man much, but respect his eager intellect, his zeal for the King's Navy, his love of music, books & plays, his delight in acting, & every now & then his telling comment on men & misdeeds.

He is best in his description of the Fire of London, which of course he saw at very close quarters. He lived just to windward of the Fire's outbreak. If the wind had changed, he would have been an early casualty.

458

. . . It had not occurred to me that the pourer might be for chocolate.[1]

I do not quite know how the late 18th century people made their chocolate, nor, indeed, how our earlier coffee-house people made it. The making of it was (in the early times) rather hard work; for it was made from Cacao nut that had to be crushed & squeezed & pounded to get away the oil, which was said (otherwise) to make the drinker "too full of Blood". When the oil was out of the nut the nut-meat was (I think) dried a little in the (tropic) sun, before being brewed into chocolate by (?) boiling water mixed with vanilla & sugar.

The Spaniards along the Spanish Main drank it 5 or 6 times a day, without getting uncomfortably full of Blood: & the English took to it at once (about 1680, say).

. . . The cocoa used in our Navy is made from blobs of pressed cacao nut from which the oil or butter has not been wholly extracted; & I suppose that this drink makes the Navy, if not full of Blood, partly full of Beans.

[1] JM had a fine collection of early blue-and-white Worcester porcelain. This refers to a coffee or chocolate pot, with the blue underglaze crescent mark, which he had sent to ANS.

❧

459

. . . You were right in your judgement of the [*Arabian*] *Nights* & Burton's translation. He was a sort of cast-iron man who could endure any hardship to get to the back of beyond, but in the beyonds that he reached he found nothing that men have not cast away.

. . . I never saw Burton, but Swinburne was much attached to him, and I did know a man long since who knew him a little. This last thought him extra-ordinary, for a kind of tireless cast-iron toughness, with a knowledge of savage beliefs and practices seldom attained by anyone. He went to Mecca, as you may know; & was (popularly) supposed to have been recognised there in the Holiest Place, and had just 20 seconds in which to kill the recogniser before the recogniser could betray him. My friend disbelieved the story, but said that Burton liked people to believe it: & it may be true, or partly true.

❧

460

. . . I thank you for your welcome letter, here this Tuesday night in a gale, and me cowering in the dim, at the thought of tomorrow in London,[1] having to make a speech, & no Reyna to prompt me when I forget what comes next: and Willy in Paradise in his gold hat looking down, & saying, "Look at the muggins; I ask you; all dried-up like last year's snow, and ME his subject."

Well, coming away, if not lyncht by the indignant crowd, I shall at least see the Avondale doorway, & wish that it was August again.

My host is a Mr Cloudesley, & I feel sure I shall call him Mr Shovell, & then try to alter it by saying, "I mean Mr Spade".

You ask me about Mr [Wilfred] Owen.

He wrote some beautiful things, full of feeling, like those rare utterances of Mr Grenfell.

Both wrote in a high mood, & both must have been extraordinary spirits, for which one cannot find words of praise enough.

People sometimes ask me, "Were they not England's great loss in the war?"

To this, I say, "Such spirits are a loss to any land, but (to me) the great loss was Charles Sorley.[2] He surely, might have done anything, had he not been killed."

But these things are Destiny, & the allotted portion, or denial of a portion, and it is a Justice of sorts, & as the Widow said in Synge's play, "We must be satisfied" (even if we can't be).

I must marvel again at the posts from here. They too are our Destiny, but they get worse, & are already like the Devil on 2 sticks . . .

[1] At the restored rooms of W. B. Yeats in Woburn Walk, Bloomsbury.

[2] Charles Hamilton Sorley, (1895–1915), a poet greatly admired by Sassoon and Graves, and especially by JM.

461

. . . Thank you for your dear enquiry about the London day . . . The room there is all spic & span & bright & tidy: and nobody, of all the old of 60-odd years ago, was there except myself, one of the two youngest . . . .

The day was hard going, but I got thro' it, & said my say, & Willy, if he heard it, thro all his halo (& the gold hat) didn't (I hope) blush for me.

I think he must wear the kind of clothes Chopin would wear, a kind of Jodh-pore trowsers of the purest mother of pearl, or that film of opal that covers so many rocks in Australian deserts.

. . . You must not be sad at being a woman. You are a lovely woman & beloved & clever & dear & wanted by all who know you; & you are a very fine woman; & good at all sorts of things that you have learned by being a woman, & could not have learned as a man. It was your Destiny to be a woman: you have made it a high Destiny.

There are other ways of order & beauty & power than running fast up steep rope ladders to tie cords round wet canvas . . .

462

. . . I send some lines I wrote for *The Times* (Monday's issue, the 25th).

It is hard to speak from the heart when stunned by the news.

John Fitzgerald Kennedy
All generous hearts lament the leader killed,
The young chief with the smile, the radiant face,
The winning way that turned a wondrous race
Into sublimer pathways, leading on.

Grant to us, Life, that though the man be gone
The promise of his spirit be fulfilled.

Nov. 22. 23. 24. 1963.

❀

463

. . . I am in the throes of Christmas writing; which I dread & shrink from when otherwise very busy.

I always try to counter its torment by extensive study.

Some men would yield to drink or drugs; or do cross-word puzzles, or chess problems, or go every evening to the Turkish Bath, or a prize-fight, or read about detectives such as Dr Watson's friend, or that other Frenchman who used to talk to Mr Ricardo (I forget this wonder's name).[1]

I do none of these things. I begin again on the good old Battle of Waterloo. Modifying the negro spiritual I sing:

> Gimme that old time confusion
> He's good enough for me.

Wellington, who figures largely in the tales of confusion, discouraged study of it by the famous remark, that the history of the battle would be like the history of a ball.

This is a good remark, & discourages (as perhaps it was meant to) enquiry into what a general remembers with qualms. But most of those at a lively ball have lively memories of bits of it, and were influenced by some of it, perhaps profoundly; and, bit by bit, one probing into a welter of memories begins to see & disentangle, tho much remains in the mud, & all the smoke has now blown away.

I suppose that a quarter of a million men fought in it, & 700,000 were killed or hurt or ruined by it: and the memories of those who were there are very queer.

I jot down (from memory) what some of those there said about it.

"I don't remember much about the Battle, but I'll never forget the night before."

"I was hoping to get a little sleep . . . but not a bit of it . . . and beyond that slice of bread I had nothing all day."

"In his purse were 20 louis, which we took as a good omen for the day."

"I wondered if there were battles in which everyone was killed, & if this was one of those battles."

Wellington was overheard saying, "By God, Adam, I do believe we'll beat them yet."

"The other officers in the battery said that we were beaten, but I said 'No, I think we've won, for the firing sounds further away.'"

[1] A. E. W. Mason's French detective, Inspector Hanaud of the Sûreté.

464

. . . Thank you for your word about Tim & the Red Indians.

It is strange to remember that only 100 years ago, the American frontier was still pretty much the Mississippi, and that those that went beyond that barrier might be scalped almost anywhere: and that Lincoln, as a young man, was in an Indian war in Illinois & found one of his regiment dead & scalped.

When I first came to these parts there was an old man alive who had been chased by the Cheyennes, who would have scalped him had they caught. This would have been only 100 years ago, I suppose, with Lincoln alive, & the Civil War not over.

It would be hard for me to say what intense delight the tales of the Wild West were to my childhood. It was not then the *Wild & Woolly* West; it was the Wild West before the cowboy was there, before the ranchers were on the ranges, when the only trails were the Indian trails.

Of all that wilderness, from Florida, west to the Pacific, Captain Mayne Reid wrote magically in novel after novel, in the mid-Victorian *Chambers Journal*, to all of which I had access, unknown to all authority, to my intense delight.[1]

I do not think that any mortal could have enjoyed his writing more than I did, or half as much, or anything like as much: and Mayne Reid himself was only 12 miles away, & I may have seen him, unknowing, may even have seen him often, "brushing my shoulder unguessed-at", for he was living in those parts, & I think he died there.

[1] There were many bound volumes of contemporary periodicals in the Library at The Priory, Ledbury, home of JM's grandfather.

465

... Generally on Christmas Day, as soon as I have fed the hens & robins & blackbirds who watch for me then (probably thinking me a silly muggins to be throwing food away, & hardly human, as far as that goes, not having a gun even), it is my plan to begin the day by writing to you. At Christmas time, ankle-deep in envelopes & in despair of ever being tidy again, I feel like the Naval officer in 1918 who cried, "Hurray, Hurray, the war is over, and now I can get all hands back to Battle Practice."

When I have written a few letters, I, too, will turn-to & really tidy-up, & get my room straight again.

Your sword paper-cutter,[1] has been invaluable: it seems to slice open each envelope by an instinct of where to strike: & this year has been a mass mail: the biggest ever, I think, for many strangers have written to me this time.

Do you read Dickens ever? He did some good Christmas writing in his day; in the little book about Scrooge; & in the child's Christmas in the first few pages of *Great Expectations*.

[1] ANS had given JM a paper-knife for a birthday, a silver reproduction of the Coronation sword, with the special hall-mark for Coronation year.

466

... Now that the fury of the storm of Christmas has blown by, it occurs to me to ask: would you care to have the marine cards & so forth? Usually there are some, & often rather good, but I daresay this particular kind of grass-hopper has become a burden, for I must have sent you a good many such; and papers can be a menace when they pass a certain point. I have a nice one of a Brig, going in to Avonmouth: rather jolly: & one or 2 of the old London barges.

We had similar craft on the Mersey, of old. We always called them "mud-flats", but it was a caution to see them when a sea was running.

Talking of the sea, brings in the *Lakonia*, & I hope no friends of yours were in her.[1]

I have been unable to find any dependable account of whereabouts her fire was, nor what the weather was at the time, nor the time of day, nor where she was when all began, so I cannot begin to imagine, nor try to reconstruct.

The men who towed her and tried to get her to Gib must have had a nightmare time of it; she still on fire and listing, a big sea running, and she a brute of a big tow, barging about like Satan's own, and I suppose towing with chain cable & a great span of cable out. Golly, my own, quel joi.

I wish that people would understand the difficulty in lowering a boat from a boat deck to the sea, with the ship in any motion at all, & the crew & passengers in the boat, & 50 or 60 feet of drop, perhaps, before the boat is in the water, & can be cast loose: & 2 passengers wanting to go back & get their passports, & 2 to get their cigarette case & to send a wireless home.

It is a grim thing to picture.

Once, going to the US I had a steward who had been in the *Titanic*: and, indeed, I had the picture very vividly from him.

[1] The Greek-owned passenger liner *Lakonia*, bought from the Dutch in December 1962, sank a year later in the Atlantic, 180 miles north of Madeira, following a fire on board due to an internal explosion—she had set sail in a poor state of repair. Of the 1,000-odd passengers and crew, mostly British, 91 are known to have died and some 900 were rescued by US Airforce helicopters based in the Azores, by RAF Shackletons, and a number of ships in the vicinity, including the *Montcalm* and the RN aircraft-carrier *Centaur*. According to the ship's master, Captain Zarbis, the fire started in the barber's shop.

467

... For the time, I have laid aside the battle of Waterloo, & have taken to the re-playing of famous games of chess, by Masters of chess; & revive some memories of long ago, when I used to follow chess-tournaments closely. You must not think that I am good at chess; I am not; but I am interested in seeing what the Masters can do, with their slowness that is suddenly sudden, & the shock it brings to the situation.

I think that the Russians have a genius for chess, as they have for ballet; and that modern world-politics are outside their spiritual natures, & that we mis-judge them.

A Barge.

1964

468

. . . I thank you for answering my question about Dickens.

People read him less & less, of course, as the life that he describes becomes incomprehensible.

I saw Victorian England after 50 years of agitation for reform; & some reform had been made, but it was still a terrible place: and London an appalling place, much as CD describes it.

Of his books, I like best *Great Expectations* as in that (I feel) he is most like a poet, & has touches of beauty. It is a tale of the criminal code, & its effects on society, & a few chosen characters: and some of the writing is very fine & deeply felt, & done in a high mood.

I find it difficult to read some of his books now, but in most of them there are things of power—scenes, descriptions, poignancies & things well put; & these I often & often read; scenes in prisons for debt, scenes in lodgings & boarding-houses; drives at night in coaches, in frost, in smashes; in eating-houses; in dens & Newgate, & in fear of the gallows.

Some of his Letters are admirable: and often he has a marvellous page or two, quite perfect as prose & charm & character.

I think that some of his accounts of childhood, & the child's mind are marvellous, too: I know nothing to match them.

It is a staggering thought to me, that he would pledge himself to do a book, say, in 12 or in 24 monthly numbers, not having begun the book, but having perhaps the first number ready for press . . . & a general scheme, of course. Then he, a busy, convivial spirit, going everywhere . . . would try to keep the numbers going in time for press . . . . Ah, my Reyna, he was sorely put to it sometimes, but he never quite collapsed: the book went on.

Artemus Ward[1] (it is said) wrote a remark to an imaginary youth of whom he disapproved: "Young man, if you were my Son, I would order your Funeral for tomorrow ... and the corpse should be ready." Easier to do this than write ½ of a book.

I really do not know how CD could have kept these long tales going, & made them on the whole so very good. He had a sense of character as lavish as Nature's, & when bored with the characters in any book, he would invent new ones, which gladdened the moment when things pressed. Mrs Gamp is one such.

He had something of the native power of the old very good low comedian, who could go on before a sticky audience (while the Hamlet was being sobered up, perhaps) & keep them rocking with laughter, or sobbing real tears, (or both) for an hour if necessary; like "the little quiver fellow" in the play of K Henry the IV, part II, who took the Musketry squad before Mr Justice Shallow, at Mile End.

Like the old low comedian, CD could act or read in public inimitably well.

In his books, sometimes, he writes prose as if he were doing bad blank verse in the Old Surrey Theatre of Melodrama, a haunt of his. You can turn whole pages, easily, at these points, into blank verse, by leaving out a few words.

He died 94 years ago: and I have only met 1 person who heard him read: a Lady, who said that it altered life for her: it was so moving.

[1] Artemus Ward was the pseudonym of the American humorist Charles Farrar Browne (b. 1834); he came to England in 1866 to lecture and edit *Punch*; he died the following year.

469

... I think that "to a T" must refer to the mechanical T-square, a wooden appliance, used by draughtsmen & artists in marking lines with precision.

Du Maurier mentions the T-square in *Trilby*, as laid on the floor and danced over in the Morris.

The Xmas feast: p 168 or so, "The Laird danced a sword-dance over two T-squares, and broke them both."

Usually, in the sword-dance, you dance over crossed swords. In the Morris, now, you dance over crossed church-warden tobacco-pipes, & pick them up with pride at the end to show that you have not broken either.

It is a very real feat, not to break either.

I think that the letter T was used to impress the young with a sense of exactness. Children had to cross the T with care.

❧

470

. . . I must confess that I do not know the words Ropy & Tatty, [1] except that Tatts used to be a slang word for Dice, & especially loaded Dice. A man using dice was called a Tatts-man. The word was associated with fraud. Ropy has a meaning of slimy, and was applied to ships' drinking-water, which smelt horribly and had a green slime in it when drawn from cask (or even from tanks). Marines were called *Mrs Ropers*; and the frequent hanging of criminals caused a good many allusions to ropes in thieves' slang: *Mr Roper*, for *Hangman*, & *John Roper's window* for a *Noose*, etc.

. . . You ask about a poet, did I know him. [2]

I met him very long ago at WBY's rooms, & did not take to him. He then wore Turquoise Ear-rings, & these I might have admired in a sailor, but disliked very much in a young man. Long afterwards, I met him again, & the ear-rings had gone, & I liked him better, & thought better of his work, but did not really take to him, nor his work, & the world has accepted the work, remember, and it may have merits, or must have. To me, it does not appeal. To some it does appeal, and Poetry is a large expanse, & all can find flowers after their hearts there.

In the *M of Venice* someone says of his Father that "He did something smack, something lean to, He had a kind of taste". It was something like that.

Thinking over a long-ago lady with dingle dangle ear-rings, I have the feeling that her ear-rings hung down a full two inches on each side, or even a tiny [bit] more, and that the lady kept still, to avoid the jingle, and thereby gave the illusion of tranquillity.

The ear-rings gave an effect of beauty: they were things of grace.

While I am on this theme, I beg you will be so kind as to tell me if the ears so pierced are now healed. And will you tell me what colour of ear-rings you most affect, when you dress up for special occasion, with your Tea Tray spread, all shining, and crumpets perhaps, for tea, if such things still exist?

I do not think I have seen a real crumpet since 1899.

Crumpet was, for a while, & perhaps still is, in some circles, a term for the human head.

Long long since, I read with joy, in a weekly paper, the phrase: "With my new Cady on my crumpet" (Cady meaning hat).

Long afterwards, I found that it had been written by Jack Yeats, WBY's brother.

... Now as to your question about story-telling. I feel that we are all born with certain aptitudes, for this or that: you with aptitudes for beauty, friendship, music etc, and myself, say, for old rigging and gratitude to those who like me.

Wm Morris, who was one of my masters, said that a good artist was always telling himself stories.

Then the Welsh Triads[3] say that the *Three Foundations of Judgement* are:

Bold design, Constant Practice and Frequent Mistakes.

If you wish to tell stories you must try to do it, taking a difficult big theme and going at it hard. One may come a purler, or go west of the flag, but the attempt will teach, & the attempt must be made again, ribs gone or not, till you learn how to do it, or that it is not really a thing that is best for you. Even so, the effort will have been helpful in many ways.

[1] The *OED* gives "Ropy or Ropey: of poor quality, inferior, bad (1942)"; and "Tatty: Tattered, shabby, tawdry (1933)".

[2] This is one of the times when I regret that none of my letters survived. I cannot remember the poet's name! ANS.

[3] The Welsh Triads. In ancient Welsh literature these were verses on traditional subjects, such subjects or statements being arranged in groups of three.

47¹

...You always write with genius about music & musicians that delight you: and I loved to hear of your Wagner time & of your new partner. In writing, one sometimes meets a man of genius, a fellow who makes one say: "He has it ... He will knock down the bars & let some light in," and then, what joy when he ups & does it.

Excellence is rare, however, even in the very good. As a terrible Spanish proverb says, "There are more days than sausages".

When I was very little, I used to hear much about the Kabul rising, when Afghans murdered all the members of the English Embassy (some hundred of staff & officers & guards) but latterly I have been reading that not all were killed, because there were lots of children among them & fair-haired & comely; so that to this day there are lots of English looking Afghans, who are survivors & do not know what their real names were, but were saved from slaughter, & brought up as Afghans & servants of the Prophet.

The Afghans were in time a bit tamed by their Amir Abdurrahman, whose ways suited the country, which is mostly rocky. He had an English governess for his children, & once told her "I'd like to kill all the fools in this foul den of my Kingdom." She said "Even if you did, there would still be one fool left." It took him some time to see what she meant, but when he saw the point he yelled with laughter & praised her.

472

. . . I expect you will find even the shadow of California, circa 1900, exciting.

Rabelais has a naughty proverb, "Even the shadow of an abbey-spire is fruitful;" (hinting at a failure of discipline in the Abbot), and the shadow of California in 1900 would be the shadow of violent wild life in a sunny, gambler's paradise.

Old San Francisco, the centre of this, was wrecked by earthquake in 1906 & then nearly wiped out by an appalling fire: and what had been strange & wild became legend.

There were terrible tales of an underground China town, perhaps 7 storeys of cellars deep, where what went on is shocking even as fiction.

Then, in the Bay, where the ships came for grain & fruits & timbers, the crimps lay in wait for the ship as she came in, and boarded her, in armed gangs, & took her crew by force (or by temptation of alcohol) & then sold the men for 40 dollars a man to a ship eager to sail elsewhere.

This went on until the Earthquake: and so did the thieves' paradise, the Barbary Coast, as it was called, where any seaman coming ashore, or any landsman going unwarily, might be slugged or drugged & sold as a sailor at any time of day or night.

SF—"Frisco"—was a live burg then, in need of the Last Judgement that it got.

I did not see SF in its wild days, but I have been there 3 or 4 times since; and the Barbary Coast was a quiet place of ice-cream parlours, and Dreamy Shaves only 15 cents, & the cheap dentistry with Painless Extraction.

A "Conway" of my time had a cigar-store there at the earthquake time, & news of the city's doings used to come thro to me, but the disaster wiped him out I think; or perhaps he got sold for 40 dollars:

I never heard. If you got slipped a Micky Finn, the Micky Finn was sometimes very strong, & the taker never woke.

473

... When I first saw SF harbour, the Alcatraz Island was a government building: it looked like a huge battleship, very splendid. When I next saw it, it was a prison, and was called "Al Capone Island" from its chief prisoner, a Chicago gangster, who is very likely now buried there.

Sir F. Drake must have known the harbour, but the general view is that he careened and re-fitted his ship in another inlet a few miles S & W from SF, which I have been near, but not actually to. This was in his circumnavigation voyage, when he was all crusted with Spanish plunder, & a long long way from home. There are some whitish cliffs where he careened the *Golden Hind*, which reminded people of Dover Cliffs: so they called the place Nova Albion & took possession of it for Q Elizabeth. These cliffs are not as high as Dover, but they help still to identify the place.

... My thanks for your enchanting letter about Mr Walton's[1] work.

The new mind has to quote Scripture to itself:

"Marvel not, if the world hate you." Any new view, any new method, will be assailed.

If the new mind does not know any Scripture, there is a proverb (from the Balkans) that is more consoling, & very fine: "The dogs bark: but the caravan passes."

Unfortunately, in modern times, artists are more in special compartments than formerly: they seldom meet & work with artists of other arts than their own, & do not often know or practise other arts. I once had the great privilege of working with Holst, but that experience showed me how utterly the arts need each other & are bettered by each other: and how utterly loutish I remain, only doddering along with some clumsy verses, or dull prose, while the Spirit of the Vale of Tempe, clothed like April, divinely pipes to the spirit to awake awake!

1 Sir William Walton (1902–83), the distinguished English composer (knighted in 1951).

474

. . . I have a kind of dread that your China Tea may be drawing to an end, & I ask you therefore, please, may I replenish? So, will you, dear Carpenter, sound the well, & let me know?

I had an astronomer here long ago, who gave me a view of the size of the universe by a lively illustration. Since he gave it, I have felt "chawed up considerable small", like the man in Dickens (or in my memory as Dickens, a very different thing).

He sat, where you sat when you first came here, & he said: "Where I sit represents the sun. Now, to my left, the river there (say 80 yards away) represents the outermost planet about the size of a pea, at his extremest distance, of an 80 yards radius. Now where do you suppose the nearest fixed star would be?"

I said, in my cheerful way, "I suppose about at Abear's Farm there" (say 1500 yards).

"No," he said. "About New York City."

I am so glad to hear that you like Holst, & had met & liked his daughter. He was the moving spirit in getting the play done in Canterbury Cathedral, 36 years ago;[1] & I have the baton he conducted with, which I must give to you, my dear dear girl, when next you come.

He conducted his Quire, of the Heavenly Host, & was in all ways a living marvel of fun and friendship, & fervour for any triumph of art. What I had to offer to the cause seemed chawed up considerable small.

Still . . . I can tell you these things, & it is strange to think that nobody else can, in just this way, so that what I offer, is, in its way, unique & only comes to you, or can come from me, so this cheers me up much bigger.

But before I begin to swagger, let me say that I hope you *may* be coming hither not too long hence? What chance of that?

I am reading Old Nosey again, the D of W, old Blue Nose, his Peninsular Letters: a marvel of a man, who in earlier days had been a very choice violinist.

[1] JM's *The Coming of Christ*: see Letter 39.

475

. . . The other day, reading about the Hundred Days, I came upon a mention of the Gloucestershire Regiment, the old 28th.

Perhaps some of the Officers were at the Duchess of Richmond's

Ball, but anyway the 28th were in Brussels on the 15th June, 1815, waiting for already too long delayed orders to move South. At 4.30 a.m. on the 16th they stood to arms from where they had slept in the streets & marched out of Brussels to the tune of one of Thomas Moore's Irish melodies: "The young May moon is beaming, love . . ."

I send you a suggestion of the time. [He wrote out the melody.] The verses are light enough:

> The young May moon is beaming, love,
> The glow-worm's lamp is gleaming, love
> How sweet to roam thro Morna's grove
> When the drowsy world is dreaming, love.

The tune may be traditional, I do not know. I suppose the Regimental Band Master adapted it to a quick-step for drums & fifes.

The Regt marched 18 miles in a hot day, the 16th, to Quatre Bras, where they were in tall rye, then usual in Belgium, 6 feet tall, in full furious fight with Ney, before 3 p.m.

I thought that perhaps you, the dear daughter of Gloucestershire, might like to have the tune & the suggestion of the words.

Thomas Hardy in *The Dynasts* mentions the 28th, marching out, but not the tune they marched to. The thing touched me very deeply, for they had a fearful time at Quatre Bras, & worse on the 18th at Waterloo, where they were rather to the L of La Haie Sainte, near the English Centre, where Picton was killed (well to the L of the Belgian Lion). Moore says that the tune to which his words went was that of a song "The dandy O", some glimmering of which song I seem somehow to have in what I call my mind, tho it is liker a kind of ragbag.

Moore refers us to some work that I have not seen for an account of Morna's Grove. It sounds like a place in Macpherson's *Ossian*, where somebody drank the wine of death from getting the bright bronze too heavily on his crumpet.

. . . But about Astronomy & Morna's Grove. RLS [Robert Louis Stevenson] wrote feelingly about the difficulties of Astronomy in Literature:

"How troublesome the moon is."

You will see, above, how T. Moore says how sweet it might be to rove in Morna's Grove when all others are asleep under the young May moon. The young May moon would be visible soon after sunset, not for very long. Even late in May a young moon would not be up very late, & it may well be that Morna's Grove would be rather like the *Bounty*, with lots of men saying, each of them, "I do desire we may be better strangers."

... She [the *Bounty*] was a tiny thing, & people were jammed together in her and every word uttered on board was always overheard by somebody, and repeated falsely, so as to be overheard by everybody. It must have been so. R. L. Stevenson ought to have remembered this in writing *Treasure Island*, for the *Hispaniola* was smaller than the *Bounty*, a good deal; nothing could have been secret in her.[1]

[1] See also Letter 237.

476

... The other day, I sent you a little cutting showing the American replica of the *Bounty*[1] about which I meant to ask you a question.

I noticed that her fore & main topsail yards were both hoisted (the 2nd yards from the water-line upwards) though the sails were not set. This struck me as odd in any ship, but impossible in a ship in Naval command.

It occurred to me that the oddness may have been a part of the mutiny: that in the script of the film Bligh may have ordered hands to square the yards, & the hands may have said that they had squared enough yards, thank him kindly, & let him square them himself.

Please, was there any such moment in your film?

The appearance of the yards shocked me, for the yards, when not sailing the ship, are lowered & squared, the sails furled & perhaps unbent.

It is possible that for some reason the sailors who sailed the ship for the film were at dinner or doing some other film, & that the actors didn't feel quite up to meddling with the gear: but the matter puzzled me. I suppose that the topsail yards would have weighed about ½ a ton each, which is a weight that does damage if it suddenly falls from a height onto a working upper deck, where a film is being done. If you can remember the events of the film, please, will you tell me if the yards were mentioned at all.

[1] The model built at Hollywood for the first film of *The Mutiny on the Bounty*. Many years before, in California, JM had seen and been much impressed by the *Bounty* model.

477

... Someone was here the other day telling a tale of Wellington, in Spain about 1812. Wellington suddenly found that his army was not concentrated, & that the French were advancing in force to scupper him.

He sent a most urgent call to the Light Division to come in at once from its exposed situation, & stamped (& very likely swore) till it was there.

When Craufurd,[1] its Comm[r], reported next morning, he said, "Well, here you are at last." Craufurd said, "O yes, Sir: all was well; I was in no danger whatever."

Wellington said, "I'm not talking about you. I WAS!"

Craufurd just let the wind blow; and when W left the room, he remarked, "He's —— crusty this morning."

[1] Major-General Robert Craufurd, commanding the Light Division, joined Wellington after the battle of Talavera, having marched sixty-two miles in twenty-six hours.

478

... It is so kind of you to take an interest in things that I study.

Many years ago, I tried to get to know something about Napoleon; & from this came to know Wellington: & of late have studied W rather more than N: & have come to admire him much more, as a genius & a gentleman.

Napoleon was a genius who saw that any great national impulse is itself genius, & with proper weapons can impose itself anywhere. He gave the French Revolution proper weapons, & the order that such weapons demand, military order, and at once almost was Ruler of France and Dictator to Europe.

He was not a gentleman, and concluded that genius would suffice, if coupled with military order. He did certain appalling things; but did also, surely, maintain what social good the Revolution had started.

Wellington was a gentleman, with an unusual instinct for War, and an honesty & probity in making all his military service remarkable. As a regimental officer (in a drunken time) he made the 33rd Foot the one faultless battalion in the Br. Army, then (I fear) the by-word & the mockery of all the world.

Going early to India, parts of this Army, under him, broke the French effort to seize India, & brought India to be mainly ours to direct.

When he & Napoleon were both about 40 years old, Napoleon made his infamous grab at Spain; & soon after this W was sent to Portugal, and left in Portugal to out-do and defeat the French & drive them from the Peninsula.

Consider, on the one hand: *Napoleon*, Ruler of France, Dictator of Europe, able to order all France, Italy, Belgium & much of Germany, to send him what troops he needed; & having his Brother a King in Spain, & perhaps 160,000 troops in Spain.

And on the other hand: *Wellington* in Portugal, dumped into Portugal, with but 20,000 men, to hold Portugal, & save Spain from her oppressors, and just to do it, & not be a bother.

479

... I wish that I could so mend my pens that I could write better poetry, or even better letters to darling you;[1] but pens cannot be so mended, but I do know a little about the pleasure of an improved tool to work with, such as a new, sharp, sparkling marline spike, or a chisel or plane, really sharp, or a fine drill that didn't bend, or a saw that I had toothed up with a file or 2. Still the results of these were not like music, even to unmusical me.

[1] My Gagliano violin had been re-set and overhauled, and was much improved. ANS

480

... Thank you for your praise of my lett about Boney & Old Nosey (or Blue Nose).

I would like to return to these thrilling themes, presently, if they would not weary you. You see, I met, in my childhood, people who had been scared by Boney, & saved by Old Blue Nose. Several men were still alive who had fought at Waterloo: & all still felt indebted to Blücher; & Blücher shoes & Wellington boots were still in use.

The state of England at that time was somewhat odd. We had been terrified by the French Revolution, & forced by that terror into repressions, and into war all over the place. We were at war in India & the East Indies (about 7 months' sea journey from here), & in most parts of Europe, the West Indies & the African coast as well. We had allies in these far parts, who had to be paid to keep the war going, & would not accept paper money. We had to send weapons, powder, or silver or gold. We could make the English at home accept paper, and did so, but I gather that the English had the sense to see that paper wasn't quite quite. Even so, gold & silver were scarce here: the precious metals went to keep the foreign wars going, & a scarcity of these metals made all our foreign payments precarious & uncertain.

Wellington, in Portugal, for *years*, called out for money—silver or gold—to buy the necessaries for his 30,000 men, & for the 20 or 30,000 Portuguese whom he was training. He never had enough money: never: for those at home were pressed by those at home, who had newspapers at their command: and the money went as the press clamoured, to wild-cat schemes that didn't prosper: & Wellington had to do as he could. Portugal had no industries, to speak of, save agriculture & vineyards. Spain, at first, yielded no help to the English cause. She was in trouble, a cleft-stick trouble, of her own.

This last sentence of the fore-going seems (& is) a shade sudden & odd, but I leave it in.

If you still go on with your Astronomy, do look West on any clear night this week, to see Venus in splendour. It is a last quarter moon, so she has no competitor, & will be on view for some days more.

I suppose she will last our time, but with men hoping to pollute her with rockets & clockwork who can tell?

481

. . . I see the planet Venus from my bed every night, until about midnight, though this is only if I open my eyes, which I do not always do in bed.

. . . You ask: did I ever wear a pair of Blücher shoes?

Yes, I did, in boyhood, have a pair. They were low, rather heavy shoes, strongly made for rough country, but not hob-nailed. I thought them unpleasing things for running, football, walking, cricket, climbing of trees etc, duds in fact; & I daresay mine were among the last ever worn.

Wellington boots I began to use on the *Conway*. Ours were the knee gum-boots known as sea-boots; tho, later, I had, also, a pair of leather sea-boots, Wellington in cut, & no good at all.

Wellington wore *his* boots *over* his trowsers, & I expect that the outer knee-caps flexed back, when his knee bent in riding, to keep rain from filling his boot.

His Dragoon regiments wore their Wellingtons *under* their trowsers; and many Bucks and Bloods, who had a mind to impress folk, wore theirs *under* their trowsers and caused the trowsers to fit tightly to the boot, by a strap that came under the boot & made a tight fit.

At sea, sailors always wore their sea-boots *under* their oilskin trowsers, but *over* their other trowsers, if they had any. Often they had no other, or would not pamper their flesh by wearing two pairs.

Oilskin trowsers were always lashed tight over the boots by rope-yarns, which were cut when the men undressed, if they did undress in sea-boot weather; often they didn't.

One of Old Nosey's Portuguese regiments had only trowsers for 400 of its 800 men. This 400 had only one garment apiece, a British infantry greatcoat, reaching below the knee, and held to the waist by a belt. These were the admired men, for the coats were uniform & looked well.

The Wellington Coat, now obsolete, was like a sailor's P-jacket,[1] cut short at the knee, or a shade above. (The P stood for Pilot.)

[1] More usually spelt "Pea-jacket".

482

... As it seems almost to be the Spring now I have begun to count the daisies. In the old time, men told me that Spring had not come till one could cover 9 daisy heads in the grass with one foot.

At present, I can, in one place, cover two, so things are improving.

Next week, with certain difficulties in the post, I know not when I shall be writing, but this letter brings you my blessing, & these cards of the *Siren* & the *Palgrave*. Both vessels were said to be built on the dimensions given for Noah's Ark, though the *Palgrave* was at least twice the *Siren's* size.

The "cubit" (you will know) is a somewhat doubtful measure.

The *Siren*, I would say, was the most beautiful full-rigged ship I ever saw; & I wish that she had survived to come to Greenwich, & be trodden on by two dear friends on Aug. 16th. You would have *loved* her exquisite lines, her rake, & that divine bow.

483

... I have given some thought to the opening of *The Tempest*; & how the Globe presented it.

They had the house as dark as might be, & men upstairs behind the scenes rolling cannon-balls down wooden slides, & waggling thin sheets of metal, to make thunder, while others did riskier things (still upstairs) with squibs, for lightning.

They had some supers on the stage shouting "Yo ho. Heave & bestir her" etc etc, & a lot of angry courtiers trying to make the audience know that the ship carried a noble lord, & was in peril.

As far as the seamanship went, the crew were shortening sail, & getting the topmast down: the storm having just begun. One minute later they were trying to lie-to, the storm being appalling; & one minute later the ship split having seemingly run ashore, & this in the Mediterranean, where everyone must have known exactly where the ship was, & must have had at least 2 anchors ready for letting go.

The Master, who leaves the Boatswain in charge, had some excuse, for he was probably dressing to play another part a couple of minutes later.

The fo'c's'le hands seem to have been much as usual when of English origin. Nothing could be truer to type than the Boatswain, Stephano etc.

. . . I have never practised magic myself, as magic, but it seems to me to be a use of the imagination like (in some ways) to writing or painting. Some have thought that I did once practise magic, but it is not so. Yeats did a little in that way at one time, & helped to raise the devil (in Dublin) once. And I have heard of such tricks from scholars of magical practice in Red Indian tribes. There are powers that can be summoned, very very terrible powers, that exact penalties for their favours.

In Edinburgh Museum there are some appalling exhibits of relics of wicked magic; and these must at one time have been used for evil, for very dreadful evil.

The negroes in the Southern States practise a good deal of magic, either to harm people, or to find an answer to some problem; & I have been assured that for a dollar will ask their hoodoo for the answer to a problem that besets a white: who pinched the watch; who took those water-melons: who got all them li'l pigs etc.

484

. . . I thank you for your letter with the glad news that you had a little freedom, & a sunny day for it also.

"This," as George Meredith says (of something else), "this approaches felicity."

But perhaps your next letter will tell me that you are just off to play in Timbuctoo for the Midsummer Festival.

Will you have a foreign visit this summer?

I am sending you a *Sea Letter*[1] from San Francisco, which will remind you, I hope, of Aug. the 16th. It has a photograph of the *Wanderer*, as she was, when in Oregon, loading those marvellous pine-trees, long ago. I did not know of this photograph, & perhaps the collection may have others.

There is also a nice view of the upper deck of the *Bermuda*. This will show you the sort of deck ships came to have, before sail was extinguished. I am glad that I saw a finer show, of the splendid peak achieved before steam conquered.

The *Bermuda* was Clyde-built, and had many new devices, which made for cheapness, I suppose, but not for looks. She had bathrooms for her fo'c's'le hands: a splendid thing; but I never could abide these battens instead of ratlines,[2] nor her poor bald head, where men had once set royals & skysails & perhaps even moonsails; & the house-flag, over all, brave boys, as the ship towed up the bay.

[1] A periodical published by the San Francisco Maritime Museum.

[2] Ratlines: small lines of rope running horizontally across the shrouds of a sailing-ship and used as steps for climbing the rigging. JM objected to their replacement by wooden battens.

485

... When the *Wanderer* was at Port Blakeney, the place was all fragrant with new-cut pine plank from the marvellous pine-trees of Oregon, just laid low by the murderers of the forest. The trees were truly marvels of beauty: and the slaughterers hacked them, & chopped them, & wasted them & made many into planks; & the saws were at it all the time & a sort of fragrant soul of pine-forest sweetened the desolation for miles.

I saw many of these noble trees being discharged at Liverpool; & saw, also, many & many a marvellous spar, a royal & skysail spar, towering up above many a ship, in a way never before seen, and now not ever seen.

The Oregon ports, like San Francisco, were feared by all, for there the crimps lived, who slipped the unwary, or the not wary enough, a Micky Finn, or K.O. drop, & sold the unconscious body (sometimes a corpse) for as much as 40 dollars to a Captain in need of a crew.

When the unconscious bodies recovered sense, they might be out at sea, out of sight of land, in some hard-case ship all undermanned, bound to a port 4 or 6 months away, with no clothes save what they wore, & perhaps no knowledge whatsoever of ship or sailing.

Yet I lived to see all this Micky Finning utterly done away with, & the ships, too.

486

. . . I wore your pin, my dear, as I said, but I could not get it into the furled body or knot of the tie, & it was therefore nearer my heart than what I suppose to be my gizzard, so please be not vexed.

The speech was nothing. I asked the students to speak 2 Shakespeare sonnets, one of which, 146—"Poor Soul" etc—was grievously misprinted by the scoundrel who stole the script & printed it . . .

. . . The other sonnet spoken was "Tired with all these" [Sonnet 56] & the 2 sonnets seem to me to be WS his best sonnets, & the best sonnets now in the world: but both are from a great afflicted heart, and I suppose youth would have liked something cheerier.

Tho in the poor soul sonnet WS suggests a sublime adventuring on, & in the other he tells of what kept himself going.

I don't think that that was a lady, but a spiritual power such as no other man has ever had in such glory & such variety; and that consoled and could not lightly be left.

487

. . . The speaking of the sonnets was not bad: indeed, none of it was bad. The general level was good, but I felt that the young people were all very nervous & (as usual) the men were much more nervy than the women. The women were all in their best go-ashores (and rather glad of a chance to show these, perhaps) & that (as always) gave them a comfort; & they beat the men, but I thought that 1 of the men ran her close (ran the actual winner close). I did not hear quite all of them.

I do not like many of the sonnets very much, but about 5 or 6 are superb; & a lot of them have some wonderful line or lines; he being a poet of power; none, ever, with more.

. . . I venture to send this:[1] please keep it, if you find it interesting.

I don't care about it myself, for it seems to me to make the poetry less poetical: and I don't care for the cut of the young dandy's jib, tho I must say that Hilliard's clever use of the rose leaves, on the lad's tights, is most effective.

[1] A coloured reproduction of Nicholas Hilliard's *A Youth leaning against a tree among roses.*

488

. . . Please will you tell me, if I ever sent you a copy of a little book called *A Wonderful Ghost Story* by a portrait painter, Thomas Heaphy, the Younger, 1858?[1]

His story deeply moved Charles Dickens (& many many others), and stands by itself among ghost-stories.

I do not know his paintings, but the RA people have some of his work at Burlington House, I believe: perhaps in their Diploma Gallery.

I ask, if I have sent it to you, for, in a way, you see, you are my Diploma Gallery, & when I like, or have liked, a book very much, I like to send it to you, being so sure of a response: & I have very likely sent it to you.

Academicians, when elected, send a work of theirs to the Diploma Gallery, where the big Leonardo cartoon used to hang.

I ask you this, for I found, this morning, a typed copy of the little book, now pretty rare, & I thought at once . . . "Did I send this to Reyna or only meant to and didn't?"

I prythee, sweetheart, enlighten (& forgive) the darkness of your friend on this point.

[1] Heaphy, Thomas, the younger (1813–73). Portrait and subject painter and writer. His "Mr. H—'s own Narrative" was first published in the magazine *All the Year Round* in 1861, and later re-published in separate form as *A Wonderful Ghost Story* with letters to the author from Charles Dickens.

489

. . . I send the Heaphy story. I hope that it will interest you & delight you.

Heaphy's wife lived in Oxford I believe, after her husband died, and I have met those who knew her.

It is a very strange tale, and moved Charles Dickens profoundly.

I have not seen any of Heaphy's portraits, to my knowledge, but the Academy people have some. Somebody, perhaps, still has the portrait of the Lady. It would be interesting to see that.

I once knew, for a little while, the lad I call HB in *New Chum*: a wonderful lad, who had the Second Sight. Heaphy had some visionary power, & was a Seer, but perhaps not what is called Second Sight. Dear, I do hope that you will hang the book in your Diploma Gallery.

490

. . . I hope that you are not in any civil war or revolution up in the North.

Things are peaceable here, & letters dribble through, but not newspapers; however the radio tells us the chief events: Senator Goldwater in America; & strangled ladies in garages in England.

I am now without a House-keeper; & at the moment, alas, I cannot arrange our hoped-for meeting in London in August.

This I shall still hope for, but the House-keepers are very scarce: I have dreadful fear that they are all being strangled & then hidden in garages, by some fiend in human shape.

> Ripper, thy murders check
> Red Hand, be not so stormy
> Such dames would cook my brek
> And do my dinner for me.

491

. . . At this point, thinking of the ghost story, I think of a queer ghost that Dickens saw in a dream: John Forster[1] tells the story in Dickens' words, from a letter dated (seemingly) May 30 1863.

"I dreamed that I saw a lady in a red shawl, with her back towards me, whom I supposed to be E.[2]

"On her turning round, I found that I didn't know her, and she said: 'I am Miss Napier.'

"All the time I was dressing, I thought, what a preposterous thing to have so very distinct a dream about . . . and why Miss Napier? for I never heard of any Miss Napier.

"That same night I read . . . (meaning, gave a Public Reading)

"After the reading came into my retiring-room Mary Boyle & her brother, and *the* lady in the red shawl, whom they presented as Miss Napier."

[1] John Forster (1812–76) edited the *Daily News* (1846) and *The Examiner* (1847–55); he published a life of his friend, Charles Dickens (1872–74). The *Daily News* was founded and, for a while, edited by Dickens.

[2] Probably the actress Ellen Ternan who became Dickens's mistress after he separated from his wife in 1858.

492

. . . When NYC is mighty hot, it can be pretty nearly unendurable; dogs, horses and men dropping dead all over the place: as I so often saw of old. (Not the women, for perhaps they dressed more wisely & took fewer risks, & wore sombreros & used sunshades.)

So I suppose the Hudson is still bearing the human relics out to sea, out out vile candles, with the ebbtide, & the hot hot prevalent Westerly.

I minded the nights more than the days: the nights could be frightful, from the mosquitoes.

In the days, I used to drink cold water: always the good cold Croton water; always the best drink in heat.

. . . Arizona is the State that has most moved me by its savagery, its wonder, its beauty. I know nothing in the least like it.

There is a place in it called Yuma, said to be the hottest in all America. I doubt this, but it is hot enough. It used to be said that when a bad man died in Yuma, as they frequently did, he always came back for his blanket.

493

. . . This week's letter from you, here on the 10th (yesterday) was a special joy to me, & made my old heart feel that you had come-in and tidied the place up, & left a wondrous cake for me in the embers of the hearth.

. . . Mr Heaphy's story is an undoubted true tale of fact; and I do not doubt that the portrait that he painted did save the reason of the bereaved Father, & it may even still exist.

I do not doubt that Mr Heaphy was a partial seer; like many people whom I used to meet in Ireland, he seems never to have quite known which people in his world were real, and which were spirits visible to his vision.

If you ever are in London, and free, I expect that you could see his work, or some of it at Burlington House. They have some of it there still, so Munnings[1] told me; a portrait or two, probably.

[1] Sir Alfred Munnings (1878–1959), President of the Royal Academy, 1944–9.

494

... From your summary of the monologue of the English lady showing her garden, I would say it is one of the triumphs of Miss Ruth Draper,[1] an American *diseuse* of genius. But her work was not in verse; only the perfection of skill and certainty. She had a wonderful study of that kind in her repertory: & if it be not that one, it must be some imitation of it. Her very best studies were of American types, native or Irish-American: most deeply felt (or comic).

She is no longer living, I think.

... Mdme Yvette Guilbert, in France, gave studies deeper & more wonderful, but I know of no English diseuse of such variety & charm.

[1] Ruth Draper (1884–1956), an American actress, unsurpassed in her day as a solo performer. The sketch mentioned by ANS is certainly one of hers.

495

... Toulouse-Lautrec may well have painted Mdme Guilbert in her great glory of yellow dress & long black gloves. She would have been a star of his time, & a queen in his world.

She was truly a genius, & he was much in the theatrical world, then, looking for his themes; I have not seen the portrait.

There has been no-one so great in her particular work, no-one with such a range, such power, such perfection. She could do wonderful things, religious things, & then uproarious & merry & terrible things, & could become a child or a maenad at a moment's notice.

An old man trained her, I believe, & he must have had genius, surely, to perceive what wonders she could do. I have seen & heard no-one to compare with her, for a moment.

496

... I have been twice to Yuma: & the tale of Yuma is true, dearest: one longs to go back, for other reasons than one's blanket.[1]

... I am glad that you like the *Arizona* issues. I kept thinking, when I was out there, "This is where the Aztecs came from. Out of this marvel those marvels came with their bows & conquered all of

Mexico & built great temples & sacrificed most bloodily & frightfully thousands of men, literally thousands, yet made a beauty such as no other land had seen before war, Spaniards, & small-pox exterminated them."

We know it chiefly from Spanish sources; & I wonder if you know what Bernal Diaz of Castille wrote about it, after seeing its glory in all its blood, and filling its ruin with all its carrion.

¹ See Letter 492.

❀

497

. . . Bernal Diaz was a young man of good family, who went with Cortez, a soldier of fortune, a very brave, crafty scoundrel, who was bent on his own advancement by courage & cunning. Diaz was often nearly killed, & nearly dead of fatigue & cold & wounds; & would have been eaten by Indians, who had the pots, the pepper & tomatoes all ready for his joints, had not Cortez been the cunning savage that he was.

He saw the appalling cannibal Aztec civilisation of art & beauty & handicraft, and the worship of terrible gods, needing blood from men & children daily & insisting on sodomy in their priests: it is an incredible story, told by one who saw it all & was in it all.

❀

498

. . . I venture to send . . . another Arizona paper, showing some of the designs of Indian crafts.

But these Indian crafts are uncanny widenings of life, & men who go among the Indians do not readily go back to white men, nor did the white women carried away by Indian raiders.

. . . I send you with this a card, said to contain the Rules of a Cornish Lodging House, but I know not where: but perhaps Falmouth, Truro, Redruth, or Wadebridge; a place of some resort: or Fowey.

Onion-sellers from Jersey or Brittany used to wander all S. Cornwall: & I judge, slept thus.

> *Words of an Old Cornish Signboard*
> RULES OF
> THIS LODGING HOUSE

Fourpence a night for bed
Sixpence with Supper
No more than three to sleep in one bed
No beer allowed in the kitchen
No smoking when in bed
No Clothes to be washed on Sunday
No boots to be worn in bed
No dogs allowed upstairs
No gambling or fighting here
No extra charge for Luggage
No Razor Grinders taken in
Organ Grinders to sleep in the attick.

by
IZIKIAH O' DONIVIAN
Donkeys, Chaises, Handcarts, & Durries
LET ON HIRE
MANGLING DONE HERE

I do back all the rules about the Bed: not more than 3 in any one Bed: no smoking in Bed: no boots in Bed. What wd a bed be with 4 in it, one smoking, & 1 in boots?

The Boots question was a vexed question for many of the Lodgers were travelling men, needing their boots, well-nailed & iron toed, for the roads, & liking to wear them in bed, lest they should be stolen in the night, as otherwise they would very likely be. If one wore them in bed, one would feel the thief, & with one good kick defeat the wicked felon.

I remember reading of one man who tried sleeping with his boots tied round his neck, but you see, this was not clean potato: it was wearing the boots in bed: and besides, unavailing, for the thieves could get them away without waking the wearer. The roads brought one some very odd bed-fellows.

Please, do you know what a Durry was? I judge it to be a *Dory*, or flat-bottomed small one-scull scow, in wh one could visit one's (or someone else's) lobster-pots in the bay.

In the rather crowded beds at Mr Squeer's School, Brooks' Bed was held to be full up with four boys in it.

I think that 3 men would be a full dose for most beds; & perhaps with only 3 the two first comers would expect the 3rd to sleep with his head at the foot & his feet up at the pillow.

In this arrangement, anybody wearing boots would come in for criticism.

The card seems to have been of a superior or Fourpenny Lodging.

In London, there were Twopenny Doss-Houses, where one had a share of a stove before going upstairs to bed.

There was a strange, vivid book, long since, by a man called Mayhew [*London Labour and the London Poor*, 1861–2], about the incredible lives of the incredibly poor in an incredible London. Bad as London was, I know that Liverpool then was far worse, & charged a penny for lying on the floor if there was a floor.

499

. . . Before I can send you Bernal Diaz, I have to find a missing vital volume; and, alas, even so, some child of Belial, this time not my own self, has removed some maps from another volume, so here, in pit of darkness, I sit like Job, & would very likely scrape myself with potsherds, if there were any to hand.

Still, losses, or some such, can be made good, by valiant effort, in not too long time . . . please . . .

I have been re-reading him; & have been marvelling again, how America was peopled, in the remote undated past.

It is a vast double land, & not much has been, or can yet have been, searched by archaeologists; but the general feeling is, that the Main source of Man in all America has been the Alaskan Tip, where Behring Straits makes a 50 mile gap from the Tip of Siberia, a gap dotted with islands, & frozen over in winter, but always unfriendly to Man, & unfriendly in both shores. Over this gap, Asiatics of an Eskimo type, short, powerful, adaptable, pretty savage chaps, are supposed to have begun the adventure, in very remote times.

But at some other remote times 2 or even 3, other types, 2 of them tall, & big, & savage, the other small & savage, seem, somehow to have got going, somehow, & kind of complicated matters.

When, about 1517 or so, bodies of Spaniards came exploring for gold & slaves in the Gulf of Mexico, all central America was densely populated by a highly savage, highly military invading, enslaving, nation of newcomers, the Aztecs, who could build in stone, & had a script of sorts, & amazing crafts, as well as a ferocity & bestiality not often known. They were worshippers & wholesale sacrificers to appalling gods; & ate religious feasts of the people sacrificed; & fattened multitudes for these feasts, to which they looked forward. This cannibalism existed wherever the Aztecs ruled. The priests of these gods had to be sodomites; & sodomy was much practised everywhere in the land, perhaps among the young men of war who may not have been allowed to marry until they qualified as braves.

The braves, even the sodomites, were prone to make mistresses of the women they took in war, and all Mexico swarmed with people, dominant Aztecs, or "Mexicans", and writhing subjects, expecting to be fattened, sacrificed & eaten.

It is thought that all N America & Canada together held about 750,000 hunter & rover Indians, while central America held about 4 million of these slaughterers & their prey. This about 1520 AD.

Within a few years of landing in Mexico, the Spaniards had depopulated many districts, by war, slavery, & small-pox. Mexico was in ruins, heaped with dead & wounded people; & central America was a collection of savage rebels, who found the Spaniards hateful alive, & indigestible & unpleasant when cooked. "Sour," they said.

This note of mine seems to have dwelt upon unpleasing people: cannibals etc.

It calls to mind an old tale of a South Sea Islander who saw an English child being bathed by its parents (before bed). The Islander watched with surprise, and made the comment, "There was no need for all that washing: we should have just cooked the child straight away."

The Mexicans had many little dogs that they ate, but may have been "hungry for man", as the S. Sea Islanders often were; for they had no horses, cows, pigs, or sheep, only little dogs & poultry. To a religious Mexican the sight of a plump unbeliever may have been too too altogether.

Try, soon, to rest a little: it is a good thing to rest. Sleep, good air, good water & good bells: are 4 of life's blessings, all of which I wish you.

500

... I thank you for your kind note & the portrait of Mdme Guilbert.[1]

This shows the famous yellow costume, with black shoulder-knots & long black gloves, coming well above the elbows; she was then at the height of her glory, where she remained, without rival, a peerless wonder.

I saw her then, I cannot remember where; perhaps in New York; but it was much later when I really saw what she could do: she was improved; her range was marvellous; her grace & power inimitable; & herself so great, so kind, so full of good affections & generosities.

She was of the type that the French call the Vraie Gauloise, the type of Gaul described by Caesar, large, golden impulsive, winning, merry & great-hearted. It is not common in France, but one used to meet it, & welcome it (& be welcomed by it); it is a very splendid type; & to be noticed whenever it appears.

[1] Toulouse-Lautrec's portrait of Yvette Guilbert taking a curtain-call is at the Museum of Art, Rhode Island School of Design, Providence R.I. See Letter 495.

501

... I am sending with this a book or two, that may help a little to show you the kind of thing that Mexico sprang from; & a note about Sir F Drake, well worth reading. I have been near to his Bay, in California, but not into it; save in thought. He was there, with big thoughts, all those thousands of miles from home, & one cannot but think of him with wonder.

The Indians in Diaz's time had no horses, & had never seen horses till the Spaniards brought them: & then they thought that the horseman was a kind of twin, that could divide into two selves, at will. This was a great asset in the Spaniards' hands; horses and gunpowder were too much for the Aztecs, though they faced both with much courage.

A few hundred men, & the germ of small-pox, destroyed the Aztec rule. Only about 5 or 600 Spaniards were killed in all the war, as far as one can gather.

In the pamphlet, you will see the kind of land, & bird, & beast & reptile that the Aztecs knew, & the Spaniards had to learn, but the fruits & flowers & colours are not shown, nor the scents diffused, nor the marvel of variety suggested.

The alligator was a danger in the Mexico Rivers. I never saw an alligator in Arizona.

I shall hope to send some of the Bernal Diaz at the end of the week.

The account of the first seeing of Mexico is (to me) amazing: & all the fearful account of peril, crime, greed, treachery & savagery, until the first disaster, is a wonderful story: then the fighting back, to the destruction of Mexico, is another wonder.

These two tales, in the first 2 volumes will (I feel sure) thrill & move you. Later, perhaps, you will sicken of the never-ending war, the never-ceasing treachery, cruelty, murder & devilry on both sides.

Cortez, one must admit, was a very brave man, without any limit to his greed: rather like one of Napoleon's generals, Masséna, shall we say?

I suppose that he did dis-people most of Mexico, & Central America, what with war & small-pox.

He was never in Darien, as in Keats's sonnet.[1] That was Balboa; Cortez was "stout" enough, that is stout-hearted, but never in Darien.

His eagle eyes wd not have cared 2d about the Pacific, unless he had seen some gold there: & even then, it would have to be good gold, real sizeable blobs & bars of it.

[1] The sonnet "On first looking into Chapman's Homer": as JM says, it was not Cortez who "stared at the Pacific", but Vasco Nuñez de Balboa.

502

. . . I thank you for telling me of your enforced rest: and am glad to think that you have a rest; & that you take it, being so wise.

Rest is one of the things that gives a liberation; rest of some sort must be the source of most liberation.

I think that life culminates in intense life; it is a height of life to which one has a rare access, of perceiving eternal things.

Death is a resting from life, so that the spirit may resolve life's experience into character, before proceeding on, & on, & on again, into the limitless possibilities of the universe.

503

. . . (I will not attempt anything like your dashing Italian sentence, to which I do full justice & give full admiration).

But I must add a phrase or two of Sir F Drake's own, to make him more vivid to you than the sentence you quote.

I love his remark that he only wanted to give his men "a few crownes, a few reasonable booties, a little comfortable Dew of Heaven".

This is in my mind every day, & I wish them for you, Reyna mia, in my hourly thoughts of you.

Then, next to this is a remark to his crew. He was down at the back of beyond, with a pretty mutinous crew, in the E end of Magellan's straits (a grisly place, with Magellan's gallows still standing) & Drake found that there was too much of what he called "Stomaching" or proud, insolent overbearing among his gentry to his seamen, & Drake disapproved of it, there it was, "such stomaching".

"But, my masters," he said "I must have it left."

He then enquired, very pointedly, all hands being just a little scared of what might be very near, if there was anybody who wanted to go stomaching any longer; & found that it had suddenly lost favour, all this stomaching, & did not trouble the community again.

I mention "crew", above, but it was really 3 crews being addressed together; the crews of 3 small ships, soon reduced to one, the famous *Golden Hind*.

504

... The two vols of Bernal Diaz were posted to you on the 2nd (y'day).

They are not like anything else known to me, but these two are the cream of him: there was only one Mexico in history, & that they swiftly destroyed.

Afterwards he becomes rather a boring growler, that all the war & hunger did not make him richer, in gold & slaves, after all that he had done for virtue, the state, & true religion.

He livens up a little in vols 4 & 5, here & there; & remembers odd things of the men who were with him, & also of their horses: in this he is unique among historians.

Your 2 vols are the best, but I like the 5th vol, the last, also.

I like the phrase of his that certain comments, that he could have made, had better be left in the ink pot.

I do not like Vol IV, but I am glad to think that those who destroyed so much had small profit from their destruction.

... Bernal Diaz tells of Ponce de Leon, who, at one time, was in Florida, looking for a Fountain of Eternal Youth which was said to be in Florida. He did not find it, but I think that everybody who goes to Florida still splashes around in any spring he may find, in the Hope that it may be IT, & its results be given. (I tried some Hotel taps, but they weren't IT, seemingly.)

Ponce de Leon is almost a poem, because of his search for it. It is queer to read of him in Mexico, as a sort of ordinary chap who muddled about & then died.

... Please, did you ever hear of a "Wellington colour?" (The colour of a coat.) "The coat was a hunting kersey of the admired Wellington colour" (a kersey was a somewhat rough strong woollen, a cloth woven, not a jersey knitted).

I suppose that the D of W began in the 34th Regt of Foot, which wore red; & he seems to have worn red when Goya painted him. But this is some tint in vogue long after his war time, 1835 or even a little later: and to be dark & admired.

Well, port wine was dark & admired; & the D of W made it possible for port wine again to flow, as it did flow, like Thames in the poem,[1] till many a poet ended his song.

[1] Edmund Spenser (1552–99) *Prothalamion*: "Sweet Thames, run softly, till I end my song."

505

... I hope that this fine weather will hold for your remaining rest, so that you may be in the garden, & in warmth, so that you will really be resting, & enjoying it.

You will probably have heard my old tale of the farmer who said "The victuals I like best is cold pork for supper, and then to lie awake all night feeling it doing me good".

... In one of my letters to you, I mentioned the Spanish adventurer Ponce de Leon, who was (later in life) in Mexico.

He died there of sleeping sickness, which was said to be spread by the African Tsetse fly, & I am now wondering whether he was infected in Africa, the present home of the disease, or got it from some other fly while looking for the Fountain of Youth in Florida.

Anyhow, he looked for youth, & most of these fellows looked for gold, or slaves, or both, and, by comparison, Ponce seems so like a flower.

506

... I wanted to ask you if you know the work of Georges Courteline, who, about 50 odd years ago, wrote merry tales of the lives in French cavalry barracks.[1]

He wrote a wonderful play about a Civil Service office in Paris, which had a mad success, as a farce; but the tales of the cavalry barracks are his real contribution.

He writes a very slangy French, but is worth the trouble, but I must say that here & there the life, shall we say, is a kind of a sort of a . . .

Well, the French can write about such matters, & no other people can.

¹ Georges Courteline, pseudonym of Georges Moineaux (1861–1929). His "wonderful play about a Civil Service office" is *Messieurs les Ronds de Cuir* (1893).

507

. . . Please, let me congratulate you on your garden-crops, so much better than mine.

This place is very subject to very cruel blasts from the N, whence winter evils come galore. They came this spring, & tho they killed off queen-wasps & clegs, they slew all the blossom, so that I have not one apple, one plum, one nut.

The tomatoes were under cover, & I had a half crop, very good, but small in size, and late.

Vegetables were fair, but my crab-apples have not one crab on them, & my blackberries no berry that could be eaten or bottled; this last, owing to the drought.

I have a friend, however, a fruit-farmer, from whose 1964 Bumper Crop, not yet picked, I can purchase fruits in case of scurvy or other cruel diet-deficiency: so I keep up my spirits.

> Am I not Shakespeare's countryman,
> And are you not my friend?!!

508

. . . I am sending you a folder about San Francisco, the " 'Frisco" into which so many known to me disappeared, & to which so many splendid late sailing ships went of old, from Liverpool. Stevenson was there, & Mark Twain & Herman Melville; and I believe Al Capone was in the prison in the harbour.

It was a wickedly tough port for poor seamen, as I expect you will have heard, but you will not see that in these old panoramas.

509

. . . You are a dear to be moved by "the forest of masts" in the panorama. It impressed me very much, for I used to hear about

'Frisco in the Gold Rush, 1849. A vast quantity of gold was found (in all) and myriads went to try to find it, by ship round Cape Horn, by ship to Vera Cruz or Colón, & thence overland to Acapulco or Panama, & then on, if possible, by whatever shipping could be found.

When the ships reached 'Frisco, all hands went to the gold-fields, & left the ships as they were.

I believe that the crime in 'Frisco then has never been equalled anywhere. The city of huts & tents was burnt out I think 6 times in 3 years, & had between 4 & 500 (400–500) homicides in each year, sometimes more.

I speak of *known* homicides. It was a tough burg; & became unendurable. The men formed a Society of Vigilantes or Watchmen, & kind of coralled-up the toughs & hanged a lot of them, & tarred & feathered some, & rode them on rails out of town, & said, "Now, brother, GIT, & don't stop to pick no flowers!"

They had two harvests & things quietened down a little.

510

. . . I once had a bird-bath, which was used by many hundreds of birds, & gave great delight to them, & to the watchers.

It was a stone basin. There used to be a stone-mason at Bibury, just as you turn over the water out of Bibury to go to Cirencester. He used to make them, & had a ready sale for them.

I had this for years, standing on an old tree-stump, but as far as I can recollect some accident knocked it to pieces: I think a big branch of a tree, or the tree itself, fell on it in a great gale which did fearful harm here about 16 or 17 years ago.

If you fill your Bird Bath with water every day, put near it, if you would care for it, a daily meal for the birds. Then (if you go to bed at all) you might wake up & hear them saying

"Ouak, Quak, & gogologk" & the rest of it.

Birds are very punctual things, & expect punctuality in their friends.

511

. . . I have found a few ghastly snaps of this creature; and fear that they are really what he looks like and is.

If this be so, I may well marvel at your friendship during all these years, your patience, kindness & gracious acceptance *quand même*.

In the written article that contains the view hardest to bear, I am reminded of something that Aubrey Beardsley was once heard to say. At some gathering, a lady was heard to ask him:

"O Mr Beardsley, where are you living now?"

"O", he said, "I'm living with my sister . . . not incestuously."

512

. . . I looked at some of the old views of San Francisco under a strong glass. All the ships in them were wood, & quite small, a few ships & barques (all 3-masted) & a lot of brigs & schooners: nearly all American, & some in very good order, & all square by the lifts & braces.

In 1848, Mexico ceded California etc to the USA & San F began to be American. SF then had about 200 people in it, & to these came a lot of Mormons, who were eager to get from SF to Salt Lake City, a lot of Frenchmen & Englishmen who were probably not up to much good there, & a lot of Americans who meant to make it a part of the USA. By the end of 1848, SF may have had 800 people in it, & the place was growing, having "good air, good water & good bells", & a very pleasant climate, Then, suddenly, near SF, a man who was making a sawmill found some yellow stuff, which was heavy & unusual. It seemed malleable & heavy & he thought it might be gold. His employer thought it might be gold, & they gave it a test, which seemed to convince them. A local chemist gave it a certain test which convinced them all; & it is a fact that the sawmill men, boss & man, felt that all their plans & hopes would now be utterly ruined.

"Farewell, al is y-go."

I think they were right, for the gold rush began.

A great piece of Calif is, or was, immensely rich in surface gold. It was water-borne gold, in dust, nuggets & blobs, all within 2-4 feet of the air. It was all what the miners call placer-gold (pleasure-gold) from the fact that it was a (comparatively) pleasant task to mine it. You scooped up the earth & washed it, & all the gold, being heavy, sank in your pan, & could be used as currency coin.

The amount to be had was vast, & scattered over a vast trail-less, road-less, man-less wild country; & the gold rush stirred the world, & set thousands of adventurers from all over the world to come to such a Tom Tiddler's ground.

Americans flooded in from the East, overland, in thousands, & thousands of these died in the deserts on the way, of thirst, starvation, fevers, cholera etc. Thousands came by ship round Cape

Horn, & were lost on the way, from the fortune of the sea (it was a 5 month voyage).

Myriads sailed to Panama, crossed the Isthmus, & hoped to sail thence to SF. Thousands of these died in the Isthmus from fever, before they could find shipping to the N.

Many others came to Eastern Mexican ports, & tried to cross Mexico to her Western ports to take ship for SF, and myriads of these died, I suppose, from fever, starvation, suicide, homicide and general exhaustion.

But thousands got thro to SF, & then found that any food there, & any spade & pan, & canvas for a tent, had to be paid for in gold dust; & then, when they tried to steal it, they shot the owner, or he shot them. All ship's crews left their ships & went prospecting.

I am told that the people of SF hauled a deserted ship ashore, propped her up, and used her as a gaol; but soon found that a wooden gaol was not strong enough for that sort of prisoner.

> It was great pitee
> Such birdës for to put in such a cage.

They soon had a stone one; perhaps a part of the old Spanish Presidio.

Mark Twain saw SF later, when it was a City, but it was a tough burg even then; & a lot of shooting took place in it.

I did know a lad who was murdered in it, much later: and the port had a terrible name among sailors until the great Earthquake & Fire in 1906 (I think) which removed it pretty well altogether.

513

... You asked me about Sir J.M. Barrie & his work.[1] I know not quite what to say ...

I feel this, that the Scots have a gift for communication, a national genius for it, a part of their heart & nature. It may be the clan instinct coming out.

Anyhow, they can talk from the heart better & more readily than the English can, & the English respond to this gift of theirs, & are very glad of it. It is a gift, & a precious gift, & a great gift, to be able to make people glad: & JMB had this gift pre-eminently. He was very deft in all that he wrote: & it was all trim: all square by the lifts & braces: and many millions have been glad of what he wrote; & cannot think of him without thanks & joy: this is an answer to all criticism: he made millions the gladder for his being.

Doubtless I am the poorer in many ways for not caring for his work. I have not read much of it; perhaps not a fifth part of it, and I can only say this, that when I was greedily reading, I was reading for guidance and could not read what was not touched with the qualities of poetry, abundance and music & glad excess.

Writers who had these, I read all of, all they had written, that I could find.

The only think that I like of his was *Mary Rose*,[2] which showed me that he was shedding life away & coming into the universe. The Scot in him was getting quit of Edinburgh & getting into his native land at last.

You spotted *MR* as of course you would & you also shrank from that nightmare of the Pantomime, The Principal Boy.

It is possible that you have seen now & then boys playing women's parts in Elizabethan plays. Please, what have you thought of the attempt, if you have ever seen it?

Sometimes I have been delighted by such acting: indeed, usually, I have been charmed by the acting of children, but never yet by a Principal Boy; a young woman pretending to be a boy.

Shakespeare, in the crisis of his career, was writing Rosalind and Viola & Juliet for unknown boys to act: & we do not know their names now.

. . . I am sending you some views of the desert of the Mexican Border, where the ancestors of Montezuma worshipped wild gods & looked on tempestuous & mankilling beauty, with its rocks & splendour, before they decided to move southward.

Also I send with this a snap of the *Wanderer* as she was when re-rigged in Queen's Dock, Liverpool, when I was 13: & a view of the Mexican peppers such as the Mexicans prepared, long since, to eat the Spaniards with.

Tomatoes were also to have been in the feast for I think that all our tomatoes came by Spanish hands from Mexico (over 100 sorts).

[1] Sir James Matthew Barrie (1860–1937), most famous for his *Peter Pan*, although his work as a dramatist included other highly original plays.

[2] *Mary Rose* (1920) has some of the other-worldly quality which was always to appeal to JM.

514

. . . Please let this be with you, if the posts permit, on the morning of the 24th.

It comes to try to thank you for what you wrote to me on that day twelve years ago, & have written to me since, in all these times of friendship, that have been so beautiful.

I thank you & bless you at all times, & can only hope that (as I think always happens) some sweetness & help of the heart's thought comes to the beloved, like some hidden ray of sun.

515

... The forest of masts at SF ... A lot of them stayed there, & bits of many of them are often found, still, in road repairs.

Many, being small, were hove ashore & used as stores, or houses, or broken to be groynes, or for use as building material. They were deserted by all hands; & the crews, I suppose, had the luck, or want of luck, of any gold rush, and could easily make gold-camp wages, at any shore-job, such as sexton, waiter, chucker-out, undertaker, or breaker-up of ships & maker of tents or shacks.

The California gold-rush lasted about 7 years, & a vast amount of gold was found, but the men who made most money were the capitalists who brought the rushers there, and sold them bad bacon & beans at a dollar a bite.

Did I tell you of two spectacular nuggets, one weighing 161 lbs (20 lbs of it quartz) & the other 141 lbs, each worth some thousands of pounds.

They, the miners, got all the gold from the existing streams; & later, found all the gold left by the extinct, prehistoric streams; & all the gold that both sorts of streams had left in the rocky lode, & could be got at by human greed & go.

Gold seems to exist in very ancient rocks, & again in tolerably modern rocks, but does not come much in the in-between time rocks. So, ask some geological friend to help, before you start out for a gold rush.

Long ago, I met a very clever geological chap, who had had the thrilling job of going through the waste dips of a Roman gold-mine in (I think) S. Wales, to see if the Romans had extracted all the gold, and to prove that it would pay, or not pay, to re-work the waste.

The Romans had been at the mine a long time, over 100 years, I think, and had crushed a vast mass of rock, but, as Tacitus says of his countrymen, "There is no deficiency in Roman avarice."

They had taken all the gold there was from the rock, and the lode was exhausted.

(Possibly this mine was in Monmouthshire, but I think it was further west, in Caermarthenshire, and I think that the Romans had organised a bath-house, for the miners, & a sort of works-place for jewellers, making small brooches etc to sell to tourists. "A present from Caesar's Diggings", etc.)

516

... You ask me about Napoleon's death.

It is always being suggested by interested parties that N was poisoned. It is a charge often brought against us; & it is one that should be refuted at once & firmly.

N was put in our charge by Russia, Austria & Prussia, who all wanted to hang him, both in 1814 & after Waterloo.

He was attended in St Helena by his own Corsican doctor, Antommarchi, who treated him for internal cancer.

Napoleon told him that such a thing had killed his father, & ordered him to make a post-mortem after he had died.

On his death Dr A opened the body, in the presence of the British Staff & doctors, & found the stomach ulcerous.

Had he been poisoned by a terrible irritant like arsenic, every doctor present *must* have known at once that arsenic had killed him. Few poisons can wreak more havoc on a human frame, and no doctor present thought for a moment that arsenic had caused the death.

It is possible that Dr A had, at some time, given tiny doses of arsenic to N; & that these minute doses had helped him. It was, and is, often given, with advantage, to patients, but always with risk, & in tiny doses.

The Italians & the French, who should know (& do know) that we saved N from being hung, must know that the autopsy was public & quite final in determining the cause of death.

I doubt if the stomach were returned to the body for burial. I do not know.

N gave little peace to Europe for something like 20 years, & caused the atrocious deaths of some millions of people. I think that he might be left in peace now, & not trouble our peace.

I will try to find some report of the post-mortem & will send you the result if I succeed.

517

. . . I do know what number of ships were lost in SF. There were over 500 there at some times in 1849 & 50.

Some no doubt got away, manned by broken & despairing & sick miners, who had had enough of looking for gold.

There is an old story of a sea-captain ready for sea & eager to get away, & manned by a lot of despairers. He wanted a cook, & met an old negro sea-cook who had once sailed with him, He hailed this man.

"Hey, Habbakuk. Come & ship with me & get home to Boston."

Habbakuk said, "What you give me, sah?"

The Captain said, "Why, the old rate, ten dollars a month & your slush." (The fat of salt meat, a sea-cook's perquisite for each voyage.)

Habbakuk said, "No, sah. But you come to my Restaurant, sah, I give you 25 dollars a week, & all your board, if you come as waiter. You can start right now."

SF is a sandy place, & had low sandy hills near the sea. The thousands who came into SF by sea did a lot to improve the sea approach, by driving the sea back, tumbling the dunes down onto the beach & revetting the sand with deserted ships, & so making wharves & groynes, & by great labour easing the necessity of frightful labour.

The mortality among the rushers must have been very great indeed, from scurvy, typhoid, typhus, starvation, murder, suicide, drink (of the sorts sold to them) decayed food & polluted drinking water: cholera etc, not to speak of knives & bullets.

Gold varied in price a good deal. You paid your bills, if you could pay, in gold dust, which was apparently worth as little as four dollars an ounce, or as much as 7 dollars an ounce, according to the place, & the purity of the dust.

It was a mad time, with much devilry of lawlessness & outrage.

It is said that in 1849–50, the nearest laundry to SF was in Hawaii, about a month by sea or more.

I daresay that the Chinese soon organised a laundry service nearer at hand.

Possibly, you could not wash at the diggings, for the water must have been rare in many places, & needed for "washing the dirt" away from the particles of gold.

I saw some rudiments of a gold rush in Australia once. I saw boys walking along a track with eyes intent on the track. When they saw a glint or spark, they pounced on it, & put it into a matchbox.

I asked how much they got. They said, "O, sometimes we get as much as half a crown in a week."

A lot of gold had been found in the district by accident, off all beaten tracks, & a lot of odd searches were being made.

. . . In lifting & carrying weights, much depends *not* on actual weight, but on its convenience for balancing & carrying. With some packages on their heads, or *in their teeth*, I have seen negroes *trot* with at least 100 lbs or more, in hot sun. People often sadly strain themselves by trying to carry lopsided odd weights that cannot be steadied. Do not, I beg you, go wrecking yourself by lifting grand-pianos about, even for a grandchild of Chopin.

❧

518

. . . I have done some reading about Napoleon's death at Longwood.

N often talked of his illness, saying that he would die of cancer of the stomach, as his father, & uncle, & 2 sisters had died. He disbelieved in medicine, because the doctors could not possibly see how their drugs acted.

He believed in surgeons, up to a point, because they did see what was wrong & could sometimes remove it or get directly to it.

He was autocratic, & a very difficult patient, but came to St Helena a fairly healthy active man, inclined to stoutness, but having no apparent serious ailment.

One of the midshipmen in the *Bellerophon*, on the way to St H, made a ribald sketch of him leaning on a gun, in his favourite green uniform, with red facings, of the Horse Huntsmen of the Garde. It shows him, very stout, & no longer blazing in some vast political fury, as when on a throne, in what Blake calls "all the fury of a spiritual existence".

He was unoccupied, indolent, & certain to become very stout indeed.

St Helena is a sub-tropical place, & subject to heat & flies, mosquitoes, infested water, etc; & by no means prepared as a royal residence, even as a royal prison. N had escaped from Elba, but we were not going to let him get away again & upset Europe with another Cent Jours. He was to be guarded, & to keep to rules, & to drop all his empire. He was to be "General Bonaparte", not Emperor, to all the English in the island.

Like all other sub-tropical places then, St H was not healthy to white men.

Two regiments of British Foot were in barracks there with very squalid fittings doubtless, very unwholesome diet, & perhaps a big rum ration; no great science in their surgeons, & a very poor record of health.

They had much "liver complaint", whatever that was (perhaps rum), with much absence from duty, & a lot of death; not the devastation of yellow fever, but still more death than malaria would cause, or perhaps even 'flu.

It was the popular belief that the tropics did for the white man's liver, & apparently this liver complaint was expected to visit all who came to stay in St Helena.

Napoleon, from the first, chafed at his imprisonment, & growled at his governor. Things were in a poor state at Longwood, and the little court of the prison went rather to pieces, and nerves were strained.

After a year or two at St H, N complained of pain in liver, and shoulder, as chronic symptoms, & was treated for it. The pain did not clear away, but did not get worse. N's teeth gave trouble, so did his gums. He became more & more indolent, became fatter, & less & less willing to do anything.

The English allowed a clever Corsican doctor to come to be N's physician. This was the very able physiologist Antommarchi; a brilliant lecturer, but not in any way a healer, who seems to have seen that N was suffering, but not unduly, from a sort of general liver complaint, with lethargy & lack of interest in life.

He seems to have wooed N to doing some gardening & greatly improved his condition thus.

It is supposed (by a clever English doctor Chaplin) that N's symptoms, up to this time, were those of a slowly growing ulcerous condition of the stomach, that improved, during the gardening time, and then changed for the worse.

Then, it became rapidly worse.

N thought that he had cancer of the stomach. Antommarchi was afraid that it was liver inflammation. Arnott (an English doctor there) thought that it was lack of liberty & melancholy.

The Governor was sure that something was radically astray in N's inner being.

Meanwhile, N became most frightfully assailed by sickness, pain, more sickness, more pain, and a great wasting away; and I should suppose that all saw that he was dying.

Presently, he died, and the Governor ordered an instant, most carefully guarded autopsy, attended by 5 or 6 surgeons of the island, the garrison, & the ships of war, and the operation was done by Antommarchi, a brilliant anatomist.

He found that on the coat of the stomach was a gastric ulcer with a most active cancer at one point of it. This cancer had thrust its growths almost round and across the ulcer, and that this was the cause of death.

(Later, A wrote that the cause of death was liver complaint: he being a liar.)

A few days before his death, N dictated his will, and he, being a truly champion liar, and savage against the Governor, declared that the Governor had murdered him.

To this day from time to time haters of England, in many parts of the world, where we are not loved, bring up this charge, which is one of the three great St Helena lies of the extraordinary man who died there.

The autopsy is clear: he died of cancer.

But now, my Reyna, let me thank you for your most dear gracious letter & beg you to forgive all this long tale of Longwood prison, which was a brave place when all is said, for his devoted friends stuck it, for love's sake, for about 6 years, & it was no joy to be with the poor dying Emperor, and their own lives at all times dropping away at the back of beyond on a rock ten miles by eight.

It is said that a school exercise of N's exists, a geographical paper by him, aged 10 or so, with the words "Ste Hélène—petite isle" in N's hand.

About 20 years later these brave generous men were sent by the French King to St Helena to fetch away N's body to Paris, & so they brought him home, having seen him again for 2 permitted minutes.

After the autopsy in 1821 all the body was carefully & guardedly buried in the coffin. His devoted friends opened the coffin & saw him again, the Emperor as he had been at death.

He had been beautiful in death. The English soldiers who had seen him lying in state there were most deeply touched by his beauty, as English soldiers would be. A greatness had dwelt there, & that was clear to them.

519

... Christmas is the time of year that most needs enlivening: one does long for more day-light. From Dec. 10th to Jan. 31st—O would that one were a grizzly bear in a woody cavern somewhere, near a thermal spring, with crumpets & muffins & things just in case, but really nothing to do, but sleep: & hear perhaps distant bells, or cocks crowing in the valley, yet just turn over and pull the blankets over.

... A man promised to send me some addresses where the old *Arizona Highways* [magazines] may be had in the US.

If he keeps his word, as I am sure he will, then perhaps in the New Year some time these may come, to add more romantic names to your imagination.

I marvelled at all that land when I was in it; all amazing in its beauty, all so great & so remote, and so near & full of power.

The Indians still made little boxes and amulets out of the old (debased) silver Spanish dollars, & also little beaded bags & moccasins, but the silver dollars came to an end, & the gazelles, whose skins made the bags, got eaten, so perhaps these pretty trifles are no longer made.

520

. . . I wrote to the man who made the jolly poem about the birds, and have had a jolly letter from him from the Pacific Slopes, where the humming-bird seeks entrancingly for honey, and is left alone, & the pelican plunges riskily for fish, & is then beset by Nature's pirates to make him drop it.

I doubt if we have had humming-birds, but primitive man at Glastonbury used to eat pelicans quite a lot, & I suppose ate their eggs, too, and ended them.

See how thoughts run on food at this season.

521

. . . I saw a lot of the Indian silver things when I was in New Mexico; but most of them were parts of harness: bit-cups, spangles, parts of stirrups & saddles; and things made when old soft silver dollars were to be had. The modern things were little silver boxes with bits of local turquoise on the lids; and little amulets called thunder birds.

The bead-work, of moccasins and little bags, was often lovely: but the beads were (as I supposed) of modern civilised make, not Indian at all.

I shall try to find out if any of these are still made by Indians.

In what was called the Mesa country, I would see the vast level plain, going from eternity into the undying, & here & there amid the solitudes rose the Mesas, or Tables, each rocky table 1 or 200 feet high, all built up in adobe houses, where Indians lived, in a sort of rude Troy, a hundred or two to a Mesa.

They were in their stone ages or early bronze ages, such as our forefathers were here, on Bredon & Malvern, & all over the Downs.

To look at them was to know what we sprang from, & to marvel if we had not forgotten what was precious, which these fellows would not part from for any treasure.

522

. . . Some time ago you asked me what risk my house ran of being flooded.

In the nightmare of writing at Christmas I fear that I did not answer this question, but will do so now.

Generally, at a rough guess, the river's normal surface must be about 35 feet below the lowest brick course of the house; at the grass level.

In the usual winter floods the river rises about 3 feet 6″; in bad floods about a foot more, and in my worst flood here, due to heavy rain melting a heavy snow, it rose to five feet 4 inches. About a mile below this, where the river Thame comes in, a great body of flood from this big catchment may make things awkward for some miles, but just here the flood of 5 feet 4 inches only made a mess of the lower garden, right up to the foot of the old river bank on which the house stands, about 30 feet above the flood's limit (at a rough guess).

. . . In the spring & early summer of that year, all the flooded garden bore a great crop of the pink Ragged Robin which made a fine sight, but did not re-appear next year.

I had feared that this flood might have swept away some of my lower garden, but that did not happen. It left more mud than it took, I think.

If a terrific flood should come, and unsettle the house, the Upper Thames will lose a lot of bridges, villages, & river roads; and the vast volume of water, when held up in the London area by the sea's spring tides, will play old Harry with Chelsea & other quiet spots.

You may remember how an archaeologist some time ago, digging at Ur, in Chaldea, found a fearful layer of a flood deposit, & decided, perhaps quite rightly, that this was the deposit of *the* Flood, Noah's flood, which had wiped away a civilisation & caused people to begin it all again, when at last there was a dry surface to begin upon.

523

. . . I will try to find out about the Apaches for you; the real Cochise & Coloured Sleeves & Mescalera Indians. Did you ever read a tale by Cunninghame Graham[1] "A Hegira"? about some Mescaleros?

They were a kind of tough guys; and had need to be; and though they could keep down the Mexicans, they could not keep down the Americans; and I suppose they are now pretty well penned-in, somewhere near Death Valley; a terrible place, but very great for poetry, that will come out of it when the right man goes there.

It is so strange, that so much wildness is so near modern cities, with films, and politics, and those Hereford cattle, that so often made me weep from homesickness as I passed through.

[1] See Letter 199.

1965

524

. . . I am trying to find out a little about the Red Indian origins for you.

This study is still fairly young, but not supported yet by any nation-wide search of old sites, and comparison of ancient tribal traditions. Many tribes have utterly gone, & their memories lost, with their languages.

I suppose that they were mainly hunters & raiders, and there seems to be a general surmise that USA, Alaska & Canada were peopled by the slow spreading of people from Siberia into what is now Alaska, & thence, in small gangs of hunters & raiders, into all that vast expanse as far as Arizona.

The main belief is that the main stock that came down to the romantic SW states is the Navaho stock, & that it came thro Alaska, & SW-wards, at unknown times, but keeping a language which is still, in part, in use by Indians, in Canada, & understood (it is said), in part, in far Colorado.

All this moving & hunting & raiding must have been done on foot or by canoe, for they had no horses then.

I can give no dates at all, but it is generally supposed that when white men first settled in America during the 16th century, after Columbus's discoveries, there were not more than 750,000 Red Indians altogether, counting from Mexico in the S, to Hudson's Bay in the N.

Few of these 750,000 practised farming to any useful degree. They were hunters, fishers, raiders & trappers, often at war, often quarrelling about hunting rights, & often raiding their neighbours' settlements, for booty or wives.

The coming of white settlers from Europe soon brought them into a perpetual war, in which they had much disadvantage, but learned from the whites the use of gunpowder and of horses.

With these, they made themselves very terrible to whites who settled, or tried to settle, in remote western areas where Spanish & other power could give no defence.

The main mass of the Navaho stock was not disposed to deeds of blood. They cultivated, & had learned from the Spaniards the herding of sheep & goats, and were prosperous within simple limits.

But some of the Navaho stock, the Apaches, were successful, under some of their chiefs, against the US Army commanders, and these waged war along the frontier, and made the Indian lot, as a whole, much worse than it might otherwise have been.

Gradually, the Indians lost, and were put into Reservations.

. . . Please, will you some day tell me, if, in your Naval days at sea you had to drink, each day, about one quarter of a pint of water in which a fine brand of lime had been mixed with Demerara sugar? This was a preventative of scurvy, & had to be taken by all hands.

To us, long since, in the MN [Merchant Navy], this was a glad break in the day, for the drink gave 2 new real tastes, acid & sweet, & cleared away the fog always in our mouths as tho bad men had been burning bad brown paper in them.

It is true that the Americans always called us LIMEYS, with much contempt, for the practice; but we didn't much mind that. We came away from the drinking with a song:

> So what's the use of grum-bell-ing, you
> Know you get your whack . . .
> Limejuice & vinegar according to the Ack

(Tho we had no vinegar; in the other ship the vinegar; not us, no vinegar here boys, no —— French practice here.)

525

. . . I have your letter this morning, with the poems of your friend.

The first facings of life can be pretty grim; & I suppose the first sweetness in poetry is found in its suggestions of suicide.

I speak of the multitudes of the young who loathe life, & yet are in it, and see no hope & no help; & only care for art when it suggests death.

"Death after life does greatly please"[1] etc etc. or some poisonous stanza from "The City of Dreadful Night",[2] which must have peopled whole cemeteries.

The first escape of so many is to get safely round Suicide Corner without a smash.

Most people meet young people who are in despair, & have to give what comfort they can with what understanding they can muster. The verses shown should be seen as a symptom not as art; for art is not a matter of despair, but of courage *quand même* and of sticking it, hell or no hell, as the thing to live by; in itself, enough.

It is said that a sentimental lady once said to Thomas Carlyle, "I can accept the Universe."

And Carlyle replied: "By God, Madam, you'd better."

It may be that most people have to seek help & other help, & more help & even then go seeking help, till enough comes to carry them round the bend. One must seek one's guide, & lucky is he or she who finds a guide.

Those who have no guide, can have no Order, no Power and no Beauty, wh are the three elements of the Universe, & will help one into and through the universe, and the conception of an enduring pilgrimage not limited to one life may be a help.

> To find in foolish things that live a day,
> Eternal Beauty wandering on her way.

[1] Edmund Spenser, *The Faerie Queen*.

[2] A poem by James Thomson (1834–82), first printed in 1874 and published in a collection in 1880.

526

... I fear that the desert Indians were not musical. They had a drum or two, & some rattles, & now & then they clacked bits of wood together, but I cannot be sure that they did this in rhythm or with variation.

The Aztecs in Mexico went much further than this of course. They had become almost modern men, & were ahead of the Spaniards in many ways.

The Indians were mostly hunters, I believe, and had to keep silent pretty much, wherever they were, lest they should scare the game, or rouse their enemies.

Perhaps this accounts, in part, for their not being musical like the negroes, who were always encouraged to sing at their work, being always slaves when first brought to America.

I cannot find that the Indians had any kind of harp or banjo or fiddle: but some tribes had whistles, & some had a crude kind of horn. They had lots of religious dances & for these (I suppose) there were accompaniments of thumpings or thwackings very effective & impressive (and using marvellous wooden masks).

527

. . . You must not think that going aloft is difficult or dangerous. It is, however, a thing that uses all one's muscles all the time, and when one is out of practice at it one finds out what idleness may do. Like most boys, I found it easy, but I have seen its effect on grown men who had never before tried it; & it is astounding how the matter can appear to the mature unpractised man. I have seen them paralysed, unable to go up or down, & quite likely to let go & fall.

Barefooted Navy men thought nothing of going aloft at full speed, hopping onto the yards & running out the yard-arms on the top of the yards barefooted. My feet were never hard enough for that, nor my spirit sufficiently active.

I feel that you, my Reyna, would have been aloft with the brightest, & would have been down (head first by the back-stays) before the last man was aloft.

You *are* a sailor, I would say . . .

528

. . . You will have seen humming-birds here & there.

We have the humming-bird hawk-moth, which is near enough to show the sort of thing.

Long ago, when Mt Pelée blew up in the W Indies,[1] a man showed me a humming-bird's nest from there, a tiny wonderful nest, with white ashes in the nest, & 4 tiny eggs among the ashes: all a miracle of dainty beauty.

The island blew up pretty thoroughly: & the sole surivivor (in one place) was a man in the condemned cell in the prison. I hope that he was pardoned; but I doubt the French view in these matters being like ours.

Earthquakes are not frequent here, nor severe. I passed my childhood near a geological fault, which caused occasional tremors; & I felt some of these, but since then, one or two severer ones have come. These I missed.

At present, I believe that only one man is known to have been killed by earthquake in all Britain during historic time.

He was a man at Comrie, in Fifeshire, who took shelter, in a tremor, in a doorway, which came down upon him.

¹ Mount Pelée, a volcano at the north-western end of the Island of Martinique in the West Indies, erupted violently on 8 May 1902, destroying the island's chief town, St Pierre, and killing an estimated 40,000 people.

529

. . . My gratefullest thanks for your radiant letter about the Arizona book.

I think that many of the Navaho tribe are now mingling-up with the American whites, & taking to the ways of the pale-face more readily than in the past.

They are said to have taken to coffee, which they like in quantity, weak, black, and sweetened. They also buy jam, candies, & other groceries at the stores.

Most of them still live in conical big tents, call *Hogans*, which are mainly sheep-skin, & have fires inside them, with a smoke outlet at the top. These are said to be cool in summer, warm in winter.

In these hogans, the dogs live with the family, & at night serve, in case of need, as hot-water bottles for the chilly.

The Indians do not wash much (often water is rather scarce) & are often somewhat infested, but no doubt have some remedies for this, just as our fore-fathers had.

They are a fairly industrious people, sheep-farming, basket-making, carpet-weaving etc etc, but are not provident, and do not take to regular hours.

Generally they have abundant food, but being improvident & generous they sometimes run short of things. They will then eat all manner of things not usually eaten: all the wild things in Arizona, wild-cats, their dogs and their donkeys. They say that they do not like dog-meat, nor pig-meat, but are very fond of a big Arizona field mouse, which they skin and then roast. This is their great delight; like squirrel.

In parts of the Apache country, the sugar-cane will grow; & here they have learned how to make Rum; & to add to its effects with other ferments, which they say are "Good Medicine — Him makey you more drunk."

When I was in Arizona, at some stations, there were always some big Indian bucks, in their ceremonial costume, with the eagle-feather head-dress, which is so splendid.

These men looked superb. I daresay they were there to help any Indians using the trains, but perhaps they were employed by the railways just to delight the travellers.

They all looked like Dante Alighieri, & as though they had been in the Inferno somewhere, & would go back to it presently, to eat pale-face with pepper and lots of little red & yellow tomatoes.

All those SW Indians are, like the Mexicans, weavers of cloth, & wear ponchos (and the women serapes) — highly civilised garments made of square cloths with holes for neck & arms. It is a snakey country, & they use moccasins & leggings.

. . . In this page, perhaps you will allow me to write something about chanties.

The word must come from the French *chanter*, to sing. The order would be given (now & then): "Chantez it up, now!" — "Sing it up". You would hardly say, "Shanty it up, now": or "Tumble-down — ruin it up now."

I do not understand how these songs could ever have been inflicted upon girls at school: but in the 1880s & 90s the newspapers for boys began to print chanties & music as used in the MN, & this led to some strange perversions for many years.

The life of a chanty was not very long as a rule. The words are usually bits of here & there, bits of hymn, music-hall, popular song, bits of ballad, occasional rubbish & ribaldry, & momentary comment & mockery.

The chanties mentioned by Dana[1] (say, 1840) were unknown in 1890; and in the 1890s, I just missed some famous chanties which had fallen out of use, like "Paddy Doyle" & "Limejuice".

At the same time, there were survivals from Tudor times (two anyhow).

I have no doubt that the song at the end of *Twelfth Night* was a halliard shanty lifted up by William into unusual high romance.

As a rule, the words of chanties are singularly poor & scrappy as literature: the choruses are often nonsense.

"Tibby way hay O hi O" is a fair specimen.

"Haul on de bowline, de bowline haul" is a bright specimen (and very old).

All through my youth, the sailing-ship was being driven from the seas, and finding it hard to get even the dreadful crews that shipped.

I do not think that there were many chanties in use at the end.

I have joined-in & been glad of about 35 of the best chanties; a doubtful half dozen more were known to me, & in the general repertory: one heard them.

Of the best chanties, all were used in hoisting heavy yards & sails, when setting or re-setting sail, or in getting up a heavy chain cable attached to a very heavy anchor at which the ship then lay. They were used therefore, always, either at halliards or at those capstans that turned the great windlass.

They were designed to help very severe manual work. You know, very intimately & thoroughly, the power of Music, & the miracles it will do to people.

The chanties performed that miracle, too, in their special way; & miraculous they were. The songs or tunes came from all over the place, from the back of beyond or the other side of nowhere, they were lively, & every note in them was meant; & when I first heard them I knew for the first time, & was shaken to the silly core to know, the Power of Song upon Man.

Life was never the same thing afterwards.

To this day, I recall things & scenes & the work of chanties; and the miracles happening.

How many times I have walked a deck looking on the port bow for the first sign of the Bishop's Light.

> Soon we'll sing in joyous chorus
> In the watches of the Night
> For we'll sight the shores of England
> When the pale Dawn brings the Light.

Forgive all this long stravage.

[1] Richard Henry Dana (1815–82) was an American jurist who had served as a seaman; his *Two Years Before The Mast* came out in 1842.

530

Reyna mia

I thank you for your kind nice letter.

I have been bothered with some eye trouble and cannot write an answer to it today, nor indeed, could I easily read a reply to it if I were to try to answer it properly.

Please forgive a brief note now, & please (tho it deserves no answer) may this have only a very short one, with not more than five words in a line & 3 lines to a page?

My blessings to you. Jan.

53¹

... In the turmoil I had occasion to need a book. I have several
such, as you must have seen, & this was a rare one that I have not
wanted to read for 30 years or so.

But O the fury of not finding it now.

Alas, I fear that it has been tidied away, or borrowed ... or ...
(being rare, made rarer).

You cannot guess what a pleasure it has been to look in places
where it might be.

Books have their days and demand them, & this book (nothing in
itself) demands to be re-read.

There is always a joy in finding for certain where it isn't.

53²

Reyna mia

I thank you for your most kind, welcome letter; & grieve to send
in return such a wreck as this.

Please, I am sorry, but I cannot now read much; & find that any
closely written passage is not to be read at all.

About 5 words to a line is the sort that I can manage. Any bigger
burden of words tends to blur & defeats me.

I do not expect this to get much better, being now somewhat old.

Blessings & thanks to you,

Jan.

533

My dearly loved Reyna

I thank you for your gracious letter, here this Tuesday, with the
marvellous itinerary waiting for you in April.¹

Please you must not fail to send me details of this journey long
before you start upon it. Post Early is the slogan, and please do not
forbid me to write. It is the thing I am said to do, or to have been
able once to do, and I wd like to keep that reputation the few years
remaining to me.

Your letters have been a great cheer, for long & long. My thanks
for them & my blessing. You write a most lovely letter: they are like

the birds in Chaucer who sang "all out with the full throte". I thank you for writing thus. I thank you with a full heart.

Jan.

¹ The Hallé Orchestra was preparing for another European tour.

534

. . . I am sending, in another cover, a few more copies of *Arizona*, in case they should be new to you.

It is thrilling to me to look through these things & to come upon photographs (in colour) of Hereford cattle, whose forebears I may have seen, & whose breeders I probably did see, at some old fair or other; & whose relatives, I do not doubt, put the fear of death into me as I trespassed into their pasture, & they got up to welcome me.

Hereford cows & bulls have scared me a good deal, I assure you, first & last.

I hope that you heard the football match on Sat^y last, England & Scotland, at Twickenham. A desperate game in the mud.

535

. . . I thank you for your dear kind letter, & am sad to think that you have had snow, & possibly a nipped almond blossom on account of it.

Here we have no snow, but a rising river & a lot of cold wet mud, instead of cold dry frost.

Alas, that we cannot meet, to have a good growl at what we both hate, & then a long talk of what we most love, much about ourselves of course!

HI [Henry Irving], whom I only saw act in Manchester, rather late in the day, but in all his great parts, must have died I think, in, or just off, the wings of an old-fashioned theatre in the North somewhere. I had seen him, off any stage, at Ledbury once, at some sort of flower show, & to me he was the flower, & I did not look at any other, but was very careful not to stare, or not to be noticed staring, but he was the first man of genius I had seen, & I took a good look I assure you, for he had the look of genius of the rather terrifying sort. He had a devil in him, as well as a spirit.

536

. . . Do you know the Icelandic Sagas at all, & like them at all?

They were much in vogue about 60 or 70 years ago, but I doubt if they are much read now; life is now probably much fuller of bloody doings than it was in the Victorian time, when the Sagas were first revealed to us.

They made much reading, being wonderful true stories often involving 20 families of Iceland in the 11th century or so.

It has been really hot here, though freezing a little after midnight. I have had some hours in the sun in the afternoons, listening to the birds, & hearing a good many still; though the rooks have been murdered a good deal hereabouts by various dogs in office.

I hope that you can read some of this writing.

537

. . . I am thinking that the 8th Henry only reached to a 6th wife, & that perhaps this may be only the 6th, or perhaps only the first, to reach poor Reyna in the wilds.[1]

But I am cheered to think that Reyna may be having a wondrous glad time of success & applause & national triumph.

It is astonishing how ink gets unruly with me in these days. But look at [these blots] now. One looks like a horse's head, & the other a little like a cat by the fire, and this in a fellow who calls you his friend.

He is, too, and sends you an 8th note to say so, & bless you for it.

[1] The Hallé was now on its tour of Europe.

538

. . . I wonder if you ever read the best book of an English voyage, the voyage of Anson round the world?

The writer was a chaplain,[1] not a sailor, but he was in the voyage, which was a great feat, & his book is outstanding.

It is just possible that I have given it to you. Will you kind heart please let me know if I did?

I do not remember sending you a copy, but it is easily the best English voyage. Perhaps I have given you the only book of a voyage that compares with it, the American book, Dana's *Two Years Before the Mast.*[2]

Surely I have given you one or other of the two books, or have I failed, & left you with no share, in my 2nd great delight?

[1] Lord Anson (1697–1762), who later became First Lord of the Admiralty, made his famous voyage round the world in 1740–44. His chaplain, Waters, wrote the account. Anson began the voyage with seven ships and finished with only one.

[2] See Letter 529.

539

. . . You have been back a week without a letter from me, & I have had two letters, both most dear & kind, and an Easter card from you.

For these I send my heart's thanks: & for my own defects I must plead my own defects & a pile of work that I never seem able to get done; really a lot now, and accumulations of it, & a great lessening of the power I once supposed I had to deal with it.

Ah, my Reyna, I once wrote 2 books of poems in six weeks (I did) & a history book in 30 days, and a book of criticism in 31 days; and now I leave my beloved Reyna for a week without a word. As the Welsh used to tell me in Hereford on market days, "An Inglissman is a plight on Cot's earth, look you."

540

. . . Anson's book was by his Chaplain. I do not care much for Anson. He was against Byng; and I feel that any fine intelligence would have known that Byng was murdered by a gang of politicians & 1 or 2 personal enemies.

Now, please, I would love you to have this Anson, which I know you would love; it is a masterpiece of a book; quite our best English sea-book; all about our imbecility, the deaths it caused, & the wonders done by survivors. The only real harm in the book is that it belongs to me . . . It would be such a joy to me to think that it would be yours, & that your hands will turn the pages & your eyes will brighten wherever its tide turns. It is a link the more in something that makes us friends, though I was born when we wore whiskers & thought that they were becoming (yet you forget that).

. . . I never had much chance to hear much music when young, having been rather poor and hard at work and caring madly for books of poetry. I heard some Wagner, though, 3 operas in all, I think; but I might have done better than that, had I not been so drawn by poetry & painting.

I liked the thought of Wagner; he that wore trowsers made of cloth of gold, & served a King who was as mad as a hatter. I suppose that each was quite incapable of understanding the other.

541

. . . Please, I would like to help the plan of the sealings.

I send a little very old design that is 4-square. It is a replica of a Greek seal from Persia: the seal itself is in the Ashmolean; I suppose it to be about 3 centuries BC. Each and all the cuts make a good seal.

With it I send a replica of the Florence fleur de lys badge. It is cast from a modern Italian replica that I got on the bridge at Florence about 40 years ago.

There is also a little modern ship seal; not too like a ship, but liker a ship than a motor-car.

With these you can practise; & I would so like you to have them for your very own.

In sealing, it is well to have ready a saucer with a bit of wet sponge in it. When you have dripped the hot wax onto the envelope, take the seal, dip it onto the wet sponge, and apply it to the hot wax *damp*, but not too wet.

It will serve if you will hold the seal to your mouth and breathe upon it twice. The seal must be *moist* or it will stick on the wax, but ths seal must be *moist* not really *wet*, or the water will mar the impression.

542

. . . My thanks for your dear letter & the fine seal of the fox; a fresh fox, just starting from whatever sin he was committing, and not being hunted by a pack.

I thought that the impression was very good.

I forgot to give you a suggestion that helps a sealer.

When you have dropped hot wax on an envelope from a hot stick of wax, always stir the little pond of hot wax with the hot end of your stick of sealing-wax; stir it round once or twice to take the wrinkles out, and—*then*—when the cooling blob is not cold—*then* press the moistened seal on the waiting wax, & look at the marvellous impression.

It is always easier to seal with sticks of wax that are narrow not coarser than this [a sketch followed]. Usually the stationers only supply this size in *red* wax.

. . . Please, I want to say this to you.

You have given me lovely, thoughtful & treasured gifts, leather cases, precious books, a dagger that cuts open all my mail: and you are ever generous & a wonder.

But please, I am coming to an end, & I know that within a few years I shall leave all these things, & I cannot bear to think of your dear gifts going to others.

So, please, may I ask you to give me a letter instead of a gift, in any time of gifts?

I have been thinking of all this lately; & have to tell you.

. . . Did you ever take to the Icelandic Sagas, & the similar work from Norway?

Long since I read a lot of them, & found them marvellous as social history & as story-telling, but find them less staggering now.

I am also reading a few of Heine's poems, & envy him his power of knocking a nail right dead on the centre, & knocking it into any heart that is left in me.

As you are much in that heart, I tell you not to be afraid of Heine's crowding you out.

He was a clever German Jew, who wrote the poem "The Two Grenadiers", for which I feel sure you must have played the music for some lucky Basso Profundo who would sing it?

I read him in small bits at a time when there comes a gap in the usual work. He has a way of hitting the nail on the head, in a condensed lyric way: and is then very effective.

This is the kind of thing:

> At Cross Roads, so the Law bids
> All suicides are set
> A small blue flower grows there
> It's called What Sinners Get.
>
> At Cross Roads I stood sighing
> At midnight in the wet,
> The flower nodded to me.
> It's called What Sinners Get.

But if all Poets were as brief as this the paper-makers & the ink-people wd all be ruined; & there would not be cross-roads enough. It might be well to add a 3rd stanza.

> At Cross Roads something hungers
> For every man who lives
> What Sinners get is Justice,
> But often Life forgives.

. . . I must send you a book of Greek coins, showing the marvel of the Greek mind. I have had some seals made from some of these coins, & these, too I must send, at least the 2 best, which are a bit big for general use, but are absolutely corkers for power & glory.

543

. . . It is now more than mid-May, but I have not yet heard the cuckoo here. Cats & weed-killer have put the cuckoos out on the downs. . . and it is the same with the nightingales. I used to wake in the night to listen to them, but they are gone now: and the herons are gone & the bullfinches; & I have not seen nor heard any of the woodpeckers nor of the really rare birds that I *have* seen here in the past. Nature cannot stand an English suburb, I suppose; boys, cats, dogs, weed-killer and lawn-mowers upset so many small birds.

Possibly the kingfishers are in clover, for there can be no doubt that the river is less used now; few boats & no steamers.

544

. . . To my amaze, I have a lovely letter from you, from Swansea, with words about the curlew, the most moving voice among all our birds, & a charming shell, from the beach, which I have put on my writing table & shall bless while I write.

I can see it with thought of you, by looking 15 inches to my right, or much less than that when I sit a little further from the window.

When your letter came I was translating a poem of Heine. This is what I was doing (a lyric tale):

Night was upon my eyelids
Lead was upon my lips
Annulled, in head & spirit
I lay in the Grave's grips.

How long I cannot tell you
I lay there stunned and dead
I woke . . . someone was knocking
My tombstone, overhead.

This was a cheerful note to come to, as your letter came, & it goes on, *muy bien*, or even better:

Will you not rise, dear Henry?
It's now Eternal Sun . . .
The dead are up, re-living,
Eternal Life's begun.

But this is only a first draft, and it will have to be toiled at for a long while.

. . . I saw the old England of 80 years ago: a dreadful land, so starved, so drunken, so untaught, so cruel, & now I cannot see any child unfed or lousy or beaten, or set to beg, & thrashed if unsuccessful, or sewn into clothes already ragged . . .

Millions & millions are now free from all this, & are now set free to so much: and the joy of that is O beyond all telling, all thought; it is so amazing, beyond all old hopes & prayers. O my beloved, so much is to the good. I feel myself to be the only failure going.

545

. . . These are the promised seals, with two others, one of an antelope from the Greek settlement in Persia, & one of Arion on the Dolphin's back, imitated from some other fellow in Syracuse or Tarentum (I forget now which).

. . . I feel sure that many of the designs [in the book of Greek coins] will enchant you: such beauty, such perfection, such magical catching of what is in the design to charm one, are rare, indeed, and all the designs so tiny, and done in reverse, with such life.

I would like to see you looking at the designs, and deciding which lady does her hair best . . .

546

... I am disobeying your word of no replies this week, not from any contempt of Court but because I thought you might like to hear that I thought some of your sealings very good. The man riding the dolphin ... then the very delicate creepy crawley thing in the 4-sided seal; you got all its spidery legs very well. (They are very finely cut, & I know not how they got such a fine line on a hard stone or metal.)

Now & then, when I have tried to make a seal, I have learned what marvellous men the old Greeks were. One cannot imagine a Roman of antiquity making off-hand, from power and beauty of mind alone, a little bird or beast that would draw tears from anyone, tears of joy & forgiveness & understanding. (The three best kinds of tears.)

It is always a joy to think of your enjoying a thing that I enjoy. I then feel that in bits & spots in the iniquity of my being there may be some thing not wholly evil, but of a kind of a sort of a something ... so then I take courage & look at myself in the glass again.

547

... I have been reading lately a history of the Tichborne case,[1] 1867–74: seven years of law that cost the defendants £98,000, which seems a lot to a poet, but these law fellows seem to think nothing of it, & wish it were more.

Did I ever write to you about it?

When I was in Australia, I thought the Australians would be glad to hear of an Australian place that the case had been instrumental in bringing to fame, since the claimant had been a butcher there, so asked, "Is there much to see at Wagga Wagga?"

The man looked at me with the severity of a Greek professor at a false quantity. He said: "You do not pronounce it Wagga Wagga (as you spell it). You pronounce it Wogger Wogger."

I have wondered since what Wagga means. The place must have been unusually Wagga as the name was repeated; or was it a warning, of a once bit twice shy sort, one visit to Wagga might be all right, but this repetition of Wagga might have meant, no, the second time, they'll kill & eat you. And then, why pronounce it wogger? was *wagga* irreligious or something?

[1] The Tichborne case. Roger Tichborne, heir-presumptive to the Tichborne estates,

was lost at sea in 1854. A butcher in Australia, Arthur Orton, claimed to be Roger Tichborne, but lost his claim at a famous trial in London and was imprisoned for perjury in 1872.

548

. . . I am here (as usual) writing a book,[1] & trying to get it off my chest. This is ever a difficult job, for it is then that a book really gets written & off my chest. The chest is me, my sea-chest or bag of tricks: and it is tending to be off my chest, but now sticks: & I wish it were, as Mrs Gamp says, "in Jonahdge's belly".

[1] The book must have been *Grace Before Ploughing*, published in the following year (1966).

549

. . . I grieve for the great black blob up above. It is astounding how ink gets loose on my desk, onto my hands & now onto my letter to you.

There are some old books of seamanship that tell people (of the mariner kind) how to make ink when in foreign parts. I made some ink by these directions long ago: it wasn't bad, but it saved time to buy it in big gallon jars at the stationers.

I used also to try to make inks from various flowers, but this was messy & not much good.

I also used to make pens from feathers and reeds, & sticks & bones: some of them not too bad. On the whole, I found that the modern pens were better but it was interesting to see that my own makes were useable & not too bad.

Many years ago, I knew a writer who would only use one ink: "Higgins-es Eternal INK" — which is an American INK, & very good.

Not long ago a scribe asked what ink he should use, so I said "Higgins's Eternal" and he found that it can still be had.

550

. . . You graciously ask *What my book is about?* It is about things that happened at my home over 80 years ago. The savage reviewer will say "The Poet Laureate enters his 2nd childhood", or some such tart remark.

Apart from this, I think it is mainly about water, which is a thing I am very fond of, as a drink & as a wetness, & as a thing of beauty: in all 3 varieties, it is (to my thinking) quite matchless.

There was a lot of water near my home, and luckily for me a lot of it was in springs, bursting out of the ground, lots of springs, a foot high or more after rain.

55¹

. . . Please, did I introduce you to *Huckleberry Finn*?

I came to it at the age of 14, & I have since been a good deal in the South, near the Mississippi: and I suppose I have read the book, all thro, every year since then, and can a little imagine what the South was in the slave days (which only ended 100 years ago). They do not bear thinking of.

But Reyna mia, do you also know *Life on the Mississippi* by M. Twain??? Tell me this, for I ought to have sent it to you years ago: it is a corker of a book, and tells one about the Mississippi, which is a river to be careful of, for in the Spring of many years it may be 80 miles broad in patches, & my river here has never been broader in a flood than 600 yards, but that was pretty good too, for the flood bore hundreds of Arctic skuas and gannets, all fishing.

If you go to America ever, and I hope that you will, you must be careful of snakes.

There are 250 kinds of snakes in the US & may be more. But cheer up. Of these 250 kinds only *15 kinds in all* are dangerous biters, but all these 15 are found in Arizona, for A is nice & warm & rocky & desert, & you would expect to see snakes in it; you wouldn't expect so much to see a Salvation Army with tambourines.

. . . I never met Mr Twain, but have heard much about him from some who knew him.

I do not know any writer, except Dickens, who has given folk more cheer; & here I must say *prose*-writer, for D & T are not poets, and poets have, like musicians, given deeper joy.

55²

. . . I thank you for your dear letter, & for your kind question of what gives me the shivers?

A good many things have done that, for, I have had (like everybody) some close shaves in my time, but I think that my childhood, in a rather drunken England, in a country where men bred big red Hereford cattle, made me even more terrified of bulls, bullocks, and cows with calves, that I can well express.

At any moment in my childhood I was (or might well be) exposed to the sudden appearance of a bull in a field-path, looking for somebody wicked, and I was frequently told that I was wicked, & just the sort of chap the bull would know about, & deal with.

I met 2 or 3 unexpected bulls in field-paths: & I suppose it was too soon after their lunch for them to bother; & I was not tossed, but I was given something to think about; & for years I had the most frightful nightmares of raging bulls, & me running, & then coming round a corner on more bulls, & only a deep raging Hereford river to jump into to save me.

They gave me some shivers; and then (besides these) another kind of shivers was associated with hornets, a frequent (very frequent) pest in Herefordshire & I was never stung by one, but I was terrified by the tales told of what they did to the wicked and why I was not stung was a wonder to all the righteous. They are big handsome insects, & beautiful to watch, but for years they gave me the shivers: of the coldest, awfullest kind, for they had wings & could always run me down.

. . . I have been reading in Chopin's letters of late, written in his last years: while on an English visit.

He was a great success here; & I think, liked the English & respected them, but yet makes the shattering remark: "Whatever is *not* boring here is *not* English."

He saw something of Miss Jenny Lind, a lovely Swedish singer, in about 1838, for she was singing here then.

This gave me a thrill & a shock, for, when I began to go to Church in Ledbury, about 1886, Miss Lind was often in the pew in front of me, & I could have leaned over the pew-top & prodded her had I had an umbrella.

I suppose that I heard her sing, but cannot remember.

It was long ago; & at the side of her pew was a pillar of a late Gothic period. On this pillar, a man of genius, in the 15th century, had carved, with power, a startled man's face (nothing else) that haunted me a good deal. This pillar rose from within her pew.

In repairs to the church in 1891 (or 2) this face disappeared.

553

[A note to ANS in King's Lynn]

> They warned me to beware of Sin
> And cutting throats with knives
> Lest I (like Aram)[1] should leave Lynn
> All loaded down with gyves.

[1] See Letter 212.

554

[ANS was staying at a house in Hampstead, London]

> This goes to where a Nightingale abided
> That sang to Keats, as happy fortune guided.
> Where cats are many; nightingales are few,
> But still, I hope that one will sing to you.

555

[To ANS in Bexhill]

> As I was a-sailing, a-sailing the sea
> Up rises a Mermaid and beckons to me
> With the shiny bright sea-drops her raiment was wet,
> And she said, "Your Reyna, have you heard from her yet?"
>
> And I said, "Not exactly: for the sea is so salt,
> And the posts & the postmen are often at fault."
> And the Mermaid said, "True: but believe in her still,
> If you don't hear this evening, tomorrow you will."

556

. . . Please forgive me if my letters gave too poetical a tone to my regret at having some scarcity of news of you.

Poets are creatures of excess, & when they only get 3 letters or 4, they are apt to say:

> My soul is withered to its shell
> And all my drink is tears,

& sometimes they go further, & have to be put under some constraint. I was but showing that I felt your absence. Who would not, even if only a prose-writer?

You wrote most kindly, though so busy.

M. Twain was for *years* living in a community where murders happened every day, & travelled some thousands of miles in that community where most men were killers, & nearly everybody was red with gore.

> Pop, pop, the little pistols banged
> And many died, a few were hanged.

557

. . .I have wondered if you ever cared for Edward FitzGerald and George Borrow, both perhaps less known now than 60 years, or more, ago, but both *then* famous more than most.

Borrow was a scholar in Romany or Gypsy; & FitzG. was a scholar in Persian; & FitzGerald used to say clever things.

At his marriage feast, he being then about 50, somebody offered him some blancmange (usually known as Shape).

He shrank away from it with a shudder, exclaiming "Congealed bridesmaid".

I have only just come across this anecdote; & I must say it does him credit.

He used to sail a lot on the Broads, & off the Lowestoft coast in a trim built wherry & with a handy man. He was a friend of Tennyson & Thackeray. George Borrow knew the murderer Haggart whose book you liked so.[1] Haggart was a drummer in the line regiment to which Borrow's Father was Chaplain.

But Borrow knew also a much better murderer than Haggart, who was also hanged for the public good, & I doubt if FitzG ever knew any murderer at all; as one would expect, he being a sizeable poet.

[1] See Letters 145, 191, 413.

558

. . . I believe that E FitzGerald did once have a merry meeting with Borrow, at Oulton, in Suffolk, where B (I think) died long after.

FitzG as a rule lived in other parts of Suffolk, but was much given to times at sea, & on the broads, & to stays with friends, and gaddings about, having wealth, and no very great need to toil at anything. He ran out of love with London, but he loved a lot of his friends, the 2 Tennysons, & Thackeray, & 3 or 4 scholars who were at Cambridge with him, to whom, for years, he wrote most delightful letters, talking of books & so forth that did not please him so much as those that had won him in the past.

Men told him of Miss Jenny Lind, how she would sing, but he would not hear of her. He was all for *pasta*, and for music of Handel. He could not away with Browning being all for the rather early Tennyson (not the later vintage) and I should say that the Pre-Raphaelites gave him a scunner in the mid ribs; but (to me) what they gave was necessary for the time, precious & worth the doing.

559

The tonnage of the Diplodocus[1]
Is very much a thing to shock us.
His brain was just a walnut's size,
Who says he was a poet . . .
    errs.
The frenzied figure just beneath
I cannot stand his hooky teeth,
I loathe the fellow with the frills
That make a collar round his gills
    I don't like any of the four.
    I say they marred the days of yore.

[1] JM sent this to ANS with a picture of prehistoric animals.

560

. . . I am glad to have sent some Swinburne, Rossetti & Morris to you in the past.

Rossetti was the main rose bush of these three blossoms: & was a very early influence in my life; curiously, I took as serious & marvellous art, du Maurier's mocking of Rossetti in an old *Punch*. It meant all the world to me (I being then about 5 years old).

Then when I was about 19 I came upon some real Rossetti work, & his poems came first to me, then his best paintings, the early water colours, & *Dante's Dream*, & I met people who had known him, & O the wonder & the marvel.

He was the main inspiration of us who had never seen him.

Ah, but my Reyna, my beloved friend, there were others then alive who were marvels to me.

... Do you know a musician Paisiello (1740–1820 c)?[1] He wrote operas: & the great Napoleon said he preferred him to all musicians, "because he doesn't interrupt my (N's) thoughts". (He was an Italian, who had great success in Russia, but none in France.)

[1] Giovanni Paesiello (1741–1816), composer of 100 operas, much in favour with Joseph Bonaparte at Naples, Catherine the Great in Russia, and Napoleon I in Paris.

561

... It has been a beautiful day together, and you make it live again by what I found on my table this morning on coming down—a dear uncanny gift from you of pens (one of which writes this) & a sailor's wheel: how put there by the clever you I have no imagination; but I suppose your beautiful young clever heart came somehow there (but *when* is past me).

My thanks to you for it; and I wish that I had contrived some magic gift of the kind to be on your table at the Avondale [Hotel] this morning.

It is difficult to begin to thank you for yesterday, but what a day it has been, & a memory you make in all that Didcot drive that I so often pass, & know so well; & now will be linked with you.

The ship's wheel will be on my writing table, holding the four pens given by you; & they will now be SEEN & to hand and not invisible, as in the present chaos there.

I am desolated that I could not get the famous raspberries from the local fruit farm for you: it had been a sloppy picking day & they were somewhat mooshy & blood-stained looking.

In thanking you for yesterday, I must specially thank you for what you said of your Mother, & her care for Thomas Hardy.

I will (in time) tell you all my memory of TH which is that of a disciple who loved a master & read nearly all his work, & knew its worth.

You will likely know Landor's poems, & his words to Robert Browning:

> There is delight in singing, though none hear
> Beside the singer, and there is delight
> In praising, though the praiser sits alone
> And sees the praised far off him, far above.

Hardy was well-known to me for his novels, before I began to read with sense; but I came late, as the world did, to his verse, and the verse I read & re-read: & my good golly, I read it with joy & with despair.

Then, too, he was an architect, & he could draw & illustrate his poems; and then he could take a vast subject, like "Eighteen hundred and war time", & carry it through to the night after Waterloo.[1]

(He wrote a lovely hand, too.)

I will soon be vexing your peace with Hardy. I did not know him well, remember, only as a devoted disciple, who could not mean anything to the Master, yet longed to cut the throats of anyone who doubted the Master's mastery.

[1] Thomas Hardy's three-part narrative poem, *The Dynasts: An Epic-Drama of the War with Napoleon*, published 1904–8. See also Letters 174, 475.

562

. . . Now about the grass-plot in the quiet.[1] There is a legal maxim *Let the buyer beware*, which I do not quote to you, for you are wise, and do beware (long acquaintance with me must have helped your wisdom) and you see what an old building may be: foundations insecure, a roof with cracked tiles & rotting pegs to them, the gutters gone; the plaster gone inside & creatures in the plaster, such as we do not mention; the wood & the stairs rather odd, & the rates prohibitive; all the paint perished, bats in the belfry & rats in the cellar. Then, too, no water may be laid-on, nice dependable water, & the chimneys may be foul & choked, or exposing inner timber. Then the floors, the hinges, the doors & windows may be all jammed.

But you are a clever woman and I am only an aged writer from the Victorian Time, & I see your clever eyes wrinkling up at this letter, as much to say "Elementary, my dear Watson".

Well then let the buyer beware of any possible sudden move of some Board or Ministry of Public Squander that may seize the ground for a Home for Human Misfits to cost thirty-nine million pounds by 1971.

All these things, I do see as possible; & I feel sure, too, that M, the city [Manchester], must have eyes on every bit of country near it; & must ever be encroaching.

. . . The bowl[2] will be sent as soon as I can get a really strong container. I may have to paste paper in & round the bowl, but a minute in hot water will take that off. I want to send that bowl as the Fore-mast of four masts for you; & you may call the whole a 4-masted barquentine: for the other 3 will have coloured outsides; & this has only a white relief outside, & very little blue in the inner rim. The four will go soon, but perhaps not *very* soon, for they will need careful packing, such as I saw you do, & was glad to see.

I made a sad job of the handle to your package. It should have been easy to make a wonderful handle all half-hitched to your hand.

PS Two things, please, will you very kindly tell me. A. The name, bearing, & distance of yr piece of earth from Manchester. I want please, to see it on a map (I have many motoring maps). You say 15 miles from M.

B. May I write to you a writer's advice about publishing my letters, if after my death you should wish to make a selection from them? I may be able to guard you a little.[3]

C. Another thing does suggest itself, for you to consider. Would you, who are you, but something of me as well, it seems to us, care to write a brief life of me to go with the letters?

Forgive this C. You are busy, busy, & go to bed at 3.45, if the car does not puncture, & the road isn't flooded, & the season for this draws near again.

[1] I had seen a field, on the edge of the Yorkshire moors, with an old gritstone house on it, with mullioned windows, and a woodland nearby, and had been tempted to buy it. ANS

[2] These are four more pieces of early Worcester blue-and-white china, in the same style as the chocolate-pot of Letter 458.

[3] During a brief visit to Burcote Brook, ANS had asked JM if he would ever consent to her publishing some of his letters. (See also Letters 175, 182.)

563

. . . I used to be much in Yorkshire. On the whole I was mainly in big towns, but now & then in the country, which was of an entrancing beauty, unspoiled from what it showed to the young Turner a hundred years before.

In some Yorkshire moors one used to be able now & then to pick up flint implements in exposed spots, or dried water-courses; so an

archaeologist told me, but I only found flint implements elsewhere, in a hill site in Ireland, near one of the reputed settlements of St Patrick.

There, the rains had laid bare an outcrop of rock that primitive men had flaked into weapons, knives etc, which lay about in hundreds. I am sorry to say that this site was swiftly plundered bare, but the lively natives learned how to make more, and the place still does a happy trade in them.

564

. . . I promised to tell you about TH. [Letter 560.]

To begin with, his Funeral in the Abbey. We were both wrong about the Bearers of the coffin. There were not 4 nor 6, but 10. They bore only his ashes, for the body had been cremated.

His bearers were:

2 old friends, Barrie & Gosse.

2 prose writers, Shaw & Kipling

2 poets, Bridges & A. E. Housman.

2 Prime Ministers, Baldwin & MacDonald

2 Heads of Colleges, from Ox & Camb.

565

. . . If you wish to print my letters to you, or some of them, please, will you wait for ten years from my death before they are printed, and then consult my Literary Executor? And will you, my loved, loving lovely you, write a little preface?[1]

. . . I do not think that you know the kind of contract a publisher's contract ought to be, and, if you will so far honour me, I will try to warn you, while I can, of what might be very ungenerous terms that are often imposed on the unwary; and should be refused.

. . . Generally, death quenches half the interest that a writer raised in his life. It is well to hold back publication about a writer till he has been for some years dead. His posthumous reputation can then be made, perhaps, by his letters or his literary remains; or he may be so far forgotten that no publisher will look at either.

Generally speaking, a book of letters would hold about 80,000 words; and a letter of two sides, such as this, contains about 200 words in all . . . Four hundred of these would make a volume.

. . . I will try to post to you some words about publishing before I die. Publishers and authors, both sides, wish to profit and live by their work; and I reckon that the author ought to have the bigger share. Latterly the printer and the booksellers have joined in the struggle to an alarming extent.

¹ See Letters 175, 182, 562 (P.S.).

566

. . . You kindly ask me how I am.

I used to know an old sailor, who would always answer the question with:

"O the usual thing. One foot in the grave, & the other on a bar of yellow soap."

I am well enough, but cannot do much, & have to go slowly & keep quiet; & man usually likes to exceed the speed limit & to shout "Here we go round the mulberry bush" or other folly . . . .

567

. . . I thank you for what you wrote about the funeral service of Thomas Hardy at the Abbey.

It was well done & deeply moving, & a credit to us; some people say that we do funerals better than anybody: & it is true; but apart from the Abbey Service, some dreadful things were done on that occasion, by some who should have known better and should have been quelled. I cannot write of it: & it is 40 years ago, nearly, & the people are dead. (37 years ago.)

I first saw Thomas Hardy in a London Theatre. It must have been well over 50 years ago, but I cannot tell you what theatre & play it was.

It was in the stalls, & I sat about 2 rows in front of him (by some error of fate), but between the acts I could go out & get a view of him.

I suppose that he was about 72 or so, at that time, and rather ill & shrunken & broken looking. He gave me the impression of an old Chinese saint, or very very wise man. I have seen marvellous Chinese paintings of such a one; holy & wise, past telling; & not living our life at all, but intensely in another life.

He wrote somewhere: "I never cared for life: life cared for me."

I could not doubt that he was watched and tended miraculously; one of the two such Englishmen of my time, Thomas Hardy & A. E. Housman, through whom all England spoke: all the England that is, that folk of a spiritual turn would harken to.

He spoke not from a brain, but from a nature & from a house that he built himself from his own plan, and in digging the foundations of it he found that he was building on the Graveyard of Roman Dorchester, and was thus linked with the conquerers of Mai Dun, and with our first entrance into the European Problem.

568

. . . Long since, when I was reading a lot of the Napoleonic books 1807-the end, & asked TH why he had not dealt with 1814 in the *Dynasts*. He said, "I was in such a hurry to get to Waterloo!!"

. . . I think that the last survivors from the battle lasted till about 1890–1895, but he had known his Wessex men in the 1850-1860 time, when they could really tell him what the battle had seemed to them.

. . .I met Hardy late in his life, after his first wife had died. I never saw her, but I used to see her portrait at Max Gate: and one could not avoid noticing it. The face commanded attention. The abundant hair was a wonderful colour of ripe corn grain: a wonder such as one cannot see in a day's march. This first Mrs Hardy was a very social clever hostess, smart, friendly, a good horsewoman, and actively making much of people, & a good critic of men & books. Hardy said of her: "*She is so living*." That is the effect produced by the portrait. I have seen a later portrait, that gave the face a haunted look very hard to describe.

569

. . . What a book you could write.

Cathedrals I have played, etc etc. or *How England listens to music*.

Please, will you tell me if Wells moved you as one of the most delightful places you have played in?

Winchester I do not care about, except for the fact that it seems to be built in water.

I saw, in its nave roof, once, very long ago, the biggest wasps' nest I ever saw. A kind of cloud of wasps.

You must have had a rather breathless tour of it. I hope that the weather charmed you, & was not too foggy. Keats was there in fine weather (at Winchester) in a very fruitful year; and he must have had the high barometer that has lately delighted us.

High barometer is very good for the brains. It brings the sun into the mind, and all the delights of sunlight to the world; so that the savage Briton, in his woad, could forget the native crab-apple, & in an odd way begin to imagine the coco-nut (at 3 shies a penny) & even the banana.

Did you ever come across the poems of James Thomson, who wrote "The City of Deadful Night" which might have been called "Suicide City, a plea for bigger Cemeteries"?[1]

He was at one time an Army school-master, teaching illiterate recruits. He called it "pumping undesired water into unretentive sieves".

[1] See Letter 525.

570

... I must thank you for your so kind long letter, and your account of the New Forest.

I knew it (a little) nearly 70 years ago, & was at Beaulieu; but it is now somewhat dim.

I remember a Purple Emperor that I saw, the only one I ever saw (the Forest was famous for them), and he was a fine fellow.

I saw little strings of forest ponies, too, of the good old chuckle-headed kind, that could live out of doors all the winter.

They introduced some shapely stallions there at some time that had much more comely colts, but the new breeds have to come in for the winter, I believe; and perhaps one does not now see the strings of ponies wild in the forest.

... I expect you began life (real life) with *The Children of the New Forest* by the adorable Capt Marryat. Surely you had that, had you not? I am not sure that even I could enjoy it now, but ONCE . . .!

He was rather done for in the Navy, because he wrote a brave pamphlet, against the impressment of sailors, that inflamed all landsmen and politicians.

571

... I cannot now remember very clearly, but in the last days of the small coastal sailing craft, 1850-1880, there were a lot of very fast schooners, & brigs & barquentines, working in Spain & the Azores from the South Coast (New Forest and Southampton way).

They were called *Dukey*s, I do not know why, & for a time did very well bringing fresh fruit to England at a great pace.

I was told of them long ago, I never saw them, for the craft's regular lines of steamers just killed the trade. But I do not doubt that your builders near the New Forest built many Dukeys, & ran them, while the going was good.

572

Reyna mia

Did you ever set yourself to read, over a course of years, *all* the works of any writer; and did you ever succeed??

I have tried, and failed, but have had a fair shot at a good many chaps, and I do believe that I have read *all* the Shakespeare that has survived, but know that some early work must remain doubtful, and that hundreds of pages were written by him, and cut for perform-ance, and the cuts either thrown away or burned when the Globe Theatre was burned by some unknown Muggins firing cannon during *Henry the Eighth*.

WS must always have been an abundant writer, able to write whatever the moment and the situation needed; and to begin *in fervour* at a second's notice, and to write pages in any day & at any time. Such power has never been in any other single poet known to me.

There is a sort of barmy dodderers who write that WS was a noble lord, or some such juggins with other things to do, but these stars are less frequent than once, and are less regarded.

I have read nearly all the known published work of Dickens, the nearest in power to Shakespeare, on a much lower level. I once set myself to read all Balzac's novels, but I did not get very far. Hardy: I think I have read all the published books, both prose & verse: and of Keats all the poems published during his life.

573

... My thanks to you for so kindly telling me that you have Don Roberto's[1] *13 stories* but not yet *Hope*. The *13 Stories* contains the "Hegira" story: the best thing he ever wrote. *Hope* (I think) contains the next best. On the whole, I would say that he was the most wonderful man I have ever met; on 2 days out of 3 I would say this, but on the 3rd day I would say one of the three others, & unable to choose which.

Don Roberto was the handsomest man I ever saw, either on foot or on horseback, & I trust that he now rides the heavenly fields on winged horses that never tire.

... Alas, I never came to Miss Austen's books until too late for them.

I was a reader of Miss M. Edgeworth[2] before I came to Miss A & never took to Miss A. (I was very much with Irish writers about 63 or 64 years ago; and I knew Miss E's books very well indeed.)

I must have read a fair show of Dumas, but I was fond of many French writers in early days: they were our Masters in so many ways—Pierre Loti, Anatole France, de Maupassant, & some wonderful chaps whose names are now out of mind; and of course Victor Hugo: and a wonderful Belgian who was such a sinner, & then in the midst of a sensational & scandalous time took to French cookery & going to church for 3 intolerable volumes,[3] and so sort of petered out discussing the story of Bluebeard ... I forget the chap's name, but when he was wicked he had few peers. He felt that all was not quite right in his way of life, & was advised to visit a monastery of great sanctity, & this wonderful place quite did for him as a sinner.

[1] "Don Roberto": R. B. Cunninghame Graham (1851–1936). Son of a Scottish laird, who led the Dock Strike of 1887 and proclaimed himself an anarchist. See Letters 199, 523.

[2] Maria Edgeworth (1767-1849), the Irish novelist and educationalist.

[3] See Letter 575

574

... I am much tangled up in a difficult piece of writing, trying to imagine something that there are no books about. Any sensible friend would say, "Well, more fool you for trying to imagine such", but I want to have a go at a pretty difficult fence. As Wm Blake said "Bring forth Number, Weight & Measure, in a time of scarcity".

Old Age is a time of scarcity, & I can manage Number, to some extent, but Weight & Measure are rather corkers; & are not so soon settled.

575

. . . When old age, & ignorance try to write anything it is like the old Circus that used to announce that wherever it came

"Industry pauses & Commerce holds her breath."

. . . I have been reading a good chunk of print about the pestilences that beset this Nation not so very long ago. Cholera was with us several times in the 19th century; and Yellow Fever once at least, & Leprosy once at least in my lifetime.

The leper was an old woman who cooked and sold snacks of hot pig's trotters at a London Station. (I often saw her there.)

She fell ill and went to hospital, where it was found that she was a leper of long standing. The Hospital cured her other ailment but had to keep her for treatment of the leprosy, which was then without any very certain swift cure. I never saw her again, but she may have lived until the new treatments came in.

The accounts of Plague are startling. Probably, you know Defoe's book about the London Plague[1] only about 300 years ago. That plague made its mark on the English memory, and the history books.

The Belgian writer was J. K. Huysmans,[2] who must, I think, have been French, not Belgian, but of a Dutch extraction. He lived & worked in Paris, & wrote there many books that I have not read & some that I have forgotten.

But these Parisian writers led the young writers here, & the young writers here, living in London, were eager to know all the ginger that was hot in the mouth in Paris.

Now some of the writers here, in the Wilde set, made a great scandal, & came to grief.

Huysmans wrote of a rather bad French egg, who was a scholar of queer times & passions & saw something of the Satanists, who raised the devil in mockery of religion, & were otherwise off their rockers.

He wrote a book (*A Rebours*, or Topsy-Turvy) describing some of this way of life very vividly. I judge that he had lived it. He followed it up with a series of books, to show how he was converted to better ways.

He visited the Trappist Monastery (then in France) & wrote a wonderful book about it (*En Route*), & then (as I think) the salvation got mixed up with a house-keeper who was a good cook, & the beauty of Chartres Cathedral. What with omelettes and the 13th century, one got kind of diddled which was doing the good.

[1] *A Journal of the Plague Year* (1722)

[2] See Letters 348, 573.

576

. . . Defoe was a most remarkable man, and his Plague book scared my childhood a good deal.

Shakespeare must have known several years of plague in London; bubonic plague, with a great mortality. John Fletcher died of plague in London, and plague inspired Lodge to write some marvellous lines, and Dekker to write a marvellous pamphlet of *London sick of the Plague*.

We have war, of course (*Europe Sick of the war*); but plague filled society with madmen, & thieves made mad by opportunity; and inhumanity made almost universal, & houses (shut up) with all hands dead indoors.

Lepers increased in numbers here, owing to wars in the East, but I hear that it now has some effective quick treatments. Many lepers reach a good age & die from some other complaint. It is a disfiguring rather than a killing disease, such as authorship.

. . .The difficult thing that I was trying to do is just a difficulty; or *the* difficulty, that Blake spoke of, as the artist's main difficulty (or am I wrong).

"To bring forth Number, Weight & Measure in a Time of Scarcity."

Shakespeare did it by writing *Macbeth* in the year of the Gunpowder Plot;[1] & I would say that you do it by arriving in a frozen state, in fog, to play a divine symphony at the back of beyond somewhere; & I don't think that I do it at all, but did once do something somewhere, but I have forgotten what it was.

The present task is of no known time, & of a subject that is hardly a subject, but rather an ignorance of any known fact: but you shall see what I make of it, if I make anything of it, that is, make it a thing.

Writing is difficult, even if it be possible, and gets harder daily.

[1] 1605. (Shakespeare is thought to have finished *Macbeth* in 1606.)

577

... About the seal on the chain.[1] It was dug up by a woman many
years ago, as she was planting out young fruit trees & bushes in
her garden (somewhere in Gloucestershire, I think).

How it got there, and to whom it had belonged, was never
known; and I suppose that the owner dropped it in the garden, and
perhaps trod it under the soil as he moved about. Most men used
seals till about 1850 I fancy, but gradually gummed envelopes
supplanted seals.

It used to be said that some sticklers challenged the users of
gummed envelopes, for daring to send by post envelopes that they
had licked. But gradually the sticklers got shot or prosecuted, and
all was quiet on the Potomac, or fairly so.

... Don Roberto[2] was often in London, at a house in a good
central place: probably he had a flat there.

When in London he rode a good deal in Hyde Park, in the tan
tracks of Rotten Row.

He was the Laird of Gartmore, in Menteith for his last years,
and was often in Glasgow, when in Scotland. While there, once, he
was in a two-horsed bus, such as plied in our cities then. He
noticed that one of the horses in his bus was new to the life of a
bus-horse, and was much upset by the frequent stops & strains &
trouble. He was sweating & finding it tough going.

His heart was touched & he got down to speak to the poor beast,
& found that it was an Argentine horse, with the brand of a ranch
that he knew; so at once he went to the Bus Office and bought the
horse and rode it home; & found it a weary job to get him there:
but he had a way with horses & got him there, and, later, got
another horse of the same ranch: & kept them both as pets at
Gartmore till they died. This is a characteristic feat of Don
Roberto, who was one of the most wonderful men then living: no
one like him now.

[1] JM had sent ANS a very fine eighteenth-century seal with a coat-of-arms cut in it
and a French motto.

[2] Cunninghame Graham: see Letters 199, 523, 573.

578

... I thank you for the happy pleasure of a second letter, here
yesterday, about the China Tea.

I am so glad that this has so swiftly reached you. If I meet my Tea-planter friend, I will ask him how the "smoky flavour" is produced. It seems to me a well-chosen phrase.

He always tells me that it *never* is Chinese tea, but "high grown" Indian Tea from plantations up in mountains. He thinks it quite deplorable stuff, as Tea; but when I drank tea (years ago now), I always preferred it to the poisons he sometimes sent me.

I used sometimes to drink Bitter Maté, a decoction from the Argentine, often mentioned by Don Roberto, but I never cared for it. Don R mentions it now & again in *Hope*.

Then there was Camomile Tea, another liquid.

All these drinks, I suppose, were the hopeful devices of women in the 18th & 19th centuries, to make their husbands & male guests able to articulate when they "joined the ladies" after dinner. A good many, of course, never joined the ladies, but lay in their tracks under the dinner table, with their stocks and collars loosened by the Butler, lest they should be choked.

I am writing this in another liquid, called Higgins-es Eternal Ink, which scribes used to use long since.[1] It is an American Ink, but I never heard of its being drunken. Porson, the great Greek Scholar drank some ink at dinner with Rogers,[2] but that was because he had finished all the other drinks, & the Butler had gone to bed.

[1] See Letter 549.

[2] See Letter 282.

579

... I hope that your Virginia Creeper has rewarded you by turning a lovely soft red in dying (if yours be a variety that does this in Autumn).

I believe that the variety is called Ampelopsis by the learned. There was a mocker not long since who wrote the lines,

> The Ampelopsis slowly ambles up
> The garden wall . . .

which were admired in my youth: but I like the much later lines better:

> Ampelopsis green above my head
> How much more beautiful you'll be when dead!

(The red of the dying leaf is very fine.)

"Virginia" was a phrase coined to please Queen E, for many thousands of Englishmen prayed that she might never marry, in France or Spain, & so end their happy quiet as Protestants.

Q E steered a very difficult course among a horde of pretenders and desperados; and (as I think) she liked the desperados best; especially Sir F. Drake, who had such marvellous Spanish jewels to give her, whenever he came home.

She must often have been near death by murder, & the men responsible for her safety must have been most watchful, with spies everwhere, and not only watchful but lucky.

Some of the Virginian settlements came to grief, & one of them (I believe) disappeared, leaving some of its possessions before it migrated. I believe that they left signs to show in which direction they had been lured: but nobody knows what happened to them, and I suppose that the Indians scuppered them in the wild & hove them into a river.

But I believe that they left some gear in their huts before going, and that these included some coloured drawings of Red Indians; and these (by a French artist) are now in the Brit Museum. I may be all wrong in my history, but I have seen the drawings, which are very splendid; and you cannot think how splendid they are.

You see, these lads were ruddy brown, and they were all tattooed with some stuff that showed *blue* on the skin, & the tattooing had been done with delicate skill, as well done as Oriental tattooing; & the effect of delicate blue lace on a ruddy brown skin, on neck & chest, was most rare.

I suppose it was woad that they used (like the ancient Britons); & I only hope that the Brits looked as handsome.

I think that only the Braves were tattooed; as the poem says:

> None but the Brave deserve the Blue
> As Ox & Cambridge Sportsmen do.

580

... It has been a sore week of toil & trouble, though I have not exactly raised the devil worth a cent.

I have been reading about Tattooing:[1] & find that the Maoris in New Zealand are among the chief masters of the art. Perhaps you may have seen some of the fine work done there.

It is, I suppose, usually a male weakness, but long ago I used to see some so-called tattooed ladies in English Fairs. I always felt that these ladies were only painted, in face and neck, and that the designs were washed out after the exhibition.

Perhaps the designs could be swiftly painted through special stencils in a few moments.

There used to be many vile little dens in sea ports where men would tattoo sailors for small sums.

A blue ring round a finger 1/-
A   " wrist band   2/-
A foul anchor[2] on the back of the hand, 2/6

I was never done (not having such sums), but I knew several who were done, & heard that it was a very painful business & a permanent disfigurement; and, as far as I could learn, it never moved the heart of woman irresistibly. My own feeling was that the women would have preferred the 1/- or 2/6 to be spent on sweets for themselves.

I have known some men very beautifully tattooed, from the shoulders to the finger tips. They said that it was most painful, & all regretted having done it or endured it. Possibly the result shocks people usually. It always shocks me.

[1] See also Letter 283.

[2] A "foul anchor" is the design of an anchor entwined in its rope.

581

. . . I wonder if you take a great interest in names?

I mean, especially, the place names that reveal so much, of an unknown history, when closely examined.

One learns that Evesham was the estate or ham of a chap called EOVE; it isn't much but one can't help wondering what kind of a chap he was, and whether he drank, or lived in sin, or something.

For a time in France I used to go daily down a street that had a real name: The Street of the Naked Body without a Head.

Now that is a real name. It makes one sit up and wonder.

Some say that it was very likely called after an Inn-sign in the street of old. It doesn't sound quite like an inn-sign; it suggests a real body without a head; & it does not suggest a broadcaster telling the world that Scotland Yard are inclined to take a friendly view of the case, & put it down to some medical students having a prank.

It remains one of the moving names in my memory.

Another that pleased me much long ago was a field-name in some country-estate book.

I have been in the very field.

The name (an old name) of the field is: "There an ox lay dead" and there, I don't doubt, an ox did lie dead, & the question rose, how?

There used to be a fairly frequent inn sign of

The Silent Woman,

a lady with her head off, and carried under one of her arms for coolness and quiet. It is not a sign I have seen anywhere, but it is mentioned now & again in guide-books.

582

... I thank you for your dear kind letter about the famous tattooings of NZ.

I wish that I could have seen them, but it is not an art that pleases me. I wonder at it, and am glad that it is not on me. Many sailors were marked with it, in big bold designs on hands, arms & chest: the foul anchor (an anchor with an old hemp cable round the stock); Lovely Nancy; a full-rigged ship; a portrait of some particular ship; or the skull & crossbones (the Jolly Roger: the Roger being the skull, & the jolly its grin).

Women know how to look their best without any of the above bewitching charms.

I suppose that the ancient Britons were tattooed, & not just painted: but I do not know. They may have put on war-paint before battle.

I have an old seamanship book (1863) shewing the seamanship of the Navy of that time, a wooden Navy, with muzzle-loading guns, and most of it under sail as a rule. It is incredible that such things could have existed so lately. It is wonderful (all of it, of the very best) but as obsolete as war-paint and the long bow. Yet a battle-ship of the kind (*The Nile*) was in the Mersey when the first *Conway* was begun there; & later became the 3rd *Conway*.

Much of her old gear was still in her, & I had the great privilege of seeing some of it, so that I could now understand my book.[1] Unfortunately it was all utterly obsolete at sea; & I had to learn the new seamanship, which was using wire & chains & iron where the old men used rope, canvas, hemp & muscle.

[1] JM's *The Conway*, first published in 1933 and revised in 1953.

583

. . . When I first came to London, all traffic on the roads was horse-drawn; & the entire city smelt like a stable; for every street, almost, had to have stables of some kind.

I saw one of the first motor-cars in London, broken down, surrounded by a scornful mob, not quite sure that they ought not to burn it, with the driver on top of it, but they contented themselves with mocking.

I hope that you have had a happy glad Christmas, & are not worn out with long night journeys over the moors in snow.

We had a small flood here on Xmas Eve, but it was not into the garden: only an extra breadth in the river on the Berkshire side: a 3 foot flood or perhaps only 2 feet 6″.

. . . I have seen one salmon in the river here: leaping: going up to spawn. I daresay 1 or 2 still come up each year. Salmon differ much (I'm told) & there may be a real difference in Thames salmon.

584

. . . Sometimes, I cannot get to the post here; & this (the last day of 1965) is one of them. I cannot get a letter to you tomorrow, to wish you a beautiful & glad New Year; and this cannot reach you till Monday or Tuesday, or, if you are on tour again, in snow and icebergs & things, even Wednesday.

I shall hope to send a telegram, but, alas, no letter, for Christmas has upset my toils more than can be told; I live like a lost sheep in a kind of cold chaos (mostly unanswered letters that have gotten to be jumbled up, ends from beginnings).

"Garlic & saffron, roach & dace"—Christmas here was of "the newë get", as Chaucer calls it; much unlike the old sort. There are now no carol-singings (at least I heard none) & the Mummers mum no more, though 30 or 40 years ago there were 2 or 3 teams of Mummers, playing slightly different versions of the play, within a few miles of this.

Perhaps you have never seen the Mummers. There would come a-knocking: & I would go to the door, and there would be a team of giants, dressed mainly in overcoats covered with tassels of paper, & helmets of the frills, and fearful swords of wood, and 2 or 3 lantern carriers.

Then I would ask them in, and clear a space, and then St George would fight the Turkish Champion & get killed (as often in an

English war) but then Dr Vinny would come in, & give the corpse a drink; & up St George would get, & slosh the Turkish Knight stone cold.

Then there was a general peace-making; & a song of sorts (sometimes) & the room would be swimming in Xtian & Turkish gore, of torn & crumpled paper frills.

It was an absurd play, but as Dr Johnson said of some other folly. "Sir, it promotes kindness", and I think that bits of the versions may have been mediaeval, with later additions that one could sometimes date, as from events of a past time.

It left a pleasant memory always. Any work of art that wakens encouragement makes a pleasant memory. Soul is made to speak to soul; & the souls see the priceless joy of effort and recognition, & live the more gladly for years.

1966

585

. . . I thank you for your letter, & for the good news of your Father.

It is very dark today, and winter darkness is one of the worst things that winter brings.

I used to be told that some early Christians were luminous within, & brought light wherever they came: they had only to unbutton their waistcoats: "And lo, Creation widened in their view"—but if I am one of these (as I much doubt) the waistcoat does not work.

"Total eclipse", as Milton said.

In the darkness, I cannot tell what this card is that I write on. It might be a Xmas card but it seems a sort of clear paper to write on, & I hope it will not be illegible.

I have ordered some soups to go to you, & you should have them in about a week, I think, & I do hope that they may cheer your Father & you on some cold evening. They are not a very engaging lot I fear, but may taste better than they sound.

The floods have abated for the moment, so do not think of me being washed away with all hands.

I am reading bits about the Napoleonic War, & the schemes of that clever scoundrel to conquer England by flat-bottomed boats & things: he never really took the plunge but I think that for a week or two it might have been attempted.

586

. . . I was reading the other day of an old shipwreck in the Channel about 100 years ago.

The wreck was broken to bits on the rocks, & these bits (some of them) washed ashore, & among them was a bit of iron deck-house, into which the power of the sea had driven a few gold sovereigns right into the iron.

Some power there I wd say.

❧

587

... While trying to remember some of the text of the Mummers' Play[1] as performed near here nearly 40 years ago, and is now no longer played, the rag-bag of my memory does partly recall a speech of the Turkish Knight & the bold reply of Dr Vinny.

Dr V (I often think) may have been meant to be a woman, for she was the one sensible character in the cast.

In this fragment the Turkish Knight says to Dr V:

TK: Why, thou boastful braggart, what diseases canst thou cure?
Dr V: The itch, the stitch, the Curly cues,
    The palsy and the gout,
    The pain within and the pain without.

As the players may have depended much on local memory for their text, you must not be surprised at Curly cues, but recollect that it must once have been an unusual 3-syllabled word, that had been imperfectly remembered.

I have met with no doctor who had ever met with a case of curly cues. It may well have been "the common cold" originally; and this might easily have been a term not familiar and easily corrupted.

About the year 1888 the world was smitten with influenza, then a new disease here.

Long afterwards, in Ireland, I would hear of people who had died of "the influence", or "the Russian influence". These words are easily corrupted in popular speech.

I hope that you are enjoying the days of mild sunny weather, with warmth of over 40°F. Here we enjoyed them intensely.

Our forefathers, who were all farmers, dreaded mild winters, lest growth should prosper too early, & be killed by late frost. All our spring proverbs are against a mild winter.

    If the sun shines in Febryear
    Her shines the worse for it all the year.

[1] See Letter 584.

588

... My thanks for your touching faith in me as a scholar.

You ask me about The Cid, & I have to tell you that he was liker King Arthur than anybody else in popular legend, and perhaps rather liker Warwick the King Maker in real life, with a good crimson streak of outlaw, rebel, etc, when people annoyed him.

He was Rodrigo Diaz, of Vivar, born in Spain about 1040. He died in 1099 and his bones are now in a tomb in Burgos.

He was the son of noble parents.

Cid is an Arab word Seid, pronounced more or less like Seith, which means Lord. The Spaniards call him *Campeador*, which means champion.

He *was* a champion, no doubt, and a great fellow in single combats and as an army leader. He fought the Moors as a Christian soldier; and often fought for various friends against the Christians, during a life of warfare. War was his chief business; & his feats are the subject of ballads & songs, which I will try to look up (I must have some somewhere).

Like King Arthur he was a real man, married, and the occasion of poems (of sorts).

I send this at once in a hurry, with my blessing.

Jan.

589

This book[1] containing ninety pages
Is (nearly) what the writer's age is.
If Age were Youth and Wits were greener
It would be better for Reyna.[2]

[1] These lines accompanied a copy of JM's *Grace Before Ploughing*, published that year.

[2] NB Pronounced Ra-eena.

590

... I have been looking at various photographs of portraits of Napoleon.

He lived through an inflated feverish art time, & was rather ill-served by his flatterers & inflators, and I do not take to his painted portraits, they smack of the inflated manner; but the Death Mask taken at St Helena is a wonderful thing: no mistake about the fundamental beauty there.

You will know the old tale, that N never was at St Helena, but had a Double, who went to St Helena, while he lived happily in (some say Italy, some say New Orleans or New York) for many years . . . .

It is a pleasing tale, but it cannot quite convince. But it would be fun to write the history of a saved N in some little Italian hill city.

⚜

591

. . . I'm afraid that you may be having a grim time on the moors, with snow drifts & frosts, for hours after each concert.

Here, it is sunshine on a snow that covers the view. I can only see a bright whiteness (from my window) with a dark streak across it that shows the river-bank shrubs. From the chart, I would say that this will be our lot for a week or so.

I do not mind, for I have a fearful month of toil before me, and must attempt that instead of growling. As sailors used to say of their way of life, "Growl one may, but *go* one must."

. . . I am writing & writing, with only 1 waistcoat, where last week I wore 3.

I am a shocking sight in 3.

⚜

592

. . . I went yesterday to a famous old inn near here, that I have often passed, but had never before entered. It has the enchanting name of "The Rose Revived" & I must say it is a reviving place. But who gave it the name? It must have been a poet; either Shakespeare or John Fletcher . . . or . . . was it some broken Yorkist or Lancastrian who was ruined in the war of the roses, yet recovered fortune there? I do not call myself a rose, but your dear kindness to me makes me

Your Jan revived.

593

... I am sending you a card of the *Cutty Sark*, which may not have reached you yet (I have not seen it before) & she is rather linked with us, & you may like to see her something like what she was when making a passage.

I think she would have set a flying jib & kept it flying long after the skysail came in; and a spanker, too, & very likely a big ringtail.

Still, she shows a fair amount of sail, & is evidently hopping along, and thrilling all the watch; and nobody thinking of striking for a 40-hour week, but expecting an 84-hour week as the minimum.

594

... I belong to a time that shrank from the writings of men from about 1660 to 1760.

We were unjust to them, but were born so, so that we might enjoy the Romantic Movement.

But I did once have to read a lot of Mr Ned Ward[1] & of his contemporaries, looking for qualities that I did not always find, but finding (in that century, both in France & England) a prose that was certainly a marvellous prose. (I did not find this prose in Ward, but I did find in him some knowledge of the life at sea, of that rough time when sea life was about as brutal as life can be.)

Anybody who went to sea then must have felt that the life had a rather strong taste; it had a reek of rum to it, and a bite of plug tobacco, with some mockery of any weakness such as civility.

Dr Johnson had a reek of it by going aboard a frigate in the Thames, and rashly asking a ship's boy what a box or chest or locker of some sort, was for.

"O," the boy said. "It's where the lob-lolly boy keeps his lob-lolly."

(An answer, Dr J said, "Gross, ignorant and disrespectful".)

Lob-lolly was a kind of stew, rather more liquid than lob-scouse, perhaps being more like a gruel. Slaves in the West Indies were said to weep on Lob-lolly days, so no doubt it was a grisly kind of dish to one working in the sun all day.

Lob-scouse used to contain meat, fat (all salt), ship's bread, & any old bits that were around. Both dishes were disgraces to mankind; and are now (I hope) gone from human knowledge.

¹ Edward (Ned) Ward (1667–1731) was a tavern-keeper in London who wrote humorous sketches, some of which were published in *The London Spy*.

595

. . . I have been reading lately some Dickens letter about conjuring. I fancy that he was a pretty good conjuror himself, but he met a French conjuror who left him speechless with wonder, though I think that this Frenchman was (in part) a hypnotist.

I had one experience of a conjuror a long time ago, that leaves me still speechless. I do not in the least know how it was done.

It was in the East. I was in a party of about 10 taken to see a conjuror, who did some tricks that took my breath away; & then did the wonder that has left a memory.

We ten spectators were seated in chairs in one curving line. I was about in the middle.

The conjuror was about 10 or 11 feet from us, on the same level.

I was wearing a dinner jacket, with an *inner* pocket, for a handkerchief, on the left side of the coat.

We 10 people and the conjuror were the only people in the room, so far as I know.

Presently, the conjuror produced a live yellow chicken from nowhere and said, "O the pretty little chicken. O the nice dear little chicken; O pretty chick."

But at this, the chicken disappeared; & the conjuror seemed hurt; but then looked at me, and said, pointing to me, "The little chicken in the pocket. You look in pocket." I put my hand into the coat pocket, & there the little chicken was, on my handkerchief.

How it got there, I have not the faintest notion. No-one had come near to us, as far as we could tell, but there it was.

596

. . . This is the 4th of July, when the US celebrate their first First Independence.

For a "Fourth of July" it is strangely still here, but in the US I suppose that no stillness exists: guns, cannon & crackers bang, & the bullets whistle, for in the general joy who can delay the Bang to cut the bullet from the cartridge?

It was late on a 4th of July that I saw Robert Fitzsimmons, who later became the heavyweight champion of the world; and an unusual man looks unusual; and he answered to the expectation.

He was said to have been a miner of some sort, and to have studied the kicks of horses, to make his blows as sudden and as deadly.

I think that he had been a blacksmith in Australia and had had some kicks when shoeing.

It was on a 4th of July that I saw some American boys drag a small cannon into the Avenue, load it full of powder and touch it off with a fuse on a stick. The cannon leaped six feet in the air with a royal bang, and collapsed on to the tram lines. "It was a famous Victory."

. . . I often wonder how primitive people who cannot read or write, manage when they are in love [and apart] as no doubt they often are.

Can their minds communicate, and tell each other, by what we call telepathy?

Even with us, now, in a modern land, our minds can communicate: the distant soul can shake the distant friend's soul and make the longing felt, over untold miles. What our modern minds, often so full of rubbish, can do through the rubbish, primitive minds may do like wild fire: and what can quench wild fire? It does not go at death, but it undergoes a change then.

So here we talk together on themes that you may not perhaps like to discuss; themes that perhaps music answers for you; or as some rare concerted colours answer for painters.

Your darling letters are always a joy to me, and never properly thanked. I am so glad that your friend likes the prose book. It never seemed to me to be coming along, & I was in despair when I read the proofs: it seemed to be as dead as the Dead Sea, which is pretty dead, I would say.

My heart's dear pleasure, bless you for your kind long friendship. I hope I haven't been a great pest.

597

. . . I learned very early, and cannot forget the two essentials of life Sleep and Water.

The Spaniards name three things: "Good air, good water, and good bells", omitting sleep, for Spain is a lively sort of land, & they do not sleep very much, & would much rather dance or go to a bullfight.

I like Coleridge's verses:

> O sleep it is a blessed thing[1]
> Beloved from pole to pole.

[1] This is a slight misquotation. The original line, from "The Ancient Mariner", runs: "O sleep it is a *gentle* thing".

598

. . . I used to see an old Shakespearean actor, who had a memory of Shakespeare; but it was not at all precise; he was apt to get into the wrong play, & begin a speech from *Twelfth Night* & then pass into *Macbeth*; or prompt in a pause, from a sonnet or *Coriolanus*. I used to notice this, but I never felt that the audience did. To them it was all right, being only poetry.

Women, as a rule, have better memories than men, but do not you ever get led into some phrase like the proper phrase but belonging to some other composition?.

Well, they used to tell of Lord Macaulay, who had once to wait 3 hours for a train & to pass the time repeated *Paradise Lost*, & was glad to find it still perfect.

I seem to remember, though, that he found himself a little sticky in *Paradise Regained*; but he could keep them apart.

599

. . . I am sorry to say that my memory is not too good now; & I am not sure what GM meant by my cottage.[1]

I think that about 60-odd years ago (or more) he & a friend did look in on us, when we were in rooms in a little farm in N. Cornwall; in a place now all built over and (I suppose) a "sea-side resort" and unrecognisable, but at that time utterly unknown & unpeopled.

The two came to us, & then went on (to Tintagel, I think).

I cannot remember more about it than this, but I remember the little place as it was, close to the sea, and within a quarter mile of the best bathing pool in these islands.

It was a heavenly pool about 80 yards by 40 yards, a rocky square, all from 8 to 4 feet deep, a smooth rock floor to it, so that one's first view of it always prompted the poetic line
"Eight feet deep and as clear as gin"
but not to be approached at high water.

From about ¼ ebb till ¼ flow it was sheer bliss, but in any west wind the tide came in with the curbs off, and one had to hop it for dry land.

The beauty of the pool would have made you sing; & I wish that you could have seen it.

---

[1] Unfortunately, my memory has failed me—I cannot now remember what the reference to JM's cottage was, or who GM was. GM might have been George Moore ("AE") whom JM would have known through Yeats, or Gilbert Murray, an old friend and, when the Masefields moved to Boar's Hill, a neighbour. ANS.

600

... My loving thanks, as ever, for your darling letter, and my heart's good wishes for the Viola player.[1] I hope that you will have much joy in mastering the new instrument.

Alas, writers do not have these thrills often, for the two methods of prose and verse are usually left to different people, though all poets claim that no one is much good at prose unless he can write verse, too.

Both are (as it were) liquids, but verse is a sort of wine, and prose a sort of water; and water is the foundation of both, and good water such as the Malvern Spring, is rare indeed, and is like liquid silver in the throat (someone in the 18th century said) and it used to have a magical twang to it in swallowing. I don't think it keeps this twang in captivity.

But poetry, like the rarer wines, matures, often slowly, and perhaps does not win its *real* audience for 50 years or more; after the man is dead or in a mad-house.

(As I am neither, I'm probably no good.)

... I used once, as a boy, to take huge joy in the Bab Ballads of Gilbert;[2] the nonsense verses that he published week after week in a paper called *Fun*, to which he often sent drawings also.

He was soon writing the famous Operas of Gilbert & Sullivan; and I never came to know those operas as I knew the Bab Ballads.

But I heard two of the old Savoy singers in Shakespeare, after the great days of the Savoy, and one of them, Mr Courtice Pounds, was the Star Actor of Feste the Jester, in *12th Night*, and I do think that he must have been the best Feste that ever breathed; and O if I could but see him in that part again ...

(I have seen over 60 *12th Nights*. It comes to less than one a year.)

[1] After a long career as a violinist, ANS had changed over to the viola, as Sir John Barbirolli was in need of one at the time.

[2] W.S. Gilbert (1836–1911), better known for his collaboration, as librettist, with the composer Arthur Sullivan in the Gilbert and Sullivan operettas. The Bab Ballads were published in book form 1869–73.

601

... I am glad you had the joy of sailing a big (cutter) model on a pond.

I never had that joy, but it fell to me to re-rig the wrecks of three such mastless models for young friends (or their parents) and in one case I rigged her as an old Preventive Cutter, with cannon on her deck; and genuine cutter-stay fashion forward, & a grand square topsail with a reef-band in it: a wonder to behold.

Rigging is a delight, or was a delight . . . & O the wonderful things old model-riggers did, in the last 2 centuries of sail.

602

. . . "We twa hae paidlit i' the burn". We have been companions a good while, and it has been dear to me, and undeserved.

Long since, I went to the Burns country, & saw some of the burns he paidlit in; & would have paidlit in them if it had been warmer weather.

It was pretty grim to see the cow byre opening into the living-room, but the cows to Robert Burns were fellow mortals.

This brings me to the point of asking you if you ever met an English person who had seen fairies?

Burns, I think, must have known some who had, but I do not think that he himself had. In his part of Scotland, the belief in them was strong, & still exists (or did when I was younger).

In Ireland, of course there must be many who have seen them; & been terrified by them.

I have seen many offerings to them, of flowers, & bread etc, on trees near their haunts; and (while there) I did the same, to be on the safe side.

603

. . . I doubt if Ned Ward's sailor [*c.*1700] had any uniform, but had clothes bought from the Captain's "slop-chest" and charged against his wages. The hat was perhaps a shore hat, tarred on board ship, & possibly fitted with a chin-stay, or fitting under the chin. He would be paid in cash, would receive the money in his hat, & would then (very speedily) be robbed of it by some false friend, very likely a lady.

When I first came here some 26 years ago, there were River steamers plying between Oxford & Reading in every summer: but these no longer ply, and very few boats row past: the river is hardly used at all.

... "When I was but and a little tiny boy"[1] is (in the main) a quotation from Shakespeare; but I use it now as the opening of a theme of what was then possible to an English child.

A good deal was possible to him in England, but if he went to America, well west from the Mississippi, he could get himself scalped still by Red Indians, here & there, and his little scalp might decorate the scalp-house of a Brave. Or he might go into the wilds there, to look for the supposed white race of whom some traveller told; or if he went to Africa, he might go seeking for Marimba, of which the Zulus said: "Marimba is far away, and nobody ever got there."

But that sentence alone would make any child want to try to get there.

How tame the modern prospect seems: Scalping is dead; the cowboy is extinct; and the wilderness is owned by syndicates; and out on the Desert nearly every rock bears one of two slogans painted: "PAINLESS EXTRACTION", or "Prepare to meet thy ... "

Did you ever long to go along the Spanish Main, ever westward, & then northward past Yucatan, to Vera Cruz? along the whole stretch of New Spain, given by the Pope, who had no right to give it, to Philip the King, who had no business to take it, but did contrive to extract from it fabulous sums of gold and silver, which Francis Drake contrived to get quite a pretty share of??

I have been along a good chunk of it, & wish that I had seen more of the eastern Mexic coast, where Cortez landed, and did grim things.

The Spanish Main (the Spanish Main land of America) may not have seemed romantic to you, but it was romantic to Victorian youth because of various novels & histories, then much read.

Probably, you were more attracted towards Africa & India by the books of Rider Haggard & Kipling? (They were better reading, too, than the Spanish Main writers.)

... PS I have come to the conclusion that the 1700–1750 sailor had no naval uniform, nor any safe place for his money, & that his lot was hard & usually penniless.

He was pressed into the Navy from some Merchant-ship nearing England, or in port here, and treated with every rigour till peace or death released him.

He entered the Navy or Merchant Service, with nothing, & bought from the purser, or other store-keeper, the things absolutely necessary to him. These things were *stopped* out of his wages, at the purser's prices; & I doubt if he was even "issued with a hammock" or a bag. Bags came later, I think, & were stowed in the hold, & could only be visited at stated times.

[1] From *Twelfth Night*. This line usually reads: "When that I was and a little tiny boy".

✥

604

. . . Alas, the 2 little glass blobs [paperweights] were late imitations of the things that the Shah liked so much.

I believe that his heart was set upon an earlier make in which the design was done in small clumps of coloured tiny glass sticks, that were something like sea anemones, but very skilful & beautiful. I used to think them jewels of every possible beauty, but the 2 now yours have (I think) only designs of gaily coloured paper, & are not the joy of collectors like the earlier ones.

I expect that the early ones are rather sought after by Americans now, & it is many years since I saw one in a shop.

✥

605

. . . Every human soul is stricken sad at times,[1] & a friend, even an old & worthless friend, will have but a word or two to say, and that not his own, but something he has picked up on his way, in some bad time.

There are not many of these, but some few are about; & mine you will have heard (I expect) already.

When I was lost & broken,[2] I found a line in Browning, that moved me very much: but I forget, now, where it comes. The line is: "All service ranks the same with God", and then there is the wonderful quatrain of Francis Thompson:

> *But* (when so sad thou canst not sadder)
> *Cry*, and upon thy so sore loss,
> Shall shine the traffic of Jacob's Ladder,
> Pitched between Heaven & Charing Cross.

You told me of your tears, and, like the woman who touched you, "I am sorry you are so sad": and the lines are the remedy: for all that is really felt is remedy; it is life & warmth & light, the things that we live by, the law that we call to in all disorder.

. . . One thing, my friend, you must be sure of, that each human being is unique, quite unlike any other, & therefore Unique to the ruling powers above Life, and precious to them as a rarity.

[1] ANS had not suffered any immediate loss but, as she says, was simply thinking of her mother's later sufferings, and what more she might have done for her. JM wrote three times to console her.

[2] JM lost his only son in the last war, but of this loss he never spoke. It may be that he is referring to Lewis's death.

606

... I back the Post Office, for 6 pence anyhow, to deliver this tender fragment to the wistful wanderer.

The Post Office is still an English thing, that once, long ago, received, & safely delivered, a letter addressed to

Mark Twain,
God Knows where.

607

I saw the Mail (in days of yore)
Go by me in a Coach and Four.
Later I saw them go by sea
(And very sure they used to be . . .)
And shall Reyna pine in vain
For letters travelling by plane?
                ??
Perish the thought, if by the thought
Her gentle hope be brought to naught.
Hie, Postman, let thy work be thorough,
Bring this to her at Middlesborough
By Monday next, that she may con it.
The writer ventures sixpence on it.

608

... I will try to get the Worcester [porcelain] to you.

I expect that I will be able to pack the things so that they will carry. They have all lived about 200 years, & might well survive another 200.

They are nothing much, of course, 2 or 3 small bowls about 9 inches across at their tops; 2 or 3 big quart mugs that our manly ancestors used for beer at breakfast.

I have seen several men drinking beer, or cyder, or perry, from guest mugs at breakfast; & I marvelled that such men should be . . .

Long, long ago, I was sometimes in Worcester at the pottery there, looking at the works' collection of the output, & admiring the blue period.

There will only be a few pieces in all, but if you like them, you will gladden me.

⚘

609

. . . When I first came here, the birds were so wonderful: the little owls at sunset; & the great owls in the midnight; & in the Spring cuckoos & (a distant) nightingale; and in the summer rare harriers, and a constant heron, always just across the river looking at me.

Sometimes too, there would be curlews, telling of another world than this, where men do not come, but wonder does.

⚘

610

. . . Browning was a good musician, and fond of all the arts, modelling things & so forth, & playing some instrument, I believe.

He lived in London for a time, after he left Italy, in a house N of Paddington Canal, rather a big open space of water there.

He had a tame goose in the house, that he called "The British Public", and this goose would hear the postman drop letters thro the slit in the door, and would collect them in his bill from the door-mat & bring them to Browning.

All this may be false, but it was *said* soon after Browning's death, & it may be partly true, possibly. Geese are very clever and affectionate creatures.

It was bliss to come to Browning after a nightmare of Idylls by Alfred T.

I hope that you will be able to read this: it looks pretty odd script to me.

611

. . . You must not think me too unjust to Tennyson.

He must have added at least 500 good proverbial lines that are in daily use all over the world: & I would say that only 2 or 3 English poets have entered so far into the public heart & mind. It is a great achievement.

Often a poet will stop doing any good work at about 35 years of age; and very few do really good work later; & only 1 or 2 go on into the grave; but those who do are the surpassing ones; the real nightingales who go on after dark.

Browning was a man of strong intelligence and supplied much to young men, who needed a manner rougher on the tongue than AT. He did some noteworthy things, but time has changed the world since his time, and added new conceptions of life & art. Victorian times are now almost incredible to us and Mr Barrett of Wimpole Street now hardly seems possible.

612

. . . I was never at Steyning,[1] and did not see much of Yeats after he left London, and his wondrous Monday evenings came to an end. Later, too, he lived in Ireland chiefly, and I only saw him once there, while he was in Dublin.

He would be 101 years old now, if he could only have lived so long.

There was an actress, a Miss Farr, a scholar of mystical religious thought, who was often at the Mondays; & later became a Buddhist Nun in Ceylon.

The widow of Duncan Scott, the Canadian poet, did the same renunciation, & became a Nun there: & only last week a woman was here, who said that she had heard from, or of, Mrs Scott quite recently. I thought that Mrs Scott was a spiritual being from another world: & Willy was always that, and a wonder.

[1] Yeats used often to stay at a friend's house in Steyning during the 1930s.

613

. . . I venture to bother your kind heart with yet another illegible letter, to ask about Yeats at Steyning.

I know Steyning a little, but never saw Yeats there, nor did I know that he was there at any time as a resident. I saw very little of WBY after his marriage; for usually we were living far apart; he in Ireland & London, and myself a good deal in the country; moving about; and always at work at absorbing tasks. (A wrong way to adopt towards life, it often seems.)

There is an Indian proverb: "Obey thy Guru in all things"; but the Guru is the teacher of youth; and when youth passes, the youth sees the full complexity and vastness of the problem, and that the Guru knew them and could not help more than with the sudden utterance.

"The laws were made for half the world; but the Breaker of the Laws has half."

Yeats had all the wisdoms and was known to have all the wisdoms, all the admired ways of art, all their practices, all their defects, all their attainment.

I am shocked that I never knew of his being at Steyning.

. . . Dunnage is a sea word meaning the stuff, of straw, or stuffing, used to keep cargo from shifting and smashing.

Any stuff that protects cargo is dunnage; and personal luggage is dunnage; and pretty nearly everything that helps to make a safe package is dunnage, and anything that does not look like dunnage, is probably something that could be used as dunnage, in case of real need.

I think that it was used as a bedding in a ship's hold of *brushwood* or *shrubs* on which cargo could be laid.

The first spelling (about 1630) was Dynnage: a word sent by Heaven to rhyme with spinach, but seemingly never so used.

> A torn coat needs a pinnage.
> Haste, brother, bring some dynnage.
> Etc . . .

614

. . . My grateful thanks to you for your dear letter about WBY.

I loved your account of leaving the car and venturing down that alley, risking imprisonment and fine, past where Willy's old door once stood, as he loved to say, "next door to a lapidary's shop".

The lapidary was still there when I first went there; & the alley was always quiet. Later on, it was never quiet, and one reach of it was peopled seemingly with people who never went to bed till midnight.

WBY was only there as a rule (in the days when I first went there, almost 70 years ago) from about November till about April, when he went back to Ireland, to spend the summer in all sorts of tasks and deeds, making a new Ireland.

He rented and furnished the two upper floors of the house. The ground-floor was held by Mrs Old & her husband (who was, I believe, a carpenter, but I never saw him). Mrs Old came from near Oxford somewhere. She was a big upstanding Englishwoman whom I last saw in Canterbury where she wept in my presence remembering "those blessed days with Mr Yeats: for they *were* blessed days". (My golly, I would say they were.)

I should explain that the house was tiny. Willy's sitting room was not big, and had a tiny little kitchenette with a gas stove adjoining it. I never saw his bedroom on the floor above; & I feel that the owners have changed the old bedroom floor to make a big room for big hotel occasions, dances, feasts, concerts etc etc: that was my impression.

I have been writing out of a cloud of memories of Willy and his London home. I can only *give* you the confused shadow of what these things were, that were so marvellous in the having that I cannot but stagger blindly again in the light they gave. I would so love to tell to you if only I could.

But I am old & blind & crazy & I make but a poor show at it.

615

... I lived in London for 20 years or more, and knew it (as it then was) very well, all of North of the River, & a good chunk of South of the River.

I knew it well, from walking all over it, for I determined to know it intimately well, for the fuller understanding of my favourite writers, all of whom had a dose of it, or more than a dose; and I longed to know where one could escape from it the soonest, for *then* (not now) one could always walk out of it.

I knew Bloomsbury very well indeed, having lived in it a good deal, & gone looking for books in it, and finding many a blessed bargain in the 2d boxes of old times.

Woburn Bldgs was almost touching what I took to be St Pancras old church, but it was no such thing. That church was gone & had not been in that place but elsewhere (N and E).[1] The old church was where Shelley went courting Mary Godwin, who was (I felt then) not much of a wife for Shelley, but a most admirable Widow.

We are two rather linked by the heart; & in this matter of the heart, please let us share what we can of the places of pilgrimage.

¹ The church near Woburn Buildings is the Parish Church of St Pancras. The "old church" is in Pancras Road.

✂

616

. . . My special thanks for your lovely kind letter and for the offer (so generous) of the records of poetry readings.

Alas, dear, I am rather deaf now & can only make out about one word in three, which I find is not enough.

It makes even Milton rather odd. See now:

> Of Man's . . . disobedience . . . the fruit
> Of that . . . tree . . . whose . . . taste . . . etc etc

But I thank the dear thinker of the dear thought.

I am going to write (in this) more about WBY, for he was much in my life of priceless help to me; and that (in letters) can be shared to some degree, I hope.

In the old days when Woburn Bldgs was still a quiet little alley of rather tiny neat houses, the busy main road to the West of it (Upper Woburn Place) was shaded with plane trees, and at the northern mouth of Woburn Buildings had a (then) small hotel, that recently became the main entrance of the main big modern hotel.

In the old days of the Monday Evenings, after dark, this was the pitch or standing place of a blind man, who stood there night after night selling matches. He was supposed by us all to be a romantic figure, who worked all day at the Stock Exchange, & adopted this business as a change, and fresh air, after the day in the City. Some supposed that he was all manner of other things: but to me he was always a poor blind man, like Homer, but with no audience, like Homer, for people panting to hear of the rage of Achilles or of Odysseus' long journey home after the Siege.

To most of us, perhaps, he seemed a part of the miracle, the Keeper of the Gate, to whom we were bound to pay something (if we had it) as an entrance fee.

He had a small tray slung at his chest, with matches. He was rather a little man, never very clearly seen nor very clearly heard, though he may have kind of mumbled. I do not suppose he knew of WBY but none of us will ever forget him. He was always there near that quiet door, in the dim, with the plane leaves trembling, & he himself trembling, and we, all, trembling together, too, for what was up the alley, on the first floor, opening to Paradise.

. . . It is now nearly 66 years since I first went to WBY's; and I know that I cannot certainly name any man or woman who is now alive to tell you of his Mondays as they were in the great days.

Then, always, at a Monday there were some scholars of Righteousness; about a dozen in all, whom I never knew well, for they were men of 35 or 40, & I was only 22, but they were all wonderful beings, kind, helpful, generous, and righteous, knowing (seemingly) all knowledge, somehow, & unlike anybody I had ever seen anywhere.

Some of these would be present, and though I never knew them well, I felt that they were divine figures watched by guardian spirits.

Then, there were usually 1 or 2 Irish journalists there, consulting him about Irish politics or tendencies, & often some lively young Irish writer, whom one saw perhaps only once; and often an English journalist would be there with questions about the Irish Movement.

Usually 1 or 2 such would dine with WBY at about 6.45 before the Evening began about 8 p.m. These in all made about 20 more, whom I never knew well: and those whom I did know, alas . . . I think they are all gone into the world of light, & I alone sit sorrowing here.

617

. . . I have wanted to ask you, do you know the unfinished book of Charles Dickens, *The Mystery of Edwin Drood*? I ask, because it was only half done (if half) when Dickens died; & I want to discuss it with you. Undoubtedly he began the book meaning Edwin Drood to be murdered by his wicked Uncle, who wickedly loved the girl ED was pledged to marry.

But I think he saw the chance of shaking the civilised world with a great surprise; having no murder, but the wicked Uncle believing that he *has* murdered his nephew, & the nephew (seeing his Uncle's wicked plan) escapes far away, & lies low.

. . . The wicked Uncle takes opium a good deal, & has some pretty noisome fancies.

Anyhow, some 50 years ago, a party of criminal jurists raised the point that CD meant to end the whole case with a happy surprise, though I do not know how they thought he would (or could).

I feel, on reading what we have of the story, that the matter had occurred to CD & that he took some care to leave the gates open for a general happy ending.

The jurists were eminent men of letters bent on re-writing the tale, I think. G.K. Chesterton was (I believe) the moving soul among them.

Please, my Reyna, if you are interested in this, may I send you an *Edwin Drood*, if you have not one (the tale has much merit) & see how you think CD could have used the existing draft had he decided on the happy end?

. . . It may be possible, now & then, to put down in some letters to you some few notes about the Yeats household as I knew it between the years 1900 and perhaps 1907, in which latter year I moved out of London for some years.

I never met Mrs Yeats, the Mother of the 4 children, but Yeats had a group photograph of the family showing Mrs Yeats, who died (I believe) really long ago.

I saw from this photograph that she was very like Yeats's sister, Lolly: a beautiful woman from Sligo, with dark-brown hair, and I should say an imagination of wonder & delight.

I met the Father once only, when he was about 75 or so. He was a portrait painter who had been trained in Paris (like du Maurier) in the days of the last Empire when (to the English mind) a French painter's brush was just a little dipped in hellfire.

The school to which he belonged was not welcomed here, but much opposed.

One quality in his painting was most marvellous. He would seize, in one minute, the essential being of his sitter; a lightning likeness that could not be bettered. He made a lightning sketch of Synge that (to me) is un-surpassable: and this quality made him very famous in New York as a painter or sketcher of children.

He was an unusual lively talker.

WBY always said that he (WBY) was only memorable as a talker when he quoted his father.

Once I heard WBY say (to Another, not to me): "A prophet is an unreasonable being raised up by Providence, when Providence is going to be unreasonable."

Later in the evening I said to WBY that I had delighted in his definition. He said, "That is my Father . . . I am always quoting my Father."

In a land where few good talkers come, such talk is very rare, but the main body of WBY's talk was wise & final: it hit the nail on the head & that was that.

For WBY himself, I have to say that he wished to be a painter, but he had some deficiency of sight, which gave him a lot of trouble in his youth; & I suppose made him give up art for letters.

At all times, he talked about painting like a painter: and cared much, as we all cared, for D.G. Rossetti, Burne-Jones, the young Millais and the little water-colours of Blake.

Now & then (once a year or so) I met the two sisters, "Lily and Lolly Yeats", who were then running two Arts & Crafts [centres] in Dublin.

Miss *Lily* Yeats ran a press called the Cuala Press, which published many of WBY's shorter works and Miss *Lolly* Yeats ran a craft [concern] which provided all sorts of Celtic goods, I know not quite what, but mostly decorative.

I only saw their works once, long ago, and forget what Miss Lolly's special works were: but they were a sterling couple of brave souls, those two.

Of course I knew many of the Cuala Books, which were all short stories, verse, etc, all by the lively men & women in the Movement: Synge & the others; with much of WBY.

When Miss Yeats died, Miss Lolly kept the press going.

618

... This is the 66th anniversary of my first visit to 18 Woburn Buildings, so to mark it, may I send you this deplorable book,[1] so unworthy of the day, and you.

I was ill when I wrote it, but ought to have been well enough to write better.

Still, the drawing shows what the old front of the house was, and links you with No 18 & the Mondays after 8 pm.

[1] *Some Memories of W.B. Yeats* (1940).

619

... In this, I hope to tell you of Jack Yeats, the youngest of the family.

He was much in Sligo as a child, but lived & was taught to draw in London; and at an early age (like his father) he was often noted for a facility of catching the very mood ... [the rest of the sentence is indecipherable].

He contributed drawings & prose to a vast comic press for many years. He was said to be the only comic artist in all that press who could make his own jokes. I think that this was probably near the truth.

He attended boxing-matches, races; whippet races; concert singing etc; & drew them with jocund joy. Donkey racing, too, & contests in eating & drinking, & feats of arms, when cavalry men would behead a dead sheep, or cut him in two.[1]

Jack lived in Ireland part of each year, but at other times lived in Devon, in the Gara Valley near Slapton. The Gara comes towards the sea, & is then forced west, for about 2 miles, in what is a sort of Lagoon, kept from the sea by a vast mass of shingle, which the river can only seldom break.

The river is alive with otters, & rather deathly with adders; it is wise to walk carefully. Start Point is near its exit to the Sea.

Every week he kept going a weekly comic; & every year he painted scenes in Ireland; very ably & feelingly: & wrote also very well in wise & witty ways to the huge delight of the Irish, who thought that WBY was just Mr Yeats's brother.

The *Manchester Guardian* sent him with John Synge to write about & paint the wilds of Connaught (about 1905) & this tour was a wonderful test of two most unusual talents.

Please forgive a bed-ridden letter, it is so hard to write lying down.

All blessings to you.

Jan

[1] See also Letter 226.

620

. . . I am sad I could not write to you yesterday to say how glad I was that your Sister could come to help you in your sea of troubles.[1]

I am not to go to hospital yet at any rate, but I suppose that all old age has to go there in time: so what a good thing to have a grand time while the going is good & then feel in the mood for going.

My blessings to you through your troubles, & health to your Father.

. . . Please, does Manchester still honour Miss Annie Horniman, who gave the City her first Repertory theatre? I hope they do not forget her yet.

She looked like an Egyptian princess of some high generous religion; she was one of those often at the Mondays at WBY's London flat.

Woburn Buildings was always quiet & discreet and rare; but so near it were alleys & gulleys which were (seemingly) Satan's very own.

[1] ANS's father had become very ill.

621

. . . I ask you not to write during the time of stress, but to use any leisure that should befall for sleep.

"Blessing on the man who invented sleep." Cervantes wrote it, and the whole world agrees with him.

As a little boy I once found a local gardener dead drunk in a wheelbarrow on the top of the lawn-mowings; & I must say that he was an image of inner and outer peace.

But looking after illness forbids that kind of peace, which is for few, and I am hoping that you can sleep some of each night as a matter of course.

622

. . . I had a strange dream last night, that I was in 3 beds, having a nightmare, & that the 3 sets of bedclothes were all on the floor, & that I fished for them, & found all sorts of woollen clothes that could be used, but were all very small, & had to be used about 8 to one suit, but all very warm & fine.

So I in my three beds decked myself with about 24 woollen garments, all letting in cold air at the joints.

And lo, in the morning, there was only 1 bed, & one me, and only 2 blankets on me & all the other blankets on the floor.

The question arises, was this hallucination or poetry, or were my wits astray?

But it was a shock to be only one, not 3 and that one in only one bed, & the fine woollen suits only blankets.

623

. . . I am sending you a sort of copy of the *Edwin Drood*, reprinted on a smaller scale from the old edition.

It was to have filled just twice the space it has, but Dickens' death left it (with some bits of it cut) only this to go upon, & the notes given in the Life by Forster.

From the work & these notes as they stand, it is clear that Dickens meant Drood to be the victim of his wicked uncle, who meant to marry the girl called Rose formerly engaged to Edwin.

I think it is just possible that D would have made a great change & hurrah my hearties in a complete upsetting of the plan, & making the wicked uncle, the opium fiend, believe that he has killed Drood, while Drood, finding his Uncle not quite a safe Xtian companion, fled away silently to Egypt.

I say that D *might* have done this, to startle his readers, so show that the sin had only been done in thought, & that all would end happily.

But D would have deeply missed the giving up of the detective work & the justice that they would bring upon the murderers.

He was ill when he wrote some of it, & was in a mess with his plot, I think, and aching to get into a mood of power, either to go on, with a great arrest and trial, or to fling over all his plans, & make a great change, with Drood alive, the uncle perhaps a suicide or a victim to some chunk of opium in his waistcoat pocket.

"The world was all before him where to choose." He was both ill & tired & dying, but a wave of health might have restored him, & ready to startle anybody with sudden surprise & any number of new characters.

Some of the book is quite fair good Dickens character-writing.

624

. . . I am glad that the Drood book may be of interest.

I say that D meant to hang the wicked Precentor[1] after a searching trial, in which each character had a chance of proving the scoundrel guilty.

But I am sure that Victorian England would have called for mercy, and to no one louder than to D who might so easily have seen the ways to twist the plot round, & show Edwin D not dead & the Precentor not guilty, save of taking too much opium.

There was a version of the story dramatised about 1910 in London; a very bad piece (I thought), but I did not stay to see how it ended. It had nothing to do with the suggested happy end, so I suppose the Precentor was hanged.

I still think that D might have welcomed a happy end, as being a chance not often given of Surprise and Mercy & Thanksgiving.

I suppose that the town meant is Rochester.

[1] Edwin Drood's uncle, John Jasper, was Precentor of Cloisterham (Rochester) Cathedral.

625

. . . This is Boxing Day here, & I am writing on the precious pad you have given me, to thank you for your letter & the charming kind useful gift.

I wish that it were Boxing Day in Ledbury, with you, for the Hounds meet on that day in the Town, at a cross-roads, about 300 yards from my old home: & I should be able (perhaps) as of old, to tell you which was *Billicock* & which was *Marigold* in the pack, & then we could have gone up into the woods, & perhaps seen a fox break to leeward somewhere, with the hounds at Head & Marigold whimpering blue murder & scarlet sin just ten yards from his brush & men yelling *Hoick*! to Marigold, & the pack (as one hound) saying, "You silly asses, do you think we need telling?"

I would hate to have a pack of hounds after me, for all their sweet looks.

Several cases are known of packs eating their huntsmen or hunt servants; & Ireland is said to have had beggars eaten quite often; perhaps 1 in every 10 years.

But I once knew a rogue hound, a real beauty of a hound, whom I had the honour of taking back to kennel. Now to get there, I had to open a closed 5-bar gate, a horse gate at least 5 foot high, & as I went to the gate-head to open it, this hound, without any seeming effort whatsoever, took it in a cold jump in a clear leap, that made me marvel. He went clear over it without any thought.

A hound must weigh nearly 80 pounds, & to lift 80 lbs 5 feet in the air like a tennis ball would puzzle a strong man.

But these are old memories, &, I fear, likely to bore you a good deal, so I cease bidding you Hoick to Marigold or Billicock either, but end by saying that the 3 Welsh men agreed about them.
First: "They were the finest hounds I never tid see."
Second: "Neither tid I either."
Third: "Either tid I too."

1967

626

... This will be but a poor short note, for the Xmas mail was a heavy one, & is not yet cleared away.

I hope that you had some holiday from nursing, & saw your people & had some lovely hours with seldom-seen friends.

Some of all these things generally reach one at Xmas, which exists by their presence.

Reading Dickens, one finds that the early Victorian Xmas was much unlike anything that we know or now have. The Xmas card did not exist, & the Xmas stocking had not begun; but many shops kept open on Xmas Day (if a week day) and many people contrived to get drunk.

The Carol singers went round (they no longer sing here) and the lavish giving of gifts had hardly begun.

I hope that you are happier to have it over for the year, and that this year may bring you great happiness & love & friends.

Blessings to you.

Jan.

627

... I thank you for your kind, and loving note on this so memorable day.

I grieve that I cannot write a fitting note now, having a rather grim piece of work to try to finish.

But my blessings & thanks.

I hope that all is well with you.

Jan.

FINALE

So, on the "so memorable day", the fifteenth anniversary of our first meeting, these letters are finished. He did try to write one or two more, and after that was obliged to dictate answers to my letters, but "the grim piece of work" he spoke of proved to be his brave fight for life. During the following weeks his daughter Judith wrote to me:

. . . So many thanks: the beautiful apples he was not able to eat. He just takes eggs and porridges, & dozes most of the day, as he takes such a lot of sedatives. In spite of pain he seems cheerful & fairly happy. He takes in questions and can answer, so that if you would like to ask me I could obtain an answer . . .

. . . Father has been in hospital, & they tried in vain to get circulation restored to his bad leg. He is confined to his room & will never walk again. He is not going to get well. His letters have piled up & gone unanswered, and though he cannot see to write he is loth to let anyone touch them. Our C-H [Companion-Housekeeper] has begged to help write a few letters, & I have taken two, but he is like the Captain of a Ship, who likes to command to the end; & the end is not far distant.

Homer, our cat aged 17, brought in *2* baby bunnies to show him . . .

This is his last message to me, written in his Housekeeper's hand:

. . . I grieve that my letters must be scattered & brief, but I shall ever be grateful for the many years of friendship with which you have helped my Pilgrimage.

Good luck, & blessings to you.

He died on 12th May 1967, aged eighty-eight, and he lies in Westminster Abbey, near Browning and Tennyson.

AUDREY NAPIER-SMITH

EDITOR'S EPILOGUE

Be with me, Beauty, for the fire is dying;
My dog and I are old, too old for roving.
Man, whose young passion sets the spindrift flying,
Is soon too lame to march, too cold for loving.
John Masefield, "On Growing Old"

There is a sadness about John Masefield's last letters to Reyna, much of which is in our own minds, as we perceive approaching death. Certainly it was not in Jan's nature to rail against the inevitable, or to burden others with his troubles. His quintessential good manners forbade him to complain, to indulge in vain regrets, or to do more than hint at his physical sufferings.

"I am well enough but cannot do much, and have to go slowly and keep quiet," he says at one point, and later comments briefly on his increasing deafness. He makes light of his failing sight with jokes about blots on his letters, and surprise that so much ink has got about on his desk. In the last autumn of his life he is ill in bed, and asks Reyna to forgive a bedridden letter: "It is hard to write lying down."

Throughout these letters one is aware of a prose style admirably suited both to high gravity and to simple fun. It is a style founded on good classical models, stately sometimes, but always supple and strong. Some of his observations have a crispness, a trenchancy about them which is memorable. On Voltaire, for example, he writes: "His genius was not to give light, but to shatter darkness"; on Hardy: "He spoke not from a brain but from a nature"; on Flaubert: "The work is that of labour, not of power." Power was a key-word to John Masefield. He did not mean by it any earthly power, but a universal, benevolent force, essential to art, and coming sometimes to the aid of human beings in danger or distress. He writes of this to Reyna more than once. "A Power" or "the Powers" appear again and again both in prose and verse. He is often amusing, his humour having an unemphatic but delightful ironical tinge, as in this observation on Ruskin: "He was consumptive in youth, and some-times mad in his maturity, so that the curtain comes down on his performance a good deal." It is there again in a spoof speech by Napoleon to his army; in "When England led the world in things she is good at: marine affairs, domestic comfort, decency, honesty, political imbecility etc."— "Having people to breakfast seems like smothering the day in its cradle" — "M.J[ames] did not murder sleep. He was a Christian scholar; he just scared sleep out of the bedroom." He liked to vary his style sometimes with slang and morsels of old English or old French: "All is y-go!" — "Golly, my own, *quel joi!*"

Jan was writing regularly almost to the end of his life. "I have been doing some verse this week" is a typical remark in one of his letters, flatly modest in tone, as though writing poetry were on a par with doing some weeding in the garden. By the time of his death, one month before his eighty-ninth birthday, he had been England's Poet Laureate for thirty-seven years. Those had been troubled years for his country, encompassing the depression, the Second World War, and all the shifts and changes of the two post-war decades. Through no fault of his own Dr John Masefield OM had become a remote figure to most people, many years before his death. He had lived on into a society which, for all his honours, largely neglected, mis-understood or belittled him, if it had any knowledge of him at all. It is small wonder, then, that he should turn his mind most often to the heady days of his youth and his apprenticeship to literature, and to the giants (as he saw them) who had had all his reverence when he was young. "Swinburne, Rossetti and William Morris were the voices of a generation, and every such voice has something marvel-lous and of that time, and is the bread of that day." He writes that it distresses him "that anyone should speak of ACS [Swinburne] with disrespect".

John Masefield situated himself firmly in the Romantic Move-ment, from Gray onwards until the explosion of all traditions in 1914. It is hard to tell, from these letters, how closely he studied modern developments in poetry after 1920, but I feel that if T.S. Eliot, for example, and later Auden, Spender and Day Lewis (his successor as Laureate) had meant much to him he would have written of them to Reyna. Nevertheless, and with his usual generos-ity, he would probably have conceded that those poets were indeed "the voices of their generation".

From time to time in his letters Jan touches on the changed existence of artists and writers, and we feel that he was unhappy that contemporary verse was becoming arcane, unexplicit, solipsistic; that poets seemed deliberately to be seeking obscurity, setting up barriers to comprehension, as though their poetic nerves were too delicate, their themes too personally precious, for open display to the public gaze. "Artists are more in special compartments than formerly," he writes to Reyna. More than once he repeats his opinion that "writers do not often work much together; but all young writers belong to a gang or clique", and notes that they are inclined to turn in scornful rage on those whom earlier cliques had thought admirable.

The years after 1945 saw a general cooling of the passions among writers, a narrowing of interests, an increasing politicisation, a lowering of sights. Those were the days of the "picaresque" novel and the "anti-hero"; and "high heart, high speech, high deeds 'mid honouring eyes" were not on the list of things that poets thought it right to celebrate. More and more, therefore, Jan turned his eyes away to an era before the shattering of all certainties, the disruption of a long continuum, brought about by wars and revolutions. Hence his delight in sharing with Reyna the discoveries made by a lonely boy in an American town in the last years of the Victorian age. Most significantly, he wrote to her: "When I was greedily reading, I was reading for guidance, and could not read what was not touched with the qualities of poetry: abundance and music and glad excess."

It is natural for people in old age, if they are neither curmudgeonly nor self-centred, to hark back to youth, and to love the young for an unblunted enthusiasm, an undamaged faith in the possibilities of change, an unsatiated appetite for life. When Jan first met Reyna she was a mature woman, an accomplished musician, well-read, well-travelled, with much experience of the world in both war and peace. Yet it pleased him, often, to treat her in his letters as being very much younger, even, than she was. He was, after all, twice as old as she, and had long passed the point in life where trivial differences of a few years here or there have much meaning, where the important thing is what might be called the poetic age of someone who is loved and admired. As the letters proceed, Jan's deepening affection causes him to scan the whole of Reyna's existence, and to address her sometimes as the young girl, and even as the child that she had been. It would be harsh to call sentimental what was simply an exploration of the many dimensions of love. It also gave Jan pleasure to contemplate Reyna's wartime service with the Navy, and to imagine her at sea, even though her duties had been mainly the driving of every sort of transport, from ten-ton trucks to the Admiral's car. "You mariner girls", he writes somewhere; and the English popular image of the "sailor-girl" no doubt had great appeal for one so deeply versed in the folk-lore of his people.

"You must not think of me as a Church man." Jan's childhood experience of church in Ledbury, and the unappealing religious conventionality of his elders, had evidently given him what Scots call a "scunner" of organised religion. That he had a compelling mystical gift is evident from much of his writing, particularly the sonnets. For long he agonised over the dissolution of the body and what should happen to its inhabitant, the soul; and, like any other writer he feared the impermanence of what had been wrought with such exaltation and so much pain.

> Yet for a few short years an influence stirs,
> A sense or wraith or essence of him dead,
> Which makes insensate things its ministers
> To those beloved, his spirit's daily bread;
> Then that, too, fades; in book or deed a spark
> Lingers, then that, too, fades: then all is dark.

In later life Jan came to study Buddhism, and it may be that the impersonality, the calm acceptances of that creed were comfortable to him. Of human beings, he writes to Reyna: "Are they not all struggling to be out of a perishing self into an eternal universe?" When he speaks at the unveiling of a memorial to Keats and Shelley, in Westminster Abbey in 1954, it is noteworthy that he says: "This great building is consecrate to the Eternal Spirit abiding above all change and chance. Whatever creed they hold or rebel against, all poets worthy the name seek to enter the light of that power, and are poets solely as they are worthy to perceive it. What they perceive in the truth of that light may absolve utterly the weakness of the perishing hand that held the pen, and abide for centuries, having in it that touch of the undying."

The immediate cause of Masefield's death was a damaged toe-nail which had gone septic. Gangrene set in and spread up through his foot and leg. It could have been stopped by amputation, and this might have prolonged his life, but the poet would have none of it. John Masefield died on 12th May 1967, twenty days short of his eighty-ninth birthday.

It was in Westminster Abbey, on 20 June 1967, that a memorial service was held for John Masefield. The casket containing his ashes stood between the burial places of Tennyson and Browning, where it was to be interred. Jan had once written to Reyna of the refreshment which Browning had brought to his generation, "after a nightmare of idylls by Alfred T". Now the younger poet, whose humility would never have allowed him to imagine his dust so honoured, but who had loved the idea of the poets throwing their pens into Spenser's grave, was to have his resting-place not far from Spenser's, between two giants of his early days, all differences, one may believe, composed. Extracts from "The West Wind", *Dauber* and *The Everlasting Mercy* were read by Cecil Day Lewis, the Poet Laureate designate, and an address was given by Robert Graves whom, as a young man, Masefield had befriended. At the close of the service Day Lewis read from *A Consecration* to the assembled company all standing. Outside a light rain was falling; the Abbey's flag flew at half-mast; its magnificent peal of bells rang half-muffled. It had been assured for John Masefield's memory that all, now, could never quite be dark.

INDEX

Index compiled by Peter Tickler.